Open(ing) Education

Open(ing) Education

Theory and Practice

Edited by

Dianne Conrad and Paul Prinsloo

BRILL
SENSE

LEIDEN | BOSTON

Cover illustration: Messe Basel – New Hall, Basel Switzerland

All chapters in this book have undergone peer review.

Library of Congress Cataloging-in-Publication Data

Names: Conrad, Dianne, 1956- editor. | Prinsloo, Paul, editor.
Title: Open(ing) education : theory and practice / edited by Dianne Conrad and Paul Prinsloo.
Description: Leiden ; Boston : Brill | Sense, 2020. | Includes bibliographical references and index.
Identifiers: LCCN 2019058074 (print) | LCCN 2019058075 (ebook) | ISBN 9789004422964 (paperback) | ISBN 9789004422971 (hardback) | ISBN 9789004422988 (ebook)
Subjects: LCSH: Open learning. | Education and globalizaton. | Web-based instruction. | Education--Effect of technological innovations on.
Classification: LCC LC5800 .O635 2020 (print) | LCC LC5800 (ebook) | DDC 371.33/44678--dc23
LC record available at https://lccn.loc.gov/2019058074
LC ebook record available at https://lccn.loc.gov/2019058075

Typeface for the Latin, Greek, and Cyrillic scripts: "Brill". See and download: brill.com/brill-typeface.

ISBN 978-90-04-42296-4 (paperback)
ISBN 978-90-04-42297-1 (hardback)
ISBN 978-90-04-42298-8 (e-book)

This book is printed on acid-free paper and produced in a sustainable manner.

Contents

Foreword

Opening Education: Complex Is as Simple as It Gets

It is an honour and a privilege to write the foreword for this book for three reasons. Firstly, I have great confidence in the intellectual integrity of the editors and their ability to attract and curate rigorous and finely-tuned contributions to the theory and practice of openness. Secondly, I believe that this book is important on its own terms because it offers a rich and necessary counter-narrative to dominant marketized discourses in higher education where data surveillance is the new normal. Thirdly, the editors and the authors have consistently refused to offer simplistic or essentialist accounts of very complicated territory. In an era of techno determinism and easy promises in higher education, this commitment to nuance is exemplary; indeed, complex is as simple as it gets.

While the 47 authors from 20 countries approach the theories and practices of open(ing) education with multiple lenses and at different levels, there is coherence in the shared understanding that simple binaries are not useful, and specifically that simple oppositions of "open" and "closed" do not illuminate the intersections of policy, practice and discourse through which education is opening up. Thus, the book is held together by the metaphors of networks, ecologies and rhizomes which are threaded through the chapters.

While this book offers a sophisticated counter narrative, it is not a sci-fi utopian imaginary being provided; there is a form of principled pragmatism manifest in the cases studies and the macro and meso level analysis. At the micro level, it is in the real world of politics, social contestation, economic tension, discourse entanglement and profound contradictions that attempts at changing the foundations of education are being explored, experienced, trialled, researched and made visible. These case studies from different contexts framed by diverse disciplinary context, regulatory policies and cultural concerns insist on asking the hard questions of power and agency, history and structure. It is through the answering of these questions, that decisions can be made in order to negotiate new models of education holding on to the value of decades of experience, expertise, and understanding of the past. Yet at the same time, the imagination that shines through these narratives makes it possible to shape the future on the basis of new materialities and options.

It is because of these deep reflections, these robust accounts and this critical reflexivity that the possibility of change becomes tangible. At a moment in time in education where despair is never far-off, these rich and diverse offerings provide opportunities for optimism and reasons for engaged educators, academics and practitioners to persevere.

Laura Czerniewicz
Cape Town, October 2019

Figures and Tables

Figures

Tables

Notes on Contributors

Heba Abdel Naby
is Professor of Islamic Art, History and Archaeology at the Faculty of Tourism, Alexandria University, Egypt.

Andrew A. Adams
is Deputy Director of the Centre for Business Information Ethics and Professor at the Graduate School of Business Administration, Meiji University. His research interests are in the social impact of computer and communication technology and related legislation and regulation.

Saida Affouneh
is Dean of the Faculty of Education and Teacher Training and Director of the E-Learning Center at An -Najah National University, Palestine. Her research focuses on academic staff development in eLearning, and Open Education Practices.

Anne Algers
is Associate Professor at the Department of Education, Communication and Learning, University of Gothenburg, Sweden. Her research interests include open education and technology-mediated teaching and learning within higher education. She has an interdisciplinary approach and uses the framework of cultural historical activity theory.

Ahmed Almakari
is Director of the Educational Innovation Center of Ibn Zohr University, Agadir Université Ibn Zohr-Agadir, Morocco. Professor Almakari is also an International Consultant-Trainer in E-Learning and an Expert in ICT for UNESCO and the Agence Universitaire de la Francophone (AUF).

Jo Axe
is a professor in the School of Education and Technology at Royal Roads University. In addition to holding a PhD from the University of Bradford in the UK, she is a Chartered Professional Accountant/Certified General Accountant. Jo's teaching experience includes a mix of on-campus and online deliveries, facilitating courses in both domestic and international programs. Her current research interests include open educational practice, learning community development, and student engagement in online environments.

Lisa Marie Blaschke
is Program Director of the Master of Technology Enhanced Learning (MTEL) at the Center of Lifelong Learning, Carl von Ossietzky University of Oldenburg. For a complete list of education, experience, publications, and awards, see: at: http://lisamarieblaschke.pbworks.com

Kate Bowles
is Associate Dean International in the Faculty of Law, Humanities and Arts at the University of Wollongong, Australia. She designs and teaches storytelling work with undergraduates, and her current research focuses on everyday storytelling in healthcare settings.

Elizabeth Childs
is Professor in the School of Education and Technology at Royal Roads University. She holds a PhD from the University of Calgary in Education Technology and teaches in both blended and fully online environments. Her current research interests include open educational practices, flexible learning environments, fully online learning communities, and design thinking and maker research.

Dianne Conrad
is a retired post-secondary educator who continues to write and teach in her areas of interest: adult education, open and distance learning, assessment, teaching and learning. She has co-edited the *International Review of Open and Distributed Learning* and instructs at graduate levels for Athabasca University.

Catherine Cronin
is an open educator, open researcher, and Strategic Education Developer at the National Forum for the Enhancement of Teaching & Learning in Higher Education (Ireland). Catherine's work focuses primarily on critical approaches to openness, digital identity practices, and learning and teaching in increasingly networked and participatory culture. She has been involved in teaching, research, and advocacy in higher education and in the community for over 25 years and is an international contributor to conversations and collaborative projects in the area of open education.

Laura Czerniewicz
is the Director of the Centre for Innovation in Learning and Teaching (CILT), at the University of Cape Town. She has worked in education in a number of roles with a continuous focus on inequality, access and digital inequality. An NRF-rated researcher, Laura has published widely, both formally and informally.

Tanya Elias
is a doctoral student at the University of Calgary. She works as a learning and training advisor and is a strong advocate for open, flexible and distributed approaches to learning.

Roberto B. Figueroa
is a PhD candidate in Educational Technology at the International Christian University, Tokyo, Japan and an Assistant Professor at the University of the Philippines – Open University (UPOU). He is interested in virtual reality (VR) and its effective integration in learning activities.

Kathryn B. Francis
is a Lecturer in Psychology in the Faculty of Management, Law & Social Sciences at the University of Bradford, UK. She has a PhD in Experimental Psychology from the University of Plymouth and previously held a Postdoctoral Research position at the University of Reading in psychology and philosophy.

Geoffrey Gevalt
an award-winning journalist for 33 years, founded Young Writers Project in 2006 to help youths gain voice and express themselves better. YWP has trained 2,000 teachers and connected with 110,000 youths in school, at workshops and online at https://youngwritersproject.org, a supportive, civil youth community.

Jenni Hayman
is Chair, Teaching and Learning, at Cambrian College, Sudbury, Ontario. She has recently completed her doctorate candidate at Arizona State University conducting research on use of OER in post-secondary contexts.

Leo Havemann
is a postgraduate researcher at the Open University (UK), and a Digital Education Advisor at University College London, having previously worked as a learning technologist at Birkbeck, University of London, as well as in various teaching, library and IT roles.

Rebecca Heiser
is an Instructional Designer for The Pennsylvania State University's Lifelong Learning and Adult Education online graduate program with World Campus. Her research interests include identity-centered design, inclusive and equity-centered design, online learning communities design, learning analytics, informal learning spaces, aesthetic design, and OER.

Kristina Ishmael
is a Senior Project Manager, Teaching, Learning, and Tech in the Education Policy Program, New American. She previously served at the U.S. Department of Education's Office of Educational Technology, Nebraska Department of Education, and is a former classroom teacher.

Jeremiah H. Kalir
assistant professor of Information and Learning Technologies at the University of Colorado Denver School of Education and Human Development, is currently chair of the American Educational Research Association's Media, Culture, and Learning Special Interest Group. He is Co-PI of ThinqStudio, CU Denver's digital pedagogy incubator, and serves on the board of directors for InGlobal Learning Design.

Tharindu R. Liyanagunawardena
is a learning technology researcher and the chair of the Online Learning Research Centre at the University College of Estate Management. Her principal interest lies in the area of the social implications of information and communication technologies, especially eLearning.

Frank Loesche
is interested in creative, non-obvious, and playful problem solving. As a PhD candidate within the CogNovo programme at Plymouth University, he focuses on the temporal aspects of Eureka moments from a multidisciplinary perspective.

Klara Łucznik
completed her PhD in Psychology as a part of CogNovo at Plymouth University, focused on group creativity and flow in dance improvisation. Her research interests include embodied cognition and group dynamics in collaborative processes.

Diego S. Maranan
is an artist and educator who investigates the use of technology for reimagining our relationship with the body and the environment. He is Assistant Professor at the Faculty of Information and Communication Studies at the University of the Philippines Open University, and co-founded SEADS, a global network of artists, scientists, designer, and activists.

Wolfgang Müskens
is a researcher at the Carl von Ossietzky University of Oldenburg, Faculty of Educational and Social Sciences. With over 15 years experience in the Recognition

of Prior Learning field, he helped establish Germany's first PLAR-service at University Oldenburg (2017). He holds a doctorate in psychology.

Paul Prinsloo
is a Research Professor in Open and Distance Learning at the University of South Africa. He holds a DLitt and Phil and has published widely in books and journals. He keynotes globally and researches in the areas of learning analytics, student success and retention and postgraduate identities and supervision.

Laura Ritchie
is Professor of Learning and Teaching at the University of Chichester. She designed and leads both undergraduate and postgraduate f2f and distance courses, and advocates open-learning through an open music class. Laura's book *Fostering Self-Efficacy in Higher Education Students* brings her research to everyday classrooms.

Lloyd Hawkeye Robertson
is a counselling and educational psychologist in northern Saskatchewan, Canada. He also teaches a graduate class for Athabasca University. He has published on the structure of the self and has presented on prior learning assessment, self-structure, counselling in northern and remote communities, the psychological effects of Indian residential schools, suicide treatment and prevention, and community development in mental health.

Trevor John Robertson
is an Assistant Professor of English at Woosong University, South Korea. He has published research on the student-teacher relationship in international education.

Dulce Torres Robertson
is an educator with over 20 years experience who has taught education and graduate school courses in the Philippines. She has also published several English textbooks, provided personnel training, and crafted administrative policy and procedures. She is currently an Assistant Professor of English at Pyeongtaek University, South Korea.

Kristin M. Rouleau
is an experienced teacher, principal, and district administrator. She is currently senior director of Learning Services and Innovation at McREL International. Her research interests focus on educator social learning ecologies and how these networks lend themselves to developing educator practice and creating more open environments for teaching, leading, and learning.

Pamela Ryan
has retired from full-time academia and now works as an academic consultant and advisor for the University of South Africa, helping young academics with their research papers and funding applications, and editing theses, dissertations, and academic books. She has been a research fellow at St Edmund's College, University of Cambridge since 2003. With a background in English Studies, her interests are in Sylvia Plath, modern women's fiction, psychoanalysis, open learning and digital literacy.

Aska Sakuta
is a PhD Candidate and Associate Lecturer in Dance and Sports Psychology at the University of Chichester, focussing on the cognitive and performative aspects of Flow experiences during movement improvisation.

Sujata Santosh
is Assistant Director in the National Centre for Innovation in Distance Education at the Indira Gandhi National Open University (IGNOU), New Delhi, India. Her research interests focus on open education resources, massive open online courses, e-learning, and digital libraries. She also has interest in latest developments and innovations in distance education

David Starr-Glass
is a mentor with the International Programs (Prague) of SUNY Empire State College. He has earned master's degrees in business administration, occupational psychology, and education. When not in Prague, he lives in Jerusalem and teaches economic and business-related courses with local colleges.

Cristina Stefanelli
is a senior project manager at UNIMED, the Mediterranean Universities Union (Rome, Italy), where her work focuses primarily on activities relating to eLearning, Open Education and Virtual Exchanges in higher education.

Seddik Tawfik
is the Secretary General for the Council of Private and National Universities in Egypt and former Vice President of Alexandria University for Graduate Studies and Research. Professor Tawfik's work includes supporting opportunities for young researchers to excel in the international field, and on the improvement and reform of higher education in Egypt.

Ilaria Torre
is a Marie Skłodowska-Curie Postdoctoral Research Fellow in the Department of Electronic and Electrical Engineering, Trinity College, Dublin. She has a PhD in Psychology from Plymouth University, UK.

Adiy Tweissi
is an Instructional Technology Expert and Educational Content Designer and Assistant Professor in Business Information Technology at the Princess Sumaya University of Technology (PSUT). Dr Tweissi is also Director of the E-Learning Center at PSUT.

George Veletsianos
is a Professor and Canada Research Chair in the School of Education and Technology at Royal Roads University. He holds a PhD from the University of Minnesota and has held faculty positions at the University of Texas at Austin and the University of Manchester (UK). His research examines the practices and experiences of learners and educators in digital settings, particularly online education and social media. George writes about his research at http://www.veletsianos.com

Arjen E.J. Wals
is a Professor of Transformative Learning for Socio-Ecological Sustainability at the Education and Learning Sciences Group of Wageningen University in the Netherlands. He also holds the UNESCO Chair of Social Learning and Sustainable Development. His blog on www.transformativelearning.nl signals developments in the emerging field of education, learning and capacity building for sustainability.

Keith Webster
has been an educator in various roles and institutions for over 30 years. He is currently Associate Director, Centre for Teaching and Educational Technologies at Royal Roads University and an Open Learning Faculty member at Thompson Rivers University.

Shirley A. Williams
is a national teaching fellow and an emeritus professor at the University of Reading, UK. Her research interests include learning technologies, communities, social networks, digital identity and knowledge transfer. She is currently exploring the use of Artificial Intelligence in Online Learning.

Katherine Wimpenny
is Lead for Intercultural Engagement and Global Education, in the Research Centre for Global Learning: Education and Attainment, Coventry University, UK. Her research examines how higher education institutions are integrating ethical, social, cultural and moral dimensions into the purpose, functions, design and delivery of learning experiences.

Gabi Witthaus
is an open educator based in Leicester, UK. She works at the University of Birmingham as a learning design advisor and is also an independent consultant. Gabi's research interests include online learning design and widening participation in higher education, with a focus on inclusion of refugees. She blogs at www.artofelearning.org

Tara Zaksaite
is an Experimental Psychologist working as a Research Associate at the Open University. She is interested in human learning, memory, and decision-making, as well as how we can best combine experimental and applied research methods.

Olaf Zawacki-Richter
is Professor of Educational Technology at Carl von Ossietzky University of Oldenburg, Institute of Education, and the Director of the Center for Open Education Research (COER, http://www.uol.de/coer/).

Open, Opening, Opened and Openness: An Introduction

Dianne Conrad and Paul Prinsloo

'Open': a provocative movement that has snowballed into an educational enterprise in the last few years. I use the metaphor of a snowball rather that of an avalanche because the movement's shape and speed has been slow – rather than torrential – and steady. The notion of 'open' in education has been creeping forward like the proverbial snowball gathering size as it rolls downhill. Beginning at first with open educational resources (OER) and the dawning realization of their value to educators and gaining size and attention with the first massive online open course (MOOC) in 2008, we have now arrived at a place where the concept of openness is globally ubiquitous and very diverse. We embrace and contend with OER, MOOCs, open research, open science, open learning, open publishing, open scholarship, open institutions. The terms are 'big' terms and can be somewhat confusing as to their scope and meaning. Language is contested in this regard. Additionally, a critical tension exists between the notions of open and its supposed binary, 'closed.' In this volume, we propose understanding ecologies of 'open' in education as existing in the nexus of political, economic, social, technological, environmental and legal frameworks and agendas and as entangled with contestation, incongruities and obstacles.

We put this challenge out globally in 2018, asking these questions, among others: Who/what are the gatekeepers in the discourses on 'open,' 'openness,' 'opening,' and/or 'opened?' How do they impact on the future of 'open?' How can a culture of openness be fostered within institutions, programs, researchers, or culture?? What design innovations/strategies will foster a culture of openness in research and scholarship? What constraints do inter-disciplinary researchers face? What types of leadership skills are required to further the interdisciplinary agenda? How can communication practices – personal and institutional – foster openness and connectedness within institution and beyond? What is the value of a culture of openness to individuals, to community, to society? What innovative technologies can promote, initiate, or sustain a culture of openness?

Researchers from over 20 countries responded to our call, resulting in this volume's extraordinary breadth and providing not only a fine overview of 'open' in all its varied contexts but also detailed insight into open's many

 | DOI: 10.1163/9789004422988_001

facets. We are honoured and happy to write an introduction to this collection to showcase what has been well-said by our 47 authors.

The language used in this collection is obviously themed around the concept of open. The opposite of open is usually closed. That's all logical enough; but there's much more meaning embodied in each. In *closed,* we have nuances of oppression; of hierarchy; of tradition, often unhappy; of hegemony and power; of boundaries. With open, we have opening, opened up, openness, being open. But, more than that, we have a metaphoric presence of images that imply 'things not closed': freedom, sharing, collaboration, mentoring, and building. Building bridges, building knowledge, building connections, building resources, building on experience. Building a future.

The chapters within this volume make it clear that there is more to open than just being 'not closed.' Open has history and foundational philosophy. Those who are deconstructing it here are examining it through myriad critical lenses – and have found a lot to talk about. In Part 1 of the text, four chapters present discussion at the macro level, focusing on theory and concept. We see some fine examples of critical thinking in these chapters, beginning with Cronin's crisp and thoughtful chapter. Here is the perfect opening, the perfect challenge. Cronin throws down the gauntlet, drawing initially on Lane's (2016) division of open education initiatives into two streams: those that open structures by removing barriers to access; and those that attempt to transform the structures themselves. Cronin shines the light immediately on issues of inequality, social transformation and justice. Her subsequent references to the United Nations 17 Sustainable Development Goals – specifically Goal 4 – are the first of several throughout the book's pages, and rightly so, as the trajectory of open was clearly outlined in the UN missive (2015). Cronin concludes with references to the privileges of the Global North, and by implication, the hardships of the Global South, themes that are also repeated in subsequent chapters – themes that echo her calls for justice and equity.

The concept of open is explored equally broadly but differently in Robertson et al.'s chapter, as the authors bring forward their rich discussion from a psychological perspective. The Robertsons' chapter stands apart from the others in several ways: it traces a history of 'mind' and its relationship to 'self'; with this foundation in place, the authors then consider the cultural adaptation that permits and gives space to notions of open. It is a provocative read that comments on the role of education in terms of self.

Ryan's beautifully literary-referenced chapter positions open in another way, looking at the space between open and closed, the threshold, or the limen, noting the threshold as a pivotal entryway between places. She sees potential here, in the freedom of this space, and asks what kind of productive thought can emerge from time spent here. Her exploration takes her to our pedagogical practice in this digital age: how *will* we use the limen and the affordances of open? Ryan's final call uses an architectural metaphor that has us contemplating future practice as if through glass – an opening up. Witthaus, in the chapter that follows, continues that theme against the backdrop of the knowledge economy. She does this primarily by carefully contrasting two documents that speak to the issues of 'open,' each in a different way, each having important implications for the higher education landscape.

With this foundation established, we move next into several discussions of the quality and nature of 'open' as it exists in various applications: place, purpose, people – learners, teachers, administrators. Part 2, in the meso sense, considers the application of the mandate of open as presented conceptually, illustrating that the practice of open, or open educational practice (OEP), is at work worldwide in varied and exciting contexts. Part 2 of the text presents discussions and research on OEP across three continents. Algers and Wals, from Sweden, ask how open education can address sustainable development challenges. They illustrate the value of a culture of openness to not only individuals but also to community and society. Starr-Glass focuses on another application of open, examining the established practice of mentoring. Once the purview of the mentor and mentee, Star-Glass views mentoring as connected to a more expansive and ecological landscape of learning in broader contexts.

One of the core concepts of openness is inclusivity. The earliest incidences of open related to open access in institutions labelled 'open' universities, the prime example being the Open University in the UK. Liyanagunawardena, Adams, and Williams' chapter asks what is 'open' for the disabled. They note that in spite of the fall of many barriers to access, significant barriers for those with disabilities still exist. Open is not always open. This theme recurs in several chapters, highlighting the folly of binary thinking.

So too, the boundaries of private and public become blurred. Rouleau and Kalir look at educational systems in the United States, observing that teachers must navigate open and closed systems, must be connected while being isolated, must collaborate innovatively while being held individually accountable for traditional standards. They present a social learning ecology to frame these seeming contradictions and tensions.

The remaining two chapters in Part 2 are concerned with types of openness in higher education. From Germany's Carl von Ossietzky University of Oldenburg, Blaschke, Müskens, and Zawacki-Richter consider the challenges to and options available to institutions attempting to transition to open practice. They also describe the university's use of prior learning assessment and recognition (PLAR) as an open tool to increase access and inclusivity. Likewise,

Santosh recognizes the breadth of the open movement in India, which already has 14 open universities. She suggests that Indian distance education institutions are revisiting their policies to face the challenges of global competition, changing educational needs, shrinking resources, and rising costs and considers the resulting changes at institutional, pedagogical and individual levels.

Part 3 of the text comprises six chapters that we have described as case studies in that they each present a bounded situation of the application of open concepts in practice, again spanning huge geographical distances. Wimpenny, Steffanelli, Affouneh, Almakari, Tweissi, Abdel Naby, and Seddik's chapter describes their look to openness to build knowledge-sharing communities in the Mediterreanean. OpenMed is a large project with 14 partners, focusing on how universities from the designated countries and other South-Mediterrean countries can join as community partners in the adoption of strategies and channels that embrace the principles of openness and reusability within the context of higher education. Similarly, Torre and her colleagues Łucznik, Francis, Maranan, Loesche, Figueroa Jr., Sakuta, and Zaksaite viewed openness through the lenses of multiple disciplinary collaborations and presented a case study on the ColLaboratoire initiative. From this successful venture, they accepted interaction, learning, unlearning, and reshaping as necessary steps toward collegial openness in research.

The question of what is open – and what is closed – runs thematically through many chapters and through many educational contexts. In their K to 12-focused chapter, Hayman, Heiser, and Ishmael consider what is open for curriculum developers at K-12 level. Exploring another context, the continuing education world, Havemann investigates the language of open and closed, using a Birkbeck College case study, noting that in an initiative designed to be 'open,' there is still closure; once again, our binary-themed world is questioned. Havemann's chapter, in particular, focuses on the complex issue of language in the 'open' world. The old joke, 'When is a door not a door?' comes to mind. Answer: 'When it's ajar.' Nothing is as it seems.

Fostering openness, however, detecting the space between open and ajar, is rife with tensions, as was pointed out in previous chapters. Childs, Axe, Veletsianos and Webster consider the tensions and opportunities that underlie developing a sense of openness in a higher education institution in Canada, contributing to the discussion about what openness looks like in practice.

The final chapter in Part 3 demonstrates another type of application of open as Elias, Ritchie, Gevalt, and Bowles investigated the pedagogy of 'small.' Using two relatively small, non-profit platform projects as examples, they revisited the community-centered philosophy of open pedagogy found in early work and asked new questions about scale while searching for productive ways to release open learning practices from their current institutional harness. Again, an important focus of their work is community, interaction, and the ability of participants to fully and creatively engage with each other on open platforms.

The virtual geographical reach of our material in this book is evident; but where is the certainty; where is the solid ground? As many of our authors have noted, it is less 'there' than we are often comfortable with – 'we' as academics and scholars and 'we' as society. And at the end of it all – at the end of these thousands of words in many chapters – have we explored sufficiently the nature of open, its interstices and intersections – its ability to make a difference in the world? Or, more succinctly and to the point, do we yet know what IT is? Or perhaps the question is: Do we *have* to? This is not a binary world we live in; it is not black-and-white. As academics, researchers, and thoughtful people, can we appreciate the greyness in which we live? Perhaps the answer is 'some more than others.' That potential philosophical treatise aside, does the answer or definition depend on, as so many questions do, your postal code? On the width and strength of your Internet connection? Or, perhaps even more basically, whether you have enough food to eat and go to bed in safety and security each night?

The advent of open has prompted another serious investigation into – without being flip or Monty Python-esque – the meaning of life. For when we examine *who* is privileged to learn through the auspices of 'open' and who is not; *who* is advantaged and who is not; *who,* in fact, is leading the charge, and who is not – we are looking at no less than the quality of life afforded various populations across the globe.

In searching for meaning, we often turn to metaphor; in this instance, my search resulted in our finding a simile, which was presented as an analogy. 'Open source is like sharing your baked bread.' But the analogy extended until it was akin to the old adage about giving a man a fish versus *teaching* him to fish – for his own fish, for his own food, for his own well-being. The bread-baking analogy waxed on:

> Sharing the recipe also means that you and your friends can bake together, strengthening your relationships, and potentially drawing others into the bond you share – because you now possess a common language for collaboration. Sharing a recipe for bread isn't like sharing bread itself. When you share a recipe, you haven't lost anything; both you and your friends can work with and enjoy the same knowledge at the same time, passing it on without consequence – unlike bread that's already been baked, which effectively disappears when you've given it up or eaten it. (Behrenshausen, 2012)

This is warming and comfortable. But what about the potential bakers who can't read the recipe, who don't have access to flour, or are gluten-intolerant? Chris Wanstrath, CEO of GitHub, reflected in 2016: 'It's not an open source/closed source world – it's more nuanced .... The world is much more gray [sic] today than black and white' (Katan, 2016). Wanstrath maintained in his short piece that both open and closed approaches to life and work allow for diversity and create difference; and he concluded that open is 'about people making a real difference in the world.' I think, at the time of writing, we need to remember that; I specify the 'time of writing' because the situation of today may well change in the future.

Open is a privileged tension and we have been privileged to have had so great a reach into various cultures and geographies, worldwide, in the work within this book. We delighted that this has been the case. We have been as 'open' as we could be.

References

Behrenshausen, B. (2102, June 2). *An open source analogy: Open source is like sharing a recipe.* Retrieved from https://opensource.com/life/12/6/open-source-like-sharing-recipe

Katan, T. (2016, September 20). 50 shades of open source [Blog post]. Retrieved from https://blog.axosoft.com/50-shades-open-source/

Lane, A. (2016). Emancipation through open education: Rhetoric or reality? In P. Blessinger & T. Bliss (Eds.), *Open education: International perspectives in higher education.* Cambridge: Open Book Publishers. Retrieved from http://www.openbookpublishers.com/htmlreader/978-1-78374-278-3/contents.xhtml

United Nations. (2015). *Transforming our world: The 2030 agenda for sustainable development* (No. A/RES/70/1). New York, NY: United Nations. Retrieved from https://sustainabledevelopment.un.org/post2015/transformingourworld/publication

PART 1

Open in Theory and Concept

CHAPTER 1

Open Education: Walking a Critical Path

Catherine Cronin

> There is no technology for justice. There is only justice.
>
> URSULA FRANKLIN (quoted in Meredith, 2016)

•••

> If the advice of the experts worked in the past, why then are you here now?
>
> If you are here now because you were not satisfied with the results of the other way of working, why didn't we pick this way? Why not walk another road?
>
> MYLES HORTON AND PAULO FREIRE (1990)

∴

This chapter explores justifications for and movements toward critical approaches to open education. While 'open' is often framed as an unequivocal good, the deceptively simple term hides a 'reef of complexity' (Hodgkinson-Williams & Gray, 2009, p. 114), much of which depends on the particular context within which openness is considered and practiced. Critical approaches to open education consider the nuances of context, focus on issues of participation and power, and encourage moving beyond the binaries of open and closed. As a starting point, I draw on Lane's (2016) analysis that open education initiatives can be considered in two broad forms. The first seeks to transform or empower individuals and groups within existing structures, e.g. by removing specific prior qualifications requirements, eliminating distance and time constraints, eliminating or reducing costs, and/or improving access overall. A second form of open education seeks to transform the structures themselves, and the relationships between the main actors (e.g. learners, teachers, educational institutions), in order to achieve greater equity. Many critical educators have planted their flags in the latter territory, advocating the use of an explicit inequality lens to support social transformation and cognitive justice. This

 | DOI: 10.1163/9789004422988_002

chapter presents an argument for critical and transformative approaches to open education. After a brief overview of open education, I explore several different critical analyses of open education and then widen the lens to consider critical analyses of the networks and platforms on which many open practices rely. The chapter concludes with examples of and recommendations for critical approaches to open education.

1 Open Education

Education is a fundamental human right, globally recognised as a foundation for peace, human dignity, social inclusion, and environmental sustainability (UNESCO, 2016). Since 1948, universal access to education has been included in global policies and initiatives, most recently as one of the 17 Sustainable Development Goals (SDGs): 'inclusive and quality education for all' (United Nations, 2015). Multiple constraints and restrictions act to limit access to and engagement with this fundamental human right for many individuals and groups. These include physical circumstances, geographic remoteness, financial constraints, technological barriers (e.g. digital divide), prior achievement barriers, and/or cultural or social norms for particular individuals and groups (Brown & Czerniewicz, 2010; Lane, 2009). Open education seeks to eliminate as many of these barriers as possible, with the aim of improving educational access, effectiveness, and equality. Explicitly-named 'open education' movements emerged during the latter half of the 20th century in different educational contexts and geographical locations. All can be seen as part of a longer history of global social, political, and education movements seeking to reduce inequality. Despite this connecting thread, a precise definition of open education remains elusive. Over 35 years ago, Noddings and Enright (1983) wrestled with the challenges of openness in their consideration of 'the promise of open education.' Much of their analysis retains its relevance today:

> Part of the problem of definition stems from the careless, if evocative, use of the term *open* by educators and the popular press to describe the wide variety of educational innovations which proliferated at the same time as open education classrooms were being developed. (p. 183)

More recently, the term MOOC (massive open online course) has been used to refer to explicitly connectivist projects (cMOOCs); online courses offered by universities and for-profit providers, often without any openly-licensed content (xMOOCs); and myriad hybrid models (Bayne & Ross, 2014). With the exception of the definition of open educational resources or OER (UNESCO, 2002), open education definitions continue to be diverse and often contested. Today, the qualifier 'open' is used to describe access to education, resources, learning and teaching practices, institutional practices, educational policies, digital tools, the use of educational technologies, and the values underlying educational endeavours. Despite this diversity, proponents of open education tend to share a fundamental philosophy that knowledge is a common good and that its creation and access should be as open as possible.

In practice, educators who espouse open education attempt to build opportunities for learners to:

- access education, open educational resources, open textbooks, and open scholarship,
- collaborate with others, across the boundaries of institutions, institutional systems, and geographic locations,
- create and co-create knowledge openly, and
- integrate formal and informal learning practices, networks, and identities.

Such values comprise the rationale for the use of open educational practices (OEP) – a broad descriptor that includes the creation, use and reuse of OER, open pedagogies, and open sharing of teaching practices (Cronin, 2017). Through the use of OEP, open educators seek to acknowledge the ubiquity of knowledge across networks and attempt to facilitate learning that fosters agency, empowerment, and global civic participation.

2 Critical Analyses of Open Education

Critique plays an important role within education theory as a counterpoint to over-simplistic thinking – often evident in the form of 'generalisations, unsubstantiated yet dominant discourses, and questionable binaries' (Gourlay, 2015, p. 312). Open education narratives have been criticised in each of these respects, as well as for an overall tendency towards idealism and optimism. Recent years have seen a rising call for greater critical analysis of, and critical approaches to, open education. It is worth clarifying the precise definition of the term *critical* as it is used here and throughout this chapter. Firstly, 'critical' refers to a process of critique on the part of educators, as described by Michael Apple (1990):

> Our task as educators ... requires criticism of what exists, restoring what is being lost, pointing towards possible futures; and sometimes it requires being criticized ourselves, this being something we should yearn for since

> it signifies the mutuality and shifting roles of teachers and taught that we must enhance. (p. xii)

Beyond this disposition, however, critical analysis and critical approaches are so called because they are informed by *critical theory*, the core concern of which is power relations in society (Freire, 1996; Giroux, 2003). This use of the term 'critical' is less an epistemological focus (as in *critical thinking*) than a focus on the concrete operations of power and a rejection of all forms of oppression, injustice, and inequality (as in *critical pedagogy*) (Burbules & Berk, 1999; hooks, 1994). Critical analyses of open education, then, begin by asking questions such as:

- Who defines openness?
- Who is included and who is excluded when education is 'opened', and in what ways?
- To what extent, by whom, in what contexts, and in what ways do specific open education initiatives achieve their stated aims of increasing access, fostering inclusivity, enhancing learning, developing capacity and agency, and empowering individuals, groups, and communities, if at all?
- Can open education initiatives, in practice, do the opposite of what they are intended to do?
- What does emancipatory open education look like?

Following is a short summary of three key strands of critical analysis of open education.

A foundational point in many critical analyses of open education is citing the false dualism of 'open' vs. 'closed,' and, indeed, moving beyond a simple or deontological understanding of openness (Archer & Prinsloo, 2017) and the comfort of binaries. If open is not the opposite of closed, how then to define open education in a meaningful way? Wiley (2009, para. 6) has espoused the continuous construct: 'A door can be wide open, completely shut, or open part way. So can a window. So can a faucet. So can your eyes. Our common-sense, everyday experience teaches us that 'open' is continuous.' Others reject the binary as well as continuous constructs of openness, viewing openness, for example, as boundary-crossing (Collier & Ross, 2017; Oliver, 2015) or an interplay (Edwards, 2015). Acknowledging that selectiveness and exclusions are inherent in all curricula and pedagogical approaches, Richard Edwards (2015) articulates a key question: 'not simply whether education is more or less open, but what forms of openness are worthwhile and for whom; openness alone is not an educational virtue' (p. 253). Recognition of this interplay of openness and closed-ness in all educational practices provides strong justification for a more critical approach, taking individual, social, and cultural contexts into account.

Another strand of critical analysis of open education focuses on the tendency toward idealism. Some open education narratives are criticised as utopian fantasies of democratisation, where the workings of systemic power and privilege around race, gender, culture, class, location, and sexuality are absent or suspended (Gourlay, 2015). In her analysis of MOOC narratives, for example, Tressie McMillan Cottom (2015a) notes that many MOOCs appear to conceive of open learners as 'roaming autodidacts – self-motivated, able learners that are simultaneously embedded in technocratic futures and disembedded from place, culture, history and markets' (p. 9), and almost always conceived as Western, white, educated, and male. Such optimistic assumptions about open education, be they naïve or intentional, serve to divert attention from structural inequalities and shift responsibility away from educational institutions. Idealistic 'openness' narratives also tend to conceal the complexities of academic labour inherent in open education. The creation of open educational resources, for example, relies heavily on institutional resources and the appropriation of academic labour, yet many OER narratives fail to address the inherent tension between open, networked possibilities of abundance and the corporatised, educational institutional structures on which they rely (Winn, 2015).

A third strand of critical analysis of open education advocates a greater theorisation of openness, particularly by moving beyond the dominant but limited interpretation of open as 'access.' An over-emphasis on removal of barriers obscures and often prevents a deeper analysis of associated relations of power (Bayne et al., 2015; Dhalla, 2018; Nobes, 2017; Oliver, 2015, Piron, 2017; singh, 2015; Watters, 2014). Knox (2013) has argued, for example, that the 'open as access' approach masks underlying assumptions of instrumentalism and essentialism, potentially masking the ways in which networks, systems, and codes of open education might affect or transform the learning process. Beyond deconstructing 'open as access' narratives, conceptions *of* open access also have been subject to critical analysis. Global South scholars, most notably, have highlighted how alienation and epistemic inequality arise from narrow, Global North-centric conceptions of open access (Czerniewicz, 2013), for example:

> ... a conception of open access that is limited to the legal and technical questions of the accessibility of science without thinking about the relationship between centre and periphery can become a source of epistemic

> alienation and neocolonialism in the South. (Piron, 2017, translated in Nobes, 2017)

If open education serves only to reinforce the normative universalism of Global North institutions, publications, research priorities, funding, and metrics, then efforts to 'open' education may simply be exacerbating rather than challenging inequality. This is a challenge that must be faced and addressed by all engaged in open education.

3 Critical Analyses of Networks and Platforms

Beyond theorising open education itself, the underlying structures and mechanics of open practice also have been the subject of critical analysis: namely, networks and platforms. The concept of the network as model and metaphor has been used widely in describing changes in society, learning, and education.

Other network constructs include *networked publics* (boyd, 2010), the *network society* (Castells, 2010), *networked individualism* (Rainie & Wellman, 2012; Wellman, 2002), and *networked learning* (Dirckinck-Holmfeld et al., 2012). In recent years, critical theorists have added nuance to, and sometimes challenged, these conceptual and analytical frameworks by exploring how power and privilege operate in networks – and the implications for individuals, institutions, and society. Broadly speaking, critiques of networked explanations of social behaviour assert that human social life cannot adequately be explained by the concepts of social ties and social capital, and furthermore, that networks can as easily exacerbate as reduce inequality. All hierarchies are not flattened.

One compelling avenue of critical analysis has highlighted the limitations of the network episteme itself (Light, 2014; Light & Cassidy, 2014; Mejias, 2011, 2013). Networks are not just metaphors, but actively organise and shape our social reality. Mejias's critical theorisation of networks includes the concept of the 'paranode,' defined as that which fills the interstices between the nodes of a network and resists being assumed by the network: 'it is only the outsides of the network where we can unthink or disidentify from the network, from the mainstream' (Mejias, 2011, p. 49). While network logic or nodocentrism defines paranodal space as 'empty,' Mejias (2013) counters that the paranodal serves to 'animate the network' (p. 153) and also to uncover the politics of inclusion and exclusion encoded in the network. In a similar vein, Ben Light's (2014) theory of disconnective practice, asserts that disconnection is an active part of engagement in social networking sites (SNS). In Light's analysis, disconnection is complex and contextual enacted not only in terminating an account or opting out of engaging in a SNS, for example, but also prior to and during engagement in social networks. A prevalent reason for disengagement from networks (or, conversely, engagement in disconnective practice) is resistance to surveillance and preservation of privacy. Privacy is of enormous individual, institutional, and societal importance in an increasingly open and participatory culture in which data is persistent, replicable, searchable, and scalable (boyd, 2010) and our interactions tend to be public by default and private through effort (boyd, 2014).

As networked, participatory culture has evolved, so too has our conception of privacy. While definitions of privacy traditionally relied on spatial distinctions (public/private) and on limiting access to and control of information, more recent and complex understandings of privacy have shifted the focus to context. Helen Nissenbaum's (2010) influential work considers privacy within a *framework of contextual integrity*. According to Nissenbaum, social activity, occurring in specific contexts, is governed by context-specific norms; among these are informational norms regarding the appropriate flow of information between parties. Contextual integrity is preserved when informational norms are upheld and violated when they are contravened. Nissenbaum's framework of contextual integrity has been adopted and further developed by many researchers, practitioners, and policy makers. Patricia Lange (2007), for example, used the framework to explore variation within a particular context, i.e. video sharing on YouTube, proposing the concepts of 'publicly private' (revealing one's identity but limiting access to content) and 'privately public' (sharing content but limiting access to one's identity) to describe individuals' nuanced behaviours in relation to privacy. And in her empirical study of teens' use of social media, danah boyd (2012) coined the term 'social steganography' to describe another variation of privacy behaviour: sharing identity and content but limiting access to meaning: 'only those who are in the know have the necessary information to look for and interpret the information provided' (p. 349). These examples illustrate an important point: engaging in paranodal or disconnective practice does not demand wholesale rejection of networks, including social media and SNS (an unrealistic option for most). Rather, it entails critical questioning of the terms of engagement within networks and enactment of creative and alternative modes of being within and beyond networks.

Beyond these complex and contextual reconceptualisations of the concept of privacy, is the extent to which suppression of privacy lies at the heart of the business models of most digital and social media platforms. The concepts of 'platform capitalism' (Srnicek, 2016) and 'surveillance capitalism' (Zuboff, 2019) lay bare these new business models as directly reliant on the appropriation of data and the convergence of surveillance and profit. Corporate and platform surveillance practices track and monetize our locations, our connections, and our every click (Zuboff, 2019). The challenge for educators, and particularly for open educators, is clear. Many of the tools and platforms we use to engage in social connection and open educational practices, tools intimately woven into our personal and academic lives, embody values stemming from libertarian, neoliberal beliefs – designed to allow and encourage some behaviours and prevent others (Gilliard & Culik, 2016; Marwick, 2013).

In summary, critical analyses of open education, networks, and platforms present a set of critical lenses –epistemological, theoretical, social, political– with which to examine existing forms of, and conceptualise new approaches to, open education.

4 Critical Approaches to Open Education

Critical approaches to open education vary considerably by scope, location, and specific intention, but all address issues of power and offer ways to reconceptualise and reframe (open) education in ways that are both participatory and emancipatory. This section briefly describes a few examples.

Open pedagogy is a key pillar of critical approaches to open education. DeRosa and Robison (2017) and Rosen and Smale (2015) frame their definitions of open pedagogy and open digital pedagogy, respectively, as versions of critical digital pedagogy. Critical digital pedagogy focuses on the potential of open practices to create dialogue, to deconstruct the teacher-student binary, to bring disparate learning spaces together, and to function as a form of resistance to inequitable power relations within and outside of educational institutions (Stommel, 2014). Examples of open pedagogy include working together with students to: use, adapt, and create OER; edit Wikipedia; engage in conversations beyond institutional boundaries; contribute to local, global, and disciplinary communities and projects; and ask critical questions about openness. A recent definition of open pedagogy by DeRosa and Jhangiani (2018) eloquently summarises the tenets of critical approaches to open education:

> 'Open Pedagogy,' as we engage with it, is a site of praxis, a place where theories about learning, teaching, technology, and social justice enter into a conversation with each other and inform the development of educational practices and structures. This site is dynamic, contested, constantly under revision, and resists static definitional claims. But it is not a site vacant of meaning or political conviction.

Beyond open pedagogy, we also consider critical approaches to developing *open courses*. MOOC development at the University of Cape Town (UCT), for example, is grounded in a social inclusion perspective (Gidley, Hampson, Wheeler, & Bereded-Samuel, 2010). Critiquing the elite, neo-colonialist, closed, and broadcast mode of many institutional MOOCs, UCT developers have conceptualised MOOCs as an intentional *process* rather than a *product* – acknowledging the importance not only of access, but also of participation and empowerment (Czerniewicz & Walji, 2017). UCT MOOCs such as 'Education for All' and 'Introduction to Social Innovation' are embedded in a theoretical approach to openness that focuses on inclusive content development, enables engagement with learning in multiple ways (not solely online), and liaises with and empowers local communities (Arinto, Hodgkinson-Williams, & Trotter, 2017; Czerniewicz & Walji, 2017).

Openness is contextual, but it is also personal and continually negotiated (Cronin, 2017); thus, it is important to consider critical approaches to open education on an individual level also. The creation and enactment of *open, networked identities* on various platforms is considered a necessity by many as education institutions and wider society 'become enmeshed with digital practice and culture' (Hildebrandt & Couros, 2016, para. 5). Such enmeshing is not uncomplicated, however. Educators who use OEP, for example, typically create and enact open, networked, 'Resident' digital identities (based on White & Le Cornu's, 2017, Visitor/Resident typology), leaving myriad traces of their social and scholarly engagement on the web (Stewart, 2016). Critical approaches to openness can prompt us to acknowledge, and even facilitate, less obvious avenues of openness, however. In the context of increasing surveillance, the use of anonymity may be seen as fostering freedom from the commodification of the social. Indeed, anonymity, conceptualised as 'constellations of partial unknowability, invisibility and untrackability' (Bachmann, Knecht, & Wittel, 2017, p. 243), can be considered socially productive and adding value to networked experience (Light & Cassidy, 2014). And what of the many educators who use open tools to curate resources for themselves and their students and develop their own and their students' digital literacies, but without making themselves openly visible online? Such individuals would be classified as 'Visitors' in the Visitor/Resident continuum, i.e. engaging on the web without leaving a social trace (White & Le Cornu, 2017). By not creating open, networked identities themselves, these individuals might not be considered 'open educators.' And yet, educators making such strategic choices educate and empower students about issues such as digital identity, surveillance, and privacy. These strategies align with critiques of networks by Light (2014) and Mejias (2011, 2013), i.e. paranodal, disconnective practice as both resistance and pedagogy.

While we cannot readily untether participatory culture, software platforms, and corporate interests, development of digital literacies (broadly conceived) can promote critical awareness of issues such as algorithmic bias, surveillance, and privacy for all engaged in education. The conceptualisation of digital literacies continues to expand rapidly with recent work in the areas of *web literacy* (Caulfield, 2017), *critical digital literacies* (Alexander et al., 2017; Brown et al., 2016), *critical data literacies* (Hinrichsen & Coombs, 2013; Pangrazio, 2016), *digital citizenship* (Almekinder et al., 2017; Couros & Hildebrandt, 2017), *critical digital citizenship* (Emejulu & McGregor, 2016), and literacies of *participatory culture* (Jenkins et al., 2015). All include critical reflection on the ways in which networks and platforms foster connection as well as surveillance, inequality, and even 'epistemic enslavement' (Mejias, 2011). Fostering the development of digital/web literacies may range from teaching and modelling digital identities and literacies to teaching *about* digital literacies without interacting with students on the open web. Whatever the method, this is complex work, as acknowledged by Maha Bali (in Alexander et al., 2017):

> The role of higher education, and educators, is to work on nurturing digital literacies across the curriculum, taking into account the inequalities of access to opportunities to develop digital literacies before and outside of higher education, and keeping in mind the intersectionality of incoming students and how their priorities within digital literacies will differ. (p. 21)

A key to critical approaches to open education is to develop critical digital/web literacies and to foster agency on the part of all learners and educators regarding whether, how, and in what contexts they *choose* to be open. In other words, using Edwards' (2015) framing, all should have the capacity and agency with which to manage their own personal interplay of openness and closedness.

5 Conclusion

As noted at the start of this chapter, Lane (2016) outlined two broad approaches to open education: empowering individuals and groups within existing structures and transforming the structures themselves in order to achieve equity. Critical approaches to open education focus on the latter, seeking to reframe open education to be participatory and emancipatory, as well as being more accessible. Those advocating critical approaches to open education seek to expand access, including the concept of access, but also to further justice.

> What I do need are specifics about how this moment is not like those other moments, those old moments of educational expansion that were shaped by powerful white interests, wealth, and racism to expand access without furthering justice. (McMillan Cottom, 2015b)

Critical approaches to open education require that we ask difficult questions about power and participation. In addition to specific questions related to openness (see p. 5), we also must ask: Who is in our classrooms and institutions, and why? Who is not in our classrooms and institutions, and why not? Who is excluded and who may be silenced by systems, policies, and practices which skew attention and rewards toward white, male, privileged, Global North experiences and priorities? In the words of Audrey Watters (2014): 'We need an ethics of care, of justice, not simply assume that 'open' does the work of those for us.'

The work of critical open educators, researchers, and advocates is individual, collective, and multi-layered: decentering Global North epistemologies; furthering personal and institutional understanding of intersectional inequality; challenging traditional power relations, within and beyond classrooms and institutions; connecting with/via formal and informal learning spaces (digital and physical); recognising that resistance to openness is a personal, and possibly radical, choice; and ongoing self-reflection. Critical approaches to open education represent intentional efforts to transform structures, in all contexts, to achieve greater equity.

References

Alexander, B., Adams Becker, S., Cummins, M., & Hall Giesinger, C. (2017). *Digital literacy in higher education, Part II: An NMC Horizon project strategic brief. Volume 3.4*. Austin, TX: The New Media Consortium. Retrieved from https://cdn.nmc.org/media/2017-nmc-strategic-brief-digital-literacy-in-higher-education-II.pdf

Almekinder, A., Bryant, E., Caines, A., Lukens, K., Marksbury, N., Narashimhan, A., … Spohrer, J. (2017). Digital citizenship + Liberal Arts = Students empowered for life. *EDUCAUSE Review*. Retrieved from https://er.educause.edu:443/articles/2017/6/digital-citizenship-liberal-arts-students-empowered-for-life

Apple, M. (1990). Foreword. In S. G. O'Malley, R. C. Rosen, & L. Vogt (Eds.), *Politics of education: Essays from radical teacher*. Albany, NY: Statue University of New York Press.

Arinto, P. B., Hodgkinson-Williams, C., & Trotter, H. (2017). OER and OEP in the Global South: Implications and recommendations for social inclusion. In C. Hodgkinson-Williams & P. B. Arinto (Eds.), *Adoption and Impact of OER in the Global South*. Cape Town & Ottawa: African Minds, International Development Research Centre & Research on Open Educational Resources. https://doi.org/10.5281/zenodo.1043829

Archer, E., & Prinsloo, P. (2017). Some exploratory thoughts on Openness and an ethics of care. In D. Singh & C. Stückelberger (Eds.), *Ethics in higher education: Values-driven leaders for the future*. Geneva: Global Series Globethics.net. http://uir.unisa.ac.za/handle/10500/21903

Bachmann, G., Knecht, M., & Wittel, A. (2017). The social productivity of anonymity. *Ephemera: Theory and Politics in Organization, 17*(2), 241–258. Retrieved from http://www.ephemerajournal.org/sites/default/files/pdfs/contribution/17-2editorial.pdf

Bayne, S., Knox, J., & Ross, J. (2015). Open education: The need for a critical approach. *Learning, Media and Technology, 40*(3). https://doi.org/10.1080/17439884.2015.1065272

Bayne, S., & Ross, J. (2014). *The pedagogy of the massive open online course: The UK view*. Heslington: The Higher Education Academy. Retrieved from https://www.heacademy.ac.uk/knowledge-hub/pedagogy-massive-open-online-course-mooc-uk-view

Beetham, H., & Sharpe, R. (2010). *Digital literacy framework*. Retrieved from http://jiscdesignstudio.pbworks.com/w/page/46740204/Digital%20literacy%20framework

boyd, d. (2010). Social network sites as networked publics: Affordances, dynamics, and implications. In Z. Papacharissi (Ed.), *Networked self: Identity, community, and culture on social network sites* (pp. 39–58). New York, NY: Routledge. Retrieved from http://www.danah.org/papers/2010/SNSasNetworkedPublics.pdf

boyd, d. (2012). Networked privacy. *Surveillance & Society, 10*(3–4), 348–350. Retrieved from http://library.queensu.ca:80/ojs/index.php/surveillance-and-society/issue/view/Open_Dec2012

boyd, d. (2014). *It's complicated: The social lives of networked teens*. New Haven, CT: Yale University Press.

Brown, C., & Czerniewicz, L. (2010). Debunking the 'digital native': Beyond digital apartheid, towards digital democracy. *Journal of Computer Assisted Learning, 26*(5), 357–369. https://doi.org/10.1111/j.1365-2729.2010.00369.x

Brown, C., Czerniewicz, L., Huang, C.-W., & Mayisela, T. (2016). *Curriculum for digital education leadership: A concept paper*. Commonwealth of Learning (COL). Retrieved from http://oasis.col.org/handle/11599/2442

Burbules, N. C., & Berk, R. (1999). Critical thinking and critical pedagogy: Relations, differences, and limits. In T. S. Popkewitz & L. Fendler (Eds.), *Critical theories in education: Changing terrains of knowledge and politics*. New York, NY: Routledge.

Castells, M. (2010). *The rise of the network society* (2nd ed., Vol. 1). Hoboken, NJ: Wiley-Blackwell.

Caulfield, M. (2017). *Web literacy for student fact-checkers* (Self-published). Retrieved from https://webliteracy.pressbooks.com/

Collier, A., & Ross, J. (2017). For whom, and for what? Not-yetness and thinking beyond open content. *Open Praxis, 9*(1), 7–16. https://doi.org/10.5944/openpraxis.9.1.406

Couros, A., & Hildebrandt, K. (2017, June 5). What kind of (digital) citizen? [Blog post]. Retrieved from http://educationaltechnology.ca/2804

Cronin, C. (2017). Openness and praxis: Exploring the use of open educational practices in higher education. *The International Review of Research in Open and Distance Learning, 18*(5). http://dx.doi.org/10.19173/irrodl.v18i5.3096

Czerniewicz, L. (2013, April 29). Inequitable power dynamics of global knowledge production and exchange must be confronted head on [Blog post]. Retrieved from http://blogs.lse.ac.uk/impactofsocialsciences/2013/04/29/redrawing-the-map-from-access-to-participation/#more-10331

Czerniewicz, L., & Walji, S. (2017). MOOCs, community orientation and reclaiming the social justice agenda. In *GO-GN*. Keynes: The Open University. Retrieved from http://go-gn.net/webinars/webinar-moocs-community-orientation-and-reclaiming-the-social-justice-agenda/

DeRosa, R., & Jhangiani, R. (2018). Open pedagogy. In *Open pedagogy notebook*. Retrieved from http://openpedagogy.org/open-pedagogy/

DeRosa, R., & Robison, S. (2017). From OER to open pedagogy: Harnessing the power of open. In R. S. Jhangiani & R. Biswas-Diener (Eds.), *Open: The philosophy and practices that are revolutionizing education and science*. London: Ubiquity Press. Retrieved from https://www.ubiquitypress.com/site/chapters/10.5334/bbc.i/

Dhalla, A. (2018, May 7). The dangers of being open [Blog post]. Retrieved from https://medium.com/@amirad/the-dangers-of-being-open-b50b654fe77e

Dirckinck-Holmfeld, L., Hodgson, V., & McConnell, D. (Eds.). (2012). *Exploring the theory, pedagogy and practice of networked learning*. New York, NY: Springer New York. Retrieved from http://link.springer.com/10.1007/978-1-4614-0496-5

Edwards, R. (2015). Knowledge infrastructures and the inscrutability of openness in education. *Learning, Media and Technology, 40*(3), 251–264. https://doi.org/10.1080/17439884.2015.1006131

Emejulu, A., & McGregor, C. (2016). Towards a radical digital citizenship in digital education. *Critical Studies in Education*. https://doi.org/10.1080/17508487.2016.1234494

Freire, P. (1996). *Pedagogy of the oppressed*. Harmondsworth: Penguin.

Gidley, J. M., Hampson, G. P., Wheeler, L., & Bereded-Samuel, E. (2010). From access to success: An integrated approach to quality higher education informed by social inclusion theory and practice. *Higher Education Policy, 23*(1), 123–147. https://doi.org/10.1057/hep.2009.24

Gilliard, C., & Culik, H. (2016, May 24). Digital redlining, access, and privacy. Common sense education [Blog post]. Retrieved from https://www.commonsense.org/education/privacy/blog/digital-redlining-access-privacy

Giroux, H. A. (2003). Critical theory and educational practice. In A. Darder, M. Baltodano, & R. D. Torres (Eds.), *The critical pedagogy reader* (pp. 27–56). New York, NY: RoutledgeFalmer.

Gourlay, L. (2015). Open education as a 'heterotopia of desire'. *Learning, Media and Technology, 40*(3), 310–327. https://doi.org/10.1080/17439884.2015.1029941

Hildebrandt, K., & Couros, A. (2016). Digital selves, digital scholars: Theorising academic identity in online spaces. *Journal of Applied Social Theory, 1*(1). Retrieved from http://socialtheoryapplied.com/journal/jast/article/view/16

Hinrichsen, J., & Coombs, A. (2013). The five resources of critical digital literacy: A framework for curriculum integration. *Research in Learning Technology, 21*(1). https://doi.org/10.3402/rlt.v21.21334

Hodgkinson-Williams, C., & Gray, E. (2009). Degrees of openness: The emergence of OER at the University of Cape Town. *International Journal of Education and Development Using Information and Communication Technology, 5*(5), 101–116. Retrieved from http://ijedict.dec.uwi.edu/viewarticle.php?id=864

hooks, b. (1994). *Teaching to transgress: Education as the practice of freedom*. New York, NY: Routledge.

Horton, M., & Freire, P. (1990). *We make the road by walking: Conversations on education and social change*. Philadelphia, PA: Temple University Press.

Jenkins, H., Ito, M., & boyd, d. (2015). *Participatory culture in a networked era: A conversation on youth, learning, commerce, and politics*. Cambridge: Polity Press.

Knox, J. (2013). Five critiques of the open educational resources movement. *Teaching in Higher Education, 18*(8), 821–832. https://doi.org/10.1080/13562517.2013.774354

Lane, A. (2009). The impact of openness on bridging educational digital divides. *The International Review of Research in Open and Distance Learning, 10*(5). http://dx.doi.org/10.19173/irrodl.v10i5.637

Lane, A. (2016). Emancipation through open education: Rhetoric or reality? In P. Blessinger & T. Bliss (Eds.), *Open education: International perspectives in higher education*. Cambridge: Open Book Publishers. Retrieved from http://www.openbookpublishers.com/htmlreader/978-1-78374-278-3/contents.xhtml

Lange, P. G. (2007). Publicly private and privately public: Social networking on YouTube. *Journal of Computer-Mediated Communication, 13*(1), 361–380. https://doi.org/10.1111/j.1083-6101.2007.00400.x

Light, B. (2014). *Disconnecting with social network sites*. London: Palgrave Macmillan UK. Retrieved from http://www.palgrave.com/gp/book/9781137022462

Light, B., & Cassidy, E. (2014). Strategies for the suspension and prevention of connection: Rendering disconnection as socioeconomic lubricant with Facebook. *New Media & Society, 16*(7), 1169–1184. https://doi.org/10.1177/1461444814544002

Marwick, A. E. (2013). Online identity. In J. Hartley, J. Burgess, & A. Bruns (Eds.), *Companion to new media dynamics* (pp. 355–364). Malden, MA: Blackwell. Retrieved from https://www.academia.edu/26435230/Online_Identity

McMillan Cottom, T. (2015a). *Intersectionality and critical engagement with the internet* (SSRN Scholarly Paper No. ID 2568956). Rochester, NY: Social Science Research Network. Retrieved from http://papers.ssrn.com/abstract=2568956

McMillan Cottom, T. (2015b). Open and accessible to what and for whom? [Blog post]. Retrieved from https://tressiemc.com/uncategorized/open-and-accessible-to-what-and-for-whom-reflections-on-icde-2015/

Mejias, U. A. (2011). Towards a critique of digital networks for learning. *Progressive Librarian, 34/35*, 46–49. Retrieved from http://www.progressivelibrariansguild.org/PL_Jnl/contents34_35.shtml

Mejias, U. A. (2013). *Off the network: Disrupting the digital world* (Vol. 41). Minneapolis, MN: University of Minnesota Press. Retrieved from https://www.upress.umn.edu/book-division/pdf/off-the-network

Meredith, M. (2016). *All problems can be illuminated; not all problems can be solved.* Presented at 9th Berlin Biennale for Contemporary Art. Retrieved from http://bb9.berlinbiennale.de/all-problems-can-be-illuminated-not-all-problems-can-be-solved/

Nissenbaum, H. (2010). *Privacy in context: Technology, policy, and the integrity of social life*. Stanford, CA: Stanford University Press. Retrieved from http://www.sup.org/books/title/?id=8862

Nobes, A. (2017, December 8). Must we decolonise open access? Perspectives from Francophone Africa [Blog post]. Retrieved from http://journalologik.uk/?p=149

Noddings, N., & Enright, D. S. (1983). The promise of open education. *Theory into Practice, 22*(3), 182–189. https://doi.org/10.1080/00405848309543059

Oliver, M. (2015). From openness to permeability: Reframing open education in terms of positive liberty in the enactment of academic practices. *Learning, Media and Technology, 40*(3), 365–384. https://doi.org/10.1080/17439884.2015.1029940

Pangrazio, L. (2016). Reconceptualising critical digital literacy. *Discourse: Studies in the Cultural Politics of Education, 37*(2), 163–174. https://doi.org/10.1080/01596306.2014.942836

Piron, F. (2017, September 19). *Qui sait? Le libre accès en Afrique et en Haïti.* Retrieved from http://www.laviedesidees.fr/Qui-sait.html

Rainie, L., & Wellman, B. (2012). *Networked: The new social operating system.* Cambridge, MA: MIT Press.

Rosen, J. R., & Smale, M. A. (2015). Open digital pedagogy = Critical pedagogy. *Hybrid Pedagogy.* Retrieved from http://www.digitalpedagogylab.com/hybridped/open-digital-pedagogy-critical-pedagogy/

singh, s. (2015, June 27). The fallacy of 'open' [Blog post]. Retrieved from https://savasavasava.wordpress.com/2015/06/27/the-fallacy-of-open/

Srnicek, N. (2016). *Platform capitalism.* Cambridge: Polity Press.

Stewart, B. (2016). Collapsed publics: Orality, literacy, and vulnerability in academic Twitter. *Journal of Applied Social Theory, 1*(1). Retrieved from http://socialtheoryapplied.com/journal/jast/article/view/33

Stommel, J. (2014). Critical digital pedagogy: A definition. *Hybrid Pedagogy.* Retrieved from http://www.digitalpedagogylab.com/hybridped/critical-digital-pedagogy-definition/

UNESCO. (2002, July 8). *UNESCO promotes new initiatives for free educational resources on the Internet.* Retrieved from http://www.unesco.org/education/news_en/080702_free_edu_ress.shtml

UNESCO. (2016). *Education for people and planet: Creating sustainable futures for all.* Paris, France: UNESCO. Retrieved from http://en.unesco.org/gem-report/report/2016/education-people-and-planet-creating-sustainable-futures-all/page#sthash.WPPWZzsa.ytg88C7J.dpbs

United Nations. (2015). *Transforming our world: The 2030 agenda for sustainable development* (No. A/RES/70/1). New York, NY: United Nations. Retrieved from https://sustainabledevelopment.un.org/post2015/transformingourworld/publication

Watters, A. (2014, November 16). From 'open' to justice #OpenCon2014 [Blog post]. Retrieved from http://hackeducation.com/2014/11/16/from-open-to-justice

Wellman, B. (2002). Little boxes, glocalization, and networked individualism. In M. Tanabe, P. van den Besselaar, & T. Ishida (Eds.), *Digital cities II: Computational and sociological approaches* (pp. 10–25). Berlin, Germany: Springer. https://doi.org/10.1007/3-540-45636-8_2

White, D., & Le Cornu, A. (2017). Using 'visitors and residents' to visualise digital practices. *First Monday, 22*(8). http://firstmonday.org/ojs/index.php/fm/article/view/7802

Wiley, D. (2009, November 16). Defining 'open' [Blog post]. Retrieved from http://opencontent.org/blog/archives/1123

Winn, J. (2015). Open education and the emancipation of academic labour. *Learning, Media and Technology, 40*(3). https://doi.org/10.1080/17439884.2015.1015546

Zuboff, S. (2019). *The age of surveillance capitalism: The fight for the future at the new frontier of power*. London: Profile Books.

CHAPTER 2

The Opened Mind: An Application of the Historical Concept of Openness in Education

Lloyd Hawkeye Robertson, Dulce Torres Robertson and Trevor John Robertson

This chapter will argue openness in education is an expression of the development of the human mind that allows the individual to seek an objective stance relative to received tradition. The capacity to think as an individual led to such advances in cultural evolution that it has become universalized with education becoming a project promoting nothing other than the further development of this capacity. This promotion of thinking skills may be constrained or uneven. For example, universities have traditionally exercised a gatekeeping function determining which classes and categories of people are permitted entry. Such a function will restrict the opportunity of some classes to develop those thinking skills we associate with education. Also considered in the concept of openness is the development of accepted canons and the ability of faculty, students and the public to challenge those canons. Since education involves self-change, it also changes the cultures of those who participate; and the discussion of openness must also include consideration of the receptivity of cultures to education.

Referencing earlier work, we will suggest that an evolved self-structure allowed us to situate ourselves temporally and contextually with notions of objective reality leading to our self-definition as a rational species. As will be seen, since such learning may effect changes to the worldview and to learners' 'self,' issues with respect to the transformative nature of education such as the balancing of the individual and the collective, and implications of democratization are discussed along with issues of content and historical tradition. The receptiveness or openness of cultures to education-enhancing transformative education in the development of mind will be examined. We conclude with a paradigm on the transmission of cultural meaning. Fundamental to this discussion is what is meant by the term 'mind.'

 | DOI: 10.1163/9789004422988_003

1 Cultural Evolution and the Development of Mind

Johnson (2003) defined *mind* to be an evolved cognitive program that included algorithms for objective belief, individual volition and internally consistent thought. After studying three-millennia-old written work, he declared that ancient Egyptians and Greeks lacked such minds. Although we cannot be certain when humans obtained the ability to situate themselves temporally and contextually as individuals with accompanying notions of causality, at some point in human history our ancestors would have lacked these abilities. It can be said, however, that significant developments in human cultures with inevitable applications to self-construal occurred during the period referenced by Johnson. Noting an outpouring of philosophical and religious thought across numerous human cultures during the period from 800 to 200 BCE, Jaspers (1951) declared this period to be the 'Axial Age' when 'the man with whom we live today came into being' (p. 135). Mahoney (1991) called this epoch 'a time of turnings … of unprecedented reflective and spiritual activity when humans first 'formally' discovered the universe within themselves and the powers of faith and reason' (pp. 29–30). Robertson (2017) argued that the self evolved culturally during this period with humans defining themselves using cultural memes for volition, constancy, distinctness, and social interest. Central to this development is the sense that there is an 'I' capable of such thinking with self-reflection the inevitable spandrel to the exercise of these abilities.

The evolution of the individual self was not without cost. Homo sapiens owe their success as a species to the ability to take collective action in response to environmental challenges (Harari, 2016; Pinker, 2002), but prior to the development of an individual volitional self such action would be dependent on genetically and culturally programmed behaviour sequences that responded to triggering stimuli. While the 'cultural wisdom' contained in such response systems was less efficient in addressing new challenges, it had eminent application to conditions in which they evolved. Creative individual action could result in less effective responses than those already present in the collectivity's repertoire. Individual self-interest could destabilize the collectivity by challenging assumptions upon which the collectivity was based. Thus, the Axial Age was as much about placing limits on the volitional self as it was on embracing new knowledge creation, with resultant implications for openness in education.

Education prior to the Axial Age would have largely consisted of the rote learning of culturally mandated customs and responses. With notions of an objective reality that exists outside of such cultures, education necessarily became concerned with epistemological questions such as, 'What constitutes evidence?' Initially, education that developed rational thinking abilities was restricted to small classes of people with limits placed on inquiry to protect the collective interest. In today's parlance, societies that attempt to limit inquiry in the interests of the society are often termed 'traditional' or 'collectivist,' while those advocating a more radical paradigm are called 'individualist.'

Yet people in societies deemed to be collectivist are capable of individual volition. For example, a recent study involving 1,660 Chinese adolescents (Li, Wang, Zhou, Kong & Li, 2016) found that a majority (85%) had a belief in their own individual volition and they scored higher on scales of cognitive and affective well-being than those who did not share this self-belief. Conversely, individuals in societies marked as individualist engage in collective identification and action because such abilities are fundamental to social organization. Defining individualists as those who perceive themselves to be stable autonomous entities and defining collectivists as those who view themselves as dynamically defined by their social context, Chiao and his associates (2009) used functional magnetic resonance imaging (fMRI)[1] to modulate neural representations underlying these social cognitions during the processing of general and self-judgments. They found that such imaging positively predicted how individualistic or collectivistic a person is across cultures; however, subjects from Japan were as likely to be individualistic or collectivistic as those drawn from the USA. In a qualitative study using a cross-cultural sample, Robertson (2010) identified memes for both collectivism and individualism in the selves of every participant. Psychologists from a variety of therapeutic schools have reported that approaches assuming individual volition and/or self-regulation are effective in cross-cultural settings (Deci & Ryan, 2008; Freire, Koller, Piason, & da Silva, 2005; Robertson, Holleran, & Samuels, 2015; Seligman, Steen, Park, & Peterson, 2005). An implication of this research is that the dichotomous designation of societies as 'individualist' or 'collectivist' is too simplistic and such designations may reflect the official ruling political ideologies more than the constituents themselves.

Education has the potential to be personally transformative (Conrad, 2008; Robertson, 2011a). It is argued here that from its earliest beginnings, the project of education has been based on an evolving vision of our human potentiality that includes conceptualizations of objective belief, individual volition and logically coherent thought. Issues involving the scope of what is taught and to whom it is taught and openness with respect to content and access flow from this beginning.

2 Education as a Response to the Needs of the Individual and the Collective

In this chapter, openness references opportunities given to those classes of people permitted to gain the knowledge that promotes capacities of selfhood. The ability to question and develop the mind is a powerful advantage that is promoted as a practice of power. At the same time, the individual thus formed and promoted must also be contained and enabled within the collective cultural matrix. From this perspective, history is a balancing of the forces of collectivism and individualism. Democratization is a process of extending the rights of citizenry and education to increasing classes of people and extending the rights of the educated to question existing knowledge the ultimate triumph of individualism. Open access to a university education is part of a three-millennia process of the formation of the individual and the democratization of knowledge with open universities and Massive Open Online Courses (MOOCs) representing a further and more recent extension. As the field of MOOCs expands in education, there's also accompanying diversification in its implementation. This diversification posts a challenge to higher education within the 'landscape of educational provision' (Czerniewicz, 2014; Weller, 2017).

The balancing of the forces of individualism and collectivism is best accomplished through the individual's conscious appropriation of tradition, where tradition may be seen as the accumulated responses and patterns of the collective and conscious appropriation may be seen in the ability to individually respond to tradition as a dimension of objective reality. Based on an understanding of the mimesis at the basis of cultural transmission and development (Girard, 1977), it may be seen that the formation of the individual is at the same time the individual's appropriation of culture. Education thus needs to have a definite historical and cultural content which is subjected to a hermeneutic retrieval (Gadamer, 2013) which will be explored further in this chapter. Quality education must offer the understanding of tradition which was espoused by the liberal arts together with the capacity for a critical reception. This capacity to receive culture and give it a personal meaning is a central aspect of meaningful creative living (Winnicott, 1971/2005). This necessity for creative cultural transmission indicates that the content and practice of quality university education necessarily involves cultural sources that are not arbitrarily chosen but historical. The process of opening minds is also the process of becoming cultured within a specific historical situation, and debates about culture and multiculturalism are at the heart of education as a meaningful enterprise.

Two further recent developments in university education pertain to the implications of this perspective on the opened mind. The first is the inclusion of increasing numbers of students in universities to the point that it became necessary to focus on preparing students for specific careers. Societies cannot support leisure classes of an unlimited size and the university is now perceived as much as a path to employment as a place for self-development. While an older system of higher education served the needs of the aristocracy, Simon Marginson has described higher education in terms of a national status competition in which students and institutions co-produce social status (Marginson, 2004). According to Marginson, this national status competition continues to be a key factor for understanding how higher education is conducted, with lower-status institutions more likely to become determined by economic market competition or eventually a fully capitalist development. It should be noted here that our argument begins from what Marginson calls 'the pre-market world of lived educational practices' (2004, p. 182), although the model of status markets and economic markets in higher education could be used to describe delimitations on the activity of education from the side of the collective. It should also be noted here that open education cannot be reconciled with a status market insofar as the status market is premised precisely on a limit to the number of high-status positions, a point which Marginson makes effectively throughout his argument. Insofar as education is part of a national status market, the economic empowerment of the individual is circumscribed within the roles afforded within the system. Thus, the balancing of individual and collective is repeated in terms of employment and economic roles, where the individual seeks both empowerment and self-development through knowledge with economic implications.

The second, still more recent development, is the rate of change in technologies associated with attention formation. Donald (2001) defined attention formation as the abstraction of components of event percepts and the isolation of common features of those percepts noting:

> Given our invisible habits of shared attention, and some cultural control over how experience is processed, a common language will allow us to share mind better, by defining a common representational framework. This gives us a new cultural domain, a stock exchange of the mind, where ideas and impressions can be traded, tested, and recombined at will. (pp. 294–295)

Attention formation is both a collective and an individual activity. If the rise of the educated individual is the formation of the capacity for attention, these dynamics may be heightened or curtailed by new technologies that are addressed specifically to attention. Weller (2017) predicted that technical and cultural changes could significantly impact the new domain of higher education over the next decade with implications for cognition. Stiegler (2010/2008) thematised that a number of technologies must be of concern without ascertaining the status of any technology as 'poison' or 'cure.' Among the new technologies that catch his interest are television and websites targeted to youth and children, technological developments in marketing, video games, and 'universities with global outreach.'

3 Self-Reflexivity and Curricular Content

The desire for openness, economic development, technological development, and the process of democratization lead to increasing rates of participation in university education. This may be understood as increasing openness provided the activity of mindful cultural transmission is being meaningfully achieved. Were these educational institutions to focus on career preparation without developing those qualities of mind essential for reasoned thinking skills, there would be little overall gain in openness as it relates to what we have described as the historic project of education. Reasoned thinking skills are grounded in self-knowledge and the ability to understand new perspectives. While the self may be constructed through the unconscious appropriation of cultural sources (Damon & Hart, 1988; Harter, 2012; Robertson, 2014), making this appropriation conscious along with its cultural and historical antecedents increases the capacity of the individual to make meaningful decisions.

In the older educational mandate of opening the mind, it was necessary to grapple with traditionary sources. This involvement with historical tradition cannot be superseded insofar as the educated individual is formed by conscious appropriation of the historical sources which are received objectively. For this reason, it is of vital importance to discern which cultural content should be transmitted and how it should be appropriated. As all perspectives and materials are historically bounded, the very task of including material, let alone establishing a canon, may become exclusionary. In the worst cases, cultural transmission becomes indoctrination. As for expanding the group that is to be enabled to operate as individuals through employment, the university must also attain a standard in which students are able to advance their lives through education: to be a worker is by no means to achieve emancipation in all cases, as there is also the possibility of being exploited as a worker and even having one's psyche further regimented by a technological work process that requires further training.[2] We contend that the educated individual will have combined career and vocational training with cultural understandings, broadly defined, and cross-cultural awareness. The autonomous individual capable of objectivity and employing the evolutionary advantages of selfhood is compatible with the aims of the collectivity for two reasons: this individual has a prescribed social role within existing power relations where volition may be employed in the cause of the existing order; and, this individual is formed by grappling with tradition and giving plausible expression to its points of continuity.

Broadly speaking, liberal arts education in Europe had its roots in educating ruling class youth in the humanities to prepare them for a genteel ruling class life. While early educational initiatives by craft guilds, independent learners, and later trade unions presaged our current debates in open education (Peter & Deimann, 2013), for the most part higher education was controlled by the church or state. The liberal arts component was initially considered to be an important component of an educated citizenry; however, increased enrolments in the universities since the mid-twentieth century coincided with an increase in skills training for specific careers and a decrease in liberal arts programs (Lind, 2006; Zakaria, 2015). But if the ability to grapple with and speak on behalf of a tradition is needed for a well-educated citizenry that balances the needs of the individual and the collective, does not the diminution of a liberal arts education represent closure to that ideal? If the long history of the emergence of the individual provides the mandate for the university, liberal arts must remain central as it represents the way in which the individual becomes critically responsible for the collectivity represented by tradition. We would argue that while inclusiveness in the form of increased rates of participation is to be welcomed, what is to be feared is a qualitative change which would defeat the potential of increasing openness through these institutions, and that the democratising potential of this development can only be actualised if education continues to promote the development of individuals capable of grappling with tradition.

If the development of learners' fullest potential as creators of meaning is viewed as a primary goal, a discussion of openness must include consideration of best practices for the delivery of quality education. In a discussion of the limits of evidence-based practice in education, Gert Biesta (2007) argues the best means for educational interventions should not be allowed to limit the values judgments of educational practitioners. What is characteristic of education is that it is not merely technological, as is a discussion of means, but that the question of ends must be continually negotiated. 'A democratic society is precisely one in which the purpose of education is not given but is a constant topic for discussion and deliberation' (Biesta, 2007, p. 18). The negotiation of what is to be valued as the end of the educational practice is not merely central but constitutive, as Biesta writes 'values are not simply an element of educational practices, but they are actually *constitutive* of such practices' (Biesta, 2010, p. 501). What may be added is that the end goal of educational practices is the self that reflexively makes meaning from tradition.

Here we are not simply looking at quality as a set of public standards to be set, implemented, and evaluated but we are also exploring its important dimension of cultural transmission and social representation. The sense of meaning is created through a social negotiation rather than through a structured and defined process and for this reason its explication may well require an appreciation of the social environment. As Serge Moscovici (1963, 1973) forwarded in his Social Representation Theory:

> Systems of values, ideas and practices with a two-fold function; first, to establish an order which will enable individuals to orientate themselves in their material and social world and to master it; secondly, to enable communication to take place amongst members of a community by providing them with a code for social exchange and a code for naming and classifying unambiguously the various aspects of their world and their individual and group history. (p. 252)

We may view education as a means of fostering discourse within the social representation framework.[3] According to Mascovici's theory of representation, a network of meaning is woven to form social relationships or collective understanding. This collectivist approach in an individual learner's creation of meaning is significant in advancing intra-group communication to establish constructs within the educational system that respond to specific needs of learners. In the same context, administrators and policy makers, educators or professors, and, most significantly, student representatives, should sit together and discuss curricular content. Citing Vygotsky (1978) and Dewey (1930), Troller and Knight (2000) forwarded that making meaning can be facilitated by the activity systems and community of practice. Here, actions toward change are taken as a social engagement with the world with individuals in distinct roles engaged in the same process of change operating on the basis of shared rules and conventions.

As Vygotsky (1978) believed, community plays a central role in the process of 'making meaning,' and the role of social interaction among educators is fundamental to the development of the learners' cognition. Reflective practice is not a new concept but rather has ancient roots in Axial Age philosophies; the practice of reflection as a form of contemplation in the search for truth was considered the noblest way to spur wisdom. In education, we become familiar with this concept from the ideas of Piaget (1950), Dewey (1930), Rogers (1961), Kolb (1984), Schön (1983), Brookfield (2009), and more recently, Larivee (2000) and Mezirow (2000). As reflective practitioners, members of the educational community do not just operate based on knowledge and skills but rather move to the point where knowledge and skills are internalized to formulate new strategies to fit a specific purpose or educational goal (Larivee, 2000).

Reflective practice is defined here as the recurring process of conscious application of learning from experience so that the quality of our actions is dependent upon the developmental insight we gain from our experiences bringing together theory and practice (Schön, 1983). Learning to reflect-in-action (RIA) and reflect-on-action (ROA) articulates extracting meaning from experience, and together forming a reflective repetitive process for decision-making and professional development. In the context of institutional processes and curricular enhancement, a cycle of periodic assessment or review is imperative. While curriculum can determine contents and assessment methodology, it cannot control the core processes of imparting those contents and skills (IWA, 2003).

An institution should be grounded on assessing its curricular content, testing it in new learning situations, and transforming it continuously to meet the learner's needs. This process of reflection in and on action paves the way for institutions to look back at what has been implemented in a more objective way involving both critical inquiry and self-reflection (Larivee, 2000). This also builds on Dewey's (1930) notion of a purposive reasoned process to allow reflective judgement; that is, being flexible and not constrained by a set of rules, and being ready to implement the necessary changes to ensure quality. In a similar view articulated by Rogers (1961), critical reflections are vital for promoting learning and self-assessment which lead to professional growth.

Key to this reflective practice is ensuring that curricular offerings in institutions help transform learners into individuals who can creatively appropriate tradition. Quality education includes the ideal of the opened mind as a creative generator of meaning embodied in a self-reflexive individual who understands the value of cultural resources. Universities are not only expected to develop learners' intellects but to also help them to flourish as active citizens who contribute to economic, social, and community development. In ensuring quality of education, universities are expected to equip learners for life in a broader sense (Ashwin, 2015). This commitment to the development of full cognitive potential facilitates democratizing education and helps prepare learners for engaged and participatory citizenship (Cronin, 2017). This transformation[4] (Kolb, 1984) can reflect educational institutions' commitment to be open and flexible with the goal of continuous improvement.

4 Cultures Open and Closed

This chapter has outlined a historical process whereby a cultural adaptation related to the structure of the self has led to our self-definition as a rational, thinking species. Although people from all cultures have the capacity for individual volition and the qualities of mind that education aims to foster and support, it would not be correct to say that all cultures are equally endowed to take advantage of modern educational initiatives. Cultures may be outward-looking and capable of encountering a range of influences from other cultures without fear of losing what is essential or positive in their own traditions. However, a culture may also become inward-looking and fearful of losing its essence in the process of assimilating new values, practices and concepts. In this situation, the self may have a capacity for the adoption of new cultural elements that outstrips what is defined, not without difficulty, as the 'traditional culture.' Here we examine the relationship of the individual to his or her collective culture or cultures.

Culture as defined here is the totality of a group's normative behaviour, artifacts, social structure and socially transmitted learning. Hofstede (2011) said that cultures collectively program the minds of group members for certain normative behaviours such a tolerance for ambiguity or it's opposite, avoidance of uncertainty; however, it is equally true that change at the individual level can, staying with the computer analogy, effectively re-program the collective 'software.' Since normative behaviour can be changed by a volitional self, capable of intentionality, with this paradigm, culture will be expected to change or evolve in tandem with the introduction of new behaviours of those recognized as part of the constituency that constitutes that culture. Earlier, we defined collectivism as a societal response to potential threats to community inherent in individual volition. Allocentrism, defined here as an individual differing to the collective good, may be thought of as a counterbalancing tendency to the individualism inherent in a volitional self and is only possible in societies consisting of individuals capable of making choices based on self-interest. Allocentrism may be understood, therefore, as a learned cultural response to the presence of an ego capable of independent action.

Studies involving the concept of allocentrism have failed to demonstrate a clear demarcation between societies labeled as 'individualist' or 'collectivist.' A study of mate preferences in a sample of 414 western European, South Asian, Italian and Chinese post-secondary students found that all subgroups rated congeniality, tradition and status traits in the same preferential order (Lalonde, Cila, Lou, & Giguere, 2013). Although the western European sample demonstrated lower family allocentrism connected to these traits, Italians resembled South Asians with respect to status and the Chinese with respect to tradition. In a study of 727 students from Thailand and the USA (Christopher, D'Souza, Peraza, & Dhaliwal, 2010), Thais were more likely to describe themselves as interdependent compared to the US sample; however, independent self-construal negatively predicted distress in both cultures.

Although all societies provide for both collective and individual responses, the act of defining a culture sets conditions for group membership. For Phinney (2002), acculturation includes (a) identification with the original culture; and, (b) adaptation to a dominant, host, or 'new' culture. In such a view, a culture may be 'lost' with its renewal dependent on education. Abadian (2006) warned that such renewal can be 'toxic' if the narratives used are disempowering or falsely empowering at the expense of others.

A retrospective study into the experience of Chinese immigrant children in Canada found they were frequently seen by their parents as 'too Canadian' with these parents sometimes using harsh discipline to restrict cultural appropriation (Mac, 2006). An anti-colonial movement incorporating the concept of 'historic trauma' has urged people aboriginal to North America to reject assimilation (Brave Heart, 2003; Kirmayer, Gone, & Moses, 2014; Robertson, 2015), thus fostering resistance to 'western education' (Richards, 2014; White, Spence, & Maxim, 2013). Widdowson (2013) lamented:

> This denial that knowledge develops with technological advancements such as literacy and numeracy is common in current examinations of aboriginal educational policy. This obscures the nature of the educational problems that many aboriginal peoples are currently experiencing. Because hunting and gathering/horticultural societies lack a culture of literacy, incorporating aboriginal traditions will not facilitate the values, skills, and attitudes that aboriginal people will need to obtain a scientific understanding of the world and participate fully in modern societies. (p. 303)

Education has the potential to be transformative (Robertson & Conrad, 2016), but the reification of culture may have the effect of closing minds to new knowledge. If we view all cultures as aggregates evolved from earlier (vertical) and contemporary (horizontal) appropriation, then each participant in the cultural project becomes an authorized speaker capable of investing in culture in creative ways with applications dependent on context and purpose. The creativity of the individual self engaged in the appropriation and development of culture may be aided or hindered by the collective responses of the culture(s) in which the self is emplaced. Transformative education is an instance of open culture.

The intersection of culture and education was demonstrated in a study of cultural bias in intelligence testing conducted in a western Canadian city (Robertson, 1990). The responses to a USA-normed intelligence test by a random sample of 235 Amerindian, Métis and people whose ancestry was not considered aboriginal to the Americas (non-aboriginal Canadian) public school students were examined using rank order, correlational, and transformed item difficulty techniques. Cultural bias was found to negatively affect Amerindian and non-aboriginal Canadian student scores (although not on the same items or to the same extent); however, this bias was not demonstrated as affecting Métis. It was suggested that the Métis sampled had lived in this urban area for three generations and this coupled with a lack of culturally-enforced European traditions resulted in greater openness to US cultural influence. Following a more recent study on aboriginality in self-construction, Robertson (2014) noted:

> Perhaps the original Métis were not concerned with building a distinctive culture, but were simply building communities to survive in their environment. It fell to later generations to conceptualize the beliefs and practices as culturally distinctive, but by the time they did so those beliefs and practices would have necessarily changed. (p. 10)

Historically in Canada, people of mixed ancestry who were raised in Amerindian communities were accepted as Indian by both those communities and the federal government. The Métis were of mixed ancestry who identified with neither the Amerindian communities nor Canada. Métis educational achievement outstrips that of other aboriginal groups (Richards, 2014; Richards & Scott, 2009), and it is a reasonable speculation that openness to appropriating new ideas has contributed to this achievement.

A relativist position that all cultural tenets are of equal truth or value nullifies the cognitive revolution; however, the capacity to take an objective stance can be applied to the interpretive understanding of textual and oral tradition. We hold that it is possible to be inclusive of cultures even if their basic texts are contradictory, provided the process is of being challenged by tradition and working to adopt it in the manner appropriate to one's own historical circumstance and in preparation for the pluralistic situation of living with other people. All groups appropriate cultural knowledge innovatively; but as Hofstede (2011) observed, 'there is no reason why economic and technological evolution should suppress other cultural variety' (p. 4). To receive culture in order to use it for creative living is the basic human condition which should be further developed through education. If the encounter with culture has been rigorously undertaken, there is much more that is available for the adoptive process of creative living. The group that is undertaking the cultural project should themselves be involved in the assessment of this rigor, as it is their process of creative appropriation which is driving it.

International students inevitably appropriate elements of the host cultures, often leading to difficulties on returning to their home country. Arthur (2003) noted that such changes, particularly for women coming from countries where women's roles are restricted, may lead to social isolation and censorship. The effects of this acculturation may be uneven. For example, one study found that Filipino immigrants living in San Francisco had lower levels of ethnic identity and higher levels of psychological distress and alcohol dependence than those Filipinos living in Hawaii (Gong, Takeuchi, Agbayani-Siewert, & Tacata, 2002).

The evolved self requires a sense of stability to the extent that the person we are today is in some important sense the same person we were in the past and will be in the future. This self-stability requires cultural validation (Chandler & Lalonde, 1998; Ishiyama, 1995; Kwiatkowska, 1990). In fulfilling its mandate to develop the mind, education is a process of community self-change (Conrad, 2005; Robertson, 2011b). Effective education must therefore meet the twin objectives of self-validation and self-growth. Such identity construction necessarily includes self-examination and reinterpretation of successes and failures, particularly for those events related to meaningful work, learning, community and leisure activities (Johnson, Thomas, & Krochak, 1998). From a memetic perspective, openness is enhanced by a multicultural education that maximizes the number of memes students may appropriate to their selves. Cultures that are open to such change serve their members well.

6 D. W. Winnicott and the Transmission of Cultural Meaning as a Measure of Openness

'The place where cultural experience is located is in the *potential space* between the individual and the environment (originally the object). The same can be said of playing. Cultural experience begins with creative living first manifested in play' (Winnicott, 1971/2005, p. 135).

Opening the mind to its potential can be approached playfully with the student experimenting with different interpretations of cultural meaning. When Winnicott defines play in a manner that expands to include all cultural experience, he provides a model for the approach that hermeneutics and the project of education should take to cultural meaning. With memes and cultural evolution, we are given a content that does not have any meaning unless it is culturally transmitted and individually appropriated. The notion of cultural memes is, one may say, atomistic, with units of cultural transmission that are so small that they do not constitute any meaningful whole. Meaning is nonetheless achieved in the attribution of meaning that is shared between individuals. Thus, cultural meaning may be achieved across generations. This is the basis of Gadamer's (1960/2013) hermeneutic of retrieval, which seeks to provide a fresh understanding of ancient texts that allows the reader to be challenged by the text. The reader is able to ask, 'What would this historical source mean for me'; and thereby also increase the range of the answer to the question, 'Who am I'? The creative activity of culture is an ability to encounter historical sources along with other people in a way which keeps meaning in play and developing. The focus on traditional sources is by no means conservative, as Gadamer is interested in a mutual questioning between the source and its reception in a way that unfolds their mutual meaning towards the future. It is contended here that this model of self-development as creative dialogue with tradition and other people is an ideal for both the opened mind and open education.

This view is embraced by Bernard Stiegler (2008/2010, 2010/2013), who also draws our attention to specific contemporary challenges which may be identified once we have seen the link between creativity and meaning. Using Stiegler's terms, we may characterize the continual formation of the individual self as attention formation. The capacity to remember, the ability to perceive oneself in a unified way over time, the ability to live in such a way that there is something about oneself which is essential which is represented and preserved after one is gone – these are all historical accomplishments. What Stiegler adds is that they are always technologically mediated, for example, by writing. It may not be sufficient to say that attention formation is aided by technologies such as books; attention formation may only be possible by way of cultural memory systems. Such an observation may cause us to look once again in a new way at open universities and the technological systems that they presuppose and propose to profitably exploit. However, in *What Makes Life Worth Living* (2010/2013), Stiegler is also concerned with the 'short circuiting' of attention formation which happens with technologies such as radio, television, the Internet, and smartphones. He reminds us of what is very much on the surface of our advanced technological society – that the advertising industry proposes to capture and sell attention. The media environment is such that attention is continually divided; and, if anything, the current technologies may be undoing the attainments in attention formation of previous times. We may ask if traditional culture is liquidated and nullified by this weakening of attention, and if the university should, as Stiegler (2008/2010) claims, participate in a battle of and for intelligence.[5]

If education is truly to be directed toward the opening of minds, the capacity must be formed to retain and be attentive to traditional sources and the historical dialogues which have developed around them. The ability to read canonical texts and respond to them in considered writing and speech has been a basic technique for the formation of individuals from beginnings which well predate the modern university. This by no means is to suggest that any canon should be closed, as the purpose of a canon is to assemble the texts most able to challenge their readers and inspire thinking on a deep enough level to question the canon. However, it is incumbent upon universities to retain sources which allow students to wrestle with ongoing traditions with the intensity that allows for self-formation and genuine dialogic openness with both tradition and other selves. These basic objectives should be accounted for at the core of quality assurance in higher education. Openness may only be achieved when a self is produced that is capable of wrestling with tradition and investing it with creative meaning.

7 Conclusion

It has been contended here that the historical emergence of the volitional self gave rise to educational institutions as both an aid in self-formation and as a means of structuring it in the collective interest, and that the extension of this knowledge to greater numbers of people is a process of democratization. The volitional self with its implied individuality predicts consequences of potential actions on the basis that there is an objective reality against which to measure possibilities. It was argued that the process of democratization includes both increasing the availability of education to greater numbers of people and releasing the educated individual from constraints to knowledge seeking. From this paradigm, the post-Enlightenment scientific revolution was an advance in humanity's quest for openness.

The self was described as having subjectively felt attributes of volition, uniqueness and continuity. An open education includes expanding the horizon of possibilities from which historically grounded self-construction evolves and was thus described as transformative. The Internet and other information technologies have given rise to a generalized fragmentation of attention and this was described as potentially detrimental to the process of attention formation. Considering the arguments of Winnicott, Gadamer, and Stiegler, it is our opinion that educational institutions must continue to pursue the project of attention formation with a creative, hermeneutic engagement with traditional sources. Using the technologies available today, the inhabitants of the university must form themselves and each other as individuals capable of being questioned by the most question-worthy historical sources. This is the hermeneutic process of self-formation which should be at the core of our understanding of both openness – and quality – in higher education.

The concept of openness is meaningful insofar as an individual is formed that is capable of meaning. Meaning is developed in a creative appropriation of culture, in the process whereby an individual obtains a sense of self as a response to objective reality that includes the traditions of the collective. If the process of education that has been operating for 3000 years has now reached a moment for a dramatic increase in inclusiveness, this can only be actualised if these qualities of selfhood are indeed enhanced. Everything that has been achieved in tradition that retains the capacity to challenge a self capable of questions should be considered for inclusion in the canons which engage and enhance the self. We recommend that universities be open cultures, where vertical and horizontal appropriations are enabled to allow individuals to form a rich texture of creative living. An evolving canon should be formed which is open to any cultural source which in turn promotes the opened mind. While the parameters of such a canon and program of education cannot be delimited in advance, what can be stated on the basis of the present argument is that the contents of education should be precisely those materials that allow the self to enhance its self-reflectivity.

Notes

1 Functional magnetic resonance imaging or functional MRI measures brain activity by detecting changes associated with blood flow.

2 Assessing transformative and democratising education has been an acknowledged problem in the quality assurance literature from the Bologna Accord (1999), and our argument suggests that these gaps in quality assurance frameworks should be filled.

3 Quality assurance is a social construction that advances a community of scholars and other members of higher educational institutions working in social

representation for learners to make sense of the world (Voelklein & Howarth, 2005). In the same light, as argued by Lane and Van-Dorp (2011), increased participation in higher education through open education, specifically, Open Education Resources (OER) (Cronin, 2017; Weller, 2018), needs to foster a better collaboration between various stakeholders.

4 The details of Kolb's dialectic and cyclical process consisting of four stages can be found in his book *Experiential Learning: Experience as the Source of Learning and Development.*

5 For Stiegler's initial thoughts on the role of the university in the 'battle of and for intelligence' see Stiegler (2008/2010, pp. 30, 63–71).

References

Biesta, G. (2007). Why 'what works' won't work: Evidence-based practice and the democratic deficit in educational research. *Educational Theory, 57*(1), 1–22.

Biesta, G. (2010). Why 'what works' still won't work: From evidence-based education to value-based education. *Studies in Philosophy and Education, 29*, 491–503.

Brave Heart, M. Y. H. (2003). The historical trauma response among natives and its relationship with substance abuse: A Lakota illustration. *Journal of Psychoactive Drugs, 35*(1), 7–13.

Brookfield, S. D. (2009). The concept of critically reflective practice. In A. L. Wilson & E. Hayes (Eds.), *Handbook of adult and continuing education* (pp. 33–48). San Francisco, CA: American Association for Adult and Continuing Education, Jossey-Bass Wiley Company.

Chandler, M. J., & Lalonde, C. (1998). Cultural continuity as a hedge against suicide in Canada's First Nations. *Transcultural Psychiatry, 35*(2), 191–219. doi:10.1177/136346159803500202

Chiao, J. Y., Harada, T., Komeda, H., Li, Z., Mano, Y., Saito, D., et al. (2009). Neural basis of individualistic and collectivistic views of self. *Human Brain Mapping, 30*(9), 2813–2820. doi:10.1002/hbm.20707

Christopher, M. S., D'Souza, J. B., Peraza, J., & Dhaliwal, S. (2010). A test of the personality-culture clash hypothesis among college students in an individualistic and collectivistic culture. *International Journal of Culture and Mental Health, 3*(2), 107–116. doi:10.1080/17542863.2010.491707

Conrad, D. (2005). Building and maintaining community in cohort-based online learning. *Journal of Distance Education, 20*(1), 1–20.

Conrad, D. (2008). Revisiting the Recognition of Prior Learning (RPL): A reflective inquiry into RPL practice in Canada. *Canadian Journal of University Continuing Education, 34*(2), 89–110.

Cronin, C. (2017). Openness and praxis: Exploring the use of open educational practices in higher education. *International Review of Research in Open and Distributed Learning, 18*(5), 1–20.

Czerniewicz, L., Deacon, A., Small, J., & Walji, S. (2014). Developing world MOOCs: A curriculum view of the MOOC landscape. *Journal of Global Literacies, Technologies, and Emerging* Pedagogies, 2(3), 122–139.

Damon, W., & Hart, D. (1988). *Self-understanding in childhood and adolescence.* Cambridge, MA: Cambridge University Press.

Deci, E. L., & Ryan, R. M. (2008). Facilitating optimal motivation and psychological well-being across life's domains. *Canadian Psychology, 49*(1), 14–23.

Dewey, J. (1930). *Individualism, old and new.* New York, NY: Minton Balch & Co.

Donald, M. (2001). *A mind so rare: The evolution of human consciousness.* New York, NY: Norton.

Freire, E. S., Koller, S. H., Piason, A., & da Silva, R. B. (2005). Person-centered therapy with impoverished, maltreated and neglected children and adolescents in Brazil. *Journal of Mental Health Counselling, 27*(3), 225–237.

Gadamer, H.-G. (1992). *Hans-Georg Gadamer on education, poetry, and history: Applied hermeneutics.* Albany, NY: State University of New York Press.

Gadamer, H.-G. (2013). *Truth and method.* London & New York, NY: Bloomsbury Academic.

Girard, R. (1977). *Violence and the sacred.* Baltimore, MD: Johns Hopkins University Press.

Gong, F., Takeuchi, D. T., Agbayani-Siewert, P., &Tacata, L. (2002). Acculturation, psychological distress, and alcohol use: Investigating the effects of ethnic identity and religiousity. In K. M. Chun, P. B. Organista & G. Marin (Eds.), *Acculturation: Advances in theory, measurement and applied research* (pp. 189–206). Washington, DC: American Psychological Association.

Harari, Y. N. (2016). *Sapiens: A brief history of humankind.* Toronto: McClelland & Stewart.

Harter, S. (2012). *The construction of the self: Developmental and sociocultural foundations.* New York, NY: Gilford Press.

Hofstede, G. (2011). Dimensionalizing cultures: The Hofstede model in context. *Online Readings in Psychology and Culture, 2*(1), 1–26. doi:10.9707/2307-0919.1014

Ishiyama, F. I. (1995). Culturally dislocated clients: Self-validation issues and cultural conflict issues and counselling implications. *Canadian Journal of Counselling, 29*(3), 262–275.

IWA 2. (2007). *Quality management systems – Guidelines for the application of ISO 9001: 2000 in education.* Geneva: International Organization for Standardization.

Jaspers, K. (1951). *Way to wisdom: An introduction to philosophy.* New Haven, CT: Yale University Press.

Johnson, D. M. (2003). *How history made mind: The cultural origins of objective thinking*. Chicago, IL: Open Court Books.

Johnson, E. A., Thomas, D., & Krochak, D. (1998). Effects of peer mediation training in junior high school on mediator's conflict resolution attitudes and abilities in high school. *Alberta Journal of Educational Research, 44*(3), 339–341.

Kirmayer, L. J., Gone, J. P., & Moses, J. (2014). Rethinking historical trauma. *Transcultural Psychiatry, 51*(3), 299–319. doi:10.1177/1363461514536358

Knight, P. T., & Trowler, P. R. (2000). Department-level cultures and the improvement of learning and teaching. *Studies in Higher Education, 25*(1), 69–83. doi:10.1080/030750700116028

Kolb, D. A.(1984). *Experiential learning: Experience as the source of learning and development*. Englewood Cliffs, NJ: Prentice Hall.

Kwiatkowska, A. (1990). Sense of personal continuity and distinctiveness from others in childhood. In L. Oppenheimer (Ed.), *The self-concept: European perspectives on its development, aspect, and applications* (pp. 63–74). Berlin: Springer-Verlag.

Lalonde, R. N., Cila, J., Lou, E., & Giguere, B. (2013). Delineating groups for cultural comparisons in a multicultural setting: Not all westerners should be put into the same melting pot. *Canadian Journal of Behavioural Science, 45*(4), 296–304. doi:10.1037/a0023257

Larrivee, B. (2000). Transforming Teaching Practice: becoming the critically reflective teacher. *International and Multidisciplinary Perspectives, 1*(3), 293–307. doi:10.1080/713693162

Li, C., Wang, S., Zhao, Y., Kong, F., & Li, J. (2016). The freedom to pursue happiness: Belief in free will predicts life satisfaction and positive affect among Chinese adolescents. *Frontiers in Psychology, 7*(2027). doi:10.3389/fpsyg.2016.02027

Lind, M. (2006). Why the liberal arts still matter. *The Wilson Quarterly, 30*(4), 52–58.

Mac, L. (2006). *A qualitative inquiry into the experiences of Chinese immigrant children in Canada: Adult reflections on childhoood experiences*. Paper presented at the Canadian Psychological Association Annual Conference, Calgary, AB.

Mahoney, M. J. (1991). *Human change processes: The scientific foundations of psychotherapy*. New York, NY: Basic Books.

Marginson, S. (2004). Competition and markets in higher education: A 'glonacal' analysis *Policy Futures in Education, 2*(2), 175–244. doi:10.2304/pfie.2004.2.2.2

Mezirow, J. (2000). *Learning as transformation: Critical perspectives on a theory in progress*. San Francisco, CA: Jossey-Bass.

Moscovici, S. (1963). Attitudes and opinions. *Annual Review of Psychology, 14*, 231–260.

Moscovici, S. (1973). Foreword. In C. Herzlich (Ed.), *Health and illness: A social psychological analysis* (pp. ix–xiv). London: Academic Press.

Osterman, K. F. (1990). Reflective practice: A new agenda for education. *Education and Urban Society, 22*(2), 133–152.

Peter, S., & Deimann, M. (2013). On the role of openness in education: A historical reconstruction. *Open Praxis, 5*(1), 7–14.

Piaget, J. (1950). *The psychology of intelligence.* London: Routledge & Paul.

Pinker, S. (2002). *The blank slate: The modern denial of human nature.* New York, NY: Penguin.

Rhoades, G. (1983). Conflicting interests in higher education. *American Journal of Education, 91*(3), 283–327.

Rhoades, G., & Slaughter, S. (2009). *Academic capitalism and the new economy: Markets, state, and higher education.* Baltimore, MD: John Hopkins University Press.

Richards, J. (2014). *Are we making progress? New evidence on aboriginal education outcomes in provincial and reserve schools.* Vancouver: CD Howe Institute.

Richards, J., & Scott, M. (2009). *Aboriginal education: Strengthening the foundations.* Ottawa: Canadian Policy Research Networks.

Robertson, L. H. (1990). *Cultural bias on Wechsler intelligence scale for children – Revised information subtest: Canadian and Native concerns.* Regina, SK: University of Regina.

Robertson, L. H. (2010). Mapping the self with units of culture. *Psychology, 1*(3), 185–193. doi:10.4236/psych.2010.13025

Robertson, L. H. (2011a). An application of PLAR to the development of the Aboriginal self: One college's experience. *International Review of Research in Open and Distributed Learning, 12*(1), 96–108.

Robertson, L. H. (2011b). Prior learning assessment and recognition in aboriginal self (re) construction. *Pimatisiwin: A Journal of Aboriginal and Indigenous Community Health, 9*(2), 459–472.

Robertson, L. H. (2014). In search of the aboriginal self: Four individual perspectives. *Sage Open, 4*(2), 1–13. doi:10.1177/2158244014534246

Robertson, L. H. (2015). The trauma of colonization: A psycho-historical analysis of one aboriginal community in the North American 'North-West.' *Interamerican Journal of Psychology, 49*(3), 317–332.

Robertson, L. H. (2017). Implications of a culturally evolved self for notions of free will [Hypothesis and theory]. *Frontiers in Psychology, 8*(1889), 1–8. doi:10.3389/fpsyg.2017.01889

Robertson, L. H., & Conrad, D. (2016). Considerations of self in recognising prior learning and credentialing. In S. Reushle, A. Antonio, & M. Keppell (Eds.), *Open learning and formal credentialing in higher education: Curriculum models and institutional policies* (pp. 187–204). Hershey, PA: IGI Global.

Robertson, L. H., Holleran, K., & Samuels, M. (2015). Tailoring university counselling services to aboriginal and international students: Lessons from native and international student centres at a Canadian University. *Canadian Journal of Higher Education, 45*(1), 122–135.

Rogers, C. (1961). *On becoming a person: A therapist's view of psychology.* London: Constable.

Schön, D. (1983). *The reflective practitioner: How professionals think in action.* London: Temple Smith.

Schön, D. (1987). *Educating the reflective practitioner: Towards a new design for teaching in the professions.* San Francisco, CA: Jossey-Bass.

Seligman, M. E., Steen, T. A., Park, N., & Peterson, C. (2005). Positive psychology progress: Empirical validation of interventions. *American Psychologist, 60*(5), 410–421.

Stiegler, B. (2010/2008). *Taking care of youth and the generations.* Stanford, CA: Stanford University Press.

Stiegler, B. (2013/2010). *What makes life worth living.* Cambridge: Polity Press.

Vilhauer, M. (2010). *Gadamer's ethics of play: Hermeneutics and the other.* New York, NY & Toronto: Lexington Books.

Voelklein, C., & Howarth, C. (2005). *Controversies about SRT.* London: Institute of Social Psychology.

Vygotsky, L. (1978). *Mind in society: The development of higher mental processes.* Boston, MA: Harvard University Press.

Weller, M. (2017). The development of new disciplines in Education – The open education example. In S. Ferreira, G. Martins, L. da Silva Rosado, L. Alexandre, & J. de Sá Carvalho (Eds.), *Education and technology: Critical approaches* (pp. 464–486). Rio de Janeiro, Brazil: Universidade Estácio de Sá.

White, J., Spence, N., & Maxim, P. (2013). A new approach to understanding aboriginal education outcomes: The role of social capital. In F. Widdowson & A. Howard (Eds.), *Approaches to aboriginal education in Canada: Searching for solutions* (pp. 161–179). Edmonton: Brush Education.

Widdowson, F. (2013). Native studies and Canadian political science: The implications of 'decolonizing the discipline'. In F. Widdowson & A. Howard (Eds.), *Approaches to Aboriginal education in Canada: Searching for solutions* (pp. 340–356). Edmonton: Brush Education.

Winnicott, D. W. (1971/2005). *Playing and reality.* London & New York, NY: Routledge Classics.

World Bank. (2009). *Literature review on equity and access to tertiary education in the East Asia Region.* Washington, DC: World Bank. Retrieved from http://www.ehea.info/cid100210/ministerial-conference-bologna-1999.html

Zakaria, F. (2015). *In defense of a liberal education.* New York, NY: WW Norton & Company.

CHAPTER 3

Open Sesame! And Then? Connection, Connectivity, and Liminal Thinking

Pamela Ryan

> ... the hiding-places of Man's power
> Open; I would approach them, but they close.
> WILLIAM WORDSWORTH (*The Prelude*, Book XI)

∴

To begin, let us consider some of the apposite terms with which we are occupied in this book, *among them 'open,' with its concomitant, 'closed,' which are, in ordinary contexts,* easily understood in relation to objects, as in the door is open; the window is closed. Under these material conditions, the words themselves denote a condition wherein something is open, allowing passage, entry, access; or closed, suggesting privacy or coziness or secrecy, as is hinted at in the Wordsworth quotation that frames this chapter. However, in non-material realms, the words take on additional connotations, often emotive, always suggestive. In politics, for example, closed systems or organisations are deemed secretive, often dangerous, such as the Freemasons, the Ku Klux Klan, the Kremlin. Behind closed doors, political interests can be secretly nurtured, sinister plans or decisions can be made.

The opening phrase in my title, 'Open, Sesame,'[1] also signals some of the ambiguity associated with passwords, especially in relation to so-called 'open' sites. The story of Ali Baba and the Forty Thieves has come down to us as tokening a magic password to a cave of treasures, yet this phrase is mired in confusion. The story segued into western culture via the French author, Anton Galland, as 'Sésame, oeuvre-toi' or 'Sesame, open yourself,' but it may be associated with the Arab word 'simsim,' which, in addition to our received meaning of the grain sesame, also means 'gate.' In yet another possible translation, the Greek word 'syssemon' meaning 'signal' has been suggested (Balashon, 2007). It is worth noting that in Galland's translation of the story, Ali Baba's brother-in-law forgets which grain is associated with the signal or password, and

 | DOI: 10.1163/9789004422988_004

he is sealed in the cave. Think now of the confusion we suffer when trying to remember our passwords to Internet sites or apps. If we cannot remember our password, we are prevented from entering the site. But what if we were locked inside a dark web, for example. As Castells says, in the opening sentence of *The Rise of the Network Society* (2010, p. 1): 'We live in confusing times,' explaining this confusion by interrogating the openness and exclusion practices of networks, which have no boundaries but which nevertheless exclude those who are not connected (Castells, 2010).

Suffice it to say then that open and closed are overdetermined[2] concepts. Being 'open' is generally regarded as a good thing. It means one is trustworthy and transparent. This is particularly the case when discussing the Internet, which is our current keyword for an open system, that is, until its openness is threatened by political interests. According to Technopedia (accessed 26 September 2018), the OI or open Internet is a 'fundamental neutrality concept in which information across the world wide web is equally free and available without variables that depend on the financial motives of Internet Service Providers.' And because the Internet is a central facilitator of open education and open educational resources (OER), openness in higher education is a concept that has been accepted as a given; and is thus rarely interrogated and seldom theorised. In this chapter, I link the concept of openness to the idea of connection, attempting to uncover and unravel ideas pertinent to both the relationship between openness and connection and to its implications for an educational future. In doing so, I will rely on ideas drawn from disciplines such as anthropology, literary studies and philosophy in order to forge an underlying theory from which other discussions can flow. To start this process, let us consider that within an ecology of open and closed systems, which facilitate or deny connections and communities, there is a forgotten space – the threshold. It is this space that forms the starting point for what follows.

The connection point between open and closed lies in the space between them, that is, the threshold, and its companion, the limen. A threshold is a point in space marking the division between inside and outside, operating as a pivotal point for entry or departure. A threshold is also a boundary line marking the entry point to another space. A limen is a state of existence experienced on the threshold, signifying, in social anthropology, a transition from one kind of existence to another. It is used by anthropologists such as Victor Turner to describe the hiatus in a ritual which engenders an ambiguity or disorientation, being neither here nor there, neither this nor that. This condition of uncertainty is immensely productive. Being in a liminal space implies that one is neither entirely inside nor outside, not caught inside nor free to roam outside. The liminal space is also a productive space because it operates as a clearing ground for old cultural habits and as a rehearsal for new adoptions. In his 'Frame, Flow and Reflection: Ritual and Drama as Public Liminality,' Turner explains liminality thus:

> This term, literally 'being-on-a-threshold,' means a state or process which is betwixt-and-between the normal, day to day cultural and social states and processes of getting and spending, preserving law and order, and registering structural status. Since liminal time is not controlled by the clock it is a time of enchantment when anything might, even should, happen. (1979, p. 465)

According to Turner, liminality is a magical space capable of producing something extraordinary, something unexpected. He pushes the meaning still further:

> Liminality is full of potency and potentiality. It may also be full of experiment and play. There may be a play of ideas, a play of words, a play of symbols, a play of metaphors. In it, play's the thing. Liminality is not confined in its expression to ritual and the performative arts. Scientific hypotheses and experiments and philosophical speculation are also forms of play, though their rules and controls are more rigorous and their relation to mundane 'indicative' reality more pointed than those of genres which proliferate in fantasy. One might say, without too much exaggeration, that liminal phenomena are at the level of culture what variability is at the level of nature. (1979, p. 466)

Turner bases these ideas on liminality on the Belgian folklorist, van Gennep, who originally used the term to designate a 'rite of passage' in cultural rituals, a transitional phase marking significant life events such as the transition from childhood to adulthood or from single status to marriage, or, most pertinently for this chapter, a state in which a whole culture or civilisation faces a turning point, such as war, famine, an epidemic, and so on. It was Turner who introduced the element of 'play' into the concept of liminality. In the long essay quoted earlier, Turner explains the several forms of liminality, including secret and public forms and extends this to social formations which have dominant forms of public liminality depending on the era in which they occur, for example, ritual, carnival, festival, theatre and film. Turner uses the variation 'liminoid' to refer to those instances of public liminality that are bounded in time and space, cordoned off, so to speak, but which are perceived as dangerous because they are by nature subversive. Such subversive liminoid acts or performances can take the form of novels, plays, marches, and parades all of which are 'framed' (Turner's word), thus bordered in discrete spaces. The liminoid, therefore, is not strictly a threshold space since it is bounded or framed and acts like an interior space.

Using Turner's ideas as a starting point, the idea of the liminal or liminoid becomes, in this chapter, a creative resting place, or an observer's platform, if you will. While residing in the limen, the properties and potentials of openness and connection, or connectivity, which is the process of, or the potential for, being connected, can be considered dispassionately as well as being proposed as a condition of liminality.

Earlier, 'open' and 'closed' were named as over-determined concepts, particularly when used in a context of teaching and learning. Scholars and thinkers as well as the media regard them both emotively and metaphorically. For instance, the poet, Elizabeth Bishop, equates knowledge with the Atlantic Ocean:

> It is like what we imagine knowledge to be,
> dark, salt, clear, moving, utterly free,
> drawn from the cold hard mouth
> of the world, derived from the rocky breasts
> forever, flowing and drawn, and since
> our knowledge is historical, flowing and flown.
> ('At the Fishhouses' from *The Complete Poems, 1927–1979*)

For the speaker in the poem, knowledge is 'utterly free,' 'flowing and flown' as if its natural habitat were the ocean, where knowledge bobs on the surface or sinks to the depths but is constantly in flux. This chapter will trace the perception of openness as 'good' but also show that that is only a perception. When tested against current realities, openness as a beneficent state in teaching and learning as well as in politics is an ambiguous concept, prone to change. It is possibly more productive rather to regard openness as flow, a state of flux, conditions that seems neutral rather than value laden (a 'good thing'). Zygmunt Bauman's choice of the term 'liquid modernity' in place of postmodernism implies a recognition of the shifting nature of reality where societies are in transition, people are on the move, and economies are forever gaining and losing ground. Bauman uses the metaphor of liquidity, in a similar way to Elizabeth Bishop, shifting 'the ground' from solid earth to water and uncannily prefiguring the melting of ice that is occurring on both our Poles:

> First of all, society is being transformed by the passage from the solid to the liquid phase of modernity, in which all social forms melt faster than new ones can be cast. They are not given enough time to solidify, and cannot serve as the frame of reference for human actions and long-term life-strategies because their alleged short life-expectations undermines [sic] efforts to develop a strategy that would require the consistent fulfilment of a 'life-project.' (2005, p. 303)

The words used here suggest a significant shift in the way we communicate. In his stark defence against liberal capitalism, Bauman points the way to an ethical view of our topic, extending the conversation beyond good and bad. Bauman thinks of open and closed spaces in terms of class. He speaks out against the 'ghettoisation' of people who are different and who are kept inside while others roam freely. He calls these ghettos the 'dumping grounds of unnecessary people and [how they become] greenhouses of hatred' (*The Guardian*, 2003). Bauman also acknowledges that the inside/outside effect is exacerbated by our consumerist culture and the habit of comparison borne on social media. The 'haves' advertise their material blessings, while the 'have-nots' feel humiliated. He calls this 'the crime of humiliation' (The Guardian, 2003). Bauman's central thesis is that modern forms of social organisation, far from indicating human evolution, are in fact crucially lacking in social and moral responsibility. As proponents of openness in higher education, we need to be especially careful in our understanding of what Bauman is saying as too often the concept is not sufficiently interrogated in terms of who has access to 'open' forms of education and who is excluded. Not everyone has the password to open access. As Catherine Cronin says:

> The deceptively simple term *open* hides a great deal of complexity, much of which depends on the particular context within which open practice is considered. Thus it is imperative to move beyond open-versus-closed dichotomies and even beyond unified conceptions of openness. Openness requires a critical approach. (2017)

1 Thinking about Connection

We turn now to the second thread in my argument: connection. Again, it may be useful to consider the associations that gather around the terms 'connect' and 'connection' since they are central to my exposition in this chapter.

Turning once more to literature and using 'connection' as a form of community, we can consider EM Forster's exploration both in *Howards End* and in *A Passage to India* of the idea of connection as an artistic and human ideal. In the case of the former novel, a link is drawn between poetry and prose, signaling emotion and practicality. In Forster's view, if these two conditions are connected we have an ideal state of human interaction. In the conclusion to his later novel, *A Passage to India* (1924), Forster returns to the theme of longing for connection. In the early pages of the book, Aziz asks the framing question of the novel: 'whether or no it is possible to be friends with an Englishman.' Forster answers this question at the book's conclusion:

> 'Why can't we be friends now?' said the other, holding him affectionately. 'It's what I want. It's what you want.' But the horses didn't want it – they swerved apart: the earth didn't want it, sending up rocks through which riders must pass single file; the temple, the tank, the jail, the palace, the birds, the carrion, the Guest House, that came into view as they emerged from the gap and saw Mau beneath: they didn't want it, they said in their hundred voices. (2005, p. 306)

The more mature author adopts a tentative position regarding the possibility of connection in a context fraught with complexity. Notice that the barriers to connection in this passage (the temple, the jail, the palace and the Guest House) are all buildings that either exclude others or trap people inside a ghetto. This is not so far removed from the considerations around connection that are examined in this chapter. For instance, delving into the meanings of the word 'connect,' it is interesting, frustrating even, that in searching for a definition one is caught up in a loop: 'connection' is defined as a relationship in which a person or thing is linked with something else; 'link' is defined as a relationship in which something or someone affects another; and 'relationship' is defined as a connection between different parties. Words circle back on each other and often confuse rather than clarify issues.

The concept of a network, which is a component of connection, unearths a similar complexity. It can be an arrangement of intersecting vertical and horizontal lines as well as a group of interconnected people or things. A computer network is two or more computers connected by nodes in order to share data, of which the most prominent example is the Internet, a term coined in 1974 by Vinton Cerf, Yogen Dalal and Carl Sunshine at Stanford University to describe 'a global transmission protocol network which are the rules that govern the transmission of information that crisscross the Internet'

(Wikipedia, 2018).). In 1989, Sir Tim Berners-Lee created the www or World Wide Web which is built on top of the Internet and connects web pages containing text, images, videos and other multimedia. In 1997, broadband networking allowed for high speed Internet searches and lent a new meaning to the word 'networking.' This led to the founding of Google, our most commonly used search engine, which works on the principle that the most relevant information is gleaned from web pages with the most 'hits' or linkages to them from other web pages. From here, as Thomas Friedman explains in his book, *Thank You for Being Late* (2016), software development caught up with already established hardware through such innovations such as Hadoop, whose algorithms 'made hundreds of thousands of computers act like one giant computer' (2016, p. 60), and the open-source movement, which includes Github, where anyone can use a software development 'off the shelf,' evaluate it, develop it further, hopefully improve it, and put it back on the shelf for the next user.

We are now, all of us, seemingly, connected as nodes in a network. We communicate across vast distances as if space did not exist, where context is collapsed,[3] and where time is only a barrier if we are trying to communicate across time-zones. Connection and community as forms of human collaboration recall Forster's idea yet are vastly different in their contemporary format. We now exist in a world where an invisible (to us) network of interconnecting nodes sweeps over us on an hourly basis either in the air via fibre optic networks which work through pulses of light, under the ground, or conveyed by pipes under the sea, and in which we are figuratively immersed. Surveying these seeming miracles of human skill and imagination from the threshold, it would appear that, to quote Friedman: 'There is something wonderfully human about the open-source community. At heart, it's driven by a deep human desire for collaboration and a deep human desire for recognition and affirmation of work well done – not financial reward' (2016, p. 72).

Friedman is idealistic here but he is covered by the admission in the title of his book that it is a guide for optimists. For in truth, these broadband networks are fragile, easily destroyed by a power failure or extreme weather or by hackers or high-jackers, and open-source may be free for its users but it costs vast sums of money to start up and maintain, and the 'open-source' community is in fact a multitude of open and closed circles or circuits in which there can be free and open discussion or in which a group closes itself off to public view so that its conversations about various specialised or sensitive topics can be shared in secret. We have circled back to the beginning. We are back at Wordsworth's 'hiding places.'

2 Exploring Ideas Prefiguring the Ecology of the Open Internet

When we are thinking about the Internet as part of an ecology, as this chapter proposes, we can move in two directions. We can cross the threshold or stay outside. But there is a third proposition. We can choose to remain for a while in the liminal space created by the threshold, which is where the bulk of the thinking in this section occurs, recognising that a liminal space is also a fertile and playful one, positioned in the never-land of neither here nor there, part of Bauman's liquid reality and allowing the freedom to play with concepts, to be creative. In order to think about the open Internet as a liminoid state, we must surrender our desire for hierarchy, order, and fixed meanings. We must also leave the horizontal plane, trusting that other places exist that we don't see, beneath the ground, for instance, or in the air. Under our feet, roots delve and shoot off sideways by means of rhizomes. Indeed, a more recent scientific discovery is that of mycorrhizae (meaning 'fungus-root') which extend from roots to supply trees and other plants with water and nutrients. In turn, the plants provide the mycorrhizae with the carbohydrates needed to grow. Thus, an eco-symbiotic set of relations and connections is busy below the ground 'creating vast community structures, known as common mycelial networks. These networks can be indefinitely huge, spawning – some believe – entire continents' (Tree, 2018, p. 20). Human connection mimics plant connection or vice versa. Deleuze and Guiattari built upon such ecologies to propose a theory about rhizomes which has been taken up by more recent proponents of connection, Dave Cormier's ideas about rhizomatic education, for instance or Stephen Downes and George Siemens' theory of connectivism (Cormier, 2008; Downes, 2007; Siemens, 2004).

Both of these more recent theoretical concepts are worthy of further exploration. What is mooted by both connectivism and rhizomatics is a decentred model allowing for a participatory culture which 'creates a social setting in which citizens become active agents in culture production' (Jenkins & Ito, 2006) and there are provocative similarities here between Tim O'Reilly's description of the 'magic ingredients,' Google, Wikipedia and the Web, as 'the architecture of participation, enabling countless small acts of self-interest like publishing a web page or sharing a link to add up to a public good that enriches everyone' (quoted by Rheingold, 2012, p. 2) and Pierre Levy's argument that a networked culture gives rise to new structures of power which stem from the ability of diverse groups of people to pool knowledge, collaborate through research, debate interpretations, and through such a collaborative process, refine their understanding of the world (Rheingold, 2012). However, it seems that the heady days when we spoke about the magic of the open Internet may be over. Bonnie Stewart speaks of the period 2006–2007 when participatory culture was at its peak, when Twitter, and other social networking sites, opened up conversations and created social ties. She calls this time 'Twitter As We Knew It.' In more recent years, the acceleration of 'algorithmic and status quo interests' threatens, says Stewart 'to choke a messy but powerful set of scholarly practices.' To choke is to block the passage of air, the flow of oxygen and so, of ideas. Stewart concludes that the free play of openness is disappearing. 'Open Sesame' is the incorrect password.

Despite this, the Internet for open teaching and learning is still open but it needs a corresponding pedagogy to make open teaching and learning participatory and effective. So, beginning with Forster's 'only connect' and continuing through rhizomatic thinking to the architecture of participation, these various gestures towards a participatory culture in different sectors of society pave the way for higher education to take cognisance of the change that is occurring and to fashion a pedagogy (to reiterate the general theme of this book) to accompany new ways of interacting online as well as new routes through which knowledge is both gleaned and shared.

Connectivism, as explained by Stephen Downes, is one such pedagogy. Connectivism, says Downes, is 'the thesis that knowledge is distributed across a network of connections, and therefore that learning consists of the ability to construct and traverse those networks; knowledge is literally the set of connections between entities' (2007).

This set of connections is directly associated with the ways in which Internet technologies have facilitated greater access to information, easier paths to connection with others, and opportunities to both participate in and share information, thus broadening the knowledge base in countless ways. Connectivism's central tenet is that learning occurs outside the individual since knowledge is no longer the prerogative of discrete thinkers or lodged in tactile objects such as books. Knowledge is now 'stored and manipulated by technology' and we acquire knowledge through our connection not only with the Internet but, through the Internet, with other users. Siemens' definition of connectivism extends our thinking on the possibilities of the theory:

> Connectivism is the integration of principles explored by chaos, network, and complexity and self-organisation theories. Learning is a process that occurs within nebulous environments of shifting core elements – not entirely under the control of the individual. Learning (defined as actionable knowledge) can reside outside of ourselves (within an organization

> or database), is focused on connection-specialized information sets, and the connections that enable us to learn more are more important than our current state of knowing. (2004)

The terms 'nebulous,' 'shifting,' and 'not entirely under the control of the individual' echo those words already mentioned earlier that shift the solid ground from under our feet and remind us that what we know about our current reality is changing so rapidly that the future of teaching and learning is wide open and uncertain. Such uncertainty should give us pause and should, ideally, provoke institutions of higher learning into more innovative curriculum design.

Both connectivism and rhizomatics form part of an ecology since they deal with the relations between people and their environment, between people and other people, between people and nodes, and nodes with other nodes. This is, in fact, the epitome of an ecology. It is becoming clear that new words for new processes and behaviours signal a reformulated practice in communication and community, in the way people relate to each other online through social media and in the several ways teaching and learning can adapt to this ecology.

At the time of writing (2018), digital connectivity, regarded by most as a prerequisite for open educational resources, is accepted as a human right, whilst in reality it is still a privilege for the majority of the world's populations. It is also regarded by some as a panacea for education, and in particular, higher education. It has by now been proven to be a subversive space, in which tweets, blogs, and Facebook posts can be used to incite, gain support for political and social causes, or raise money through crowd-sourcing for projects and community challenges. But they can be censored, struck off the public space, interrogated and used as reason to ban a person from entry to various countries. Given these three conditions or perceptions, a right, a panacea and a form of political activity, and given the suggestion that productive thinking can take place in a liminal space, it remains for us to consider the implications of open teaching and learning.

3 What Would an Open Ecology for Teaching and Learning Look Like?

In thinking about openness for teaching and learning, there are several points to consider. Firstly, a reasonable starting point would be the relatively recent flood of possibilities for open learning brought about by open educational resources or OER which, to use the Commonwealth of Learning (COL) definition, are deemed as providing more equal access to knowledge and educational opportunities by making educational resources open to all.[4] Here, the idealistic language we saw earlier, is still apparent. Neil Butcher and Sarah Hoosen (2012) state that 'knowledge is the common wealth of humankind and should be freely shared,' while Wiley, Green and Soares (2012) state that, 'For the first time in human history we have the tools to enable everyone to attain all the education they desire.'

The OER referred to in these descriptions are modules, and other university level educational materials that are intended to be freely available, without cost, digitally accessible, reusable and open to all. Similarly, open access publishing refers to research publications that are available free of charge (without a paywall) under an open license. In reality, each of these descriptions should carry the additional phrase, 'open to all who have access to the Internet,' and this might exclude significant numbers of people across the globe, those who do not have a constant electricity supply, those who have no electricity, those who cannot afford data costs, those who can only access the Internet (connect) while at work, the poor, the elderly, and so on. 'All,' in these descriptions, is ambiguous, an exaggeration or just plain mistaken. For those who cannot connect, there is no openness. What does this imply for teaching and learning?

> Let us begin with familiar binaries. We are told that traditional, that is space and time-bound, face to face teaching in higher education is mainly hierarchical, transmission-based, and often exclusionary, whereas, we believe that digital teaching is fluid, continuous, unbound by time or space and inclusive. Not so fast. This description is a perfect example of closed thinking, resorting to homogenous categories to leverage support for a well-word and hide-bound dichotomy. Where is the liminal thinking about the in-between? Who benefits from digital teaching? Is all digital teaching open teaching? Is all face to face teaching hierarchical? Who are the digital teachers? What do they look like?

Let us begin with access since this is where the chapter began. Before openness lurks access. The cave won't open without a password and the password is a secret shared between the haves or the know-it-alls. If the cave is knowledge and the password is access, who benefits? As Cheryl Brown and Laura Czerniewicz suggest (2007), we need to approach the complexities of access through a multi-layered and interpretative approach. We cannot assume that we know who has access and why, who is digitally literate and in what ways. A homogenous approach will lead us back to the beginning in a closed circle of assumptions and misinformation. Brown and Czerniewicz are careful to factor in the importance of context when discussing access and they wisely distinguish between access and use. They found that access to digital resources does not equate with use: 'Lack of access is a constraining factor for use but not vice versa. High access alone does not guarantee high use' (2007, p. 735).

Moreover, they found that some students with restricted or no access found ways to exercise their agency in accessing learning materials, while those with easy access often did not make constructive use of the materials. Appropriate here too is a reminder that students and scholars on the so-called periphery do not have similar points of access to facilities that students and scholars in the 'centre' take for granted. In this regard, the Asian scholar, A. Suresh Canagarajhah (2004) explains how the politics of location impacts on conditions attached to performing as an academic. He describes the moment after he had posted his bulky article in India to a journal in the US as a revelation: 'I realised that one has to be rich to publish academically' (p. 169).

And before we assume too hastily that in 2018 he would not have had to use the post office but simply attach the article to an email, consider his context had he stayed in the same village: some miles distant from a connected hub; paying for transport to the hub; living without steady or any electricity; poor Wifi connections and speeds; weighing the costs of Wifi, and so on.

Castells had already reached a similar conclusion to Brown and Czerniewicz some years previously (2010). He urges concerned academics to distinguish between using digital resources as 'delivery mechanisms of information' and using them to create knowledge (p. 10). He speaks too of the necessity to differentiate between formal access and effective access (p. 20). Above all, he gives us a caveat: Don't treat ICT as a homogenous concept:

> This plurality of technologies is complicated further when the content that is provided via ICTs is considered – the 'soft'ware rather than the 'hard'ware. In other words, the digital divide can also be seen in terms of the information, resources, applications and services that individuals are capable of accessing via new technologies. (p. 21)

We need to range further than the simple binary, access/no access, and consider rather the levels of connectivity 'in terms of the capability and distribution of the access concerned' (p. 22). Quoting Wilhelm (2000), Cassells refers us to 'an access rainbow' of physical devices, software tools, content, services, social infrastructure and governance, or 'various shades' of marginality between 'core access, peripheral access' and non-access (p. 22). In sum, access to technologies and thus to the Internet, and from there to new knowledges, is complicated by context (social and economic circumstances) but also, more profoundly, by people's relationships with digital resources and devices, and with the kinds of connection and contact that are attempted. It is not simply whether Jill Blogs is in possession of a digital device but how she relates to that device and how she uses it. As Zournazi, with Massumi, states: 'The present's 'boundary condition,' to borrow a phrase from science, is never a closed door. It is an open threshold – a threshold of potential' (2002, p. 211).

In this chapter, there are hints, which I hope slowly accrue, about openness as a concept that stretches far beyond the terrain of digitality, further even than higher education. It spills over into the state of the world, or rather, the world as it could be, a potential world. The previous quotation is extracted from a book about hope and it is worth pausing here to read how the book was conceived and constructed:

> This is about collaboration – in writing, in thinking, in politics – how working ideas together, across different styles and traditions, can let new ideas, views and expressions emerge. This involves a sense of trust and a 'faith without certitudes' about where hope may lie in thinking about the future. In secular times, when hope has moved out of the religious sphere, the turn towards the future may be found in struggles for individual justice, and in political activity across the globe. (Zournazi, with Massumi, 2002, p. i)

Neil Selwyn, who led me to this book, talks about 'thick' descriptions as a necessary development in our accounts of digital technologies and their uses instead of the predictions and forecasts that usually take the place of proper discussion (p. 12). And in '[T]he 'new' connections of digital education,' Selwyn reminds us that the urge to connect (everything with everything) springs from its antecedent, disconnection, which 'underpins the organisation of all aspects of human life, from the biological and social, to the economic and technological' (p. x).[5]

This disclaimer applies equally to those other, by now ubiquitous, forms of open education, MOOCs, which have proven to be productive kinds of learning opportunities for those who already have an advanced education and who wish to expand their repertoire for whatever purpose (change of career, enhancement of job prospects or promotion), and the leisured class who wish simply to learn something in their spare time. But their avowed intent is to offer free and open learning to 'all.' George Siemens and Stephen Downes, who, as we have seen, are the proponents of Connectivism, also ran the first MOOC, an event that propelled the explosion of MOOCs that is occurring exponentially. A recent Internet report indicates that in the past six years, 800 universities offered 8000 MOOCs, and over three months in late 2017, more than 200 universities advertised 560 free online courses. While we are yet to see the fulfilment of the MOOC promise to step into the gap formed by slow and unresponsive conventional universities to adjust to new ways of teaching and learning, it would seem that there is no stopping the promotion of these massive courses even though their acolytes are not the uneducated masses but the already degreed members of the middle class who need an extra qualification or who do the MOOC out of intellectual interest. Moreover, we should be cautious about lauding MOOCs as an unqualified form of open learning since they are subject to the same restrictions as all Internet transactions. They are open only to those who have access to the Internet and who have the means to support extensive use of Internet time. The second 'o' in their acronym, which stands for 'open,' is again hugely overdetermined and it is only in the few most effective MOOCs[6] that we see a truly innovative form of pedagogy. In most cases, MOOCs merely imitate the conventional lecture, fulfilling all the criteria for a transmission mode of teaching, with a talking head behind a desk or a moving hand writing on a blackboard. The promise of the early MOOCs that they would be the panacea for higher education and lifelong learning is sadly misguided. They are expensive to design and to run. They do not reach the people who need higher education and they have not been a solution for massive education.

This description of OER and MOOCs is by no means meant to be comprehensive. It is tangentially related to the central themes of this chapter and is intended to point to examples of openness and connectivity and to demonstrate the ways in which they do not live up to their declared intentions. But what of open universities?

Again, these institutions, spaced across the globe, are intended to provide opportunities for people who may not have the necessary entrance requirements for university study, or for those who live at a distance from a university, or for those who do not have the money to afford a conventional (face-to-face) education. Alan Tait defines open universities as 'innovative distance-teaching higher education institutions that have used distance in radical ways to improve openness' (2008), yet, by his own admission, he does not explain or evaluate the term openness. He reaches the conclusion that open universities are aimed at development, not just for teaching and research, since they are driven by values and are purportedly remedying social ills in the name of social justice (Tait, 2008). Tait analyses the mission statements of open universities across the world and notes how many of them have words such as 'inclusive,' 'access,' 'the removal of barriers,' 'equality of educational opportunity,' 'accessible to all,' and 'social justice' in their mission statements. He queries whether, in the majority of cases, these mission statements can be matched to reality

(2013). Certainly, several open universities charge fees (some at a reduced rate in comparison with face to face universities) so they are not 'open" to the poor. Others have barriers to entry in terms of entrance qualifications, thus these are not open to those who have not had the benefit of a matriculated education. Some still teach by means of traditional distance methods which use paper and the postal system, thus cannot be said to be radical innovators for openness. What are we to conclude about open education?

However, two new forms of open universities fulfil most of these criteria – the OERu and P2Pu – both of which offer interesting models for the future. P2Pu is the older of the two institutions, launched with the assistance of the Mark Shuttleworth Foundation and modelling itself on an ethos gleaned from the 2007 *Cape Town Open Education Declaration* among whose tenets is the idea that given 'adequate social support, anyone can learn almost anything online for free.'[7] OERu is a consortium of already established open and distance learning institutions which offer selected courses from their already established curricula free of charge but with the proviso that accreditation with assessment is paid for by the student. The OERu was established with funding from the Bill and Melissa Gates Foundation. These are two very different organisations. P2Pu takes its social mandate very seriously, so much so that in 2014 it made a strategic decision to stop teaching exclusively online and to use cities to facilitate face to face groups who learn together under the guidance of a tutor and who pledge to support each other in the group. Several of these urban centres are now in place.[8] The OERu seems to work on the principle of sustainable online education, taking the least expensive route, since the courses in place are either replicas of existing online courses or adaptations of courses. Both of these initiatives, however, provide examples of how teaching and learning can be modelled according to the principles of openness, connection and connectivity.

P2PU's policy of reintroducing face-to-face classes in the cities should give us pause. It is a reminder of the importance of contact and connection in teaching and learning. These additional components of connection can be mitigated by the design of the online course which should ensure that the online classes/groups are large enough for meaningful interaction yet small enough for effective monitoring by the online tutor. Then again if the course is designed to elicit student interest and engagement, peer conversations and indeed peer review, can reduce the sense of isolation, help with difficult material and provide a sense of community.

Turning now to current pedagogies and practices, it is well documented[9] that the Internet in general and social networking in particular have caused a possible change in the way our brains work and in the ways that we acquire and apply knowledge. Our attention is as acute as ever but takes in with amazing rapidity a vast number of bytes of information. Seldom do we focus on a single text for the purposes of analysis or interpretation. Instead we engage in rapid scanning, sifting, sorting processes creating textual collages or mosaics of mashed texts. We become bricoleurs, not of permanent literatures but of flexible, expandable or expendable literacies that become forms of accretion, texts leading to other texts across a web of information.

Recent research, however, questions the extent to which universities should adapt their ways of teaching and align their practices with the digital practices of students and with burgeoning information on the effects of digital technologies on our brains. For instance, Lea and Jones (2011) suggest that claims about students' inability to participate in conventional academic practices or academic literacies 'is akin to a deficit model of student learning and writing' and goes on to propose that we need much more engaged and in-depth research into the process of meaning-making for student learners in a digital age (p. 379). An understanding of the skills and literacies of the so-called networked generation should persuade us into adapting our teaching practices to accommodate 'poaching' and 'sampling' (see Jenkins, 2006), and shift our thinking to take into account accretive literacies rather than insisting on analytical practices. The skills of connection that occur when students build new texts, which may have a brief and impermanent lifespan, while accruing bits/bytes of information to make a new collage, may be just the appropriate skills needed for future work. Peter Norvig is quoted as saying:

> When the only information on the topic is a handful of essays or books, the best strategy is to read these works with total concentration. But when you have access to thousands of articles, blogs, videos, and people with expertise on the topic, a good strategy is to skim first to get an overview. Skimming and concentrating can and should coexist. (2011, p. 112)

Alan Jacobs claims that we are perhaps being unrealistic when we expect students to engage in deep attentive reading of long texts since this can be regarded as a relatively temporary and unsustainable phenomenon located in a relatively brief period in educational practice. Instead, says Jacobs,

> education is and should be primarily about intellectual navigation, about – I scruple not to say it – skimming well, and reading carefully for information in order to upload content. Slow and patient reading, by contrast, properly belongs to our leisure hours. (2011, p. 112)

Above all, by connecting with our students, we could go some way in facilitating more productive, more engaged and more innovative academic practices through the kinds of assignments and tests we design which rely less on producing long essays on topics or texts and more on encouraging critical filtering skills through a diverse range of texts and practices. Lea and Jones (2011) spent hours in conversation with students as they learnt about the way in which students engaged with digital and other texts and their attempts at meaning-making. They conclude that 'the boundaries of the texts students are engaged in are fluid and unstable' and their findings reveal a 'significant shift … to engagement in a wide range of hybrid texts, requiring *a sophisticated level of rhetorical complexity in bringing these different texts together* [emphasis added]' (2011, p. 381). But more significantly, these authors show that students follow the lead of their lecturers and tutors in guiding what material to source, their searches being determined by institutional requirements around assessment, and the authenticity of those sources being a concern for the students who want to know that their choices are validated. Through this two-way connection between the institution and the students: 'New forms of knowledge are being brought into the academy and validated by the university through departmental and tutor practices' (2011, p. 388).

As Siemens (2009) says:

> Information can now be acquired in any manner desired by the individual. Learners piece together (connect) various content and conversation elements to create an integrated (though at times contradictory) network of information. Our learning and information acquisition is a mashup. We take pieces, add pieces, dialogue, reframe, rethink, connect, and ultimately, we end up with some type of pattern that symbolises what's happening 'out there' and what it means to us. And that pattern changes daily … The fragmentation of information has resulted in an emphasis on individuals creating personal frameworks of coherence to understand sources information. Control over *personal coherence making* has significant implications for higher education ….

Making sense of fragmented information through networks of peer learners offers an indication of future learning tasks and even pedagogical models. But how rapidly should/can universities respond to larger social and communication technology trends in society? Current research on the impact of communication technology on learners and the learning process is still underdeveloped. Researching versus responding to societal trends will be a challenging field for academic institutions to navigate.

4 Open and Online Learning Re-Examined

Thus far the limen, which is a state of incompletion, has been the prevailing metaphor with which to begin thinking about openness and connection. However, we can now add another term, that of 'not-yetness,'[10] which is used to describe emerging technologies which are constantly evolving in 'hype-cycles' and which satisfy two (not yet) conditions: not yet fully understood, and not yet fully researched. The term was coined by Amy Collier in a blog[11] relating to teaching and learning in higher education and later expanded in a chapter in a book edited by Veletsianos (Ross & Collier, 2016). Amy Collier explains emergence as 'not-yetness' and as a productive space in which negatives are turned into possibilities, 'creating space for emergence to take us to new and unpredictable places': 'Not-yetness is *not* satisfying every condition, *not* fully understanding something, *not* check-listing everything, *not* tidying everything, *not* trying to solve every problem … but creating space for emergence to take us to new and unpredictable places' (2016).

Collier is reacting to a current rhetoric in educational practices where digital technologies are touted as the overall and simple answer to educational challenges, pushing 'simplification, ease, efficiency and measurability.' Ever since the idea of excellence was trumpeted, taken up, then denounced, technocrats have pushed their totalising tactics ('best practice,' accountability, students as clients) as a marketing tool that militates against innovation, creativity and emergent learning: 'Simplification is an over-pursuit of accountability run counter to our view that education is complex, messy, creative, unpredictable, multifaceted, social and part of larger systems' (Collier, 2016, n.p.).

Openness in the arms of digital connectivity in higher education is a high ideal that will not succeed if we do not resist the tactics and rhetoric of those who urge simple solutions based on new technologies. What is needed instead is a strategic plan by universities, particularly those in the ODL mode, to craft appropriate pedagogies for an environment characterised by complexity, which Noel Gough describes thus: 'Complexity invites us to understand that many of the processes and activities that shape the worlds we inhabit are open, recursive, organic, non-linear and emergent' (2017, p. 1).

In his *Pedagogy for Online Learning*, Jesse Stommel (2012) cites as one of the principles of this pedagogy, the following: 'Community and dialogue shouldn't be an accident of by-product of the course. They should *be* the course' (emphasis added). By this he means that shared discussion should not be left to chance when designing an open platform for learning. Such a platform must actively facilitate interaction by modelling constructive interaction. Similarly, Sean Morris (2014), in 'What is Digital Pedagogy,' speaks directly to an ecology of learning when he compares a face to face classroom with a digital learning space. In the latter, he says:

> ... when we teach digitally – whether online, or in hybrid environment ... – walls become arbitrary. All walls. And all seats and all podiums and all chalkboards, too. LMSs have ... shortcomings, but the biggest dilemma they pose is that they create the illusion of digital learning without really ever encountering the Internet. Like all illusions, this is misleading because digital learning (and by necessity, digital pedagogy) takes place all over the web.

The LMS is an attempt to build walls around the learning experience by creating a structure (one size fits all) within which learning is expected to take place, thus mimicking the shape and form of the traditional classroom and perhaps echoing the ghetto or secret hiding place mentioned in this chapter. But walls, whether these are real or illusory cannot contain today's learners who are connected by means of their smart devices to a universe of exploration and whose digitised actions make meaningless the idea of a wall or boundary. As Morris says:

> We cannot compensate for all the ways that students will choose to process and curate their learning in digital spaces, and so it becomes vital to teach students not about particular tools, but about how to choose tools for their use ... Digital pedagogy is different from teaching online because it allows us to open up learning and teaching in ways that gravity-bound education doesn't permit. when we bring the Internet into our teaching, truly embrace all that the digital engenders, we open our students (and ourselves) to a whole new world of networked, connected learning. (2014, n.p.)

While open educational resources are available for researchers as well as teachers to make use of, adapt and refurnish as university courses, many faculty members are still unfamiliar and ill at ease with OER, regarding it/them with suspicion, preferring to spend time crafting curricula or publishing in journals that carry paywalls. Yet there is evidence of progress and change. SUNY has announced that five of their campuses are working to create a zero-textbook degree programme. And the Babson Survey Research Group's report *Opening the Textbook* shows that the number of faculty members using OER as textbooks has nearly doubled from 5% in 2015–2016 to 9% in 2016–2017. Despite this positive news, awareness of OER is still low amongst academics who cite various barriers to OER adoption, including difficulty in finding materials and insufficient resources for particular disciplines. Further, academic researchers still by and large prefer to publish research in journals with paywalls rather than sharing their findings as open resources (see Lieberman, 2018) and Lindsay McKenzie's comments on the report (2017).

The literature on open learning and open resources as well as the impact of digital technologies on teaching and learning have followed typical wave cycles starting with a gentle rise of optimism, crescendoing to cries of joy, then subsiding into gloom. The period from 2005 to 2012, for instance, seems to have been the hype period for MOOCs, and also the period in which books that were positive or overly optimistic about the benefits of connection and the Internet such as *The World is Flat* by Thomas Friedman (2005), *NetSmart: How to Thrive Online* by Howard Rheingold (2012), Clay Shirky's *Cognitive Surplus: Creativity and Generosity in a Connected Age* (2010), and *Rebooting the Academy*, edited by Jeffrey Young and Tim McCormick (2012). But around 2012, the hype became more reflective according to authors such as Nicholas Carr's *The Shallows: What the Internet is Doing to Our Brains* (2011), Cathy Davidson's *Now You See It: How the Brain Science of Attention Will Transform the Way We Live, Work and Learn* (2011), Nick Harkaway's *The Blind Giant: Being Human in a Digital World* (2012), Elizabeth Losh's *The War on Learning: Gaining Ground in the Digital University* (2014) and Ellen Rose's *On Reflection: An Essay on Technology and the Status of Thought in the 21st Century* (2013). This may be a knee-jerk reaction to the speed of information of our time which threatens to be overwhelming, but it is also a necessary counter-reaction, calling for a quiet space in which to take hold of reality as we know it and ponder awhile from the shadows of the threshold.

5 In Lieu of a Conclusion, a Virtual and Tentative Solution to a Virtual Problem

This chapter has followed a specific trajectory, in lieu of a methodology. Instead of suggesting a solution to a perceived problem or predicting a new trend in digital pedagogy, I have adopted an impartial standpoint from which to gaze dispassionately at what has been, what is, and what may be in the context of open resources and digital teaching and learning in higher education. The words used to describe various trends have been examined minutely, not only for their derivations and denotations but also for their metaphorical significance in conveying meaning. The chapter unpicks the words used to describe our current discursive realities, showing both how they adapt, alter or modify those realities and how they echo and resound as one technical generation follows another. The discourses represented here are all enacted within a context that sets itself apart from and in opposition to a dominant and dominating capitalist minority that endeavours to control the world and its discourses as well as the people who create those discourses.

By making connections between past and present and between different disciplines and discourses, and by showing that words and terms are slippery concepts inadequate for the task they are called on to perform, there is something here akin to a methodology which is better framed as an attempt at coherence, at making sense of what is often seen as a productive chaos. There has also been an attempt at uncovering the emotive and sometimes politicised connotations attached to value-driven terms in order to situate the reader at the threshold or liminal space – betwixt and between, open and closed, inside and outside. This attempt reaches towards a dispassionate vision of what openness and connection entail as an ecology. Thinking in the limen creates a necessary harbour from the real, a space from which one can think oneself into either the inside or the outside. It is a way of finding oneself in the pause between movements (to use a musical idiom) without being entangled in predictions or projections. There is no obvious methodology here because none exists for the kind of thinking proposed, that is liminal or liminoid.

This chapter also promised to identify an ecology of openness, and proposed that we consider the space in-between, the limen, as a productive sphere in which to think about the possibilities for open education. Turning now to the suggestion that we map an architecture onto the ecology, I would suggest that we envision a form of Foucault's panopticon[12] but without its sinister implications for surveillance. If we imagine a building with a wall of glass at its front door and a glassed atrium standing between the building and the outside space, we could also imagine ourselves as academics in a time of openness situated in that atrium. From this liminal space, we could observe both what goes on inside the building, standing here for Wordsworth's hiding place, harbouring inner secrets, and what is going on in the busy streets outside. Like Foucault's guards, we are in a position of considerable power, but with that goes responsibility. We are also being seen, by those inside and those outside. Breaking up the model of the Ivory Tower, our new glassed building cannot hide it practices, and we who are in the atrium can devise appropriate methods of teaching and learning in this new open space, mindful of what is going on inside but also observant of the people on the street. Above all, this in-between space could afford teachers and designers a place in which to think, to observe, and to craft appropriate pedagogies for new forms of learning. But this is not a secret hiding place. Those outside the atrium can see what is going on. They can enter at will. Stretching this architectural analogy, learners should be part of the thinking and designing that forms our new pedagogies.

This rather naive architecture is intended as a metaphorical reminder that teaching in a time of openness means that we cannot hide behind past ideologies or practices. If we place ourselves within an architecture which allows us to see in both directions, it is more likely that we will begin to cultivate an open mind, one that eschews static forms of thinking and allows for more fluidity. In this way, an inclusive ecology could be created in the interstices of a new habitat.

Notes

1 I am using 'open sesame!' as the phrase used in the story of Ali Baba and the Forty Thieves but I later discovered that it is also the name of a company OpenSesame Inc that operates a marketplace for online courses. I believe there is a nice irony here.

2 A single effect is determined by multiple cases or effects or has become known without the concept's original complexity.

3 Context collapse is a phrase used by researchers of social networks to indicate the ways in which interaction takes place through the Internet and its difference from face to face social interaction. See http://hlwiki.slais.ubc.ca/index.php/Context_collapse_in_social_media. See also danah boyd: Apophenia zephoriaorg (accessed 12 October 2018).

4 See oasis.col.org

5 For a 'thick' account of the rise of different forms of connection and interconnectivity, see Selwyn's chapter, The New Connectivities of Digital Education in *The Routledge International Handbook of the Sociology of Education* (2009).

6 While not described here, there is a difference between xMOOCs and cMOOCs mentioned in this chapter.

7 See https://www.p2pu.org/en/about/

8 See https://www.p2pu.org/en/about/

9 See for instance *The Shallows* as just one example of a book on the topic.

10 The phrase is an echo of *A Passage to India*, but there is no indication that this is deliberate.

11 See http://linkis.com/redpincushion.us/blo/gNTWs

12 Foucault used Jeremy Bentham's design for a prison building that signified a system of control whereby all the inmates could, in theory, be observed all of the time by guards. It was designed as a circular structure with guards in the middle. Since the inmates could not know when they were being observed, they acted as if they were

being observed all the time thus effecting a kind of self-regarding, self-initiated discipline in the prison. Instead of actual surveillance, the threat of surveillance acts as a form of power. This was taken up by Foucault in his book *Discipline and Punish* (1975).

References

Babson Survey Research Group. (2016). *Opening the textbook.* Retrieved from https://www.onlinelearningsurvey.com/reports/openingthetextbook2016.pdf

Bauman, Z. (1983). Education in liquid modernity. *The Review of Education, Pedagogy, and Cultural Studies, 27*, 303–317.

Bishop, E. (1979/1983). *'At the fishhouses' from the complete poems, 1927–1979*. New York, NY: Farrar, Straus and Giroux.

boyd, d. (2018). *Apophenia zephoriaorg.* Retrieved October 12, 2018, from

Brown, C., & Czerniewicz, L. (2007). If we build it will they come? Investigating the relationship between students' access to and use of ICTs for education. *South African Journal for Higher Education. NADEOSA 2006: Special Edition, 6*(21), 730–745.

Bunting, M. (2003, April 4). Passion and pessimism. *The Guardian.*

Butcher, N., & Hoosen, S. (2012). *Exploring the business case for open educational resources* (COL report). Vancouver: Commonwealth of Learning.

Cape Town Declaration. (2007). Retrieved from http://www.capetowndeclaration.org/cpt10/

Carr, N. (2011). *The shallows: What the internet is doing to our brains* [Kindle Version]. Retrieved from http://www.amazon.com

Castells, M. (2001). *The internet galaxy: Reflections on the internet, business and society.* New York, NY: Oxford University Press.

Castells, M. (2004). Afterword: Why networks matter. In *Network Logic, 17.* Demos Collection. demos.co.uk.

Castells, M. (2010). *The rise of the network society* (2nd ed.). Oxford: Wiley/Blackwell.

Collier, A. (2016). *Not-yetness and learnification.* Retrieved January 2, 2018, from http://linkis.com/redpincushion.us/blo/gNTWs

Cormier, D. (2008). *Rhizomatic education: Community as curriculum.* Retrieved January 21, 2018, from http://davecormier.com/edblog/2008/06/03/rhizomatic-education-community-as-curriculum/

Cronin, C. (2017). *Open education: Open questions.* Retrieved from https://er.educause.edu/articles/2017/10/open-education-open-questions

Davidson, C. (2012). *Now you see it: How the brain science of attention will transform the way we live, work and learn* (Reprint ed.). New York, NY: Viking.

Deleuze, G., & Guattari, F. (1993). *A thousand plateaus.* Minneapolis, MN: University of Minnesota Press.

Downes, S. (2007). *What connectivism is*. Retrieved February 11, 2018, from www.downes.ca/post/38653
Downes, S. (2012). *Connectivism and connective knowledge*. Retrieved February 21, 2018, from http://www.downes.ca/post/58207
Forster, E. M. (1972). *Howards end*. Harmondsworth: Penguin Books.
Forster, E. M. (2005). *A passage to India*. Harmondsworth: Penguin Classics.
Foucault, M. (1975). *Discipline and punish: The birth of the prison*. New York, NY: Vintage Books.
Friedman, T. (2005). *The world is flat: A brief history of the 21st century*. New York, NY: Farrar, Straus and Giroux.
Friedman, T. (2016). *Thank you for being late: An optimist's guide to thriving in the age of accelerations*. UKL Penguin, Random House.
Gore, W. (2007). *In the future of management* (G. Hamel & B. Breen, Eds.). Boston, MA: Harvard Business School Press.
Gough, N. (2017). Complexity, Complexity reduction and 'methodological borrowing in educational inquiry.' *Socialist Studies, 12*(1), 41–56.
Harkaway, N. (2012). *The blind giant: Being human in a digital world*. London: John Murray Publishers.
Jenkins, H., & Ito, M. (2006). *Confronting the challenges of participatory culture: Media education for the 21st century*. Retrieved February 21, 2018, from http://henryjenkins.org/blog/2006/10/confronting_the_challenges_of.html
Lawrence, D. H. (1915). *The rainbow*. London: Modern Library.
Lea, M. R., & Jones, S. (2011). Digital literacies in higher education: Exploring textual and technological practice. *Studies in Higher Education, 36*(4), 377–393.
Levy, P. (2005). Collective intelligence, a civilisation: Towards a method of positive interpretation. *International Journal of Politics, Culture and Society, 18*(3–4), 189–198.
Lieberman, M. (2018). *Finding OER remains challenging but solutions abound*. Retrieved January 10, 2018, from https://www.insidehighered.com/users/mark-lieberman
Losh, E. (2014). *The war on learning: Gaining ground in the digital university*. Cambridge, MA: MIT Press.
Mackenzie, L. (2017, December 19). *Lever press sets gears in motion*. Retrieved January 20, 2018, from https://www.insidehighered.com/news/2018/01/19/lever-press-gets-ready-publish-first-digital-scholarship-books
Morris, S. (2014). *What is digital pedagogy?* Retrieved January 3, 2018, from http://www.seanmichaelmorris.com/what-is-digital-pedagogy/
Norvig, P. (2010). *Response to Nicholas Carr, quoted by Alan Jacobs*. Retrieved June 1, 2018, from https://www.reuters.com/article/urnidgns852573c400693880002576d20078f22f/if-youre-stupid-its-not-googles-fault-idUS241843173620100223
Rheingold, H. (2014). *NetSmart: How to thrive online*. Cambridge, MA: MIT Press.
Rose, E. (2013). *On reflection: An essay on technology, education and the status of thought in the 21st century*. Toronto: Canadian Scholars Press.

Ross, J., & Collier, A. (2016). complexity, mess, and not-yetness: teaching online with emerging technologies. In G. Veletsianos (Ed.), *Emergence and innovation in digital learning: Foundations and applications* (pp. 17–33). Edmonton: Athabasca University Press.

Selwyn, N., & Facer, K. (2013). *The politics of education and technology*. London: Palgrave Macmillan.

Siemens, G. (2004). *Connectivism: A learning theory for the digital age*. Retrieved January 3, 2018, from http://www.elearnspace.org/Articles/connectivism.htm

Shirky, C. (2010). *Cognitive surplus: Creativity and generosity in a connected age*. London & New York, NY: Penguin Group.

Siemens, G., & Tittenberger, P. (2009). *Handbook of emerging technologies for learning*. Winnipeg, MN: University of Manitoba. Retrieved from http://elearnspace.org/Articles/HETL.pdf

Stewart, B. (2014). 'Something is rotten in the state of ... Twitter. *The Theory Blog*. Retrieved March 8, 2018, from http://theory.cribchronicles.com/2014/09/02/something-is-rotten-in-the-state-of-twitter/

Stommel, J. (2012). *Online learning: A manifesto*. Retrieved January 10, 2018, from http://digitalpedagogylab.com

Tait, A. (2008). What are open universities for? *Open Learning: The Journal of Open, Distance and e-Learning, 23*(2), 85–94.

Tait, A. (2013). Distance and e-learning, social justice, and development: The relevance of capability approaches to the mission of open universities. *IRRODL, 14*(4). Retrieved from http://www.irrodl.org/index.php/irrodl/article/view/1526

Tree, I. (2018). *Wilding: The return of nature to a British farm*. London: Picador.

Turner, V. (1979). Frame, flow and reflection: Ritual and drama as public liminality. *Japanese Journal of Religious Studies, 6*(4), 465.

Veletsianos, G. (Ed.). (2016). *Emergence and innovation in digital learning: Foundations and applications*. Edmonton: Athabasca University Press.

Wikipedia contributors. (2018, November 19). Computer network. *Wikipedia, The Free Encyclopedia*. Retrieved November 19, 2018, from https://en.wikipedia.org/w/index.php?title=Computer_network&oldid=869526861

Wilhelm, A. G. (2000). *Democracy in the digital age: Challenges to political life in cyberspace*. London: Routledge.

Wordsworth, W. (1994). The prelude, or growth of a poet's mind: An autobiographical poem. In *The collected poems of William Wordsworth*. Herefordshire: Wordsworth Editions Ltd.

Young, J., & McCormick, T. (2012). *Rebooting the academy*. Washington, DC: The Chronicle of Higher Education.

Zournazi, M. with B. Massumi. (2002). *Navigating movements in hope: New philosophies for change*. Annandale, NSW: Pluto Press.

CHAPTER 4

Talking across the Chasm: Opening up Higher Education in the Knowledge Economy

Gabi Witthaus

The focus of this chapter is on the implications of the discourse of marketisation in higher education (HE) for academics who practise (or wish to practise) open education in English universities. Academics in favour of open education often face barriers to implementing openness in practice as a direct result of national policy, which emphasises competition and exclusivity in contrast to the collaboration and inclusivity at the heart of the open education agenda. One recent policy development, in particular, is likely to increase these barriers: the Teaching Excellence Framework (TEF). To explore these differences, this chapter presents a comparative critical discourse analysis of the UK government's White Paper for the TEF, and a Science for Policy report by the European Commission on opening up education.

1 Situating the Study: The Teaching Excellence Framework and Its Role in Regulating Higher Education in England

The TEF was introduced in England in 2017 to improve the quality of teaching in undergraduate programmes in higher education (HE) (BIS, 2016). It aimed to do this by 'rewarding and recognising excellent teaching, supportive environments and ways of learning, [and] whether studying has enabled students to fulfil their potential (usually in employment or further study and training)' (HEFCE, 2018). The TEF metrics are drawn from student satisfaction ratings, retention/drop-out rates, and data about graduates' employment or engagement in further study after completing their degrees. Participation in the TEF is optional for HE institutions, but from 2020 the ability to increase tuition fees in line with inflation will depend upon successful achievement of the TEF metrics. The TEF therefore pits HE institutions against one another in a new form of ranking which reflects a dramatic intensification of marketisation of the HE sector in England. 'Marketisation' here refers to a characterisation of HE as being part of a 'knowledge economy' in which it is desirable that 'providers' (institutions) should enter into competition with one another, in the

 | DOI: 10.1163/9789004422988_005

belief that this will result in 'consumers' (students) getting the best value for their money.

To understand this trend, some historical background follows. While the earliest English universities were originally privately funded, from the late 1800s onwards, they began to receive significant state aid as the benefits to the wider society of HE and research became apparent. In 1919, the University Grants Committee was established to coordinate all government grants to universities, and it continued to operate until 1989, presiding over a strong national HE system. From 1962, HE was made free for all students, and the state also provided maintenance grants on a means-tested basis. This was partly to simplify the complex array of grants and scholarships that had evolved to support poor students (Anderson, 2016), but also a manifestation of the belief of policy makers at the time that 'the communities that have paid most attention to higher studies have in general been the most obviously progressive in respect of income and wealth' (Committee on Higher Education, 1963, para. 626).

As post-war demand for HE grew, a number of new, state-funded 'polytechnics' (HE bodies without degree-awarding powers, and with a teaching remit rather than a research focus) were established in the 60s, necessitating an increase in the national budget for HE. Then, with Thatcher's rise to power in 1979, came an aggressively market-focused view of HE as a private good, and cuts were applied to HE grants. By the 1990s, many of the grants that had not been cut were being converted into loans. At the same time, there was a competitive realignment of the sector, as all the polytechnics were converted into universities. Access to university was promoted as a universal right, unlike in the post-war years when only the top 25% or so of high school leavers were expected to opt for HE, and this added to the pressure on the treasury (Anderson, 2016). It was Tony Blair's Labour government that, in the mid-90s, introduced tuition fees of first £1000 and then £3000 per year. The state paid this upfront on behalf of students as an income-contingent loan, while continuing to heavily subsidise HE through teaching grants. In 2010, the Conservative government abolished the teaching grant altogether and allowed HE institutions to triple fees to a maximum of £9,000 per year from 2012; two years later they also raised the interest on loan repayments to 6.1%, a step which is likely to generate an average student debt of £57,000 (Belfield, Britton, Dearden, & van der Erve, 2017). Since HE is not truly a market in the economic sense of the word (Marginson, 2012), it is not surprising that most HE institutions in England chose to raise their fees to the maximum level allowed.

Against this backdrop, one of the central aims of the TEF is to try to create more of a market-like economy in the sector, making any further fee increases contingent upon the meeting of metrics which will supposedly differentiate

HE institutions according to the quality of their offers (Ashwin, 2017). Questions of the suitability of the metrics, the likely outcomes of the TEF initiative, or the social consequences of the student debt being amassed, are beyond the scope of this study; suffice it to note that much doubt has been cast on these issues elsewhere (e.g., Esson & Ertl, 2016; Frankham, 2017; Wilsdon, 2017).

The next section looks at the growing awareness of open education in English Higher Education Institutions, and the role (or potential role) of a European Commission-authored series of reports on opening up education in this context.

2 Open Education and the OpenEdu framework in English Higher Education Institutions

In a seemingly parallel universe, recent calls for greater openness and collaboration between HE institutions are backed by increasing evidence that these characteristics enhance both the learning and the teaching experience (e.g., HEFCE, 2011; Nerantzi, 2017). A significant contribution to the literature on open education has been made by the European Union, with a series of scientific and technical reports published by its Joint Research Centre under the auspices of the OpenEdu project (Castaño Muñoz, Punie, Inamorato dos Santos, Mitic, & Morais, 2016; Lažetić, Souto-Otero, & Shields, 2015; Souto-Otero et al., 2016; Witthaus et al., 2016). The final report from this project (Inamorato dos Santos, Punie, & Castaño Muñoz, 2016) proposes a strategic framework, referred to as the OpenEdu framework, comprising ten dimensions of openness. Six of these dimensions (access, content, pedagogy, recognition, collaboration and research) are described as 'core' and four (strategy, technology, quality and leadership) as 'transversal.' The report advocates that those responsible for strategic planning in HE should develop a holistic strategy that embraces all ten dimensions. Two follow-up reports (Inamorato dos Santos et al., 2017a; Inamorato dos Santos, Punie, & Scheller, 2017b) examine policy approaches to open education in all EU member states, and provide policy recommendations for open education at EU, national and regional levels respectively.

Within the UK, the notion of open education had already been woven into the fabric of the HE sector through the founding of the Open University (OU) in 1969 (The Open University, 2018), with the aim of widening access to HE through distance programmes. Through the OU, many thousands of British academics have experienced open education in the sense of open-access courses with flexible delivery – either as OU students themselves in the past, or as OU tutors or academics at some point in their careers. Many more academics learned about open education, in a wider sense, through participating in the UK government-funded open educational resources (OER) programme from 2009 to 2012 (JISC, 2013), or in the EU-funded research projects on open education and their associated online communities for sharing resources and findings. These projects focused on a wide range of applications of openness in HE – not just in terms of open educational resources, but also open educational practices and policy. By the time the OpenEdu framework report and its sister reports in the OpenEdu project were published, they therefore had a ready audience of academics within English (and other British) HE institutions who were advocating and practising open education, albeit often with limited institutional backing.

3 Everyday Obstacles to Openness in Higher Education – Three Scenarios

A few anecdotal examples (all drawn from the author's own direct or indirect experience in English HE institutions) are provided here to indicate the kinds of obstacles and challenges facing academics who wish to practise open education against the backdrop of the growing marketisation of the sector:

- At Institution A, academics in the business school who wish to publish their own teaching materials as OER are prevented from doing so by an intellectual property clause in their employment contracts, because the school's management believes that sharing in-house materials under an open licence in the public domain would be tantamount to 'giving away the family silver.'
- At Institution B, a senior academic who teaches a popular but highly specialised elective module in a postgraduate programme is close to retirement. Aware that the department has not managed to recruit a replacement for her, she proposes to the dean of the school that students should be offered the option to choose from a range of relevant massive open online courses (MOOCs) taught by experts in other universities in Europe, and which include supervised assessments and award academic credits. The dean refuses to even consider the idea, positing that students would never accept such an arrangement considering the high tuition fees they are paying.
- At Institution C, an academic course team is asked by their head of department to develop and deliver a MOOC. The team is initially excited about the opportunity to deliver open education through a high-profile university initiative. However, they soon learn that the funding for the MOOC has come from the marketing department, whose priority is to ensure that the course acts as a 'shop window' for the university, and the team is instructed

to ensure that all educational resources are fully branded and copyrighted to the university (i.e., no open licensing allowed, and no use of OER from other institutions that might 'weaken the brand message'). Also, all materials must go through an internal quality assurance procedure that takes several weeks, thus making it impossible to respond flexibly to learners' needs that arise during delivery by creating new materials.

These scenarios reflect 'old power values' such as managerialism, institutionalism, exclusivity, competition, authority, and limited overall participation (Heimans & Timms, 2014, diagram under 'A World of Difference') as well as bureaucracy and commercialism. They also illustrate the logical consequences for open education of a regulatory environment which prioritises these old power values over openness and collaboration. In any of these situations, it would not be surprising if some academics concluded that open education was not worth the struggle. In his aptly-named book, *The Battle for Open*, Weller (2014) notes that even where open education appears to be taking place – for example, as more MOOCs, OER and open access research repositories are produced – this openness is very often subject to the terms and conditions of commercial platform providers or publishers, resulting in educational offerings that are no longer fully accessible, reusable or repurposable – in other words, no longer truly open. For as long as institutions prevent academics from engaging in open educational practices or enable them to do so only for the organisation's commercial gain, the battle for open will continue.

4 Comparing the Discourse of the Knowledge Economy and Open Education – Three Questions

This study explores the challenges faced by practitioners and advocates of open education in English HE institutions through a critical discourse analysis. It first examines the view of HE as part of a knowledge economy in which providers must 'compete' to ensure that students, as 'consumers,' get the best value for their money. It then compares this view against that of HE as needing to open up to provide a better service to a greater number and diversity of learners. It addresses the following research questions:

i. To what extent does the Discourse of policy makers pursuing a market-driven approach to HE overlap with, or diverge from, that of groups who are advocating open education?
ii. What can be deduced from the answer to (i) about how close or how far apart these different players are in terms of their underlying values and assumptions?

iii. What can the open education community learn from this analysis to strengthen its position within HE?

The author's own standpoint as a proponent of open education will already be clear from the introduction and research question iii. One strand of this study is therefore, that as a contributor to many publications on open educational practices (including the EU's OpenEdu series of reports), the author is subjecting her own use of language to critical self-reflection.

5 Critical Discourse Analysis and Higher Education

The term Discourse with a 'big D' is used here to distinguish between two recognisably different types of language, following Gee's conceptualisation of Discourses as distinctive ways of speaking and listening (or writing and reading), which are coupled with distinctive ways of acting in the world 'in the service of enacting specific socially recognizable identities' (Gee, 2014, p. 183). Each Discourse reflects people's values and beliefs, and the identity they are assuming or choosing to portray through the language they use. This includes considering the unspoken 'figured worlds,' i.e. meanings that the speakers/writers see as so obvious that they do not need to be stated. Critical discourse analysis seeks to uncover the underlying ideologies at play, following Eagleton's (2007) depiction of ideology as possessing 'affective, unconscious, mythical or symbolic dimensions' (p. 221) and as

> an organizing social force which actively constitutes human subjects at the roots of their lived experience and seeks to equip them with forms of value and belief relevant to their specific social tasks and to the general reproduction of the social order. (Eagleton, 2007, p. 222)

Foucault (1988) also urged his readers to interrogate taken-for-granted norms and make people aware of the 'intolerable' ways in which power is exercised through such norms: 'The source of human freedom is never to accept anything as definitive, untouchable, obvious or immobile' (p. 1). The following discourse analysis shows how the language we use is consequential for our students' and our own experience of HE.

In Fairclough's 1993 analysis of the shift towards 'marketisation' in British HE discourse, he concluded that staff members of HE institutions felt helpless to resist the 'distasteful, highly promotional, highly marketized' new discursive practices in HE at the time (p. 159). He gave examples of how the wording of academic recruitment advertisements and university prospectuses had changed since the 1960s, from a blandly descriptive and genteelly authoritative tone towards a more entrepreneurial, advertorial or 'promotional' language. Academics experienced a sense of alienation, he suggested, because of the absence of discursive practices 'through which authority relations and institutional and professional identities different from either traditional or marketized forms [could] be constituted' (p. 159). He exhorted readers to use critical discourse analysis in the struggle to develop a new 'language' as a key means of building such resistance.

Subsequent work by Trowler (2001) argued that, within the English university context, four ideological stances could be discerned among academics: in addition to the enterprise and traditionalist stances mentioned by Fairclough, he identified progressivism, focusing on the personal development of individuals; and social reconstructionism, focusing on social change. Trowler thus demonstrated that staff were not necessarily 'captured by the discourse' of managerialism in HE, and that there was indeed a 'language' (or two, even) for resisting the polarised extremes of traditionalism and neoliberalism. However, he cautions that these alternatives do not emerge automatically, and that, in order to resist a dominant Discourse, people may need to be 'captured' by an alternative one.

Since the publication of Trowler's paper, government policy and regulatory frameworks for HE in England have continued to construct HE institutions in managerialist terms, branding HE with the same neoliberal stamp that is used in the governance of other facets of public life such as health and welfare – not only in the UK but also in many other Western countries (Ball, 2012; Czerniewicz et al., 2018; Marginson, 2012; McLean & Ashwin, 2017). At the same time, a new Discourse has arisen within the HE sector globally – that of open education challenging traditional structures and values of HE and potentially being transformative for the sector (see for example Bozkurt et al., 2015; Smyth, Bossu, & Stagg, 2016; Wiley, 2010). Sometimes these two Discourses overlap, with open education being portrayed as serving neoliberal market interests (e.g. Deimann, 2015; Munro, 2018); however, as Weller (2014) points out, the appropriation of open education for commercial gain is fundamentally at odds with the essential values of openness.

6 How Critical Discourse Analysis Was Applied in This Study

This study used critical discourse analysis as a qualitative methodology, starting from the assumption that insights into the multiple realities experienced by different individuals or groups can be gleaned from the language they use to talk about those different realities. The study draws on critical literature on both sides of the 'Conversation' (Gee, 2014), including critiques of both neoliberalism and open education in HE.

7 Selecting Texts

The texts selected for analysis, reflecting the Discourses of English HE policy and opening up education respectively, are:

- *Success as a knowledge economy: teaching excellence, social mobility and student choice* (BIS, 2016) – the White Paper explaining the Teaching Excellence Framework (TEF) for England, which will be now be referred to as the TEF White Paper;
- *Opening up Education: A Support Framework for Higher Education Institutions* (Inamorato dos Santos et al., 2016) – an advisory report by the European Union's Joint Research Centre aimed at governments and HE institutions in Europe, which will henceforth be referred to as the OpenEdu framework.

Both these documents present frameworks for enhancing HE and are intended by their authors to facilitate a transformation of practices in HE for the benefit of students. Both need to be considered in the context of other related texts (a concept known as intertextuality in discourse analysis): while the TEF White Paper is part of a growing body of official guidance around the Teaching Excellence Framework (e.g. HEFCE, 2016, 2017, 2018), the OpenEdu framework is the culmination of a series of reports with research evidence, which led to policy recommendations for the European Union (Castaño Muñoz et al., 2016; Lažetić et al., 2015; Souto-Otero et al., 2016; Witthaus et al., 2016), and two follow-up reports (Inamorato dos Santos et al., 2017a, 2017b).

Some important differences between the two sample texts should also be noted:

- The TEF White Paper is aimed at HE institutions in England (with optional participation by HE institutions in Wales, Scotland and Northern Ireland (BIS 2016, p. 46)) and has a regulatory purpose and a concomitant hegemonic status. The OpenEdu framework, on the other hand, is aimed at academics and policy makers in 28 countries; its purpose is purely advisory, as the EU operates on a 'subsidiarity' basis for education (UK Parliament, n.d.).
- The process for the development of the TEF White Paper was 'extremely opaque,' with no mechanism for sector-wide discussion of its principles (Ashwin, 2016), whereas the OpenEdu framework represents the culmination of an extensive and transparent consultation process.

- Although both documents were almost concurrent in their publication date, the OpenEdu framework had a longer gestation period than the TEF White Paper, and also took a longer-term view than the TEF White Paper, which was intended for immediate implementation.
- The documents were developed in different political contexts – the TEF White Paper in the context of a Conservative national government trying to claw back public funding from HE; and the OpenEdu framework in the context of a European policy agenda focused on reducing or removing barriers to education, the modernisation of HE in line with the advance of digital technologies, and the desire to bridge formal and non-formal education through accreditation mechanisms. These different contexts necessarily have their own discourses associated with them, none of which is entirely distinct from the others – this concept of blurred boundaries between discourses is known as interdiscursivity and implies that it is never truly possible to isolate a single discourse from a 'representative' text.

Despite these differences in scope and purpose, and bearing in mind the limitations imposed on any analysis by interdiscursivity and intertextuality, there are grounds for treating these documents as typical of their respective genres: the language used in the TEF White Paper is reminiscent of neoliberal discourse in HE management internationally (McLean & Ashwin, 2017), and the OpenEdu framework can be viewed as a reflection of the discourse of academics in the open education movement globally, as it includes an amalgamation of experts' voices from over 40 institutions/organisations in 17 different countries in and beyond Europe (Inamorato dos Santos et al., 2016). Academics in England who wish to be open education practitioners are likely to seek guidance from the OpenEdu framework and the other documents in the EU's OpenEdu series, whilst simultaneously being subject to institutional policies and practices that have emerged in accordance with the TEF White Paper.

8 Generating Word Clouds

The first step in the analysis was to generate 'word clouds' of the 100 most frequently occurring words/terms in each of the documents, using Wordle,[1] as shown in Figures 4.1 and 4.2. Wordle is an online tool that produces a visual map of large quantities of text (in the case of the TEF White Paper and the OpenEdu framework, 34,000 and 22,000 words respectively), showing the most frequently used words (excluding most grammatical words such as prepositions, pronouns and conjunctions) through relative font size. As noted by

FIGURE 4.1 Word cloud for the TEF White Paper

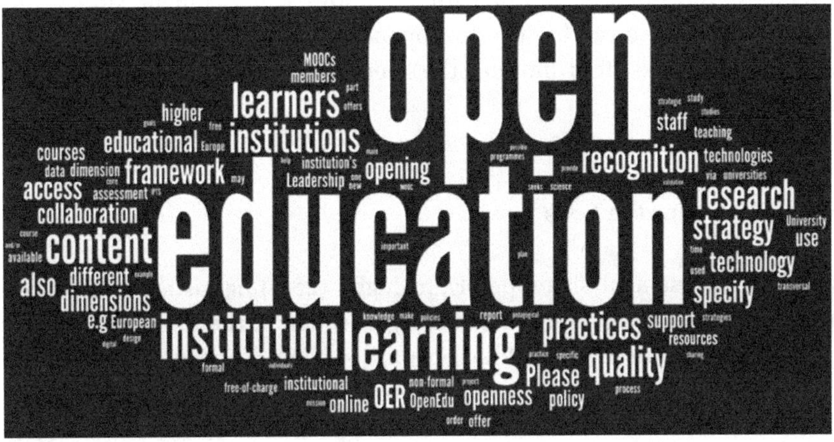

FIGURE 4.2 Word cloud for the OpenEdu framework

McNaught and Lam (2010), Wordle has limitations as a research tool, but is useful for identifying key concepts and themes.

A quick glance at the word clouds gives one a flavour of the two Discourses, with 'open' and 'education' unsurprisingly writ large in the OpenEdu framework, and 'providers' and 'students' given the greatest emphasis in the TEF White Paper.

9 Refining the Word Lists

The next step was to transfer all the words from the word clouds into a spreadsheet (final version provided in Appendix 1), and to search within the source texts to ascertain the word count of each item for each respective document. Words which were morphologically and semantically close were stemmed (e.g. collaborate/collaborative/collaboration – expressed as 'collaborat-'). Words naming administrative bodies or geographic regions intrinsically related to the domains or projects addressed in each document were removed (for example, 'UK' was removed from the TEF White Paper's list, and 'European' from the OpenEdu framework's list; also 'Office for Students (OfS)' and 'OpenEdu' respectively). Several words from the TEF White Paper list misleadingly appeared as high-frequency in the Wordle simply because they were in the document title, which was repeated on every page, but when computed as the word count minus the number of pages (84) yielded an insignificant number, and so these words were removed. (Ironically, this deprived the TEF White Paper's list of several terms – 'success,' 'knowledge,' 'economy,' 'excellence,' 'social,' and 'mobility' – that would appear from the title to be key.) The top 50 remaining lexical items/phrases for each document formed the final lists, and these can be seen in Appendix 1, with the 13 common words given in italics. These lists informed the selection of extracts from the texts for analysis.

10 Analysing the Texts

For the discourse analysis proper, Fairclough's (2010) heuristic categories of the ideational ('the representation and signification of the world and experience,' p. 94), the interpersonal ('the constitution ... of identities of participants and social and personal relationships between them,' p. 94) and the textual (the distribution of given versus new and foregrounded versus backgrounded information) – were used as a conceptual framework.

11 Ideational Features of the TEF White Paper

Several high-frequency words in the TEF White Paper reflect the general market orientation of the document, for example 'providers,' 'funding,' 'choice' (of students in deciding which institution will best 'meet' their 'needs'), 'fees,' 'delivery,' 'market' and 'finance.' This worldview is clearly spelled out in Clause

7 of the Executive Summary: 'Competition between providers in any market incentivises them to raise their game, offering consumers a greater choice of more innovative and better-quality products and services at lower cost' (BIS, 2016, p. 8). In this extract, providers (universities) are seen as businesses competing in the HE 'market,' offering 'products and services' to their 'consumers' (students). This statement reflects the 'figured world' of the TEF White Paper authors – in other words, what they think of as normal or typical. By using this 'marketplace' terminology throughout the TEF White Paper, the policy makers are setting a normative tone for the way HE is both talked about and practised, while at the same time excluding other potentially valid views and practices. The framing of HE as a regular business (which it is not, as it is subsidised by loans to students underwritten by the taxpayer, as the TEF White Paper itself is at pains to point out) leads, within this figured world, to a certain unquestionable inevitability about the need for 'market' type forces to regulate the quality of 'products' and 'services' offered.

The following extract from point 5 of the Executive Summary outlines the problems that the TEF White Paper is seeking to address:

- access remains uneven,
- courses are inflexible, with insufficient innovation
- many students are dissatisfied with the provision they receive,
- employers are suffering skills shortages, and
- around 20% of graduates are in non-professional roles three and a half years after graduating (pp. 7–8).

This is followed immediately by point 6: 'At the heart of this lies insufficient competition and a lack of informed choice' (p. 8). As Eagleton (2007) notes, where the rhetorical force behind a statement carries an implication that a particular action is the best action to take, drawing apparently logical conclusions on the basis of evidence that is not demonstrably related, the discourse betrays the unspoken values of the authors. The lapse in coherence between the scenario of deficit, insufficiency, dissatisfaction and suffering painted in point 5 and its confident diagnosis in point 6 belies the authors' neoliberal ideology.

12 Interpersonal Features of the TEF White Paper

An attempt to unpack the identities of author(s) and readers, and the posited relationship between them, leads to different conclusions depending on which section of the TEF White Paper one reads. The first paragraph of the Executive Summary appears to set the tone for the rest of the TEF White Paper:

> Our universities have a paramount place in an economy driven by knowledge and ideas. They generate the know-how and skills that fuel our growth and provide the basis for our nation's intellectual and cultural success. Higher Education in the UK enjoys a world-class reputation, with globally renowned teaching and cutting-edge research and innovation. We have maintained our position as a world leader, with continuing success in education exports in the face of increasing international competition. But we must be ready for the challenges of the future. (BIS, 2016, p. 7)

One element of this paragraph that strikes the reader is the apparently inclusive, and almost rather cuddly, use of the first-person plural pronoun – 'our' universities; 'we' are a world leader; but 'we' must be ready. This gives the impression that 'we,' the readers (many of whom might conceivably be fee-paying students), share in the ownership of the nation's universities. However, just half a page further on, after a brief discussion about the increased proportion of students from disadvantaged backgrounds entering HE, the limits of this shared ownership become apparent:

> In 2010, we took steps to enable England's higher education system to adjust to these new demands. In 2012, 13 years after tuition fees were first introduced, we took the decision to put higher education funding onto a more sustainable footing. (BIS, 2016, p. 8)

The situated meaning (Gee, 2014) of 'we' in this section is clearly different from that of the 'we' in the first paragraph. This is an authoritative 'we,' a 'we' that isn't afraid to make harsh decisions for the good of the nation – the 'we' of a government that tripled university fees for students in 2012 and labelled this a 'progressive' reform (Coughlan, 2010).

Another view of the identities of the intended audiences of the TEF White Paper, and their relationship to the authors, is offered via the repeated sports metaphor. The government is depicted as the disinterested referee, whose role is to set a 'high quality bar,' 'ensure a level playing field,' and monitor the 'track records' of providers, who are, by implication, the players. The lapse into colloquial phrasing here invites a temporary camaraderie between reader and writer – this could be an excerpt from a dialogue between mates at a pub while cheering on their team on the telly. However, the reader should not get too comfortable, because the relationship soon reverts to 'us' and 'them':

> But we must accept that there may be some providers who do not rise to the challenge, and who therefore need or choose to close some or all of

> their courses, or to exit the market completely. The possibility of exit is a natural part of a healthy, competitive, well-functioning market .... (BIS, 2016, p. 10)

There is a tension throughout the TEF White Paper between the term 'providers' (meaning all providers) and 'incumbents' (meaning existing providers). Incumbents are repeatedly contrasted with 'high quality new providers' (BIS, 2016, p. 9), suggesting that established universities are like sports veterans who cannot (and should not) be protected from the competition of a new generation of rising athletic stars. 'Exiting the market' is a euphemism for a kind of Darwinian institutional extinction, as the newest, strongest, fittest and richest institutions are expected to win out in this now no-longer-friendly competition for survival.

The word 'student/s' has the second highest frequency count after 'providers.' Students are unambiguously positioned as consumers – individuals who 'pursue' higher education as a 'sound financial and personal investment' (BIS, 2016, p. 7). Students are constructed as rational decision-makers, whose primary need is to make the 'right choices' between an array of different 'product' and 'service' options, on the basis of 'information' provided, 'pursuing' their own best interests in a linear fashion. As consumers, students need to not only be 'supported,' but also 'protected' (from institutions that 'choose' to 'exit' the 'market'). Through this language, the relationship between provider and student is reduced to one of a mere commercial transaction in which the student's primary responsibility is to make informed choices about the provision they require.

13 Textual Features of the TEF White Paper

There are three significant omissions in the TEF White Paper. Firstly, a search within the entire TEF White Paper for the term 'teaching excellence' yields no definition – the paper is loudly silent on its nominal topic. The whole universe of learning and teaching, with all its attendant complexities, is parsimoniously and conveniently encapsulated in the notion of a one-way commercial transaction between a supplier and a consumer.

Secondly, academic staff are all but invisible in this HE policy document, in keeping with Sabri's (2010) work on the 'assumptive worlds' of policy makers. Indeed, academics receive only three mentions in the entire TEF White Paper – and in one of those instances they are referred to as being 'distracted': the TEF White Paper cautions against allowing the development of a 'crafty mutually convenient disengagement contract among distracted academics and instrumentalist students,' as has reportedly been seen in the American higher education system. As noted by Sabri (2010), this lack of connection between HE policy and the lived experience of academics, who ultimately are responsible for carrying out government policies on behalf of their institutions, unsurprisingly results in many academics disengaging from national policy debates.

A third omission from the TEF White Paper is any mention of open education, even though the Higher Education Funding Council for England (HEFCE) invested government funds in the UK OER programme from 2009 to 2012 (Jisc, 2013). This omission stretches beyond the White Paper to UK policy for HE in general – the EU's report on policy approaches to open education observes that 'open education is hardly mentioned in policy circles in England' (Inamorato dos Santos et al., 2017, p. 132).

To summarise, the TEF White Paper has set out a policy context that depicts students as consumers who enjoy HE as a private good, that omits any reference to academics as the main actors in students' education, that encourages fierce competition between HE providers, and that disregards the legacy of open education in the UK HE sector built on previous government investment. As will be seen in the next section, a very different picture emerges in the Discourse of open education.

14 Analysis of the Ideational Features of the OpenEdu Framework

The word cloud for the OpenEdu framework contains two strikingly large key words: 'open' and 'education,' illustrating the exceptionally high frequency with which these words occur (959 and 615 respectively, including 371 instances of the collocation 'open education'). This indicates a consistent focus on the central concept of 'opening up' educational practices. The following is offered by way of definition:

> In the OpenEdu project, open education is seen as a way of carrying out education, often using digital technologies. Its aim is to widen access and participation to everyone by removing barriers and making learning accessible, abundant, and customisable for all. It offers multiple ways of teaching and learning, building and sharing knowledge. It also provides a variety of access routes to formal and non-formal education, and connects the two. (Inamorato dos Santos et al., 2016, p. 5)

Here, open education is presented as a universal good (for 'everyone' and for 'all'), facilitated by digital technologies. As the referent of 'Its' and 'It' in the above extract, open education is positioned as an agent with superhero properties, belying the fact that open education is itself a social construct, with no earthly agency to achieve the aims described. Hidden or assumed within this statement is a not insignificant number of human actors with very particular skills, with access to technologies and digital capabilities that are not readily available to all HE learners and academics (even in relatively well-resourced European countries such as the UK), acting with intent within a range of institutional and political contexts, and most likely sharing the belief that open educational practices can become, in the words of the OpenEdu framework, 'a strong tool for social and economic development' (p. 6). The term 'open education' is being used in a situated way as a kind of shorthand for the wider scenario just described.

The depiction of open education here is heavily dependent on intertextuality, in that it alludes to the other texts produced within the OpenEdu project which explore the details of implementation in different contexts (Inamorato dos Santos et al., 2017a), and emphasise the need for a change of mindset in the HE sector (Inamorato dos Santos et al., 2017b). Nevertheless, this text indicates how idealistic the Discourse of open education may appear to be to newcomers who do not share the same background knowledge and vision for education as the authors. Ironically, use of this Discourse could reinforce the perception of the open education community as being isolated and marginal to mainstream HE, rather than the open, welcoming, inclusive and ubiquitous community it seeks to be.

The quotation above from the OpenEdu framework is just one instance of many manifestations of this overstatement of the hoped-for benefits of open education in the wider literature on openness in HE. Bayne, Knox and Ross (2015) note that openness 'has become a highly charged and politicised term …' which 'has acquired a sheen of naturalised common sense and legitimacy and formed what seems to be a post-political space of apparent consensus.' They further argue that:

> It is precisely this view of openness – as a virtue of natural worth – that is problematic, not only because it masks alternative perspectives, but also because it does so with an apparent moral authority that renders the critic at best a technophobe and a cynic, and at worst an elitist and a champion of the status quo. (p. 247)

At the time that Bayne et al. (2015) wrote this critique, the OpenEdu series had not yet been published, and the discourse they were referring to centred mainly around OER, where this kind of romanticisation of openness was particularly prevalent. While the OpenEdu framework expands the concept of openness to ten dimensions (of which only one, content, is specifically about OER), the basic tenet of openness as being an unquestionable moral good is nevertheless deeply embedded in the ideational features of the text.

15 Interpersonal Features of the OpenEdu Framework

In the OpenEdu framework, the authors use a rather formal academic tone, which would fit comfortably within the genre of articles in social sciences journals. This may be a consequence of the fact that many of the authors and named contributors are themselves academics who publish regularly in such journals. It is possible that readers with a background in the social sciences will find this Discourse more 'natural' than will those in STEM fields and other disciplines.

The first half of the OpenEdu framework is essentially a research report, and readers are referred to in the third person. The intended audience for the OpenEdu framework is described as:

> university management and decision makers, that is, anyone who is in charge of open education or who can propose it as an important part of the overall institutional strategy. The report is also directed at those staff members of HE institutions who actually design educational strategy. (Inamorato dos Santos et al., 2016, p. 6)

Despite this spelling out of the audience, a repeated feature throughout the first half of the document is the personification of institutions and states, which sometimes makes it hard to discern who the intended recipients are in human terms, for example: 'If a university were to decide' (p. 8); 'institutions should consider' (p. 30); and even '*Europe* should act now providing the right policy framework and a stimulus to introduce innovative learning and teaching practices in schools, universities, vocational education and training' (cited from an EU Communication, p. 30, emphasis added). The effect of this conflation of individuals and groups with vastly different viewpoints into a single entity in each instance is to homogenise the readers, obscuring many a heated debate and glossing over much unresolved conflict within academic teams who might be attempting to simultaneously fulfil the requirements of market-oriented policies/regulations and implement open education. The second half of the report remedies this situation, as it contains two annexes with templates to support the application of open education in institutions, along with guidance for the use of the templates, where the reader is addressed in the second person. This shift from readers as an unspecified 'they' to 'you' serves to mark the transition from reporting to advising, and to narrow down the target audience to those staff who 'actually design educational strategy' (p. 6). The tone is tentative here, with frequent use of the modal 'may' (as in 'you may wish to refer to …') successfully positioning the authors as friendly advisors rather than authority figures, in keeping with the purpose of the document, the principle of education's subsidiarity within EU policy, and the general ethos of collaboration that characterises open education.

16 Textual Features of the OpenEdu Framework

Any discussion of textual features in a document that is part of a series, such as the OpenEdu framework, needs to be undertaken with the caveat that the foregrounding or omission of certain elements cannot be fully evaluated without taking the other texts into account. The OpenEdu series of reports on opening up education includes concrete examples of practices, beliefs and strategies around the implementation of open education (Castaño Muñoz et al., 2016), case studies (Lažetić et al., 2015), and detailed proposals for enabling the accreditation and validation of open learning (Witthaus et al., 2016); however, as the OpenEdu framework is the final document in the series and contains summaries of the other studies, it is likely that some readers will read it without referring to the full set of texts.

What is foregrounded in the OpenEdu framework is open education in its many manifestations, implying that there is another kind of education which is 'closed,' and which by definition suffers from a lack of all the benefits attributed to open education, such as those outlined in the following extract:

> Through open education each and every individual, at every stage in their lives and career development, can have appropriate and meaningful educational opportunities available to them. These include access to content, courses, support, assessment and certification in ways that are flexible, and accommodate diverse needs. Barriers, as regards for example entry or cost, are reduced or eliminated. (Inamorato dos Santos et al., 2016, p. 5)

This statement contains an implied false binary (Oliver, 2015), which may appear extreme to some academics. For example, in a recent study in an Irish HE institution, academics identified open educational practices as any and all 'collaborative practices that include the creation, use, and reuse of OER [open educational resources], as well as pedagogical practices employing participatory technologies and social networks for interaction, peer-learning, knowledge creation, and empowerment of learners' (Cronin, 2017, p. 18). This definition includes aspects of education that are not necessarily 'open,' such as closed social networks and collaborative practices between staff in a single institution.

An omission from the language of the OpenEdu framework (and many other texts written by proponents of open education) is any explicit discussion around the difficulty readers may experience of finding a balance between open education and traditional ('closed') education, arising out of the fact that any form of open education that fulfils all the functions described above can only succeed as one aspect of a wider HE system in which mainstream, formal, education remains strong. The OpenEdu framework advises readers to integrate their open education strategy into their overall institutional mission and vision, and yet the inevitable tensions and contradictions that this must lead to – for example, fears that open education will 'cannibalise' mainstream provision (Miao, Mishra, & McGreal, 2016, p. 132) are not addressed in the document. Dilemmas and drawbacks to opening up education are, however, extensively discussed in the OpenCases report (Lažetić et al., 2015), again drawing attention to the importance of intertextuality.

17 Similarities and Differences between Discourses of the TEF White Paper and OpenEdu Framework

This section returns to the first two research questions of the study. Firstly, *How far does the Discourse of policy makers pursuing a market-driven approach to higher education overlap with, or diverge from, that of groups who are seeking to open up education?*

It is clear from the above that the two Discourses reflect vastly different worldviews and value systems. The analysis has shown that neoliberal Discourse is replete with deficit notions of all the key actors in HE: we have 'distracted' and mostly absent academics; students who are 'instrumentalist' and narrowly focused on the commercial value of their education; and providers that need to be monitored, regulated and 'stimulated' by manufactured 'competition' who will be somehow motivated by the expectation that those who are not able to 'raise their game' sufficiently will have to 'exit the market.' Open education, by contrast, offers a resoundingly optimistic and positive alternative way of framing HE, promising amongst other things, abundance, inclusivity, transparency, universal access and collaboration.

TABLE 4.1 A comparative look at the use of some of the other high frequency words and phrases that are common to both texts

TEF White Paper	OpenEdu framework
The market needs to be *opened up* (to new providers)	Education needs to be *opened up* (to more, and more diverse, learners)
New entrants (i.e. institutions) need *access to* the market	Learners need greater *access to* education
Consumers (students) primarily need protection from institutions that may fail them, as well as *support* to succeed	Learners (students) need *support* to succeed
Widening *participation* means bringing more young people into HE	Widening *participation* means bringing more people into lifelong learning
Consumers (students) require information about the *content* of courses – in order to be able to choose the 'best' institution to enrol at	Learners (students) should have access to openly-licensed *content* (materials and resources for learning, including research outputs)
Recognition of new HE providers will help to stimulate competition (between institutions) in the sector	*Recognition* of prior learning is an essential element in opening up HE to all
High quality *research* as an indicator of the reputation and competitiveness of an institution	Openly published *research* as a way of removing barriers to access to knowledge, and broadening participation in research

Further to these observations, Table 4.1 provides a comparative look at the use of some of the other high frequency words and phrases that are common to both texts.

From the table, it is clear that, even when the same vocabulary is used, the TEF White Paper consistently depicts a closed, competitive and consumer-focused model of HE as the goal, while the OpenEdu framework consistently expresses a vision for an open, inclusive model. While the TEF White Paper Discourse is hierarchical and sometimes condescending, the OpenEdu framework Discourse reflects the ideal of a collaborative, mutually supportive world.

The second research question – *what can be deduced from the above about how close or how far apart these different players are in terms of their underlying values and assumptions?* – is addressed below.

Both texts address many of the same issues, such as the need to 'widen participation' in HE, and to provide learners with the best quality education possible to enable them to be active citizens in 21st century work and social life. However, the positions of the HE-as-market-economy Discourse and the opening-up-education Discourse differ substantially in their views of the nature and purpose of HE. To the extent that the two Discourses reflect mutually incompatible standpoints and value systems, it is worth pointing out the obvious, that (in England at least), the TEF White Paper Discourse represents social and legislative power, and so academics and institutional leaders who want to both open up education and be 'winners' on the 'level playing field' of the TEF will have to find creative ways of doing so – as will be illustrated by a return to the original scenarios in the next section.

18 Considerations for the Open Education Community

The third research question for this study provides the frame for its conclusion: *What can the open education community learn from this analysis to strengthen its position within higher education?*

The foregoing discussion shows that while the TEF White Paper is preoccupied with fees, finances and funding within the parameters of a perceived competitive financial market, the OpenEdu framework is more focused on distributing the social benefits of HE throughout society. Financial sustainability is included as an element in the OpenEdu framework; and return on investment is discussed in terms of 'revenue by commercialising specific parts of the open education offer to specific types of audiences, such as assessment or credentials, or more registrations for paid-for courses) or indirect (e.g. increased reputation and enhanced internationalisation)' (Inamorato dos Santos et al., 2016, p. 62). The critical difference between the proposed commercial activity within the OpenEdu framework and that within the TEF White Paper is that, in an open ecology, any exchange of money would take place between individuals or groups who perceive themselves to be part of a networked community collaborating for the common good, as opposed to the principle of individuals paying fees for which they will reap private benefit. This has fundamental implications for all aspects of the HE 'marketplace' which can be illustrated by reimagining the three scenarios presented in the introduction:

- At Institution A, academics in the business school who wish to publish their own teaching materials as OER are supported to do so by an intellectual property clause in their employment contracts that encourages the collaborative development of teaching resources as OER. The school management believes that creation and reuse of OER will drive up the quality of materials in the sector, and are therefore reallocating finances to the production, sharing and reuse of openly licensed resources instead of the ongoing development or purchasing of copyrighted ones – as recommended by Weller (2016).

- When a senior academic at Institution B, who teaches a popular but highly specialised elective module and is close to retirement, proposes that students should be offered the option to choose from a range of relevant MOOCs, the dean examines this idea in detail. After much deliberation and discussion with the senior leadership team, the dean concludes that offering a wide range of MOOCs taught by experts from all over the world as new elective modules would not only fill the gap left by the retiring academic but would also contribute positively to student recruitment and retention. The dean therefore initiates a dialogue between Institution B and the MOOC-providing institution about ways of formally embedding the MOOC in Institution B's programmes, with a commensurate fee to make the partnership mutually beneficial. Similar partnerships with other MOOC providing institutions are envisaged for the future.
- At Institution C, the head of department decides not to commission the development of another MOOC but rather to ask an academic course team to repurpose a MOOC that they had developed last year, in order to embed it into a module for on-site, fee-paying students. The rationale for this is to provide the in-house students with a global body of peers with whom to collaborate on assessed projects, so that they can learn the skills of virtual teamwork, which is an intended learning outcome of the course. The students will work in virtual teams to co-create online resources as an assessed project. Future cohorts will edit and add to this body of resources. The head of department wants students to be encouraged to publish the resources as OER, partly because of the opportunity this affords the students for skills development, and partly to showcase Institution C's excellence in teaching to the world. The role of the academic team is to facilitate the development of these OER by the students, ensuring that they follow rigorous peer feedback procedures for quality assurance purposes.

These reimagined scenarios could be further developed with reference to the strategy advice contained in the annexes of the OpenEdu framework. They all demonstrate 'new power values' (Heimans & Timms, 2014), such as open source collaboration, crowd wisdom and sharing, as opposed to the 'old power values' illustrated in the original scenarios described in the introduction. They reflect some of the possibilities for opening up HE in practice, while still meeting institutional needs for reputation management, responsible use of resources, and student recruitment and retention.

In conclusion, while academics may be put off by the hegemonic Discourse of government regulation and attracted by the positivity of the Discourse of open education, more work is needed to develop the language of openness in such a way that it speaks to the lived reality of academics. The tangible meanings of 'open' need to be explored with colleagues in concrete contexts related to their practice, being careful to avoid implying the inherent superiority of openness. Proponents of open education in English HE institutions should inform themselves of the many ways in which open education is being practised in institutional contexts elsewhere (for example, Cannell, Page, & Macintyre, 2016; Inamorato dos Santos et al., 2017a; Ossianilsson, Williams, Camilleri, & Brown, 2015), to help them argue for a review of outdated institutional policies which hinder or prevent openness in practice.

Open educators would also do well to interrogate their own use of language for signs of acceptance of (and possibly resignation to) a world in which they 'package' education and 'deliver' it to students in ways that reinforce closed practices, or celebrate their institutions' successes in terms defined by legislators who would create classes of 'gold,' 'silver' and 'bronze' performers competing for resources and students, rather than an open, collaborative community of HE educators working for the common good. As Foucault said, in a debate with Chomsky in 1971:

> The real political task in a society such as ours is to criticize the workings of institutions that appear to be both neutral and independent, to criticize and attack them in such a manner that the political violence that has always exercised itself obscurely through them will be unmasked, so that one can fight against them. (Foucault & Chomsky, 2006, p. 41)

This is as true today as it was then. The learners for whom openness matters most – the disadvantaged, the mature working students with families to care for, and all those targeted in the 'widening participation' agenda – need academics now more than ever to watch their language – and to push the boundaries in practising open education to show that there is another way.

Acknowledgements

The author wishes to thank Andreia Inamorato dos Santos and David Hawkridge, as well as the two anonymous reviewers of this chapter and the book editors for their helpful comments and advice on earlier drafts. The author also acknowledges the support of academic staff of the Doctoral Programme in Higher Education Research, Evaluation and Enhancement at Lancaster University from which this publication has arisen.[2]

Notes

1 http://www.wordle.net/

2 http://www.lancaster.ac.uk/educational-research/phd/phd-in-higher-education-research,-evaluation-and-enhancement/

References

Anderson, R. (2016). *Policy papers: University fees in historical perspective.* Retrieved from http://www.historyandpolicy.org/policy-papers/papers/university-fees-in-historical-perspective

Ashwin, P. (2016). 'Bizarre' TEF metrics overlook so much about teaching excellence. *Times Higher Education Blog.* Retrieved from https://www.timeshighereducation.com/blog/bizarre-tef-metrics-overlook-so-much-about-teaching-excellence

Ashwin, P. (2017). What is the teaching excellence framework in the United Kingdom, and will it work? *International Higher Education, 88*(2017), 10–11. doi:10.6017/ihe.2017.88.9683

Ball, S. (2012). *Global Education Inc.: New policy networks and the neoliberal imaginary.* London: Routledge.

Bayne, S., Knox, J., & Ross, J. (2015). Open education: The need for a critical approach. *Learning, Media and Technology, 40*(3), 247–250. doi:10.1080/17439884.2015.1065272

Belfield, C., Britton, J., Dearden, L., & van der Erve, L. (2017). *Higher education funding in England: Past, present and options for the future* [IFS Briefing Note BN211]. London: Institute for Fiscal Studies. Retrieved from https://www.ifs.org.uk/publications/9334

BIS. (2016). *Success as a knowledge economy: Teaching excellence, social mobility and student choice* [White paper]. Retrieved from https://www.gov.uk/government/uploads/system/uploads/attachment_data/file/523546/bis-16-265-success-as-a-knowledge-economy-web.pdf

Bozkurt, A., Akgun-Ozbek, E., Yilmazel, S., Erdogdu, E., Ucar, H., Guler, E., ... Aydin, C. H. (2015). Trends in distance education research: A content analysis of journals 2009–2013. *International Review of Research in Open and Distributed Learning, 16*(1). doi:10.19173/irrodl.v16i1.1953

Cannell, P., Page, A., & Macintyre, R. (2016). Opening Educational Practices in Scotland (OEPS). *Journal of Interactive Media in Education, 2016*(1), 1–6. https://doi.org/10.5334/jime.412

Castaño Muñoz, J., Punie, Y., Inamorato dos Santos, A., Mitic, M., & Morais, R. (2016). *How are higher education institutions dealing with openness? A survey of practices, beliefs and strategies in five European countries* [JRC Science for Policy Report]. Seville: JRC Science Hub, European Union. doi:10.2791/709253

Committee on Higher Education. (1963). *Report of the committee appointed by the Prime minister under the chairmanship of Lord Robbins (The Robbins Report)*. London. Retrieved from http://www.educationengland.org.uk/documents/robbins/robbins1963.html

Coughlan, S. (2010, November 3). Students face tuition fees rising to £9,000. *BBC*. Retrieved from http://www.bbc.co.uk/news/education-11677862

Cronin, C. (2017). Openness and praxis: exploring the use of open educational practices in higher education. *The International Review of Research in Open and Distributed Learning, 18*(5), 15–34. doi:10.19173/irrodl.v18i5.3096

Czerniewicz, L., Mogliacci, R., Walji, S., Swartz, R., Ivancheva, M., Swinnerton, B., & Morris, N. (2018). Negotiating the 'new normal': How decision makers in higher education perceive marketisation in the sector. In *[Re}valuing Higher Education, 2 – 5 July, 2018 HERDSA Annual Conference* (pp. 1–15). Adelaide. Retrieved from www.herdsa.org.au/publications/conference-proceedings/research-and-development-higher-education-re-valuing-higher-3

Deimann, M. (2015). The dark side of the MOOC – A critical inquiry on their claims and realities. *Current Issues in Emerging ELearning, 2*(1), 3. Retrieved from https://scholarworks.umb.edu/ciee/vol2/iss1/3/

Eagleton, T. (2007). *Ideology: An introduction* (2nd ed.). London: Verso.

Esson, J., & Ertl, H. (2016). No point worrying? Potential undergraduates, study-related debt, and the financial allure of higher education. *Studies in Higher Education, 41*(7), 1265–1280. doi:10.1080/03075079.2014.968542

Fairclough, N. (1993). Critical discourse analysis and the marketization of public discourse: The universities. *Discourse & Society, 4*(2), 133–168.

Fairclough, N. (2010). *Critical discourse analysis: The critical study of language* (2nd ed.). London: Routledge.

Foucault, M. (1988). Power, moral values, and the intellectual. *History of the Present, 4*, 1–2.

Foucault, M., & Chomsky, N. (2006). *The Chomsky vs Foucault debate on human nature*. New York, NY: The New Press.

Frankham, J. (2017). Employability and higher education: The follies of the 'productivity challenge' in the teaching excellence framework. *Journal of Education Policy, 32*(5), 628–641. doi:10.1080/02680939.2016.1268271

Gee, J. P. (2014). *How to do discourse analysis: A toolkit* (Kindle ed.). Abingdon: Routledge.

HEFCE. (2011). *Collaborate to compete: Seizing the opportunity of online learning for UK higher education.* [Report to HEFCE by the Online Learning Task Force]. Bristol: HEFCE. Retrieved from http://www.hefce.ac.uk/pubs/year/2011/201101/

HEFCE. (2016). *Teaching excellence framework year two additional guidance*. Bristol:

HEFCE. Retrieved from http://www.hefce.ac.uk/media/HEFCE,2014/Content/Pubs/2016/201632/HEFCE2016_32.pdf

HEFCE. (2017). *Teaching excellence and student outcomes framework specification*. Bristol: HEFCE. Retrieved from https://assets.publishing.service.gov.uk/government/uploads/system/uploads/attachment_data/file/658490/Teaching_Excellence_and_Student_Outcomes_Framework_Specification.pdf

HEFCE. (2018). *Student guide to the TEF*. Retrieved from http://www.hefce.ac.uk/lt/tef/students

Heimans, J., & Timms, H. (2014). Understanding 'new power.' *Harvard Business Review, 92*(12), 48–56.

Inamorato dos Santos, A., Nascimbeni, F., Bacsich, P., Atenas, J., Aceto, S., Burgos, D., & Punie, Y. (2017a). *Policy approaches to open education – Case studies from 28 EU member states (OpenEdu Policies)*. Seville: JRC Science Hub, European Union. doi:10.2760/283135

Inamorato dos Santos, A., Punie, Y., & Muñoz, J. C. (2016). *Opening up education: A Support framework for higher education institutions* [JRC Science for Policy Report]. Seville: JRC Science Hub, European Union. doi:10.2791/293408

Inamorato dos Santos, A., Punie, Y., & Scheller, K. (2017b). *Going open: Policy recommendations on open education in Europe (OpenEdu Policies)* (Y. Punie & K. D. A. Scheller, Eds.). Joint Research Centre, European Union. doi.org/10.2760/111707

Jisc. (2013). *Open education* [Archive]. Retrieved from https://www.jisc.ac.uk/rd/projects/open-education

Lažetić, P., Souto-Otero, M., & Shields, R. (2015). *OpenCases: Catalogue of mini cases on open education in Europe* [JRC Technical Report]. Seville: JRC Science Hub, European Union. doi:10.2791/778862

Marginson, S. (2012). The impossibility of capitalist markets in higher education. *Journal of Education Policy, 28*(3), 353–370. doi:10.1080/02680939.2012.747109

McLean, M., & Ashwin, P. (2017). The quality of learning, teaching and curriculum. In P. Scott, J. Gallagher, & G. Parry (Eds.), *New languages and landscapes of higher education* (pp. 84–102). Oxford: Oxford University Press.

McNaught, C., & Lam, P. (2010). Using wordle as a supplementary research tool. *The Qualitative Report, 15*(3), 630–643. Retrieved from http://nsuworks.nova.edu/tqr/vol15/iss3/8

Miao, F., Mishra, S., & McGreal, R. (2016). *Open educational resources: Policy, costs and transformation*. Paris: UNESCO and the Commonwealth of Learning. Retrieved from http://unesdoc.unesco.org/images/0024/002443/244365e.pdf

Munro, M. (2018). The complicity of digital technologies in the marketisation of UK higher education: Exploring the implications of a critical discourse analysis of thirteen national digital teaching and learning strategies. *International Journal of Educational Technology in Higher Education, 15*(1). https://doi.org/10.1186/s41239-018-0093-2

Nerantzi, C. (2017). Quality teaching through openness and collaboration – An alternative to the TEF? *Compass: Journal of Learning and Teaching, 10*(2). doi:10.3402/rlt.v23.26967

Oliver, M. (2015). From openness to permeability: Reframing open education in terms of positive liberty in the enactment of academic practices. *Learning, Media and Technology, 40*(3), 365–384. doi:10.1080/17439884.2015.1029940

Ossiannilsson, E., Williams, K., Camilleri, A. F., & Brown, M. (2015). *Quality models in online and open education around the globe: State of the art and recommendations* (Online Submission).

Sabri, D. (2010). Absence of the academic from higher education policy. *Journal of Education Policy, 25*(2), 191–205. doi:10.1080/02680930903428648

Smyth, R., Bossu, C., & Stagg, A. (2016). Toward an open empowered learning model of pedagogy in higher education. In S. Reushle, A. Antonio, & M. Keppell (Eds.), *Open learning and formal credentialing in higher education: Curriculum models and institutional policies* (pp. 205–222). Hershey, PA: IGI Global.

Souto-Otero, M., Inamorato dos Santos, A., Shields, R., Lažetić, P., Castaño Muñoz, J., Devaux, A., ... Punie, Y. (2016). *OpenCases: Case studies on openness in education.* Seville: JRC Science Hub, European Union. doi:10.2791/039825

The Open University. (2018). *History of the open university.* Retrieved from http://www.open.ac.uk/researchprojects/historyofou/#

UK Parliament. (n.d.). *The principle of subsidiarity.* Retrieved from https://www.parliament.uk/business/committees/committees-a-z/lords-select/eu-select-committee-/committee-work/parliament-2017/subsidiarity/

Weller, M. (2014). *The battle for open: How openness won and why it doesn't feel like victory.* London: Ubiquity Press.

Weller, M. (2016). The open flip – A digital economic model for education. *Journal of Learning for Development, 3*(2), 26–34. Retrieved from http://www.jl4d.org/index.php/ejl4d/article/view/152/142

Wiley, D. (2010). The open future. Openness as catalyst for an educational reformation. *Educause Review, 45*(4), 15–20. Retrieved from http://er.educause.edu/articles/2010/8/openness-as-catalyst-for-an-educational-reformation

Wilsdon, J. (2017). Responsible metrics. In *Higher education strategy and planning: A professional guide* (pp. 247–254). London: Routledge.

Witthaus, G., Inamorato dos Santos, A., Childs, M., Tannhäuser, A.-C., Conole, G., Nkuyubwatsi, B., & Punie, Y. (2016). *Validation of non-formal MOOC-based learning an analysis of assessment and recognition practices in Europe* (OpenCred). *JRC Science for Policy Report*. Seville. doi:10.2791/809371

Appendix 1: 50 Most High-Frequency Words in TEF White Paper and OpenEdu Framework

TEF White Paper			OpenEdu framework		
No.	Word	Count	No.	Word	Count
1	provid-/provision	430	1	open- (openness/opening)	959
2	student/s	354	2	education-	615
3	research	250	3	institution-	437
4	higher education	232	4	learning	227
5	quality	188	5	learner/s	166
6	able	152	6	technolog-	161
7	funding	140	7	strateg-	160
8	innovat-	140	8	content	157
9	Year	128	9	dimension/s	145
10	institution-	127	10	access	141
11	system	126	11	practice/s	140
12	sector	116	12	research	135
13	teaching	115	13	quality	128
14	work	113	14	collaborat-	122
15	new	106	15	recognition	112
16	part	101	16	support	112
17	university/ies	96	17	framework	103
18	time	94	18	course/s	100
19	ensure	92	19	offer/s	98
20	access	89	20	OER	97
21	DAPS	88	21	part	95
22	level	86	22	policy/ies	93
23	need	85	23	MOOC/s	91
24	high	81	24	university/ies	85
25	review	79	25	assessment/assess	77
26	support	78	26	free	76
27	Choice	76	27	different	74
28	take	76	28	staff	69
29	set	75	29	online	68
30	compet-	74	30	member/s	64
31	current-	74	31	use/ used/ uses	63
32	data	73	32	higher education	62

TEF White Paper			OpenEdu framework		
No.	**Word**	**Count**	**No.**	**Word**	**Count**
33	future	69	33	formal	58
34	fee/fees	63	34	leadership	57
35	meet	63	35	resources	55
36	assess-	60	36	provide	54
37	full-	58	37	pedagog-	53
38	approach	57	38	design	52
39	power/s	57	39	make	49
40	information	56	40	study/ies	49
41	first	56	41	data	48
42	participat-	55	42	process	47
43	function-	55	43	plan-	45
44	deliver-	54	44	knowledge	44
45	number	52	45	non-formal	39
46	consult-	51	46	main	38
47	make	51	47	new	38
48	outcomes	50	48	mission	36
49	market	50	49	programme/s	35
50	financ-	46	50	science	35

PART 2

Open in a Learning World

CHAPTER 5

Transformative Sustainability-Oriented Open Education

Anne Algers and Arjen E. J. Wals

How can open education play a role in making academia more responsive and responsible in addressing ill-defined and ambiguous, but ever so urgent, sustainable development challenges? In this chapter, a case study from the field of sustainable development of food systems will provide a narrative that illustrates the possible impact of open education; and the value of a culture of openness to individuals, to a community, and to society. First, we provide a contextual background on the implications of openness in higher education. Second, we introduce the subject of sustainable development (SD) of our global food systems; and third, we discuss the concept of education for sustainable development (ESD). Fourth, by means of *thick* description (Geertz, 1973), we report a case study on open education which we discuss in light of learning theory, critical pedagogy, and sustainable development. In the end we argue for a radical interpretation of open education which we refer to as transformative sustainability-oriented open education, where 'open' refers to inviting and expressing critique and marginalized perspectives in controversial societal issues, while transformative refers to enabling learners to bring about change.

1 Openness in Higher Education

Open can be both an adjective and a noun. As an adjective it is defined in the dictionary as 'allowing access, passage, or a view through an empty space; not closed or blocked' while as a verb it refers to 'unfold or be unfolded; spread out.' 'Open' in open education has emphasized the more instrumental adjectival meaning over the more emancipatory active verb meaning, although the latter meaning has gained support in recent times. The definition of open education has evolved over time, amid many differences in terminology, from the concept of open access to a *product* – conceptualised as open educational resources (OER) – to an emancipatory *process* – Open Educational Practices (OEP) (Hylén, 2006). One of the definitions focusing on agency and empowerment is the definition by Kanwar, Balasubramanian, and Umar (2010):

 | DOI: 10.1163/9789004422988_006

> The phenomenon of OER is an empowerment process, driven by technology in which various types of stakeholders are able to interact, collaborate, create, and use materials and pedagogical practices, that are freely available, for enhancing access, reducing costs, and improving the quality of education and learning at all levels. (p. 77)

A newer definition is that OEP is a catalyst for free and wide reflection on knowledge and pedagogies (Farrow, 2017). A more technical definition is related to the use of creative commons licenses arguing that the power of OER lies in the five Rs, which are the rights to retain, reuse, revise, remix and redistribute the OER with an open license (Wiley, 2014). Wikipedia, which is the most pronounced example of Open Educational Practice (OEP), is globally used as a *scientific reference point* while, on the other hand, being held in suspicion by a range of scientists – whether their concerns are founded or not. However, in small subject areas, in particular, there is a need of a constantly critical user. This is related to the transparency of both the content and the process by which it is created. Clicking on the tabs that appear on every page allows us to read across time, which make critical reflection possible (Brown & Adler, 2008) as long as the reader is aware of each tab representing a choice made by someone else that steers in a particular direction. Wiley and Gurrell (2009) claim that an OER has two dimensions, one that is context-free and has to do with the accuracy of the content; and one that has to be assessed in the context between a specific user and a specific resource. One could argue that the first dimension is about the accuracy of the OER *per se* and the second dimension about its contextual values or legitimacy. Thus, we agree with Schulman (1999) that learning is most powerful when it is shared, contested, examined, and challenged in public and least useful when it is private and hidden However, there is a risk of hidden monitoring and analysing of learner behaviour not with the intent of enhancing learning but rather of influencing this behaviour that can even increase inequalities (e.g. when learning analytics is used *of* learning rather than *for* learning) or to enhance consumerism (e.g. big data mining for commercial purposes). Open education can be regarded a potential solution to contemporary challenges as knowledge is socially challenged and therefore more robust (Camilleri et al., 2014) and invites both creativity and transgression of taken-for-granted normalized routines when open implies open to alternative perspectives, to marginalised groups and to critique and questioning. Viewed as such, OER can be a powerful force in tackling wicked problems such as climate change, toxification of water, soil, air and bodies and loss of biodiversity, that are characterized by complex interdependencies where solving one aspect of a wicked problem may reveal or create other problems (Ritchey, 2013). Such a transformative interpretation of OER can also provide a response to a commonly expressed critique that the flow of OER is most often in one direction, from the Northern to the Southern hemisphere (Hodgkinson-Williams & Arinto, 2017; Kanwar et al., 2010) which can be seen as one way to fuel neocolonialism and neoliberalism. Transformative sustainability-oriented OER, instead, has the potential to nourish, for instance, social justice when it helps to create the conditions and techniques for collaborative knowledge creation that extinguishes or at least diminishes the societal power order. Daniels et al. (2010) posit that the capacity to recognise and collaborate on shared and open resources is a reaction to experts' groupthink and fragmentation; and conclude that by focusing on tensions and contradictions, transgressive learning situations will develop, since what chafes can lead to something new and enhanced. This way of thinking is of particular interest in the context of sustainable development as we will illustrate by zooming in on a discussion of our food system.

2 Sustainable Development of Our Global Food Systems

What can open education offer for the sustainable development (SD) of our food system? Food is essential to all beings but the way humans – over nine billion by 2050 – produce and use food affects all life on Earth as it involves the use of water, land, non-human animals, chemicals, fossil fuels, labour as well as socio-cultural practices. The development of food systems that are mindful of the well-being of all animals, both human and non-human, as well as of the planetary boundaries and carrying capacity of the Earth (FAO, 2016; UN, 2018) is an enormous challenge.

The challenge of creating sustainable food systems is not defined by clear boundaries. The farming, economic, environmental and socio-ecological practices that relate to food are all inter-connected and creating sustainable food systems will need to consider all of them systemically. The United Nation's Agenda 2030 outlines 17 Sustainable Development Goals (SDG) of which 15 refer to the content of SD, roughly divided into ecological, social and economic aspects; and two SDG represent key mechanisms or processes that can help address them: SDG 4 calls for quality education and SDG 17 calls for collaboration and multi-stakeholder partnerships. Of the 15 SDGs addressing content aspects of SD all encompass so-called wicked problems (Gibson & Fox, 2013; Rittel & Webber, 1973) – characterized by complexity, uncertainty, contestation, and multiple causation, interactions, and feedback loops – several, if not all, relate to food. As such the SD of food systems can be considered a wicked problem in that they may never be solvable, but our attempt to deal with them can advance our knowledge and understanding of complexity and as well as strengthen our ability to respond to uncertainty and ambiguity. Figure 5.1 represents an attempt to capture the global food system holistically. Still, there is no one single figure that can capture all the elements, interdependencies, and sensitivities of food production, distribution and consumption. Similarly, there is no one single figure that can capture this for any of the SD challenges.

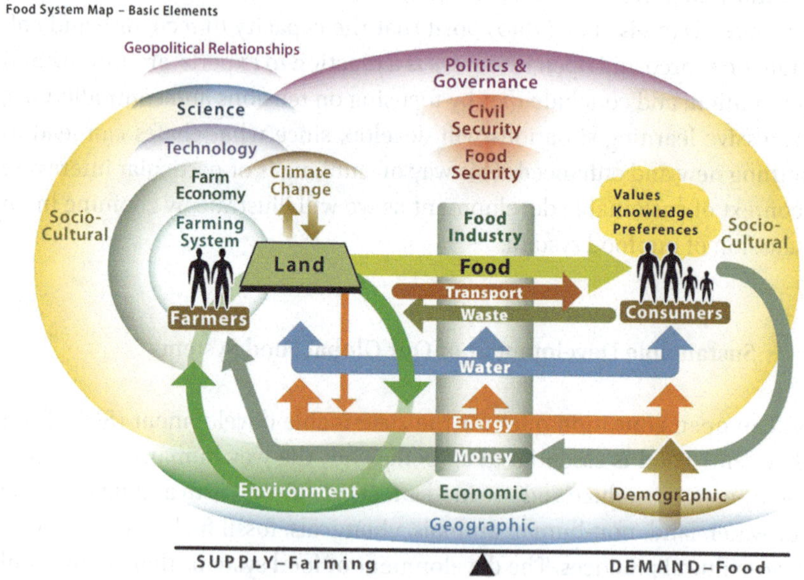

FIGURE 5.1 Basic elements of the global food systems and their relationships. The figure shows how food systems are 'nested' in other systems that connect with the world of science and technology, (geo)politics and governance, values and knowledge creation covering environmental, geographic, economic and demographic spheres and a range of chains, processes and feedback loops. (Source: GFSA at Global Food Security Alberta, ShiftN, https://gfsa.files.wordpress.com/2011/11/shiftn-global-food-system-page_1.jpeg; Open Access CC BY)

Although Figure 5.1 illustrates that food systems affect and involve many sectors and actors, illustrating that food challenges are nexus challenges requiring a systemic response, the figure also reveals a bias by centring the human and de-centring the non-human. Arguably, even the human centredness displays a bias as citizens are framed as 'consumers' which is a rather dehumanizing way of describing citizens as if their only role on Earth is to consume. A key point here is that what is often lacking in addressing global sustainability challenges is an understanding of how we can approach them more holistically and inclusively, for instance, considering the local-global element, the past-present-future, structure and agency, and the tension between the powerless and those seemingly in control.

Thus, there is a need to both disentangle complex elements and to learn to see and consider relations, perspectives and, sometimes conflicting interests and power relations (Kaiser & Algers, 2016). Furthermore, the dynamic nature of the knowledge regarding SD – what may seem sustainable today, may turn out to be unsustainable tomorrow as we continuously need to learn, (un)learn and recalibrate in light ongoing change and transformation – calls for reflexive forms of learning that facilitate a continuous search for the most sustainable and ethically tenable solution possible. Open education, as we interpret it here, advocates boundary-crossing at different levels: between informal, non-formal and formal learning; between science and society; and between disciplines but also between knowing and doing, as open education emphasises knowledge-in-action (Reiter, 2001).

The key characteristics of wicked sustainability challenges warrant that we consider the potential of open education as an emerging concept in education as a critical component of learning strategies that can contribute towards the realisation of a more sustainable world.

In this chapter, a case study from the field of sustainable development and democratic food systems will provide a narrative that illustrates the possible impact of open education; and the value of a culture of openness to individuals, to community, and to society.

3 Education for Sustainable Development

Education for sustainable development (ESD) has been around since Chapter 36 appeared in Agenda 21, the report of the UN's first Earth Summit held in Rio de Janeiro in 1992 (Meakin, 1992). Chapter 36 stressed the importance of education in raising awareness and facilitating action on global challenges around food, water, energy, biodiversity and their local manifestations. In some ways, ESD became an umbrella bringing together a number of *adjectival* educations that each had different traditions and objectives, including environmental education, health education, human rights education, and nature conservation education. Without getting into the success or lack thereof the effectiveness or impact of ESD so far (for this see Wals, 2009, 2012), we will highlight some key characteristics and a criticism of ESD (see also Wals & Benavot, 2017). First, ESD calls for the need for inter- and transdisciplinary approaches to help people understand complexity and interrelatedness. Systems thinking is often advocated as a key mechanism for realizing this, and Lane (2017) has recently suggested how systems thinking and open education in combination can support ESD. Second, ESD seeks to bridge the gap between awareness and action by encouraging exploration of real or existential issues and by creating space for attempts to make change. Concepts such as experiential learning, agency, empowerment and learning-by-doing often appear in policies, curricula and guidelines for ESD and similarly '… it is in the realms of individual and community participation and empowerment that future OER interventions hold their greatest promise and will yield their largest gains' (Arinto et al., 2017, p. 589). Third, ESD calls for deeper reflection on the values that drive what we do and what makes living sustainably easy or difficult. Value-based teaching and learning that include ethics and moral reasoning are considered critical in moving towards sustainability, and open education has been suggested as a way to be in dialogue within contested and value-based issues of societal relevance (Algers, 2015).

Fourth, critical thinking and asking questions such as, 'What is keeping things from changing?' or 'Why am I not always acting in accordance to my values?' are essential in getting underneath the structural aspects of normalized unsustainability. More recently, dealing with socio-scientific disputes and false truths has been added to the critical thinking element of ESD, especially in light of climate change denial (e.g. Algers, 2017; Wals & Peters, 2017). Fifth, as is stated quite well in the 2016 Global Education Monitor Report (UNESCO, 2016) and building on the fourth point, the continuous emphasis on *development* itself needs to be critically assessed as is done in some Latin American countries where intentional communities speak of sustainability as an *alternative to development*. This critique has led to some scholars staying away from ESD altogether and using alternative concepts such as education for sustainability (rather than for SD) or ignoring the noun 'sustainability' and adjective 'sustainable' altogether.

One struggle within ESD is the tension between instrumental and emancipatory tendencies regarding the role of education in creating a more sustainable world. An instrumental perspective suggests that education is one among many tools that governments can use to make people lead more sustainable lifestyles. Here there is a somewhat agreed-upon idea of what such a lifestyle entails and what kinds of behaviours are needed to live such a lifestyle. Along with rules, regulations, policies, subsidies, and fines, education is one mechanism that can work in an agreed-upon and often science-informed direction. An emancipatory perspective, on the other hand, does leave open what the most sustainable way of living is and suggests that this is highly contextual, time, and location dependent: it is something we need to search for but not something we can confidently prescribe. Rather than focusing on changing citizens' behaviours and lifestyles, emphasis is placed on developing the capacities and competences citizens need to become more thoughtful, considerate, critical, effective, engaged and empowered. The idea of sustainability citizenship (Wals & Lenglet, 2016) fits well with such an emancipatory approach. As educators concerned with democracy (participation, agency), equity (inter-human, inter-generational, inter-species) and sustainability (living well within planetary boundaries), we are particularly drawn to the emancipatory perspective. We believe open education has something to offer to such a perspective as it can increase space for self-determination, autonomy and co-creation. Before we present the case study that demonstrated this point, we need to declare our normative position which states that open education should contribute to a sustainable, equitable world, a world in which all people can prosper without compromising current and future planetary boundaries, including taking animal sentience and ethics into account (Fraser, 1999; 2008). In other words, we are not interested in open education as a new tool to help companies grow, expand market share, or increase shareholder value, which in our opinion accelerates unsustainability and represents a rather narrow view of education that does not serve people and planet but only the economy.

4 A Case Study of Open Education for Sustainable Development

The example we will focus on originates in the fact that farmers have kept animals in intensive systems and sometimes viewed the animals as artefacts; however, today many citizens do not accept this view on farm animals (Fraser, 2008; Special Eurobarometer, 2016). This has resulted in a dis-coordination in the food value-chain and contradictions between farmers, consumers, and citizens. Differing consumer and industry expectations on farm animal welfare may lead to increasing conflicts between consumers and the food industry, which is not sustainable in the long run (Algers, 2011). Such conflict has already resulted in arson of laboratories (Friend, 1990) and arson of animal transport vehicles for slaughter in Sweden. The issue is therefore important for society representatives to tackle (Algers, 2015). We will use what can be conceptualised as a *thick* description (Geertz, 1973) to illustrate how we see the potential of open education.

In Sweden, an OER about animal welfare at slaughter and killing was created in 2012 by a team of researchers from the Swedish University of Agricultural Sciences (SLU) in collaboration with slaughterhouses, non-governmental organizations (NGOs) and representatives from religious groups; the latter were involved in writing the sections on kosher and halal slaughter. The aim of the OER was twofold: to support local efforts to increase understanding of relevant animal welfare regulations, for example, in slaughterhouses, and to provide free access for anybody interested in gaining knowledge about animal welfare at slaughter and killing.

The OER includes each species (cattle, pigs, sheep, horses, chickens, turkeys, geese, deer, reindeer, rabbits, ostriches and fur animals) structured with learning objectives, formative assessment with feedback, and take-home messages. It includes 650 webpages, 800 illustrations and 150 video clips.[1]

During the creation phase, the team had ongoing discussions with external agents who reviewed the OER and improved the practical handling details. The target group is diverse and includes: i) slaughterhouse staff, animal transporters and farmers, ii) students in veterinary sciences and animal husbandry, iii) and the general public that wants to know how the food is produced. The characteristics of each sub-target group is described below:

i. New legal frameworks require education in animal welfare at slaughter and certificates of competence for slaughterhouse staff. The ideas guiding the framework is that people handling animals at slaughter need to understand the animal's behavioural needs and natural behaviour in order to recognise why animals must be treated in a specific way. Furthermore, staff should be knowledgeable about the causal link between animal stress and impaired meat quality as further motivation to handle animals with high animal welfare standards. The OER allows staff to learn from and comment on the content freely in time and space. A summative assessment is organised by a national organization and a certificate of competence is issued for slaughterhouse staff who have passed the examination (hitherto about 550 staff have taken the course and more than 500 have received a certificate; more than 1200 staff passed a simplified litigation due to long experience) with the result that, in principle, all the slaughterhouse staff handling animals in Sweden are educated in animal welfare (Nordensten, June 8, 2018, personal communication).

ii. Access to slaughterhouses is not self-evident and, in some countries, students are not allowed into slaughterhouses. The slaughter processes are very complex and the behaviour of both abattoir staff and animals, and how these behaviours are interconnected, needs to be understood. This is very difficult to comprehend when students are visiting a slaughterhouse. It is also difficult for groups of students who visit slaughterhouses to observe animals and therefore, the use of photos and videos, and, potentially, VR-technology such as the *i*Animal Tool (The New York Times, 2017), in the OER is critical.

iii. Citizens have very little knowledge about slaughter. In a recent focus group study, participants argued, in a pluralistic way, in favour of information on slaughter being available to the public because: (a) slaughterhouses are entities that are traditionally closed and slaughter is probably one of the most sheltered activities and, like in all other activities, citizens want transparency, (b) there are a lot of beliefs and naïve views on slaughter and basic knowledge about slaughter of farm animals is a prerequisite to have moral opinions about food, and (c) people with knowledge have an obligation to tell, not least because animals are vulnerable. Thus, there is a case for unbiased and transparent public sharing of information that is available in a way that promotes learning (Algers & Berg, 2017, p. 6).

Publishing photos and using video footage and even more powerful VR-technology showing slaughter is controversial because such images can be perceived as aversive. The slaughter industry's umbrella organizations were concerned that the OER would be used by animal rights groups to discredit abattoirs and the industry in general. This concern was, however, not voiced by the individual slaughterhouses. Slaughterhouses showed their satisfaction to tie practice to theory. They were proud of their work given the set of circumstances (Wickman, 2013), and wanted to share best practice. However, slaughter industry umbrella organizations required the material to be locked behind a password. After being put under pressure by the umbrella organizations, the Swedish Board of Agriculture (the main funder of the creation process) succumbed to the pressure and suggested a system based on restricted access to the learning resource, which in practice meant disregarding a signed contract with SLU about openness. The different opinions among stakeholders created a conflict, as a result of pressure from the umbrella organizations and the Swedish Board of Agriculture on SLU to stop the openly accessible learning material and thus to break a contract. However, after discussion with the lawyer at the university about the conflict, the lawyer wrote to the involved stakeholders: 'In the choice between meeting the requirements from upset stakeholders and safeguarding academic integrity, a university must always choose the latter' (Algers & Berg, 2017, p. 2). Consequently, the OER is still openly available. Further development with a shared medium that enhances the conversational framework to also enable learners to solve problems would be an improvement for democracy and sustainability; however, the risks of introducing false information, fake data and offensive content and the resources needed for moderating have to be considered.

5 In Light of Activity Theory, Critical Pedagogy and ESD

Geertz (1973) explains the purpose of a thick description as 'The aim is to draw large conclusions from small, but very densely textured facts; to support broad assertions about the role of culture in the construction of collective life by engaging them exactly with complex specifics' (p. 28). However, before we draw any large conclusions we need to introduce another theoretical framework in order to properly analyse the case study.

In the analysis of human interactions within the case study, the cultural historical activity system (CHAT) is used as a lens. Engeström's seminal work on CHAT (e.g. 2008; 2015) and peer-production discusses the necessary properties of a shared object for successful collaboration and argues that in order to give an object power it needs to have intrinsic properties. We argue that open education about democratic food systems has these kinds of intrinsic properties.

The object of activity addresses the relationship between the actors and their motives and concerns and gives the activities a special direction; in this case study, the object of activity is a negotiation about the accepted level of animal welfare on the day of slaughter. CHAT is based on the ideas that (1) humans act collectively, learn by doing, and communicate in and via their actions; (2) humans make, employ, and adapt tools or instruments of all kinds to learn and communicate; and (3) a community is central to the process of making and interpreting meaning – and thus to all forms of learning, communicating, and acting (Kaptelinin & Nardi, 2006). In the creation of new learning approaches to food, many actors need to be involved since different competences are needed in order to identify the instruments to enable learning, adapt the content to societal rules (e.g. animal welfare legislation and rules in higher education), take into consideration power relations between actors (which is related to division of labour) and identify learning goals and gather the content (see Figure 5.2)

Democratizing the educational process is a far more radical interpretation of openness than the democratization of access to formal education, which was the original goal of open education. Furthermore, learning on the edge of one's comfort zones and challenging taken-for-granted and normalised ways of thinking can be an effect of boundary crossing (Wals & Peters, 2017). The case study is characterized by a multiplicity of stakeholders with conflicting interests: Commercially-driven cooperative industries with a profit motive of interest, animal activist communities with an empathy motive of interest, and consumer communities that may have other motives.

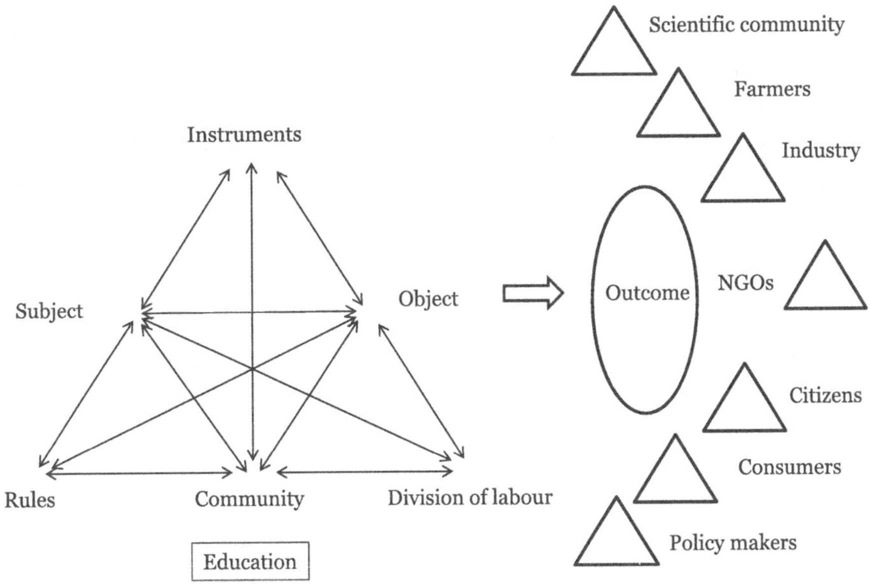

FIGURE 5.2 Activity systems involved in learning about food, with highlighted activity system for education (after Engeström, 2015)

Thus, striving to share the same object – a mutual view on animal welfare – involves a critical view and a will to revise accepted practices and their tacit rules and procedures. This integrative approach is used to analyse the motivations of actors to their practices, in this case, how slaughterhouses look at their production systems for meat, consumer attitudes to animal products and teachers' willingness to integrate learning activities about food and animal welfare into their curriculum.

Collaborative knowledge creation based on boundary-crossing can be seen as horizontal movements of knowledge between multiple parallel activity contexts and was introduced as an expansive learning theory some decades ago (Engeström et al., 1995). This is where OER come in as boundary objects. Either they are introduced as complete objects to achieve boundary activities and connect actors from different worlds (Star & Griesemer, 1989) or they are objects that are generated through a process of boundary activities (Engeström et al., 1995). The first approach can also be described as the *cathedral* model that emphasizes top-down where understanding is shared between small groups of skilled developers, as opposed to the latter – the *bazaar* model. The *bazaar* model is an open educational practice and is based on bottom-up and open development of understanding in the public (Farrow, 2017; Raymond,

1999). This aligns again with Dewey's legacy who argued that an educational system within a democracy stimulates learners' power, since it 'gives individuals a personal interest in social relationships and control, and the habits of mind which secure social changes without introducing disorder' (Dewey, 1916, p. 99).

Formative interventions contrast to linear interventions, situations in which goals are not known ahead and the expansive transformation process is owned by the participants (Engeström, 2011). Hence, in formative interventions, the key outcome is agency among the participants who take charge of the process, and the intervention must be embedded and contextualised in the participants' life (Engeström, 2011). Thus, formative interventions lead to transformation and the process does not have one actor who has the sole, fixed authority; and the work never results in a 'finished' product. Transformative agency is characterised as a quality of expansive learning (Sannino, 2015), in which the actors break away from the given frame of action and take the initiative to transform it and generate new concepts and practices that 'carry future-oriented visions loaded with initiative and commitment by the learners' (Sannino et al., 2016, p. 4). Engeström and Sannino (2010) suggest that peer production, or OEP, is one of the biggest challenges for future studies of expansive learning alongside the serious theoretical and empirical efforts that are needed in order to understand and integrate the two directions 'up and outward and down and inward' (p. 21). Peer production of learning about the food sector or animal welfare will include negotiations between the stakeholders in the food sector both because their *stakes* result in different expectations and because facts and values are intertwined in knowledge about food.

The creation and sharing of knowledge within and across organizational, disciplinary and cultural boundaries is an act of critical pedagogy, which has been described by Shor (1992), as

> Habits of thought, reading, writing, and speaking which go beneath surface meaning, first impressions, dominant myths, official pronouncements, traditional clichés, received wisdom, and mere opinions, to understand the deep meaning, root causes, social context, ideology, and personal consequences of any action, event, object, process, organization, experience, text, subject matter, policy, mass media, or discourse. (p. 129)

Critical pedagogy rejects the ideological neutrality of knowledge and argues that teaching is inherently a political act (Farrow, 2017; Habermas, 1971; Säljö, 2010) and emphasizes learners' emancipation and critical thinking. CHAT points at the transformative potential of contradictions and this is where the two might interface. When talking about sustainable development, also within the context of food and nutrition, critical questions like: What structures and routines are in place that normalize unsustainability? What alternatives might be available or can be created that can disrupt them and can lead to the normalization of more sustainable ones? Likely this will reveal contradictions. From a transformative emancipatory perspective, open education can only be open when it allows for a critical interrogation of *what is*, an open exploration of *what should be*, identification of the pathways that might get us there, and an analysis of what can help facilitate change and of what keeps change from happening.

An additional requirement or characteristic of critical pedagogy is that multiple voices are included – often those typically marginalised – and that people can contribute equally undisturbed by power relations. Dillon, Stevenson and Wals (2016) refer to civic science as a means of promoting ecological democracy (Wals & Peters, 2017) that can help disrupt, transgress, and transform unsustainable practices. Civic science here is seen as distinct from the more common citizen science to emphasize that the concerns of citizens drive forms of collective inquiry rather the concerns of scientist. In their conclusion, Dillon et al. (2016) point at the importance of

> engaging all stakeholders as co-creators and co-learners in a deliberate and systematic process of knowledge building. An important part of this process is treating emerging goals and knowledge as tentative and subject to revision based on ongoing critical and collaborative dialogue, inquiry, and action. (p. 455)

The latter points at another element of open education: the emergent and iterative nature of collaborative learning.

Using CHAT to 'read' the thick description of the case study, we can distil a number of general and critical characteristics where open education for sustainable development can be of particular relevance:

1. A transdisciplinary subject area that needs integrating both natural and social science in which perspective changes encourage disruptive thinking that goes beyond conventional ways of knowing and doing.
2. A subject area that implies affective capabilities and a sense of empathy and stewardship as well as ethical thinking.
3. A subject area that in order for societal stewardship needs intercultural communication and inclusiveness particularly for groups finding the subject highly sensitive.

4. A creation process based on a flexible and adaptable design and collaboration between academia, industry, NGOs and the public (SDG 17) for quality education (SDG 4).
5. When the object for the creation process and the outcome – the OER – never is finalized, rather a resource in flux that embraces diversities and responsiveness to societal challenges, values and norms.
6. In search for design features with abilities for enacting agency from the wider public and even from silent voices but acknowledging that the use of additional instruments has to be carefully weighed against the risk of false or fake data.
7. When navigating in complexities but, when guided properly, can result in a deeper discussion about the disadvantages for sustainable development of making hidden knowledge visible.
8. When undemocratic and sometimes fake news prescribe how people should live their lives it is academia's responsibility to take an active role on the internet. Dewey wrote that democracy is not just a means of protecting our interests and expressing our individuality, but also a forum for *determining our interests* (Dewey, 1897, cited in Wals & Peters, 2017).

6 The Way Forward

When stakes are high and the issues are complex and even wicked, as they are in matters of sustainable development, we argue that access to knowledge and learning across boundaries for *every* citizen requires the consideration of new qualities to open education (see the list at the end of the previous section) which can make OER more responsive, relevant, responsible and reflexive. The educational design principles in open education as described in this chapter involve many different stakeholders in informal learning activities leading to more robust knowledge (Camilleri et al., 2014) and is, in the best of worlds, a catalyst for free and wide reflection on both knowledge and pedagogies (Farrow, 2017).

'These collaborative forms of research and learning suggest a shift away from 'research as mining' grounded in empirical analytical, positivist and mechanistic traditions to 'research as activism' rooted in socially critical transformative and even transgressive traditions' (Wals & Peters, 2017, p. 36).

Finally, in light of global systemic dysfunction and the need to become bolder in responding to global sustainability challenges, we suggest that 'open' also should refer to academia actively expressing and inviting critique and marginalized perspectives in controversial societal issues. Inviting dissonance, even discomfort, and surprise, will be needed to break with hegemonic forces, structures and systems that currently make exploitation, oppression and over-stepping ecological boundaries the norm. The transformative potential of sustainability-oriented open education does not so much lie in optimizing practices and values that are at their core problematic, but rather in transitioning towards alternative ones that make living sustainably by choice the default.

Note

1 The OER is openly available at http://disa.slu.se/and the Swedish Centre for Animal Welfare (SCAW) has since 2013 been responsible for updating and translating the OER under a CC BY-NC-SA license (Algers et al., 2012; Algers & Berg, 2017).

References

Algers, A. (2015). *Open learning in life sciences – Studies of open educational resources in animal welfare and work-based learning in food science* (Doctoral thesis). University of Gothenburg, Gothenburg. Retrieved June 2018, from http://hdl.handle.net/2077/40580

Algers, A. (2017). Involving the general public in creation and sharing of knowledge about food. *CAB Reviews, 12*(13), 1–10.

Algers, A., & Berg, C. (2017). Open knowledge about slaughter on the internet – A case study on controversies. *Animals, 7*(12), 101.

Algers, A., Berg, C., Hammarberg, K., Larsen, A., Lindsjö, J., Malmsten, A., Malmsten, J., Mustonen, A., Olofsson, L., Sandström, V. (2012). *Utbildning i Djurvälfärd i Samband med Slakt och Annan Avlivning*. Retrieved June 2018, from http://disa.slu.se/

Algers, B. (2011). Animal welfare – Recent developments in the field. *CAB Reviews: Perspectives in Agriculture, Veterinary Science, Nutrition and Natural Resources, 6*(10), 19–30.

Arinto, P., Hodgkinson-Williams, C., & Trotter, H. (2017). OER and OEP in the Global South: Implications and recommendations for social inclusion. In C. Hodgkinson-Williams & P. B. Arinto (Eds.), *Adoption and impact of OER in the Global South*. Cape Town & Ottawa: African Minds, International Development Research Centre & Research on Open Educational Resources. Retrieved June 2018, from http://10.5281/zenodo.1005330

Brown, J. S., & Adler, R. P. (2008). Minds on fire: Open education, the long tail, and learning 2.0. *Educause Review, 43*(1), 17–32. Retrieved June 2018, from https://open.umich.edu/oertoolkit/references/mindsonfire.pdf

Camilleri, A., Ehlers, U., & Pawlowski, J. (2014). *State of the art review of quality issues related to Open Educational Resources (OER)*. Luxembourg: Publication Office of the European Union, 1–52. Retrieved June 2018, from http://www.pedocs.de/volltexte/2014/9101/

Daniels, H., Edwards, A., Engeström, Y., Gallagher, T., & Ludvigsen, S. R. (Eds.). (2010). *Activity theory in practice: Promoting learning across boundaries and agencies*. London: Routledge.

Dewey, J. (1897). The psychology of effort. *The Philosophical Review, 6*(1), 43–56.

Dewey, J. (1916). *Democracy and education: An introduction to the philosophy of education*. New York, NY: Free Press.

Dillon, J., Stevenson, R. B., & Wals, A. E. J. (2016). Moving from citizen to civic science to address wicked conservation problems. *Conservation Biology, 30*(3), 450–455.

Engeström, Y. (2008). *The future of activity theory: A rough draft*. Paper presented at the ISCAR 2008: Ecologies of Diversities: The developmental and historical interarticulation of human mediational forms, San Diego. Retrieved June 2018, from http://lchc.ucsd.edu/mca/Paper/ISCARkeyEngestrom.pdf

Engeström, Y. (2011). From design experiments to formative interventions. *Theory & Psychology, 21*(5), 598–628.

Engeström, Y. (2015). *Learning by expanding* (2nd ed.). Cambridge: Cambridge University Press.

Engeström, Y., Engeström, R., & Kärkkäinen, M. (1995). Polycontextuality and boundary crossing in expert cognition: Learning and problem solving in complex work activities. *Learning and Instruction, 5*, 319–336.

Engeström, Y., & Sannino, A. (2010). Studies of expansive learning: Foundations, findings and future challenges. *Educational Research Review, 5*(1), 1–24.

FAO. (2016). *The State of Food and Agriculture 2016 (SOFA): Climate change, agriculture and food security/194*. Retrieved October 2018, from http://www.fao.org/3/a-i6030e.pdf

Farrow, R. (2017). Open education and critical pedagogy. *Learning, Media and Technology, 42*(2), 130–146.

Fraser, D. (1999). Animal ethics and animal welfare science: Bridging the two cultures. *Applied Animal Behaviour Science, 65*(3), 171–189.

Fraser, D. (2008). Understanding animal welfare. *Acta Veterinaria Scandinavica, 50*(Suppl 1), S1.

Geertz, C. (2008). Thick description: Toward an interpretive theory of culture. In T. Oakes & P. L. Price (Eds.), *The cultural geography reader* (pp. 41–51). London: Routledge.

Gibson, R., & Fox, M. (2013). *Simple, complex and wicked problems*. Retrieved June 2018, from http://mofox.com/pdf/simple,complex,wicked.pdf

Habermas, J. (1971). *Knowledge and human interests* (J. J. Shapiro, Trans.). Boston, MA: Beacon Press.

Hodgkinson-Williams, C., & Arinto, P. B. (Eds.). (2018). *Adoption and impact of OER in the Global South.* Cape Town & Ottawa: African Minds, International Development Research Centre & Research on Open Educational Resources. doi:10.5281/zenodo.1005330

Hylén, J. (2006). *Open educational resources: Opportunities and challenges.* Paris: OECD's Centre for Educational Research and Innovation. Retrieved June 2018, from http://www.oecd.org/education/ceri/37351085.pdf

Kaiser, M., & Algers, A. (2016). Food ethics: A wide field in need of dialogue. *Food Ethics, 1*(1), 1–17.

Kanwar, A., Balasubramanian, K., & Umar, A. (2010). Towards sustainable open education resources: A perspective from the global south. *American Journal of Distance Education, 24*(2), 65–80.

Kaptelinin, V., & Nardi, B. (2006). *Acting with technology: Activity theory and interaction design.* Cambridge, MA: MIT Press.

Lane, A. (2017). Open education and the sustainable development goals: Making change happen. *Journal of Learning for Development-JL4D, 4*(3), 275–286.

Meakin, S. (1992). *The Rio earth summit: Summary of the United Nations conference on environment and development* (Vol. 317). Library of Parliament, Research Branch.

Raymond, E. (1999). The cathedral and the bazaar. *Philosophy & Technology, 12*(3), 23.

Reiter, R. (2001). *Knowledge in action: Logical foundations for specifying and implementing dynamical systems.* MIT Press.

Ritchey, T. (2013). Wicked problems: Modelling social messes with morphological analysis. *Acta Morphologica Generalis, 2*(1), 1–8.

Rittel, H. W., & Webber, M. M. (1973). Dilemmas in a general theory of planning. *Policy Sciences, 4*(2), 155–169.

Säljö, R. (2010). Digital tools and challenges to institutional traditions of learning: Technologies, social memory and the performative nature of learning. *Journal of Computer Assisted Learning, 26*(1), 53–64.

Sannino, A. (2015). The principle of double stimulation: A path to volitional action. *Learning, Culture and Social Interaction, 6*, 1–15.

Sannino, A., Engeström, Y., & Lemos, M. (2016). Formative interventions for expansive learning and transformative agency. *Journal of the Learning Sciences, 25*(4), 599–633.

Shulman, L. S. (1999). Taking learning seriously. *Change: The Magazine of Higher Learning, 31*(4), 10–17.

Shor, I. (1992). *Empowering education: Critical teaching for social change.* Chicago, IL: University of Chicago Press.

Special Eurobarometer. (2016). *Attitudes of Europeans towards animal welfare.* Report No. 442. doi:10.2875/645984

Star, S., & Griesemer, J. (1989). Institutional ecology, translations' and boundary objects: Amateurs and professionals in Berkeley's Museum of Vertebrate Zoology, 1907–39. *Social Studies of Science, 19*(3), 387–420.

The New York Times. (2017). *Animal welfare groups have a new tool: Virtual reality.* Retrieved June 2018, from https://www.nytimes.com/2017/07/06/dining/animal-welfare-virtual-reality-video-meat-industry.html

United Nations. (2002). *Resolution 57/254. United Nations decade of education for sustainable development.* New York, NY: United Nations. Retrieved June 2018, from http://portal.unesco.org/education/en/file_download.php/299680c3c67a50454833fb27fa42d95bUNresolutionen.pdf

United Nations. (2016). *The UN sustainable development goals.* Retrieved June 2018, from http://www.un.org/sustainabledevelopment/development-agenda/

United Nations. (2018). *Global report on food crisis.* Retrieved October 2018, from https://sway.office.com/lUKJJqCJlNB4wkvt?ref=Link

UNESCO. (2016). *Education for people and planet: Creating sustainable futures for all: Global education monitor report 2016.* Paris: UNESCO. Retrieved June 2018, from http://unesdoc.unesco.org/images/0024/002457/245752e.pdf

Wals, A. E. (2009). A mid-DESD review: Key findings and ways forward. *Journal of Education for Sustainable Development, 3*(2), 195–204.

Wals, A. E. J. (2012). *Shaping the education of tomorrow: 2012 full-length report on the UN decade of education for sustainable development – DESD monitoring & evaluation report.* Paris: UNESCO.

Wals, A. E., & Benavot, A. (2017). Can we meet the sustainability challenges? The role of education and lifelong learning. *European Journal of Education, 52*(4), 404–413.

Wals, A. E., & Lenglet, F. (2016). Sustainability citizens: Collaborative and disruptive social learning. In R. Horne, J. Fien, B. B. Beza, & A. Nelson (Eds), *Sustainability citizenship and cities: Theory and practice* (pp. 52-66). London/New York, NY: Routledge.

Wals, A. E. J., & Peters, M. A. (2017). Flowers of resistance: Citizen science, ecological democracy and the transgressive education paradigm. In A. König & J. Ravetz (Eds.), *Sustainability science: Key issues* (pp. 29–52). London: Earthscan/Routledge. Retrieved June 2018, from https://www.routledge.com/Sustainability-Science-Key-Issues/Konig-Ravetz/p/book/9781138659285

Wickman, M. (2013). *Knowledge and attitudes among staff handling livestock at Swedish slaughterhouses.* The Swedish University of Agricultural Sciences. Retrieved June 2018, from http://sh.diva-portal.org/smash/get/diva2:1039091/FULLTEXT02.pdf

Wiley, D. (2014). The access compromise and the 5th R's [Blog post]. Retrieved June 2018, from http://opencontent.org/blog/archives/3221

Wiley, D., & Gurrell, S. (2009). A decade of development. *Open Learning: The Journal of Open, Distance and e-Learning, 24*(1), 11–21.

CHAPTER 6

Openness and Open Practice in Mentoring: Moving beyond Strong Dyadic Linkages?

David Starr-Glass

In recent decades, there has been a growing patchwork of educational movements and initiatives focusing on 'open' and 'openness.' As an emerging paradigm, it has been said that open and openness in education 'has a history that provides much of the context and the motivating values ... part of the Enlightenment story of freedom and it cannot be separated from wider political questions concerning epistemology, ontology and ethics' (Peters, 2008, p. 14). These politically nuanced questions of epistemology, ontology, and ethics have become particularly salient in the production, dissemination, and consumption of knowledge in an age characterized by expansive social networks, the ubiquitous Internet, and increased connectivity – even though selective access to the Internet and socioeconomic digital divides have complicated, rather than clarified, how these questions are framed and who participates in the discussion (Alexander, 2017; Gilliard, 2017).

Mentoring, as a practice and a process, is increasingly being seen through the lenses of openness and ecology that have re-imaged it from 'an interaction between individuals to ... a property of whole systems' (Chandler, Kram, & Yip, 2011, p. 521). Mentoring, as a distinctive *micro-system* that includes mentor and mentee, is now seen as connected to more expansive and inclusive ecological landscapes of learning in academic, organizational, and social contexts. Much of this re-imaging has been prompted by the ecological and bricolage perspectives of Bronfenbrenner (1979) which suggest that 'the properties of the person and of the environment, the structure of environmental settings, and the processes taking place within and between them must be viewed as *interdependent* and analyzed in *system terms*' (1979, p. 41, emphases added).

Although some have argued that Bronfenhoffer's work is neither fully appreciated nor its potentials and limitations adequately recognized, ecological perspectives of education, teaching, and learning have nevertheless provided useful ways of understanding connections, connectedness, and relationship between actors, institutions and society generally (Tudge et al., 2016). There is mounting evidence to suggest that viewing mentoring micro-systems as connected, constituent, and contributive components of broader over-arching

 | DOI: 10.1163/9789004422988_007

ecologies of learning and support – rather than separated or isolated from them – provides innovative insights into the nature of mentoring and adds benefit to those engaged in mentoring programs and relationships (Chandler et al., 2011; Keller & Blakeslee, 2013; Suffrin, Todd, & Sanchez, 2016).

This chapter explores mentoring as an element of ecological systems in higher education and focuses on a critical aspect of such ecologies: openness. The following section examines the nature and experience of traditional mentoring, which brings together two individuals in an attempt to provide each with benefits derived from sharing the knowledge, experience, and perspectives of the more experienced partner. This section explores the strength, persistence, and dynamics of the dyadic relationship. The next section provides a conceptual framework by considering the constructs of ecologies, openness, and open practice with a focus on how these constructs might be applied to the mentoring process. This is followed by a consideration of mentoring in terms of weaker linkages and network connections, and then by a section that explore the means and the consequences of opening mentoring connections. The last section briefly recapitulates some of the themes of the chapter and argues that – without abandoning or undervaluing its fundamental dyadic nature – a more open mentoring practice has a valuable place in the expansive ecology of teaching, learning, and support in higher education.

1 The Dyadic Nature of Mentoring Relationships

Mentoring has an exceptionally long history that points back – perhaps in more of a mythical and metaphoric sense than a factual one – to the Homeric legends. Mentor, as a mythological presence, was the close and trusted friend of Odysseus. When Odysseus decided to regain his sense of honor and self on the battlefields of Troy, he left his young son Telémakhos in the care of Mentor, charging him to guide the young man as he matured and to provide him with advice as he negotiated the complexities of life. As an archetype, Mentor continues to inspire and inform many contemporary mentors, who see the mentoring journey as essentially an 'inner Odyssey' (Garvey, Stokes, & Megginson, 2009, p. 1).

For many practitioners, the Homeric depiction of Mentor and his interactions with Telémakhos – or perhaps *her* interactions, because it was often the goddess Pallas Athene who appeared in the guise of Mentor – offer 'provocative insights into the meaning of mentoring as a relationship that transcends time, gender, and culture' (Ragins & Kram, 2007, p. 4). Mentoring has always made connections across complex barriers and, in doing so, has always been 'fraught with the concern of how to cross boundaries, how to bridge cultural difference to show yourself, and to accompany another on their journey' (Blake-Beard, 2009, p. 15). Paradoxically, these very features of acknowledging boundaries, displaying self, and accompanying the other have often been seen as setting mentoring *apart* as a restricted and somewhat idiosyncratic engagement and not as *a part* of a more inclusive and open educational paradigm.

Because of its protracted evolution and multiple forms, it is hardly surprising that mentoring has defied attempts to be defined comprehensively or to be reduced to a unified model (Dawson, 2014). Almost 30 years ago, Jacobi (1991) recognized 15 competing definitions of mentoring taken from the fields of management, higher education, and psychology. She concluded that mentoring processes and relationships raised multiple questions and that 'until such questions are answered, mentoring remains an intriguing, but untested, strategy for enhancing undergraduate academic success' (p. 528). Almost two decades later, Crisp and Cruz (2009) found that the number of definitions in use at that time had grown to more than 50 and the authors woefully acknowledged that the 'ambiguity surrounding the definition of mentoring is further obscured by inconsistencies in how the 'mentoring" has been used throughout the literature' (p. 527).

These ambiguities and inconsistencies of definition were captured by Pawson (2004), who approached mentoring practice from what he has characterized as *evidence-based* and *realistic review* perspectives (Pawson, 2006; Pawson, Greenhalgh, Harvey, & Walshe, 2005). Considering the multiplicity of mentoring definitions, with particular focus on those used in social work and youth intervention, Pawson (2004) recognized the fluidity and flexibility of the construct, producing – with characteristic tongue-in-cheek British humour – what he referred to as his 'never-ending list' of the attributes, activities, and relational dimensions attributed to mentoring:

> Helping, coaching, tutoring, counselling, sponsoring, role modelling, befriending, bonding, trusting, mutual learning, direction setting, progress chasing, sharing experience, providing respite, sharing a laugh, widening horizons, building resilience, showing ropes, informal apprenticeships, providing openings, kindness of strangers, sitting by Nellie, treats for bad boys and girls, the Caligula phenomenon, power play, tours of middle class life, etc. etc. (p. 1)

Pawson's never-ending list hardly defines mentoring activities and behaviors, but it may strike a familiar chord with those who are engaged in the process, either as mentors or mentees (*mentee* being used in educational contexts, *protégé* in organizational ones). The common denominator of these listed items is that they are socially referenced with each referring to a connection with another person – with each predicated on nurturing, empowering, or relating to someone else. Mentoring is a relational dynamic that is purposefully grounded in the anticipation of future outcomes, expectations, and behavior. These two dimensions – social reference and anticipated outcomes – are captured in the following definition that was strongly shaped by reflections on community-based mentoring initiatives:

> Mentoring involves a one-to-one relationship between an older person and a younger one (a protégé) to pass on knowledge, experience and judgment, or to provide guidance and friendship. Mentoring programs link an adult to a younger person, with the goals of reassuring innate worth, instilling values, guiding curiosity and encouraging a positive youthful life. Distinguished from child rearing and friendship, the mentoring relationship is intended to be temporary, with the objective of helping the protégé reach independence and autonomy. (Powell, 1997, p. 4)

As a learning strategy, particularly from the perspective of the academy, mentoring belongs to a cluster of approaches that have been identified as *cognitive apprenticeships*, which center on 'learning-through-guided-experience on cognitive and metacognitive, rather than physical, skills and processes' (Collins, Brown, & Newman, 1989, p. 456). Cognitive apprenticeships are clearly socially situated, centered on the needs and aspiration of the learner, and focused on the cognitive development and expansion of those involved in the relationship. Indeed, cognitive apprenticeships explicitly understand the relationship between participants in terms of situated learning, community memberships, and the legitimate peripheral participation of the learner or apprentice (Lave & Wegner, 1991; Omidvar & Kislov, 2013; Wenger, 2010).

As a relational process, mentoring has always recognized and responded to the affective, emotional, and aspirational desires of mentees. Thus, mentoring mediates cognitive gains with an understanding that: (a) learning is inextricably situated in personal and social contexts; (b) learners and learning may need active support; and (c) learners often need active encouragment if their goals are to be achieved (Dennen & Burner, 2008).

Research on mentoring in academic, organizational, and social work contexts suggests that outcomes are recognized as mutually satisfactory and successful when *both* mentor and mentee

- are committed to the shared responsibilities and anticipated benefits of the process (McAllister, Harold, Ahmedani, & Cramer, 2009);

- perceive – or at least come to believe that – mentees are conscientious, goal-orientated, open to new learning experiences, and are emotionally stable and agreeable (Ludwig & Stein, 2008; Menges, 2015; Moberg & Velasquez, 2004);
- acknowledge that status, experiential history, and knowledge differences exist but that the other involved in the mentoring dyad possesses sufficient social and emotional, *similarities* to make the difference valuable and negotiable (Lankau, Riordan, & Thomas, 2005; Pawson, 2006); and
- recognize in themselves and in the other the desire to commit to a relationship of mutual exchange and reciprocity (Shore, Toyokawa, & Anderson, 2008).

These potential success factors underscore the relational aspect of the mentoring process that brings the individuals together into a dyadic unit and which turns their attention towards a mutual and reciprocal understanding of the benefits and responsibilities of their joint project. The traditional mentoring relationship binds self and other into a new association that is capable of engaging in altered ways of acting, knowing, and learning. Mentoring takes two separate, isolated, but potentially cooperative actors and substantially fuses them together into a single dyadic unit that becomes the primary unit of engagement. The fusion potentially brings the independent actors together in a synergistic manner, allowing them to creatively complement and supplement individual abilities and, in doing so, to recognize the value and strength of the relational bond that ties them together.

There is growing interest and research on the consequence of the dyadic connection, particularly its strength, the relational attributions of those involved, and its impact on the outcomes of the mentoring process (Eberly, Holley, Johnson, & Mitchell, 2011; Liden, Anand, & Vidyarthi, 2016; Rivera, Soderstrom, & Uzzi, 2010). The relational strength of the dyadic connection has become perhaps the key focus of interest for two reasons. First, the predicted strength of this bond is a critical factor in *selecting* optimal mentor-mentee dyads – a process that can be haphazard and ill-considered, and which is often complicated because it takes place across complex social, cultural, and gender divides (Hu, Thomas, & Lance, 2008; Kao, Rogers, Spitzmueller, Lin, & Lin, 2014; Mitchell, Eby, & Ragins, 2015). Second, the relational strength of the dyadic bond seems to be the most significant factor involved in predicting how participants will assess their *satisfaction* with the mentoring relationship (Finkelstein, Allen, Ritchie, Lynch, & Montei, 2011).

Often, it is power difference that is a key factor in the mentee initiating the relationship and in selecting the mentor. The mentor's power and authority may be seen as intrinsically valuable, or as providing the mentee with some form of future benefit or utility. It should be noted in passing that power difference refers to the perception, or the experienced reality, of unequal distributions of power within cultural, social, or organizational contexts. By contrast, *power distance* refers to the degree to which members of a national culture accept and anticipate that power will be distributed unequally (Hofstede, 2001). Both power difference and power distance are elements of mentoring systems, especially when the mentoring relationship bridges significant social, cultural, and national culture differences between mentor and mentee (Bellon-Harn & Weinbaum, 2017; Kochan, Searby, George, & Edge, 2015; Ramaswami, Huang, & Dreher, 2013).

While power difference may contribute to the ultimate strength and satisfaction of the dyadic tie, these differentials have to be first recognized and then successfully negotiated during the mentoring process (Anderson, Silet, & Fleming, 2012; Hansman, 2003). Power differences undoubtedly contribute to a perception that mentoring is exclusively restricted, hierarchical in nature, and probably peripheral in the more expansive and evolving social contexts of the academy or the organization. In other words, the very factors that underpin traditional mentoring – strong relational bonds and recognized power differences – can all too easily come to be regarded as the same elements that limit its structural openness and isolate it as part of the broader ecologies of teaching and learning. Paradoxically, power difference within the mentoring dyad has to be negotiated by those engaged in the relationship, a process that requires – but which might initially tend to inhibit – participative openness in the relationship.

2 Ecologies, Interconnectedness, and Openness

The word ecology was coined in the realm of biology about 150 years ago and its root is the Greek *oikos*. In English translation, *oikos* might be rendered as 'a house'; however, this translation obscures the original social and cultural meanings of the word. In the ancient Greek social world, *oikos* was rarely an isolated unit inhabited by a single individual or family. *Oikos* referred to a central living place, surrounded by a cluster of other dwellings and a patchwork of fields, groves, and orchards. These structures housed and supported the extended family, dependents, and workers associated with the landowner. *Oikos* was not simply a designated place, but rather a functioning, interdependent, and mutually connected assemblage of spaces, production units, and people. In English, 'community' more accurately captures the meaning. Interestingly, the same word (*oikos*) was also appropriated at the end of the 19th century to describe a new field of social enquiry: economics. Ecology is literally the *study* of the community; whereas, economics is the *management* of the productive resources of that community – although some might argue that the acknowledgement of, and respect for, the notion of *community* is more evident in the realm of ecology than it is in the other (Starr-Glass, 2014b).

In higher education, Damsa and Jornet (2016) argued that an ecological perspective involves two interconnected appreciations. The first is that 'learning is not a private, internal process, but involves transactions between people and their socio-material environment, in which both people and environments are transformed' (p. 40). The second is that 'learning involves not only intellectual dimensions, but also practical and affective ones … in learning the entire person-in-setting is transformed' (p. 40). In turn, these ecological perspectives – applied either as a means of enquiry or as a metaphor – are entwined with multiple dimensions of *openness*. In an ecological system openness fulfills a number of functions: (a) it permits flows and transfers to take place within the system; (b) it allows for mutuality and reciprocity between the constituent parts of the system; and (c) it reveals the inherently interconnected and potentially interdependent nature of the system taken as a whole.

From a dynamic perspective, it is openness to – and openness between – component parts that define the system, or the ecological unit, and which separate it from what lies beyond. Of course, separate and different ecological units may themselves be connected to, associated with, or reliant on other systems. That is, ecological units may be open to – or at least are not completely isolated from – a more extensive community of other ecological units and systems. Again, openness provides the possibility for connection, increasing complexity, and potential synergism.

Biological and social ecological systems both possess an internal openness between the elements of the system and an external openness to the environment that lies beyond that system.

For many decades, organizational theorists have explored the values of recognizing complex, responsive, and adaptive organizations as possessing differing degrees of internal and external openness (Martz, 2013; Scott & Davis, 2007). Likewise, in mentoring, it is useful to consider both internal openness (which might be understood as participative openness) and external openness (that is structural openness).

- *Participative Openness:* This is the set of dynamics and processes associated with mentoring such as the willingness, ability, and desire of individuals to enter and utilize mentoring or educational systems. It is a property of participants and actors within system, not of systems themselves. It is openness as a frame of mind – a willingness to be challenged, potentially changed, and exposed to otherness. It is an openness to life changes and experiential possibility and, as such, it is an openness that is not 'sutured over by our too quick search for definite answers and explanations ... a space in which we can dwell and observe, a space of sensibility that is not dependent upon any explanation we can give it' (Todd, 2015, p. 240). Participative openness is a critical element in both the theory and practice of mentoring and 'is not rooted in the certainty of the self, or in one's clinging to fact or reason, but ... to what one cannot know and invites a mode of response proper to that openness' (p. 241).

- *Structural Openness:* This is an aspect of the architectures through which a mentoring system is made available to those who might have otherwise been excluded, or rendered invisible, by the original social construction and design of that system. In this sense, it is openness to the surrounding world within which the system is embedded. Structural openness is not restricted to mentoring per se, but is a frequent aspect of many designed (or redesigned) systems and reflected in a whole cluster of educational systems: open institutional admission policies, open university systems, open educational experiences such as online learning and their massively open variants (MOOCs), and of course in open educational resources (Cronin & MacLaren, 2018; Weller, Jordan, DeVries, & Rolfe, 2018).

3 Mentoring as Network Links and Connections

Commenting on mentoring in workplace and organizational contexts, Ragins and Kram (2007) observed that 'while we have focused on mentoring behaviors and protégé outcomes, we have not explored the dynamic and interactive processes underlying mentoring relationships' (p. 8). However, such explorations are being undertaken and they tend to focus not so much what might be seen as the interiority of the mentoring process – that is on aspects such as participation openness – but rather on the ways in which the process is situated in, and contextualized by, the broader, nested, ecological contexts within which mentoring takes place.

For example, some have explored the cultural and gendered assumptions and dynamics within which mentoring is embedded (Buehler, 2017; Lewis & Olshansky, 2017). Others have considered the mentoring relationship as part of a more expansive, complex, and adaptive system (Jones & Brown, 2011; Jones & Corner, 2012). Yet others have investigated the relational ties of mentoring from the perspective of social network theory, with a particular interest in the implications associated with Granovetter's (1983) provocative insight on the strengths that lie in weak ties – as opposed to strong ties – in social networks.

Recognition of the strengths of weak-tie dyads has refocused attention on mentoring relationships and personal and professional development in the academy and the corporation (DeCastrom, Sambuco, Ubel, Stewart, & Jagsi, 2013; Higgins & Kram, 2001; Molloy, 2005). Increasingly, weak-tie mentoring linkages are seen as a way of contributing to structural openness by making mentoring opportunities more abundant, permeable, and diverse. It is significant to recall that the shift from an interest in strong-tie to weak-tie dyads had its roots in organizational, work-related, and career-orientated mentoring systems. In these sectorial contexts, several emerging issues suggested that mentoring might be particularly valuable if it could be recast in a more open and accessible form. These issues included:

- Careers and organizational membership were increasing viewed as unpredictable, fast-changing, boundaryless, and protean. This suggested that effective mentoring might have to be more responsive, fluid, and transitory in nature (Briscoe, Hall, & Frautschy DeMuth, 2006; Wong, Rasdi, Samah, & Wahat, 2017).
- With decreasing organizational support and investment in social and experiential capital, mentoring increasingly came to be understood as a mentee-initiated and mentee-directed advancement strategy. Career development and advancement morphed from an organizational process to a self-initiated and self-managed one, often involving strategic transitions from one organization to another (Blickle, Witzki, & Schneider, 2009).
- Those involved in mentoring relationships had less certainty about its duration, the quality of experiential capital and social capital available, and the kind of experiential capital they would require in their future. All of these concerns and uncertainties placed increased value on mentoring openness, mentoring flexibility, and the availability of – and the access to – more expansive social capital and social networks (Dobrow & Higgins, 2005; Dougherty & Dreher, 2007).
- Organizational and work-related contexts were increasingly recognized to be structured by gender, racial, and ethnic forces. Recognizing these forces and their outcomes, many concerned with mentoring initiatives began to see mentoring as a potential way of providing empowerment and support in overcoming structural barriers in the workplace, or in advancing future career trajectories (Rankin, Neilsen, & Stanley, 2007).

Although previous attention had focused mainly on the internal dynamics and processes of mentoring, changing external conditions and contexts stimulated a rethinking of the degree to which mentoring activities were in fact situationally sensitive, subject to evolutionary forces, and open to the ecological landscape of other academic and organizational systems. In particular, attention moved to the ways in which less exclusive, less powerfully linked, and more fluid mentoring micro-systems might work.

For example, Baugh and Fagenson-Eland (2005) have explored the notion of boundaryless mentoring – that is, of mentees seeking multiple mentors some of whom are inside their organizations and some of whom are outside it. Considering professional development, Murphy and Kram (2010) have placed emphasis on network opportunities that are contingent, reliant on weak-ties, and which extend beyond the corporate world. Similarly, Kram and Higgins (2009) have emphasized more openness, fluidity, and diversity in organizational mentoring because 'in today's complex, fast-paced, and global context, people's work is dependent upon many, not a single person and further, no one person can determine your destiny or fulfill every development need' (p. 1).

Mentoring, viewed as relatively transient networked engagement – rather than as a traditional strong dyadic one – has consequences for mentor and mentee:

- Mentors are no longer seen as experts separated from mentees by their high experiential or professional status – they are co-learners and co-contributors in a joint process of learning;
- Mentoring relationships are no longer exclusively characterized by high degrees of specificity, strong bonds, and temporal stability – they can be open arrangements, include greater diversity and difference, possess a multiplicity of weak ties, and recognize the temporal and spatial fluidity of the actors included in them; and
- Mentoring outcomes are no longer couched in terms of specifically defined performance goals or career advancement. They are now more open-ended and focused on increased self-awareness, the development of social and interpersonal skills, and a growing capacity for leadership (Kram & Higgins, 2009, p. 2).

4 The Opening of Mentoring Connections

Reconceptualizing mentoring as a more open, less restricted, and socially networked system has focused new interest on the possibility of expanding its reach and exploiting otherwise untapped richness that may exist in social, professional, and academic contexts. First, electronically-mediated mentoring (e-mentoring) has exploited ways in which the spatial and temporal limitations of traditional mentoring can be opened up and overcome. Second, peer mentoring has accentuated openness, accessibility, and the benefits that can accrue from operating within expansive networks of distributed assets and resources.

5 E-Mentoring and Blended Mentoring

Over the last two decades, electronically-mediated, web-based, and online mentoring systems – collectively referred to as e-mentoring – have become commonplace. E-mentoring does not necessarily imply that mentoring is considered from a network perspective; indeed, e-mentoring can be used – and indeed often is used – as a communicating and connecting instrument within traditional mentoring paradigms. However, electronic-mediation usually represents more than a simple instrumental change in the connection between mentor and mentee, or in the facilitation of their relationship. This is reflected in Bierema and Merriam's (2002) definition of e-mentoring as 'a computer mediated, mutually beneficial relationship between a mentor and a protégé which provides learning, advising, encouraging, promoting, and modeling that is often boundaryless, egalitarian, and qualitatively different than traditional face-to-face mentoring' (p. 214).

Originally, e-mentoring was predominantly facilitated via email exchanges; today, blended mentoring still uses email but complements this with other media channels that permit richer communication possibilities and which enhance the social presence of both mentor and mentee (Argente-Linares, Pérez-López, & Ordóñez-Solana, 2017; Murphy, 2011). Pragmatically, e-mentoring solves issues for those who might be physically distanced by eliminating the traditional spatial constraint of only pairing mentors and mentees from the same location. It also provides a considerable degree of temporal flexibility, allowing those engaged in the mentoring experience to schedule their contacts in ways that are mutually convenient and acceptable.

E-mentoring further expands the social reach of the mentoring possibilities and facilitates an ease and flexibility of communication that can potentially leads to greater levels of inclusion, diversity, and variety in mentor selection and mentoring relationships (Drummond, Halsey, Lawson, & van Breda, 2012; Starr-Glass, 2014a). Compared with traditional face-to-face mentoring, e-mentoring relies on and creates weaker relational ties between those involved in the process. Some may find this undesirable or in some way disadvantageous; however, in many ways, e-mentoring resonates strongly with a younger generation of mentees who are culturally familiar with social media, comfortable with extensive but weakly tied relational networks, and practiced in navigating interactive social communication.

In summary, a recent review of e-mentoring in higher education concluded that it provides additional benefits to mentors 'such as fitting into a busy schedule and minimizing status differences with mentees .... Allowed for mentoring to target students without stigmatizing ... reached out to more students, and ... enabled mentors to better manage the expectations of mentees' (Shrestha, May, Edirisingha, Burke, & Linsey, 2009, p. 123).

6 Peer Mentoring Programs

Whereas tradition mentoring relationships accentuate experiential and status differences, peer mentoring sees the advantage of bringing together those who may not be separated by a hierarchical difference but who share common, individually experienced, and uniquely varied understandings. Thus configured, the benefits are not so much in an anticipated flow of wisdom, accumulated understanding, and experiential reflection from a wiser other; rather, the benefits come from sharing and reflecting upon similar experiences that might be differently understood and variously appreciated. The anticipated flow of benefit is also not anticipated to be uni-lateral but instead bi-lateral and multi-lateral. Peer mentoring envisages weaker relational links and de-emphasizes hierarchical difference; indeed, some have explicitly considered peer mentoring – particularly the sharing of individual perspectives of faculty members in higher education – to be a primary component in a more open and inclusive 'pedagogy for equity' (Núñez, Murakami, & Cuero, 2010; Núñez, Murakami, & Gonzales, 2015).

Likewise, group mentoring – which can be regarded as a variation of peer mentoring – accentuates connectivity, commonality, and community by creating a multiplicity of mentor-mentee linkages in either synchronous face-to-face or virtual group contexts. Group mentoring further blurs the power boundaries and value flows between mentor and mentee, with group members alternatively assuming these roles in response to the dynamics of the system. This more attenuated and, as it were, more democratic expression of mentoring has proved particularly popular and effective in educational environments (undergraduate students, doctoral candidates, and faculty) and in youth-related situations. The structure and resulting dynamics of mentoring exchange provide a useful vehicle for discussing commonly-experienced problems, recognizing and exploring alternative solutions, and providing mutual support and group solidarity (Altus, 2015; Van Ryzin, 2014).

Many of those who participate in peer mentoring consider that the assumptions of traditional mentoring – specifically its roots in power and status difference – are intrinsically problematic, are unduly deferential to status quo understandings of legitimate power and knowledge claims or are essentially part of the power-related difficulties that they face in their work or career. In traditional mentoring relationships, mentors often approach their role with a sense of responsibility and a duty of care for those whom they mentor. However, there is always the problem that power and status differentials can be used – sometimes inadvertently, sometimes consciously – to create and perpetuate relationships that dominate, disadvantage, or preserve the less powerful status or perception of the mentee. From this perspective, peer mentoring can be regarded as a more democratic and more power-diffuse alternative to traditional mentoring systems (Gibson et al., 2014).

Peer mentoring utilizes lower power differentials and weaker relational ties, bringing with it the possibility of collectively reconsidering the social landscape within which participants are embedded. It provides potential benefits through re-visiting, re-questioning, and perhaps re-negotiating institutional power structures that may be considered significant for participants – particularly if they feel themselves disadvantaged, members of a disadvantaged class, or at risk of marginalization by those prevailing structures of power (Boehm & Lueck, 2016; Driscoll, Parkes, Tilley-Lubbs, Brill, & Pitt Bannister, 2009; Gibson et al., 2014; Louis, 2015).

7 Reflecting on Openness in Mentoring Practice

The nature, practice, and impact of 'open' in higher education are neither simple nor straightforward because open education 'often carries the weight of describing not just policy, practices, resources, curricula and pedagogy, but also the values inherent within these, as well as relationships between teachers and learners' (Cronin & MacLaren, 2018, p. 127). Reconsidering mentoring through the dual prisms of openness and ecological situatedness provides insights that allow mentoring systems to be more available, effective, and inclusive. Given the traditional assumptions and practices regarding mentoring, the question that might be posed is whether we should increase openness by moving beyond the strong dyadic bond that has defined it. However, perhaps the more basic and useful question is not whether this dyadic bond *should* be replaced but whether it *can* be replaced in ways that might alter the openness of the mentoring relationship while at the same time preserving the valuable outcomes of the process.

This is not to negate the valuable opportunities that arise in more fluid, tentative, and weak-tie mentoring arrangements. Nevertheless, when I personally reflect on my own international practice, it is clear that strong dyadic linkages constitute the quintessential characteristic of mentoring and that these linkages provide optimal benefits for my mentees – and ultimately for me as a mentor. My mentoring involves international students in the final year of their undergraduate business degree. I work with these mentees in the production of their capstone work – an undergraduate dissertation that explores a mentee-generated research question. Aside from this, I also work with these students in crafting their individual degree programs, advising on course selection, and supporting, motivating, and guiding them on the path towards graduation.

Ostensibly, this might suggest a *cognitive apprenticeship* model of mentoring, but I also provide a deeper knowledge and support function for mentees in their other undergraduate courses, bringing the mentoring relationship into other mentee learning domains and experiences. A restrictive and mutually inclusive dyadic relationship exists and yet the mentoring function is nevertheless diffuse, connected to other disciplinary areas of learning, and provides a new locus of engagement around which the mentee can grow, learn, consolidate, and integrate other learnings in which they are engaged. In such a relationship, structural openness to other disciplinary learning and cognitive experiences clearly exists but it is not the primary function of the relationship. Rather, openness is primarily understood as the ability to share within the dyadic relationship – a recognition of the differences that mentor and mentee bring to the process, an appreciation of the potential for joint growth and development, and an acknowledgement of the uniqueness of the relationship in building greater levels of social capital, mutual confidence, and relational trust. That is, my mentoring practice is more about openness *between* those who are defined and bounded by it, rather than about openness towards those who are *beyond* its relational boundaries (Hezlett & Gibson, 2007; Rock & Garavan, 2011).

Difference of status, experience, and knowledge in mentoring can easily ossify the relationship, leading to a sense of hierarchical deference and mentee dependency. If mentoring is conceived as primarily a process of helping and empowering, these tectonic plates of difference – which can potentially separate participants and force them apart – must be recognized and converted into productive forces that provide a more balanced system and result in mutually recognized benefits for those in the relationship. Like many other practitioners, I have found that truly advantageous and mutually rewarding relationships are a function of the amount of time invested, the degree of willingness to help and support, and openness to the mentee's unique circumstances, aspirations, and concerns. The cultivation of trust and respect is critical. Trust and respect within the relationship constitute its openness – even though that openness may, paradoxically, seem to further define the specificity of the dyad and separate both mentor and mentee from the expansive world that surround them and in which they are embedded (Gaddis, 2012).

In my own practice, mentoring takes place across significant barriers of national culture and the cultural expectations that have been created by different histories of teaching, learning, and education. For many of my mentees, there is diffidence and hesitation about entering into the relationship because – from their prior educational experiences (often in Central and Eastern European higher education) – mentoring is viewed as an inherently fractured relationship with a dominant, remote, and unapproachable figure of authority. Within such culturally and experientially charged contexts, the cultivation of internal openness is absolutely necessary. Although mentoring is often portrayed as a multinational and multimedia phenomenon,

> its essence remains the connection between individuals who have overcome the artificial barriers of experience, race, or gender to create a caring partnership or network that sustains and nourishes all, enabling them to journey together to a new and richer understanding of their world. (Kochan & Pascarelli, 2000, p. 427)

Reviewing faculty mentoring programs, Zellers, Howard, and Barcic (2008) observed the lack of evidence-based studies associated with mentoring processes and outcomes. They stressed the importance of context and culture, particularly when different national cultures seem to separate mentor from mentee. However, they argued that the potentials and positive outcomes of mentoring were more likely to be associated with re-envisaging mentoring, rather than with re-inventing it. The ongoing challenge for all of those engaged in mentoring – mentors and those whom they mentor – is to be constantly involved in a process of re-envisaging what is done and what might be done. In this continuous process of re-envisaging, many mentors and mentees might agree that,

> in retrospect, the mythological subplot of *The Odyssey* in which Athena, the goddess of wisdom and compassion, works through the character Mentor does not appear to be merely coincidental. Rather, it is an especially appropriate metaphor for the interrelatedness of the dual

> dimensions of mentoring and the holistic learning that occurs within its context. (Zellers et al., 2008, p. 583)

For those who engage in mentoring, the ongoing challenge is to accentuate the interrelatedness of its inherent duality in ways that actualize the richness of its holistic learning potential. For individual mentors and mentees – and for the organizations and institutions that seek to promote mentoring – the related challenge is to explore the ways in which mentoring can be open in relational terms, while not necessarily excluding that secondary openness to the ecological landscape of learning, teaching, and education within which mentoring is situated and embedded. These are challenges and opportunities that confront all of those who seek to explore themselves and their lived-in worlds through mentoring.

References

Alexander, B. (2017). Higher education, digital divides, and a Balkanized Internet. *EDUCAUSE Review, 52*(6). Retrieved from https://er.educause.edu/articles/2017/10/higher-education-digital-divides-and-a-balkanized-internet

Altus, J. (2015). Answering the call: How group mentoring makes a difference. *Mentoring & Tutoring: Partnership in Learning, 23*(2), 100–115. https://doi.org/10.1080/13611267.2015.1047629

Anderson, L., Silet, K., & Fleming, M. (2012). Evaluating and giving feedback to mentors: New evidence-based approaches. *Clinical and Translation Science, 5*(1), 71–77. https://doi.org/10.1111/j.1752-8062.2011.00361.x

Argente-Linares, E., Pérez-López, M. C., & Ordóñez-Solana, C. (2017). Practical experience of blended mentoring in higher education. *Mentoring & Tutoring: Partnership in Learning, 24*(5), 399–414. https://doi.org/10.1080/13611267.2016.1273449

Baugh, S. G., & Fagenson-Eland, E. A. (2005). Boundaryless mentoring: An exploratory study of the functions provided by internal versus external organizational mentors. *Journal of Applied Psychology,* 35(5), 939–955. https://doi.org/10.1111/j.1559-1816.2005.tb02154.x

Bellon-Harn, M. L., & Weinbaum, R. K. (2017). Cross-cultural peer-mentoring: Mentor outcomes and perspectives. *Teaching and Learning in Communication Sciences & Disorders, 1*(2), Article 3. Retrieved from http://ir.library.illinoisstate.edu/tlcsd/vol1/iss2/3

Bierema, L. L., & Merriam, S. B. (2002). E-mentoring: Using computer mediated communication to enhance the mentoring process. *Innovative Higher Education, 26*(3), 211–227. https://doi.org/10.1023/A:1017921023103

Blake-Beard, S. D. (2009). Mentoring as a bridge to understand cultural difference. *Adult Learning, 20*(1–2), 14–18. https://doi.org/10.1177/104515950902000104

Blickle, G., Witzki, A., & Schneider, P. B. (2009). Self-initiated mentoring and career success: A predictive field study. *Journal of Vocational Behavior, 74*(1), 94–101. https://doi.org/101016/j.jvb.2008.10.008

Boehm, B., & Lueck, A. J. (2016). Graduate student peer mentoring programs: Benefitting students, faculty and academic programs. In G. Wright (Ed.), *The mentoring continuum: From graduate school through tenure* (pp. 187–202). Syracuse, NY: Syracuse University Press. Retrieved from http://graduateschool.syr.edu/wp-content/uploads/2016/10/Boehm-and-Lueck-for-web.pdf

Briscoe, J. P., Hall, D. T., & Frautschy DeMuth, R. L. (2006). Protean and boundaryless careers: An empirical exploration. *Journal of Vocational Behavior, 69*(1), 30–47. https://doi.org/10.1016/j.jvb.2005.09.003

Bronfenbrenner, U. (1979). *The ecology of human development: Experiments by nature and design.* Cambridge, MA: Harvard University Press.

Buehler, K. (2017). *Relational cultural theory and mentoring in a science support program* (College of Science and Health Theses and Dissertations). 210. Retrieved from http://via.library.depaul.edu/csh_etd/210

Chandler, D. E., Kram, K. E., & Yip, J. (2011). An ecological systems perspective on mentoring at work: A review and future prospects. *The Academy of Management Annals, 5*(1), 519–570. https://doi.org/10.1080/19416520.2011.576087

Collins, A., Brown, J. S., & Newman, S. E. (1989). Cognitive apprenticeship: Teaching the craft of reading, writing, and mathematics. In L. B. Resnick (Ed.), *Knowing, learning, and instruction: Essays in honor of Robert Glaser* (pp. 453–494). Hillsdale, NJ: Lawrence Erlbaum Associates.

Crisp, G., & Cruz, I. (2009). Mentoring college students: A critical literature review between 1990 and 2007. *Research in Higher Education, 50*(6), 525–545. https://doi.org/10.1007/s11162-009-9130-2

Cronin, C., & MacLaren, I. (2018). Conceptualising OEP: A review of theoretical and empirical literature in open educational practices. *Open Praxis, 10*(2), 127–143. Retrieved from https://www.openpraxis.org/index.php/OpenPraxis/article/download/825/436

Damsa, C. I., & Joret, A. (2016). Revisiting learning in higher education – Framing notions redefined through an ecological perspective. *Frontline Learning Research, 4*(4), 39–47. Retrieved from https://journals.sfu.ca/flr/index.php/journal/article/view/208/322

Dawson, P. (2014). Beyond a definition: Toward a framework for designing and specifying mentoring models. *Educational Researcher, 43*(3), 137–145. https://doi.org/10.3102/0013189X14528751

DeCastrom R., Sambuco, D., Ubel, P. A., Stewart, A., & Jagsi, R. (2013). Mentor networks in academic medicine: Moving beyond a dyadic conception of mentoring for junior faculty researchers. *Academy of Medicine, 88*(4), 488–496. https://doi.org/10.1097/ACM.0b013e318285d302

Dennen, V. P., & Burner, K. J. (2008). The cognitive apprenticeship model in educational practice. In J. M. Spector, M. D. Merrill, J. Van Merrienboer, & M. P. Driscoll (Eds.), *Handbook of educational communications and technology* (pp. 425–439). Mahwah, NJ: Erlbaum.

Dobrow, S. R., & Higgins, M. C. (2005). Developmental networks and professional identity: A longitudinal study. *Career Development International, 10*(6–7), 567–583. https://doi.org/10.1108/13620430510620629

Dougherty, T. W., & Dreher, G. F. (2007). Mentoring and career outcomes: Conceptual and methodological issues in an emerging literature. In B. R. Ragins & K. E. Kram (Eds.), *The handbook of mentoring at work: Theory, research and practice* (pp. 51–93). Thousand Oaks, CA: Sage. https://doi.org/10.4135/9781412976619.n3

Driscoll, L. G., Parkes, K. A., Tilley-Lubbs, G. A., Brill, J. M., & Pitt Bannister, V. R. (2009). Navigating the lonely sea: Peer mentoring and collaboration among aspiring women scholars. *Mentoring & Tutoring: Partnership in Learning, 17*(1), 5–21. https://doi.org/10.1080/13611260802699532

Drummond, A., Halsey, R. J., Lawson, M., & van Breda, M. (2012). The effectiveness of a university mentoring project in peri-rural Australia. *Education in Rural Australia, 22*(2), 29–41.

Eberly, M. B., Holley, E. C., Johnson, M. D., & Mitchell, T. R. (2011). Beyond internal and external: A dyadic theory of relational attributions. *Academy of Management Review, 36*(4), 731–753. https://doi.org/10.5465/amr.2009.0371

Finkelstein, L. M., Allen, T. D., Ritchie, T. D., Lynch, J. E., & Montei, M. S. (2011): A dyadic examination of the role of relationship characteristics and age on relationship satisfaction in a formal mentoring programme. *European Journal of Work and Organizational Psychology, 21*(6), 803–827. https://doi.org/10.1080/1359432X.2011.594574

Gaddis, S. M. (2012). What's in a relationship? An examination of social capital, race and class in mentoring relationships. *Social Forces, 90*(4), 1237–1269. https://doi.org/10.1093/sf/sos003

Garvey, R., Stokes, P., & Megginson, D. (2009). *Coaching and mentoring: Theory and practice*. Thousand Oaks, CA: Sage.

Gibson, G., Medeiros, K. E., Giorgini, V., Mecca, J. T., Davenport, L. D., Connelly, S., & Mumford, M. D. (2014). A qualitative analysis of power differentials in ethical situations in academia. *Ethics & Behavior, 24*(4), 311–325. https://doi.org/10.1080/10508422.2013.858605

Gilliard, C. (2017). Pedagogy and the logic of platforms. *EDUCAUSE Review, 52*(4). Retrieved from https://er.educause.edu/articles/2017/7/pedagogy-and-the-logic-of-platforms

Granovetter, M. (1983). The strength of weak ties: A network theory revisited. *Sociological Theory, 1*, 201–233. https://doi.org/10.2307/202051

Hansman, C. A. (2003). Reluctant mentors and resistant protégés: Welcome to the 'real' world of mentoring. *Adult Learning, 14*(1), 14–16. https://doi.org/101177/104515950301400103

Hezlett, S. A., & Gibson, S. K. (2007). Linking mentoring and social capital: Implications for career and organization development *Advances in Developing Human Resources, 9*(3), 384–411. https://doi.org/10.1177/1523422307304102

Higgins, M. C., & Kram, K. E. (2001). Reconceptualizing mentoring at work: A developmental network perspective. *The Academy of Management Review, 26*(2), 264–288. https://doi.org/10.5465/AMR.2001.4378023

Hofstede, G. (2001). *Culture's consequences: Comparing values, behaviors, institutions, and organizations across nations*. London: Sage.

Hu, C., Thomas, K. M., & Lance, C. E. (2008). Intentions to initiate mentoring relationships: Understanding the impact of race, proactivity, feelings of deprivation, and relationship roles. *The Journal of Social Psychology, 148*(6), 727–744. https://doi.org/10.3200/SOCP.148.6.727-744

Jacobi, M. (1991). Mentoring and undergraduate academic success: A literature review. *Review of Educational Research, 61*(4), 505–532. https://doi.org/10.3102/00346543061004505

Jones, R., & Brown, D. (2011). The mentoring relationship as a complex adaptive system: Finding a model for our experience. *Mentoring & Tutoring: Partnership in Learning, 19*(4), 401–418. https://doi.org/10.1080/13611267.2011.622077

Jones, R., & Corner, J. (2012). Seeing the forest and the trees: A complex adaptive systems lens for mentoring. *Human Relations, 65*(2), 391–411. https://doi.org/10.1177/0018726711430556

Kao, K.-Y., Rogers, A., Spitzmueller, C., Lin, M.-T., & Lin, C.-H. (2014). Who should serve as my mentor? The effects of mentor's gender and supervisory status on resilience in mentoring relationships. *Journal of Vocational Behavior, 85*(2), 191–203. https://doi.org/10.1016/j.jvb.2014.07.004

Keller, T. E., & Blakeslee, J. E. (2013). Social networks and mentoring. In D. L. DuBois & M. J. Karcher (Eds.), *Handbook of youth mentoring* (2nd ed., pp. 129–142). Thousand Oaks, CA: Sage. https://doi.org/10.4135/9781412996907.n9

Kochan, F. K., & Pascarelli, J. T. (2000). Culture, context, and issues of change related to mentoring programs and relationships. In F. K. Kochan & J. T. Pascarelli (Eds.), *Global perspectives on mentoring: Transforming contexts, communities, and cultures* (pp. 417–428). Greenwich, CT: Information Age Publishing.

Kochan, F. K., Searby, L., George, M. P., & Edge, J. M. (2015). Cultural influences in mentoring endeavors: Applying the cultural framework analysis process. *International Journal of Mentoring and Coaching in Education, 4*(2), 86–106. https://doi.org/10.1108/IJMCE-03-2015-0010

Kram, K. E., & Higgins, M. A. (2009, April 15). A new mindset on mentoring: Creating developmental networks at work. *MIT Sloan Management Review.*

Lankau, M. J., Riordan, C. M., & Thomas, C. H. (2005). The effects of similarity and liking in formal relationships between mentors and protégés. *Journal of Vocational Behavior, 67*(2), 252–265. https://doi.org/10.1016/j.jvb.2004.08.012

Lave, J., & Wegner, E. (1991). *Situated learning: Legitimate peripheral participation.* Cambridge: Cambridge University Press.

Lewis, C., & Olshansky, E. (2017). Relational-cultural theory as a framework for mentoring in academia: Toward diversity and growth-fostering collaborative scholarly relationships. *Mentoring & Tutoring: Partnership in Learning, 24*(5), 383–398. https://doi.org/10.1080/13611267.2016.1275390

Liden, R. C., Anand, S., & Vidyarthi, P. (2016). Dyadic relationships. *Annual Review of Organizational Psychology and Organizational Behavior, 3*, 139–166. https://doi.org/10.1146/annurev-orgpsych-041015-062452

Louis, D. A. (2015). Cross-cultural peer mentoring: One approach to enhancing – White faculty adjustment at Black colleges. *International Journal of Multicultural Education, 17*(2), 1–19. https://doi.org/10.18251/ijme.v17i2.900

Ludwig, S., & Stein, R. E. (2008). Anatomy of mentoring. *Journal of Pediatrics, 152*(2), 151–152. https://doi.org/10.1016/j.jpeds.2007.10.022

Martz, W. (2013). Evaluating organizational performance: Rational, natural, and open system models. *American Journal of Evaluation, 34*(3), 385–401. https://doi.org/10.1177/1098214013479151

McAllister, C. A., Harold, R. D., Ahmedani, B. K., & Cramer, E. P. (2009). Targeted mentoring: Evaluation of a program. *Journal of Social Work Education, 45*(1), 89–103. https://doi.org/10.5175/JSWE.2009.200700107

Menges, C. (2015). Towards improving the effectiveness of formal mentoring programs: Matching personality matters. *Group & Organization Management, 41*(1), 98–129. https://doi.org/10.1177/1059601115579567

Mitchell, M. E., Eby, L. T., & Ragins, B. R. (2015). My mentor, my self: Antecedents and outcomes of perceived similarity in mentoring relationships. *Journal of Vocational Behavior, 89*, 1–9. https://doi.org/10.1016/j.jvb.2015.04.008

Moberg, D. J., & Velasquez, M. (2004). The ethics of mentoring. *Business Ethics Quarterly, 14*(1), 95–122. https://doi.org/10.5840/beq20041418

Molloy, J. C. (2005). Development networks: Literature review and future research. *Career Development International, 10*(6/7), 536–547. https://doi.org/10.1108/13620430510620601

Murphy, W. M. (2011). From E-mentoring to blended mentoring: Increasing students' developmental initiation and mentors' satisfaction. *Academy of Management Learning & Education, 10*(4), 606–622. https://doi.org/10.5465/amle.2010.0090

Murphy, W. M., & Kram, K. E. (2010). Understanding non-work relationships in developmental networks. *Career Development International, 15*(7), 637–663. https://doi.org/10.1108/13620431011094069

Núñez, A.-M., Murakami, E. T., & Cuero, K. K. (2010). Pedagogy for equity: Teaching in a Hispanic-serving institution. *Innovative Higher Education, 35*(3), 177–190. https://doi.org/10.1007/s10755-010-9139-7

Núñez, A.-M., Murakami, E. T., & Gonzales, L. D. (2015), Weaving authenticity and legitimacy: Latina faculty peer mentoring. *New Directions for Higher Education, 117*, 87–96. https://doi.org/10.1002/he.20145

Omidvar, O., & Kislov, R. (2013). The evolution of the communities of practice approach: Toward knowledgeability in a landscape of practice – An interview with Etienne Wenger-Trayner. *Journal of Management Inquiry, 23*(3), 266–275. https://doi.org/10.1177/1056492613505908

Pawson, R. (2004). *Mentoring relationships: An explanatory review* (Working Paper 21, Economic and Social Research Council, UK Centre for Evidence Based Policy and Practice). London: ESRC. Retrieved from http://www.kcl.ac.uk/sspp/departments/politicaleconomy/research/cep/pubs/papers/assets/wp21.pdf

Pawson, R. (2006). Evidence-based policy: The promise of systematic review. In R. Pawson (Ed.), *Evidence-based policy: A realist perspective* (pp. 2–16). London: Sage. https://doi.org/104135/9781849209120

Peters, M. A. (2008). The history and emergent paradigm of open education. In M. A. Peters & R. G. Britez (Eds.), *Open education and education for openness* (pp. 3–16). Rotterdam, The Netherlands: Sense Publishers.

Powell, M. A. (1997). *Academic tutoring and mentoring: A literature review.* Sacramento, CA: California Research Bureau, California State Library. Retrieved from http://www.library.ca.gov/crb/97/11/97011.pdf

Ragins, B. R., & Kram, K. E. (2007). The roots and meanings of mentoring. In B. R. Ragins & K. E. Kram (Eds.), *The handbook of mentoring at work: Theory, research and practice* (pp. 3–16). Thousand Oaks, CA: Sage. https://doi.org/10.4135/9781412976619.n1

Ramaswami, A., Huang, J.-C., & Dreher, G. (2013). Interaction of gender, mentoring, and power distance on career attainment: A cross-cultural comparison. *Human Relations, 67*(2), 153–173. https://doi.org/10.1177/0018726713490000

Rankin, P., Neilsen, J., & Stanley, D. M. (2007). Weak links, hot networks, and tacit knowledge: Why advancing women requires networking. In A. Stewart, J. E. Malley, & D. LaVaque-Manty (Eds.), *Transforming science and engineering: Advancing academic women* (pp. 31–47). Ann Arbor, MI: University of Michigan Press.

Rivera, M. T., Soderstrom, S. B., & Uzzi, B. (2010). Dynamics of dyads in social networks: Assortative, relational, and proximity mechanisms. *Annual Review of Sociology, 36*, 91–115. https://doi.org/10.1146/annurev.soc.34.040507.134743

Rock, A. D., & Garavan, T. N. (2011). Understanding the relational characteristics of effective mentoring and developmental relationships at work. In R. F. Poell & M. van Woerkom (Eds.), *Supporting workplace learning: Towards evidence-based practice* (pp. 107–127). Dordrecht: Springer. https://doi.org/10.1007/978-90-481-9109-3_7

Scott, W. R., & Davis, G. F. (2007). *Organizations and organizing. Rational, natural, and open system perspectives*. Upper Saddle River, NJ: Pearson.

Shore, W. J., Toyokawa, T., & Anderson, D. D. (2008). Context-specific effects on reciprocity in mentoring relationships: Ethical implications. *Mentoring and Tutoring: Partnership in Learning, 16*(1), 17–29. https://doi.org/10.1080/13611260701800926

Shrestha, C. H., May, S., Edirisingha, P., Burke, L., & Linsey, T. (2009). From face-to-face to e-mentoring: Does the 'e' add any value for mentors? *International Journal of Teaching and Learning in Higher Education, 20*(2), 116–124.

Starr-Glass, D. (2014a). E-mentoring: Mentoring at a distance. In V. C. X. Wang (Ed.), *Handbook of research on education and technology in a changing society* (pp. 974–990). Hershey, PA: IGI–Global. https://doi.org/10.4018/978–1–4666–6046–5.ch070

Starr-Glass, D. (2014b). Diverging paths: First steps into the metaphoric wilderness of macroeconomics. *On the Horizon, 22*(4), 229–238. https://doi.org/10.1108/OTH-11-2013-0060

Suffrin, R. L., Todd, N. R., & Sanchez, B. (2016). An ecological perspective of mentor satisfaction with their youth mentoring relationships. *Journal of Community Psychology, 44*(5), 553–568. https://doi.org/10.1002/jcop.21785

Todd, S. (2015). Experiencing change, encountering the unknown: An education in 'negative capability' in light of Buddhism and Levinas. *Journal of Philosophy of Education, 49*(2), 240–254. https://doi.org/10.1111/1467-9752.12139

Tudge, J. R. H., Payir, A., Merçon-Vargas, E., Cao, H., Liang, Y. Li, J., & O'Brien, L. (2016). Still misused after all these years? A reevaluation of the uses of Bronfenbrenner's bioecological theory of human development. *Journal of Family Theory & Review, 8*(4), 427–445. https://doi.org/10.1111/jftr.12165

Van Ryzin, M. J. (2014). Exploring relationships among boys and men: A retrospective, qualitative study of a multi-year community-based group mentoring program. *Children and Youth Services Review, 44*, 349–355. https://doi.org/10.1016/j.childyouth.2014.07.002

Weller, M., Jordan, K., DeVries, I., & Rolfe, V. (2018). Mapping the open education landscape: Citation network analysis of historical open and distance education research. *Open Praxis, 10*(2), 109–126. Retrieved from https://www.openpraxis.org/index.php/OpenPraxis/article/download/822/435

Wenger, E. (2010). Communities of practice and social learning systems: The career of a concept. In C. Blackmore (Ed.), *Social learning systems and communities of practice* (pp. 179–198). London: Springer.

Wong, S. C., Rasdi, R. M., Samah, B. A., & Wahat, N. W. A. (2017). Promoting protean career through employability culture and mentoring: Career strategies as moderator. *European Journal of Training and Development, 41*(3), 277–302. https://doi.org/10.1108/EJTD-08-2016-0060

Zellers, D. F., Howard, V. M., & Barcic, M. A. (2008). Faculty mentoring programs: Re-envisioning rather than reinventing the wheel. *Review of Educational Research, 78*(3), 552–588. https://doi.org/10.3102/0034654308320966

CHAPTER 7

Open to Inclusion: Exploring Openness for People with Disabilities

Tharindu R. Liyanagunawardena, Andrew A. Adams and Shirley A. Williams

The ideas of 'open' – relating to its many aspects including practices, processes and movements – have been fluid over time, gaining prominence and moving forward with technological developments. Globalisation has removed barriers and facilitated the flow of capital globally (Castells, 2000); open universities and related initiatives have enabled people who previously lacked access to university education to access it (Bates, 2005). Open Education Resources (OER) have provided access to high quality educational materials that permit reuse and repurposing by others (Atkins, Brown, & Hammond, 2007); and more recently, Massive Open Online Courses (MOOCs) have opened access to courses from institutions, including elite universities, to the world (Liyanagunawardena, Adams, & Williams, 2013). However, despite this increase in openness, there are still significant barriers for people with disabilities who want to access such open content.

This chapter introduces fictitious learner personas of Khalid, Sophie, Arun and Chamari who have various disabilities and who are keen to access open content to learn and develop themselves. The reader is invited to explore with them the obstacles they have to overcome in accessing these open resources and decide whether the difficulties they encounter may differ had these learners happened to live elsewhere in the world. The chapter presents the case for inclusion and accessibility, including legal considerations in selected jurisdictions. While highlighting the importance of raising awareness in enabling inclusion, the chapter explores the potential of open content to create 'inclusive openness.'

1 What Is Accessibility?

In the UK Equality Act 2010 (Equality Act), a person is considered disabled if they have a physical or mental impairment that has a substantial (more than minor or trivial) and long-term (12 months or more) negative impact on their

 | DOI: 10.1163/9789004422988_008

ability to do everyday activities (HM Government, n.d.). On the other hand, in the Oxford online dictionary, disability is defined more generally as 'a physical or mental condition that limits a person's movements, senses, or activities' (Oxford Dictionaries, n.d.). The authors use the term disability to denote any physical or mental condition that limits a person's ability to engage fully in everyday life be it short-term (such as having to use a wheelchair due to a plaster cast) or long-term (including disabilities due to aging).

Accessibility is a term used in various contexts with different meanings (Liyanagunawardena & Hussain, 2017). The term 'Web accessibility' is widely used to refer to whether people with disabilities can use a Web resource, the range of disabilities including (but not limited to) visual, auditory, physical, speech, cognitive, and neurological – indeed anything that could impact the use of the Web. The World Wide Web Consortium (W3C, 2005) uses the term Web accessibility to mean 'people with disabilities can perceive, understand, navigate, and interact with the Web, and that they can contribute to the Web.' In this chapter, accessibility describes equal access to content regardless of a person's disability. This may not necessarily mean that a person with a disability is able to take advantage of the full multi-sensory experience of materials, but that they can access the content in some way; in many cases this will involve the use of assistive technologies such as screen-readers (Liyanagunawardena & Hussain, 2017).

Hill (2013) reserved the use of the term 'accessibility' specifically to focus on people with disabilities, as opposed to the more general area of usability, although Hill (2013) pointed out that the two issues are related. Many accessibility requirements (such as captions or transcripts for video/audio) may improve usability for everyone (people in noisy environments such as a train, or non-native speakers who may find speakers' accents difficult to follow, can access the materials), following the principles of 'Universal Design' (Burgstahler, 2015a). Following Hill (2013), the authors use the term accessibility to mean that people can access the resource/space/setting to make full use as intended despite their disabilities or impairments. For example, a physical space such as a building can be made accessible by providing ramps, lifts, wide corridors, and toilets with wide doors and space for wheelchairs. Similarly, a digital space can be made accessible by following best practice guidelines, such as Web Content Accessibility Guidelines (WCAG), to allow equal access to people with disabilities; for example, allowing keyboard navigation options, using sufficient contrast and text alternatives for non-textual materials. WCAG 2.1, the current set of guidelines, has three levels: A, AA and AAA, with AAA being the most accessible (W3C, 2018). Such practices, for example, provide captions, transcripts and/or video descriptions for audio and video materials for the benefit of people with hearing or visual impairment while making all menus and buttons accessible via keyboard for the benefit of people who are unable to use a mouse. In this chapter, the term accessibility will mainly be used relating to digital spaces and/or resources.

Disabilities, whether physical or cognitive, can create huge challenges to learners in accessing learning. Though the need to make physical spaces accessible for disabled learners has been acknowledged for some time, not many educators are aware of the challenges learning content can pose, especially that in digital formats. For example, a learner with colour-blindness may not be able to access information differentiated solely by colour; unless supplemented by audio description, video content may be inaccessible to a learner with visual impairment. Similarly, without a transcript, a podcast may be inaccessible to a learner with hearing impairment. Unless the electronic learning materials are designed with accessibility in mind, it is not easy, or pleasant, to navigate the content with assistive technologies that provide vital support to learners with disabilities (Liyanagunawardena & Hussain, 2017).

A number of authors have reviewed the accessibility of academic websites including those delivering e-learning (Fichten et al., 2009; Kent, 2015; Seale, Georgeson, Christoforos, & Swain, 2015; Zaphiris & Ellis, 2001); and in general, over the years, websites and services have improved with regard to accessibility. However, Seale et al. (2015) point out that many learners with disabilities still find it difficult to managing their studies due to inaccessible learning places and/or learning materials; they also report that the learners with disabilities are often reluctant to over-rely on a small group of people (typically family or friends) for support, which may stop them seeking help when there are accessibility issues. Burgstahler (2015b) identified that many learners with disabilities do not disclose their problems to educators, resulting in necessary adjustments not occurring. Case and Davidson (2011) point out that proactively considering accessibility issues at design time reduces last minute scrambles to address these issues. Asuncion et al. (2010) suggest there is a role for 'e-learning accessibility specialists' within institutions to ensure e-learning material is constructed with accessibility considerations. Kent (2015) looks at the legal and moral responsibilities of institutions to provide accessible online courses. Parton (2016) covers issues with accessible technologies, particularly captioning software, which could help in making materials accessible. With improvements in technology, new and more reliable tools have been made available; some of these can be used to enhance accessibility of materials, for example, speech-to-text software can be used to generate transcripts, which in turn increase the accessibility of audio materials.

2 Open Education Resources (OER) and Massive Open Online Courses (MOOCs)

In 2001, the Massachusetts Institute of Technology (MIT)'s Open CourseWare (OCW) initiative, funded through a joint grant from the William and Flora Hewlett and the Andrew W. Mellon Foundations, sought to provide open access to materials in its curriculum and had far-reaching implications by inspiring hundreds of other universities and colleges to share their content for open access (Brown & Adler, 2008). Downes (2011) defines Open Educational Resources (OER) as 'materials used to support education that may be freely accessed, reused, modified and shared by anyone' while Butcher and Moore (2015) define OER as 'those teaching and learning materials that are available either in the public domain or under an open licence' (p. 8). UNESCO (2017) defines OER as 'any type of educational materials that are in the public domain or introduced with an open license. The nature of these open materials means that anyone can legally and freely copy, use, adapt and re-share them.'

The concept of open access to learning, pioneered by OER, was taken in a different direction with the introduction of the massive open online courses or MOOCs (Fini, 2009). MOOCs provide access to courses from different providers, either on a learning platform (such as Coursera, edX and FutureLearn) or on a bespoke course site, to learners generally without any constraints such as pre-requisites and without registration fees (although many courses now offer paid additional services such as certifications (Liyanagunawardena, Lundqvist, & Williams, 2015). Both OER and MOOCs have opened up learning opportunities for people around the world from all walks of life – albeit probably only to those with proficiency in an international language, digital skills and Internet connectivity – to access courses and learning materials from world-renowned universities, which would have otherwise been unavailable to them. Although there is no question that OER and MOOCs have expanded opportunities for learning over the years – often to those who already have significant education and opportunities (Lane, 2012) – are they truly accessible?

Accessibility of OER and MOOCs. Fichten, Asuncion, and Scapin (2014) point out that despite MOOCs and other innovative online learning options offering exciting opportunities for learners, there is a lack of substantive conversations on making such technologies accessible. Navarette and Luján-Mora (2013) review accessibility for OER materials from two perspectives: finding OER on the Web and the content of OER. They report accessibility issues in both. Lane (2012) develops a conceptual framework for OER which includes issues of accessibility; however, he points out that while OER have the potential to reduce the digital divide, they may actually exacerbate the already existing divides:

> [i]n particular the availability, accessibility and acceptability of this mode of teaching [OER] and learning is extremely variable, with socially excluded groups or communities being those who do not have much access to such technologies, may find few opportunities available to them in their circumstances and are worried that they cannot cope with these new technologies and ways of learning. (Lane, 2012, p. 12)

In its guidelines for higher education institutions, the Commonwealth of Learning (2015) points out the necessity to ensure ICT access for staff and students. Appendix 2 includes guidelines on making materials more effective and inclusive. However, following these guidelines alone is not sufficient to solve the wide-ranging accessibility issues that the creators of OER should address. See below for a further discussion of raising the awareness of OER creators about these issues.

There are a number of MOOCs offered by various providers that teach topics related to disabilities. For example, found on the FutureLearn platform, 'Disability and a Good Life: Working with Disability' by University of New South Wales; on Coursera, 'Disability Awareness and Support' by University of Pittsburgh; on Canvas Network, 'You Matter: Understanding Intellectual Disability' by London South Bank University.

However, there is little research relating to the accessibility of OER and MOOCs with Fichten et al. (2014) writing that 'conversation around accessibility of MOOCs is nascent' (p. 373). Butler (2012) indicates that the responsibility for accessibility is typically shared between platform providers and specific course providers, which Fichten et al. (2014) observe to be problematic. Iniesto, McAndrew, Minocha and Coughlan (2017b) have done some initial work on learners with disabilities and MOOCs, highlighting the need for further research; similarly, Królak, Chen, Sanderson, and Kessel (2017) have conducted a preliminary study of the accessibility of MOOCs for blind learners and indicate the need for more work.

3 Legal Frameworks That Underpin Accessibility

In many countries, legal frameworks stipulate that equal rights apply to all citizens, despite any disability or impairments. However, in reality, people with disabilities face various, usually unintentional, barriers to participating in civic society, from access to transportation to access to websites. Thus, there is often also special legal protection provided to people with disabilities, in the form of legislation and regulation, to stop discrimination in specific parts of everyday life, such as employment or education. The extent to which these enable people with disabilities to engage fully in society varies in both intent and in eventual impact.

In the next section, the authors briefly introduce such legislation in five different jurisdictions including in both developed and developing countries. These countries have been selected to illustrate the diversity of legal protection for individuals with disabilities in different regions of the world ranging from strong protection to nominal protection. The authors' knowledge of country contexts has also influenced this selection. Later in the chapter, these country contexts will be tied into the discussion with learner personas.

4 Selected Set of Countries and Their Provision for Learners with Disabilities

4.1 *Ghana*

Ghana has suffered from a poor record of disability rights and the introduction of Persons With Disability Act (PWDA) in 2006 was a major landmark for disability campaigners (Government of Ghana, 2006). However, the implementation of the PWDA has gaps in the provisions for education over which The Ghana Federation of the Disabled has expressed serious concerns (Awadzi, 2016).

Inclusive education was piloted in Ghana over two decades ago but even after 20 years of implementation, Ghana has not fully implemented its promise mainly due to inadequate resources and negative attitudes towards students with disabilities (Abraham, 2014). In their research, Abraham (2014) found that the teachers in the Effutu district had a considerable number of misconceptions about dyslexia, for example. It was also found that the level of awareness of educators with Special Educational Needs (SEN) training was not significantly different from that of general educators indicating the huge challenge Ghana faces in raising awareness among Ghanaian educators.

4.2 *Japan*

Japan ratified the United Nations Convention on the Rights of the Child in 1994 and the Convention on the Rights of Persons with Disabilities was signed in 2007 and ratified in 2014 (Forlin, Kawai, & Higuchi, 2015). The Act on the Elimination of Discrimination against Persons with Disabilities (the Disabilities

Discrimination Act) was enacted in June 2013 and the Act on Employment Promotion etc. of Persons with Disabilities was revised (Asakura, 2014). All these changes in disability laws in recent years have been necessary to provide equal opportunities for the people with disabilities in a culture where there is deep stigma against lack of productivity (or just against comparatively low 'presence') even when it is due to disabilities (Adams, 2016).

Japan has traditionally had a dual (regular and special) education system with the special education system catering for learners with disabilities. In 2011, discussions about inclusive education commenced and in 2013 a major revision to the enrolment system for public schools was made after the Articles on the Enforcement Order for the School Education Law were revised (Forlin et al., 2015). Due to recent changes in the education system, educators are likely to be teaching learners with additional needs for the first time in mainstream (regular) education and may not be prepared well to appreciate the challenges faced by these students. For example, Wydell and Butterworth (1999) state that 'the concept of developmental dyslexia is relatively unknown in Japan' (p. 278) and this contention is also supported by Uno, Wydell, Haruhara, Kaneko and Shinya (2009) who state that in Japan, due to the low prevalence of dyslexia, that it was thought dyslexia 'did not warrant special educational support' (p. 758). However, in Uno et al. (2009), a study of some 500 children, researchers identified some 6% of children with reading/writing disabilities in the Kanji script, while there were considerably less in the two syllabic Kana scripts. (For example, they found 0.2% with a reading disability with the Hiragana script.)

4.3 *Sri Lanka*

Thirty years of conflict in the Northern and Eastern parts of the country left Sri Lanka home to a large proportion of people with war-related disabilities. There are various laws and regulations (Japan International Cooperation Agency, 2002) that protect Sri Lankans with disabilities against discrimination such as:

- Article 12 (1) of the Sri Lankan constitution (right to equality and non-discrimination as a fundamental right);
- Protection of the Rights of Persons with Disabilities Act, No.28 of 1996;
- Ranaviru Seva Act 1999 (to provide care and rehabilitation of armed and police forces and promote welfare of dependents of armed and police force who have been killed or missing in action);
- Promotion of Accessibility in the Physical Environment 1998, Social Security Board Act No. 17 of 1996 (to provide pension and insurance benefits to disabled people);

- Public Administration Circular No. 27/88, 18th August 1988 (to secure job rights);
- Trust Fund Act for the Rehabilitation of the Visually Handicapped 1992.

Due to these circumstances, the Sri Lankan government introduced Public Administration Circular No. 3 in 1988 that granted 3% of public services vacancies to candidates with disabilities who hold the required qualifications; and the Ranaviruseva Act of 1999 that includes provision to ensure the well-being of security forces personnel who suffered disabilities during the course of their service to the country (Jayawardena, 2015). The National Policy for Disability (NPD) addressed newly-identified issues such as *Access to Communication and Information* (Section 13) and *Assistive Devices and Information Technology* (Section 14); however, these policies rely on simply giving ministries the responsibility for implementing suitable measures but provide no real individual enforceable rights, instead giving oversight duties to the 'National Council for Persons with Disabilities' (Ministry of Social Welfare, 2003). Jayawardena (2015) shows that despite the Disabled Persons (Accessibility) Regulations No. 1 of 2006, which stipulated a three-year period, starting from 2006, to make public spaces accessible, there are many public buildings in Sri Lanka that are still not accessible. Given this lack of progress in implementation, there are serious doubts of the usefulness of such legislation in Sri Lanka.

The Compulsory Education Ordinance applies equally to all Sri Lankan children aged 5–14 years but

> [c]hildren who have more severe degrees of multiple disability and intellectual disability have no opportunities at all. The Education System, both state and private, lacks the expertise and the capacity to deal with these children. (Ministry of Social Welfare, 2003, pp. 16–17)

Furthermore, in general, there is little understanding or diagnosis and or support for learning disabilities in Sri Lanka. Wikremesooriya (2015), after analysing the case of 11 children with learning difficulties (two with ADHD, one with Down syndrome, one with epilepsy) at a community-based rehabilitation centre in rural Sri Lanka, writes: '[a]ll the students' parents had been requested by the administrators, to voluntarily remove their children from the school they attended, because they were deemed incapable of learning' (p. 65).

What is even more disturbing is the fact that seven of these children's conditions were undiagnosed meaning they will not receive the support they require in life. Dias (2015) reports that of her sample of 15 teachers, only 75% knew about learning disabilities (such as dyslexia) and nine out of the 15 teachers did not know how to help these learners, showing the importance of awareness raising as well as challenges faced by the Sri Lankan government.

4.4 *United Kingdom*

The Equality Act 2010 legally protects people from discrimination; it replaced the previous anti-discrimination laws (Sex Discrimination Act 1975, Race Relations Act 1976 and Disability Discrimination Act 1995) in a single Act. Under the Equality Act, age, disability, gender reassignment, marriage and civil partnership, pregnancy and maternity, race, religion or belief, sex and sexual orientation are the protected characteristics for which one cannot be discriminated against. As mentioned above, to be considered disabled there must be 'substantial' and 'long-term' negative effects on one's ability to do daily tasks. However, a person diagnosed with HIV infection, cancer or multiple sclerosis meets the disability criteria under the Equality Act from the day of diagnosis (HM Government, n.d.).

Access for persons with disabilities to education, employment, housing, goods and services and associations and private clubs are protected by the Equality Act and where there are barriers, providers are expected to make 'reasonable adjustments' (Citizens Advice, n.d.). For example, a university may not be expected to employ a British Sign Language interpreter in anticipation of catering to deaf students but it may be appropriate to anticipate deaf students' needs and install a hearing aid loop in lecture theatres (Equality and Human Rights Commission, 2014). If an organisation or individual(s) do not co-operate and place a person with disabilities at a substantial disadvantage, they can be prosecuted for unlawful discrimination under the Equality Act (Tyrer, 2011).

4.5 *United States*

American with Disabilities Act (ADA) was enacted in 1990 and is a comprehensive civil rights law that protects people with disabilities from being discriminated against (Department for Justice, 2010). The ADA Amendments Act 2008 made significant changes to the definition of 'disability' after a series of Supreme Court decisions narrowed the scope of protection for individuals with disabilities including people with epilepsy, muscular dystrophy and diabetes whom the ADA was meant to protect (Benfer, 2009).

The ADA has been successful in many cases in helping to improve access to higher education for learners with disabilities. Recent high-profile cases included cases against MIT, Harvard University and University of California, Berkeley (UC Berkeley). In one case, MIT and Harvard were sued over lack of closed captions on their material: online lectures, courses and podcasts and other educational materials made available to the public (Lewin, 2015). The MOOC platform edX, a not-for-profit online learning platform founded by MIT and Harvard, reached a settlement in 2015 with the US Department of Justice (DoJ) to make its platform more accessible under a four-year agreement (Lohman, 2015).

In 2016, the DoJ issued a letter to UC Berkeley, after a complaint about accessibility, stating that the content provided by the university in public platforms such as UC Berkeley's YouTube channel, iTunes U and MOOCs offered on edX (UC BerkeleyX) should be made accessible (US Department of Justice, 2016). The remedial action required the university to make its content accessible according to the WCAG 2.0 AA standard. However, in response to this, UC Berkeley announced that the university would remove public access to these materials as the remedial measures would be 'extremely expensive' (Public Affairs UC Berkeley, 2016). There has been a storm of social media reaction to this announcement with many criticising the DoJ but others attacking UC Berkeley. However, the result has been the removal of significant amounts of materials from public access and leaving it only available behind UC Berkeley authentication, thereby removing access from most people.

Cases such as this raise difficult ethical questions. If something is not accessible to a small proportion of the population, should that the majority lose their access to it in order to maintain equality?

For example, if a library or a museum was not accessible by wheelchair, this would be seen to be unacceptable since the expectation today is that these public places should be accessible to all. However, there are many public places, including many London underground stations, that are not accessible by wheelchair and which cannot be retrofitted for accessibility. Should these underground stations be closed for the public as they are not accessible? From an ethical perspective, should the same be applied to an online space of study? Was it the right decision by UC Berkeley to take down their OER content since it was not accessible to all? Would the library or the museum that is currently not accessible be expected to stay closed until it is made universally accessible? What could other possible solutions be to resolve the situation and make these resources available again?

One possible solution could be to request donations (or crowdfunding) or charge a nominal fee to raise money for the modifications required. However, in the case of UC Berkeley, because the resources are open to the world, it would be difficult to find an appropriate 'nominal fee' considering that over 900 million people globally live under the International Poverty Line of $1.90 a day (World Bank, 2015). Such an action replaces one access limitation – disability – with another, financial means.

In the case of UC Berkeley, speech-to-text software could be used to transcribe audio material and the student community (those using these OER) and/or volunteers' support could be sought to verify them. For example, software such as Synote[1] allows students who have a login to the system to edit transcripts if they notice a mistake. However, this model requires trust between the parties. On the other hand, if the software is hosted by a third party, the cost can remain a barrier as the cost is likely to increase in line with the number of user accounts.

5 Open Content and Accessibility

For their registered students, universities and other institutions largely comply with equality laws and make efforts to offer support to students with disabilities either by providing alternative materials or by providing additional support. This is possible for many institutions as such students qualify for special financial assistance through government schemes when they are directly enrolled students of the university. However, when an institution offers open access materials, it seems from the cases of edX and UC Berkeley mentioned above, that the institutions have not considered fully (if at all) access by those with disabilities.

OER can be created by anyone and shared online either in an OER repository or elsewhere. Open courses, such as MOOCs, on the other hand, are more likely to be institutional offerings. Therefore, there may not be a third party guaranteeing the quality of an OER – a situation similar to educational publications that are controlled by education publishers (Butcher, 2015). The mindset that 'one or more dedicated agencies should take full responsibility for assuring that OER shared in repositories online are of a high quality' (Butcher, 2015, p. 12) becomes practically impossible, masking 'the reality that the definition of quality is subjective and contextually dependent' and the 'responsibility for assuring the quality of OER used in teaching and learning environments will reside with the institution, programme/course coordinators, and individual educators responsible for delivery of education' (Butcher, 2015, p. 12).

Then the question arises: Who is responsible for the accessibility of OER and other freely available content?

OER content creators can range from learners through enthusiastic amateurs and professional educators, to world authorities on the topic. Of these, only the professional educators (and possibly the world authorities) are likely to belong to institutions with quality assurance standards including accessibility standards. If an individual creates an OER and makes it available, it is not covered under equality legislation such as the ADA; individuals are not required to comply. Any educator re-using an OER as part of a formal course at an educational institution would be required to add necessary accessibility support materials such as sign language interpretation and/or closed captions, but only where they have enrolled students with those specific needs. Although such materials often could then be contributed to the corpus of OER materials, there seems little evidence of such things happening in practice.

A learner discovering an OER on a subject of interest will have to determine for themselves whether the content is accessible to them. For example, some of the video content that the authors have accessed on the JISC store[2] OER repository had no metadata about accessibility. In the MERLOT[3] OER repository, there is an accessibility statement for the site, and within the advanced search facility a flag is provided to search for content that has an 'accessibility information form' which then gives an indication of how accessible the content is. However, only a very small fraction of OER in the repository have accessibility information (at the time of writing 451 resources have accessibility information out of some 80,000 in the repository), but it is clear from MERLOT's accessibility statements that they are working towards the goal of making OER more accessible in their repository.

However, as discussed above, when it is an institutional effort such as MIT's OCW, the institution was found to be held responsible for accessibility. But when individuals create and share their work as an OER, these are not governed by equality laws, even when they are shared in an OER repository maintained by an institution. Therefore, it becomes of paramount importance that educators producing materials are aware of the importance of accessibility and the challenges faced by learners with disabilities who wish to access these materials.

6 Introducing Khalid, Sophie, Arun and Chamari

In this section, fictitious learner personas are used as an aid to explore and tease out the complex issues surrounding accessibility. Personas were introduced by Cooper (1999) as a novel method for interaction design though they have long been in other use, for example in marketing. 'Personas help define the product by replacing the abstract, elastic user with the vibrant presence of a specific user who becomes a part of the design process' (Sinha, 2003, p. 830).

Using personas gives substance to the otherwise invisible and abstract user and allows examples to be provided with which the reader can empathise.

Khalid is a young and energetic 18-year-old who attends a higher education college just a few minutes' walk from his home. He is a keen swimmer and has represented his county for youth games. He is also into computers, spending much of his disposable income on new gadgets. His house is near a main road and recently Khalid had an accident crossing the road. Since this incident, Khalid is spending more time indoors as he is no longer confident to go out on his own. Khalid is deaf and primarily communicates using sign language, but he can understand others by lip-reading if the lighting is adequate. As Khalid has been spending a lot of time on the computer recently, he has learned to program in Python using various online resources.

Sophie is a 25-year-old trainee accountant in a large accounting firm working towards her professional qualification. She is very fond of music and can play quite a few instruments. She volunteers as a music teacher at the local nursing home for the elderly. Sophie has been living in a supported accommodation for a few years since partially losing her sight due to a degenerative condition. Her parents and sister visit her often and she enjoys going to concerts with them. However, she finds that it takes her much longer to do simple tasks at work because her colleagues do not produce accessible digital documents. She gets frustrated when she has to listen to her screen reader to read through a whole document when she is only interested in the accounts section. She cannot navigate directly to the required sections because the documents are not created using heading styles that can be picked up by her screen reader. Sophie has started to use screen reader at double speed to go through documents more quickly, but she wishes her colleagues would do more to support her.

Arun took early retirement at the age of 55 a few years ago due to multiple sclerosis. He now relies on his wheelchair and has given up his driver's license. Arun gets frustrated when websites' functions/menus require a mouse to operate. He finds it increasingly difficult to operate the mouse and uses keyboard navigation. Having been a software engineer, he is a competent IT user but his condition has progressed to the point where mouse control is impossible. Arun's adapted computer provides him much needed companionship as his mobility has decreased over time, thereby reducing his links to the community and events. He is keen to stay intellectually active but is unable to afford to register on costly courses.

Chamari is 45 years old and has always dreamed of becoming an early years' practitioner. Due to dyslexia, she has had a difficult time in school. She has been working as a childcare assistant at the local nursery for many years.

The nursery wants to promote Chamari as a childcare practitioner but she must complete her language and maths qualifications to gain the promotion. Chamari dreads the prospect of having to complete the exams.

7 Exploring Accessibility of Open Content with Khalid, Sophie, Arun and Chamari

Open access content can be presented using different media such as podcasts, videos and documents (with text and/or graphics). Accessing these materials will present different challenges to Khalid, Sophie, Arun and Chamari due to their very different disabilities.

Video is a popular media and since the emergence of free video sharing sites such as YouTube and Vimeo there has been an exponential growth in the availability of freely accessible video content, some of it with educational content. Khalid and Sophie will need support to access video materials due to their disabilities. Sophie will require video description while Khalid will need closed captions or sign language interpretation or as a minimum, a transcript. Khalid may still face a challenge even if the videos were accompanied by sign language interpretation, as an accessibility aid, because sign languages are not signed versions of the spoken language but completely separate natural languages. In particular, American Sign Language (ASL) and British Sign Language (BSL) are quite different, one having one-handed individual letter signs whereas the other uses two-handed individual letter signs, for example. Australian and New Zealand Sign Languages are sufficiently different to cause difficulties, while Irish Sign Language is more or less another separate language. So, while spoken materials from the US, UK, Australia, New Zealand or the Republic of Ireland are all likely to be in some mostly understandable variant of English, any particular sign language interpretation may not be useful to Khalid.

When accessing textual documents, for Sophie's assistive technologies to work properly, the documents need to have been created with accessibility in mind. This means, for example, using heading styles, alternative descriptions for non-text materials, meaningful table/figure names, typed text rather than scanned images or images of text, and information not communicated only using colour. Chamari, with her learning disability, will face different challenges accessing such a document. Like Sophie, Chamari may also require text-to-speech software which will need actual text, not images of text. Furthermore, spacing between lines and font choice are likely to make a document more or less accessible for Chamari (Bernard, Chaparro, Mills, & Halcomb, 2002).

8 Exploring Accessibility in Different Countries

The situation which would face each persona in Ghana, Japan, Sri Lanka, United Kingdom or the US is explored below, including any support/protection they might expect to receive in various scenarios for accessing open resources. These scenarios are based on accessing open resources as a defined element of a formal education (whether mainstream or as part of special educational provision); accessing open resources informally in order to enhance their engagement in a formal educational enrollment; or discovering resources for themselves in self-directed informal education.

If Khalid were to live in any of these five countries and encountered a problem accessing materials due to his disability: if it was part of his formal education there is legislation that requires the education provider to allow necessary adjustments. However, in Japan, where the legislation for inclusive education is relatively recent, educators may find this challenging due to the lack of experience catering for students with special needs (Forlin et al., 2015). In developing countries such as Ghana and Sri Lanka resources are often lacking to support such adjustments.

If Khalid is accessing an open course as part of his informal learning the situation will be different. If Khalid were a resident of Japan, the UK or the US, and the open course were offered by an institution in his home country, then he would be able to make a request under the appropriate legal framework to seek reasonable adjustments to the materials. On the other hand, if he were a resident in either Ghana or Sri Lanka it is unlikely that he would be able to find an open course offered by institutions in these countries as the vast majority of such courses are offered by institutions in developed nations.

In whichever country he lived there is little or no legislative support to overcome the difficulties Khalid faces with the learning materials if he was discovering open resources for his own independent learning needs.

For example, if Khalid were to access video content in a course, he would be able to request closed captions or transcript as a 'reasonable accommodation' under ADA in the US or as a 'reasonable adjustment' under the Equality Act in the UK. The provider of the educational material will be bound by law to make these adjustments. As already discussed, the US DoJ has taken legal action under the ADA against providers (such as MIT and Harvard) who had fallen short of their legal obligations. However, if Khalid was living in Sri Lanka, it would be much difficult for him to access materials not only due to Internet connectivity issues but also because there is no effective legal enforcement of the accessibility laws (Jayawardena, 2015). At the time of writing, there was no known precedent for an accessibility issue similar to Khalid's situation.

Sophie's situation is similar to Khalid's with respect to her needs and availability of support. If Sophie were to live either in the US or in the UK, she would also benefit from the ADA/Equality Act which strongly protect disabled individual's rights. She would require audio description to fully access video content. In Sri Lanka and Ghana, she may struggle if the education providers were not forthcoming with reasonable accommodations for her, in a situation similar to Khalid's, as the enforcement is not effective.

Chamari's situation is a little different. There are relatively few diagnosed cases of dyslexia in Japan. There is some dispute as to whether it is less common due to the nature of the language (Wydell & Butterworth, 1999; Yamada & Banks, 1994) although the lack of a standardised test has meant cases were not always identified. Consequently, there is likely to be less experience among Japanese educators to support Chamari's needs. Many misconceptions about dyslexia among educators in Ghana and Sri Lanka have been reported with a majority of teachers admitting that they didn't know how to support a pupil with dyslexia (Abraham, 2014; Dias, 2015)

Had Chamari lived in the US or the UK she would receive the additional support to complete her maths and language qualifications as dyslexia diagnosis and support is available in these countries. The legislation would apply in similar ways to Khalid's situation, which means that for informal learning she too would struggle to get the required support.

Arun is unlikely to attend a formal course and is the most likely candidate to rely on informal courses and other online resources such as OER or MOOCs. Given his disability, he would require content to be keyboard accessible. For example, drag and drop activities would have to be keyboard accessible or, if not, an alternative for such activity would have to be introduced. He is likely to be the least supported by the legislation because he is unlikely to be taking formal courses but relying on open resources. There might be accessibility provision for his situation, if he were accessing material offered by an institution in his own country (particularly if he is in the US) but otherwise wherever he is based there is no protection or support for him. Due to his isolated status, he may also suffer from bandwidth issues that prevent reliable access to the Internet whereas the other learners are able to travel (if necessary) to college or elsewhere with better access speeds (Liyanagunawardena, 2012).

This analysis shows that the support learners with disabilities receive varies considerably according to where they live. But how does this inequity manifest when the online space blurs national boundaries? What if OER are created by individuals rather than by institutions? While Khalid, Sophie, Arun and Chamari will be protected from discrimination in countries where there is strong protection for disabled individuals, they will suffer from accessibility issues if they access content from a provider in a different country who has not designed the content for accessibility. Therefore, this is not only a matter for law but also a matter of accessibility awareness.

Imagine if our learners were each to create an OER without being aware of each others' accessibility needs. They would be working within the constraints of their own disability, and not likely to use the functionality that they themselves have difficulty accessing. Let us consider how this may look. Khalid is likely to make his material more visual and unlikely to use audio because he will create resources that he will be able to access (for editing purposes as well as from his intent). Sophie, on the other hand, is likely to create more audio materials and is highly unlikely to create anything visual. This will mean that Khalid will not be able to hear Sophie's content and she will not be able to see his visual content. Chamari, on the other hand, is likely to make her materials visual with little text and a lot of colour. She may also use video and audio as these are more accessible to her than text. Sophie will find it difficult to access Chamari's visual content and Khalid will struggle to access the audio content Chamari is likely to create (quite possibly making all her material inaccessible to both, if it relies on interleaved audio and video). Arun would likely develop material which is primarily textual in nature, with limited visual layout, due to his limitation in using graphical interfaces. Chamari might find Arun's material hard to use, but Khalid and Sophie might well find it quite accessible.

This view of our learners' own content creation shows that unless designers are aware of the wide variety of disabilities and are knowledgeable about how to support them, they may not be able to create accessible materials. This possibility reiterates the importance of raising awareness of the span of disabilities that impact learners' access to material.

9 Accessibility Awareness

Educators around the world create content and share them as OER or other freely available content. They also teach learners face-to-face and online who may have declared disabilities, visible disabilities, or hidden disabilities. In face-to-face teaching, where one meets learners, there is more chance for educators to empathise with the needs of learners with disabilities and make reasonable adjustments to the way they teach. On the other hand, if educators are creating materials to be openly accessible, they do not 'see' their learners; hence, unless they are broadly aware of the wide-ranging accessibility needs and options they will not be able to create accessible resource(s).

Further, not all educators are aware of accessibility guidelines and/or standards/requirements, especially if the country in which they live does not have strongly enforced equality laws. This is where the open content such as OER and open courses become important tools to disseminate the message of accessibility. In particular, awareness of Universal Design concepts may be crucial to improving the accessibility of content for those with disabilities and may improve the quality of the material for learners without disabilities as well. Ensuring that important elements are highlighted in multiple ways including, text, colour and graphics, for example, means that not only is material accessible to those with a specific disability, but that its importance will be recognised by all learners.

10 Open Content to Support Open to Inclusion

Open courses such as MOOCs have shown phenomenal uptake with Coursera, at the time of writing (September 2018), boasting 35 million registered learners while edX reports over 14 million learners. Even though MOOCs were originally North American-centric, they are now offered on a variety of platforms, hosted in many different countries, and offered in many different languages – for example, the Spanish/Portuguese platform Miriada X, the European MOOC platform Emma, and the Arabic MOOC platform Edraak. Many non-American and non-European educational institutions have joined major MOOC platforms; for example, South African, Indian, Taiwanese, and Argentinian providers have joined Coursera; Egyptian, Indian, Saudi Arabian (Islamic Research and Training Institute), and Colombian institutions have joined edX. The power of open courses to disseminate information is endless: for example, Liyanagunawardena and Aboshady (2017) presented a convincing case showing how MOOCs can be used to 'fulfil the unmet training needs of the health sector in developing countries.' Similarly, open courses can become an invaluable tool to raise accessibility awareness.

At present, there are already many open courses designed to educate about issues of accessibility, offered on various platforms. These courses are usually aimed at a wide audience and do not require prior knowledge, making them ideal for awareness-raising around the world on issues of accessibility. 'Professional Web Accessibility Auditing made easy' offered by Ryerson University and '(HE) Accessibility: designing and teaching courses for all learners' offered by Buffalo State, The State University of New York and SUNY's Empire State College on the Canvas platform are good examples of such awareness-raising open courses. Similarly, OER repositories such as MERLOT are endeavouring to promote accessibility in OER. However, the advice available as to how to create open resources that are accessible is not easy to find.

The community plays an important role in open courses, open content creation and support. For example, in many MOOCs, especially in FutureLearn courses, the community of learners supports each other (FutureLearn, n.d.) as the educators are unable to provide individual support for learners in such large classes. Another such example is the Coursera's Global Translator Community (Coursera, n.d.) which consists of more than 25,000 Coursera learners, fluent in various languages. They translate Coursera course videos into more than 65 languages by creating subtitles. Creating such communities of accessibility champions would raise awareness of accessibility issues. Most importantly, learners such as Arun who misses involvement with his local community may have time to spare and may be willing to get involved in online communities. Given Arun's expertise as a software engineer and his experience as a learner with disabilities, he could take a leading role in such initiatives providing accessibility testing and advice.

11 Conclusion

Learners with disabilities already face many problems in accessing education but the increased provision of open resources may or may not benefit this group of learners. As explored above using representative fictional personas situated in developing and developed countries, the difficulties faced by many learners with disabilities can easily mean that the expanding provision of open resources can increase educational inequality between learners *with* disabilities and those *without*, much as the provision of online learning in Sri Lanka benefited richer urban students more than poorer rural students (Liyanagunawardena, Adams, Rassool, & Williams, 2014), thus widening urban/rural educational inequality.

Legislation in some countries theoretically requires the provision of equal access for many disabled learners. However, the level of enforcement of such legislation varies in different countries, resulting in unequal opportunities for disabled learners globally. In some cases, such as UC Berkeley, the enforcement of accessibility requirements has resulted in the wholesale withdrawal of some institutionally produced and/or distributed open resources.

While there is much more support for learners with disabilities in formal education, especially in developed countries, there is very little support, if any at all, for them in informal learning around the world. The development of tools to automate, or ease, the provision of accessible learning material could be very helpful in allowing access to this content. The Web accessibility guidelines mentioned in the introduction, for example, are supported by toolkits developed by various organisations such as the US Association of Research Libraries.[4]

Research into accessibility issues and open resources tends to concentrate on MOOCs and routinely concludes that work is at the early stages (Iniesto, McAndrew, Minocha, & Coughlan, 2017a). MOOCs in general are created by institutions with the support of the platform provider, while OER can be created by individuals without such support. As such the creators of MOOCs are likely to have some access to support to meet quality assurance requirements in their institutions and beyond (for example the QAA in the UK), while the creators of OER may not have such help. Without suitable guidance and support, resultant resources may be inaccessible for learners with certain disabilities. Educating resource designers and creators can help to alleviate this possibility. Currently, there are some open courses available that address these issues and some tools that can be used to identify and highlight accessibility issues, though they may not offer solutions.

The real promise of making content accessible lies with the community rather than individual creators. There are examples of a community of learners producing sub-titles in over 65 different languages. If similar community action can be harnessed in helping to create accessible open content and to convert inaccessible content to an accessible form, then learners with disabilities like those of our fictional personas – Khalid, Sophie, Arun and Chamari – will be much more likely to be able to find usable resources that will enhance their potential learning success.

Acknowledgement

The authors would like to thank Asma Hussain for her comments on an earlier version of this chapter.

Notes

1 http://synote.com/
2 https://store.jisc.ac.uk/, previously Jorum.
3 https://www.merlot.org
4 Available at http://accessibility.arl.org/

References

Abraham, D. E. (2014). *Teachers' knowledge and beliefs about dyslexia: A survey of pilot inclusive schools in the Effutu district* (Unpublished BSc dissertation). Ashesi University College, Accra, Ghana.

Adams, R. (2016, August 31). *Why has Japan's massacre of disabled people gone unnoticed?* Retrieved from http://www.independent.co.uk/voices/japan-disability-rights-massacre-tsukui-yamayuriena-gone-unnoticed-a7217661.html

Asakura, M. (2014). Prohibition of Discrimination against Persons with disabilities in employment. *Waseda Bulletin of Comparative Law, 34*. Retrieved from http://www.waseda.jp/folaw/icl/assets/uploads/2016/02/d08da3c0259ba3ee3cefdf2d7cbb76e5.pdf

Asuncion, J. V., Fichten, C. S., Ferraro, V., Chwojka, C., Barile, M., Nguyen, M. N., & Wolforth, J. (2010). Multiple perspectives on the accessibility of e-learning in Canadian colleges and universities. *Assistive Technology®, 22*(4), 187–199.

Atkins, D. E., Brown, J. S., & Hammond, A. L. (2007). *A review of the Open Educational Resources (OER) movement: Achievements, challenges, and new opportunities.* Report to The William and Flora Hewlett Foundation. Retrieved from https://www.hewlett.org/wp-content/uploads/2016/08/ReviewoftheOERMovement.pdf

Awadzi, H. (2016, April 28). *Ghana's disability act: Serious gaps.* Retrieved from http://globaldisability.org/2016/04/28/ghana-disability-act

Bates, A. W. (2005). *Technology, e-learning and distance education* (2nd ed.). Abingdon: Routledge.

Benfer, A. (2009). *The ADA amendments act: An overview of recent changes to the Americans with disabilities act.* American Constitution Society for Law and Policy. Retrieved from https://www.acslaw.org/sites/default/files/Benfer_ADAAA.pdf

Bernard, M. L., Chaparro, B. S., Mills, M. M., & Halcomb, C. G. (2002). Examining children's reading performance and preference for different computer-displayed text. *Behaviour & Information Technology, 21*(2), 87–96.

Brown, J. S., & Adler, R. P. (2008, January/February). Minds on fire: Open education, the long tail, and learning 2.0. *EDUCAUSE Review*, 16–32.

Burgstahler, S. E. (2015a). *Universal design in higher education: From principles to practice.* Cambridge, MA: Harvard Education Press.

Burgstahler, S. E. (2015b). Opening doors or slamming them shut? Online learning practices and students with disabilities. *Social Inclusion, 3*(6). http://dx.doi.org/10.17645/si.v3i6.420

Butcher, N. (2015). *A basic guide to Open Educational Resources (OER) UNESCO & commonwealth of learning.* Retrieved from http://unesdoc.unesco.org/images/0021/002158/215804e.pdf

Butcher, N., & Moore, A. (2015). *Understanding open educational resources* (S. Mishra, Ed.). British Columbia: Commonwealth of Learning. Retrieved from https://oerknowledgecloud.org/sites/oerknowledgecloud.org/files/2015_Butcher_Moore_Understanding-OER.pdf

Butler, B. (2012). Massive open online courses: Legal and policy issues for research libraries. *Association of Research Libraries*, 2012, 1–15.

Case, D. E., & Davidson, R. C. (2011). Accessible online learning. *New Directions for Student Services, 134*, 47–58.

Castells, M. (2000). *The rise of network society* (2nd ed.). Oxford: Blackwell.

Citizens Advice. (n.d.). *Duty to make reasonable adjustments for disabled people.* Retrieved from https://www.citizensadvice.org.uk/law-and-courts/discrimination/what-are-the-different-types-of-discrimination/duty-to-make-reasonable-adjustments-for-disabled-people/

Commonwealth of Learning. (2015). *Guidelines for Open Educational Resources (OER) in higher education.* Paris: UNESCO & Commonwealth of Learning. Retrieved from http://unesdoc.unesco.org/images/0021/002136/213605e.pdf

Cooper, A. (1999). *The inmates are running the asylum.* Indianapolis, IN: Sams.

Coursera. (n.d.). *Coursera community – Get involved.* Retrieved from http://www.coursera.community/#gtc

Department of Justice. (2010). *Americans with disabilities act of 1990, as amended.* Retrieved from https://www.ada.gov/pubs/adastatute08.pdf

Dias, S. Y. (2015, December 3–4). *A study of the teachers' role in educating slow learners in primary schools in Sri Lanka*, Paper presented at Faculty of Arts International Research Conference, Colombo, Sri Lanka. Retrieved from http://archive.cmb.ac.lk:8080/research/handle/70130/4394

Downes, S. (2011, July 14). *Open educational resources: A definition.* Retrieved from http://halfanhour.blogspot.com/2011/07/open-educational-resources-definition.html

Equality Act 2010. (2010). Retrieved from http://www.legislation.gov.uk/ukpga/2010/15/pdfs/ukpga_20100015_en.pdf

Equality and Human Rights Commission. (2014, April 1). *What equality law means for you as an education provider – Further and higher education.* Retrieved from https://www.equalityhumanrights.com/sites/default/files/what_equality_law_means_for_you_as_an_education_provide_further_and_higher_education.pdf

Fichten, C. S., Asuncion, J., & Scapin, R. (2014). Digital technology, learning, and post-secondary students with disabilities: Where we've been and where we're going. *Journal of Postsecondary Education and Disability, 27*(4), 369–379.

Fichten, C. S., Ferraro, V., Asuncion, J. V., Chwojka, C., Barile, M., Nguyen, M. N., ... Wolforth, J. (2009). Disabilities and e-learning problems and solutions: An exploratory study. *Journal of Educational Technology & Society, 12*(4), 241.

Fini, A. (2009). The technological dimension of a massive open online course: The case of the CCK08 course tools. *The International Review of Research in Open and Distance Learning, 10*(5). Retrieved from http://www.irrodl.org/index.php/irrodl/article/view/643/1410

Forlin, C., Kawai, N., & Higuchi, S. (2015). Educational reform in Japan towards inclusion: Are we training teachers for success? *International Journal of Inclusive Education, 19*(3), 314–331. doi:10.1080/13603116.2014.930519

FutureLearn. (n.d.). *Why FutureLearn is an effective way to learn.* Retrieved from https://www.futurelearn.com/using-futurelearn/why-it-works

Government of Ghana. (2006). *Persons with disability act 2006 act 715.* Retrieved from http://www.gfdgh.org/GHANA%20DISABILITY%20ACT.pdf

Hill, H. (2013). Disability and accessibility in the library and information science literature: A content analysis. *Library & Information Science Research, 35*(2), 137–142.

HM Government. (n.d). *Definition of disability under the equality act 2010.* Retrieved from https://www.gov.uk/definition-of-disability-under-equality-act-2010

Iniesto, F., McAndrew, P., Minocha, S., Coughlan, T. (2017a, April 5–6). *How can MOOCs be more accessible?* Presented at OER17: The Politics of Open, London. Retrieved from http://oro.open.ac.uk/50679/

Iniesto, F., McAndrew, P., Minocha, S., & Coughlan, T. (2017b). What are the expectations of disabled learners when participating in a MOOC? In *Proceedings of the 4th ACM Conference on Learning@ Scale* (pp. 225–228).

Jayawardena, D. S. R. (2015, August 27–28). *Protection of the rights of the people with disabilities in Sri Lanka need for new legislation* (pp. 167–171). Proceedings of 8th International Research Conference, General Sir John Kotelawala Defence University.

Japan International Cooperation Agency. (2002). *Country profile on disability, democratic socialist republic of Sri Lanka.* Retrieved http://siteresources.worldbank.org/DISABILITY/Resources/Regions/South%20Asia/JICA_SriLanka.pdf

Kent, M. (2015). Disability and eLearning: Opportunities and barriers. *Disability Studies Quarterly, 35*(1). http://dx.doi.org/10.18061/dsq.v35i1.3815

Królak, A., Chen, W., Sanderson, N. C., & Kessel, S. (2017). The accessibility of MOOCs for blind learners. In *Proceedings of the 19th International ACM SIGACCESS Conference on Computers and Accessibility* (pp. 401–402). ACM.

Lane, A. (2012). Widening participation in higher education through open educational resources. In A. Okada, T. Connolly, & P. J. Scott (Eds.), *Collaborative learning 2.0: Open educational resources* (pp. 1–15). Hershey, PA: IGI Global.

Lewin, T. (2015, February 12). Harvard and M.I.T. are sued over lack of closed captions. *The New York Times.* Retrieved from https://www.nytimes.com/2015/02/13/education/harvard-and-mit-sued-over-failing-to-caption-online-courses.html

Liyanagunawardena, T. R. (2012). *Information communication technologies and distance education in Sri Lanka: A case study of two universities* (Unpublished doctoral dissertation). University of Reading, Reading, UK.

Liyanagunawardena, T. R., Adams, A. A., Rassool, N., & Williams, S. A. (2014). Developing government policies for distance education: Lessons learnt from two Sri Lankan case studies. *International Review of Education, 60*(6), 821–839. doi:10.1007/s11159-014-9442-0.

Liyanagunawardena, T. R., Adams, A. A., & Williams, S. A. (2013). MOOCs: A systematic study of the published literature 2008–2012. *The International Review of Research in Open and Distributed Learning, 14*(3), 202–227.

Liyanagunawardena, T. R., & Aboshady, O. A. (2017). Massive open online courses: A resource for health education in developing countries. *Global Health Promotion, 25*(3). doi:10.1177/1757975916680970

Liyanagunawardena, T. R., & Hussain, A. (2017). Online distance education materials and accessibility: Case study of university college of estate management. In G. Vincenti, A., Bucciero, M., Helfert, & M., Glowatz (Eds.), *E-learning, e-education, and online training: Third International Conference, eLEOT 2016, Dublin, Ireland, August 31 – September 2, Revised Selected Papers*, (pp. 79–86), Switzerland: Springer International Publishing. doi:10.1007/978-3-319-49625-2_10

Liyanagunawardena, T. R., Lundqvist, K. O., & Williams, S. A. (2015). Massive open online courses and sustainability. *European Journal of Open Distance and E-Learning*. Retrieved from http://www.eurodl.org/index.php?p=archives&year=2015&halfyear=2&article=709

Lohman, T. (2015, April 9). *EdX settles inaccessible online courses case*. Retrieved from http://www.accessiq.org/news/news/2015/04/edx-settles-inaccessible-online-courses-case

Ministry of Social Welfare. (2003). *National policy on disability for Sri Lanka*. Retrieved from http://socialemwelfare.gov.lk/web/images/content_image/pdf/legislation/disability_policy.pdf

Navarrete, R., & Luján-Mora, S. (2013). Accessibility considerations in learning objects and open educational resources. In *Proceedings of the 6th International Conference of Education, Research and Innovation* (pp. 521–530).

Oxford Dictionaries. (n.d.). *Definition of disability in English*. Retrieved from https://en.oxforddictionaries.com/definition/disability

Parton, B. S. (2016). Video captions for online courses: Do youtube's auto-generated captions meet deaf students' needs? *Journal of Open Flexible and Distance Learning, 20*(1), 8–18.

Public Affairs UC Berkeley. (2016, September 13). *A statement on online course content and accessibility*. Retrieved from http://news.berkeley.edu/2016/09/13/a-statement-on-online-course-content-and-accessibility/

Seale, J., Georgeson, J., Christoforos, M., & Swain, J. (2015). Not the right kind of 'digital capital'? An examination of the complex relationship between disabled students, their technologies and higher education institutions. *Computers & Education, 82*, 118–128.

Sinha, R. (2003). Persona development for information-rich domains. In *Proceeding of CHI EA '03 CHI '03 extended abstracts on human factors in computing systems* (pp. 830–831). doi:10.1145/765891.766017

The World Bank. (2015, September 15). *FAQs: Global poverty line update*. Retrieved from http://www.worldbank.org/en/topic/poverty/brief/global-poverty-line-faq

Tyrer, A. (2011, January 2). *Who is liable under the equality act*. Retrieved from http://www.stammeringlaw.org.uk/discrimination/wholiable.htm

UNESCO. (2017). *What are Open Educational Resources (OERs)?* Retrieved from http://www.unesco.org/new/en/communication-and-information/access-to-knowledge/open-educational-resources/what-are-open-educational-resources-oers/

Uno, A., Wydell, T. N., Haruhara, N., Kaneko, M., & Shinya, N. (2009). Relationship between reading/writing skills and cognitive abilities among Japanese primary-school children: Normal readers versus poor readers (dyslexics). *Reading and Writing, 22*(7), 755–789. doi:10.1007/s11145-008-9128-8

US Department of Justice. (2016, August 30). Re: The United States' findings and conclusions based on its investigation under title II of the Americans with disabilities act of the University of California at Berkeley, DJ No. 204-11-309. Retrieved from https://www.ada.gov/briefs/uc_berkley_lof.pdf

W3C. (2005). *Introduction to web accessibility*. Retrieved from https://www.w3.org/WAI/intro/accessibility.php

W3C. (2018). *Understanding WCAG 2.1*. Retrieved from https://www.w3.org/WAI/WCAG21/Understanding/

Wickremesooriya, S. F. (2015). Teaching children with learning difficulties via community-based rehabilitation projects in rural Sri Lanka. *Disability, CBR and Inclusive Development, 26*(4), 53–81.

Wydell, T. K., & Butterworth, B. (1999). A case study of an English-Japanese bilingual with monolingual dyslexia. *Cognition, 70*, 273–305.

Yamada, J., & Banks, A. (1994). Evidence for and characteristics of dyslexia among Japanese children. *Annals of Dyslexia, 44*(1), 103–119.

Zaphiris, P., & Ellis, R. D. (2001, October 23–27). Website usability and content accessibility of the top USA universities. In *Proceedings of WebNet 2001 Conference*, Orlando, Florida (pp. 1380–1385).

CHAPTER 8

Opening Educators' Social Learning Ecologies: Conceptualizing Professional Learning across Public and Private Boundaries

Kristin M. Rouleau and Jeremiah H. Kalir

For years, the professional lives of many classroom educators have been stretched across public and private contexts, leading to conflict, incoherence, and, at times, a privatization of teaching practice. Despite varied and ongoing reform efforts in the United States, many aspects of teachers' pedagogy, peer networks, technology use, and professional development have become situated at the nexus of intersecting public and private boundaries; teachers are expected to navigate open and closed systems, to be connected while remaining isolated, and to collaborate in innovative ways while being held individually accountable for conventional standards. To better understand public, private, and deprivatized dimensions associated with educator practice – and to ascertain the promise of more open educational practices and educator learning opportunities as a response to such boundary-crossings – this chapter suggests that a *social learning ecology* (SLE) (Ching, Santo, Hoadley, & Peppler, 2014) is a useful framework affording expansive and open learning pathways for educators. Educator SLEs are comprised of the people, places, technologies, and resources that educators access and connect with as they learn and develop their teaching practices. Conceptually, educator SLEs are understood from an ecological perspective on learning which posits that learners influence and are influenced by interactions with other people, proximal and distal learning resources, and their preferred modes of communication, sharing, and participation (Barron, 2004, 2006). In light of varied and increasingly public commitments to open educational movements and practices (Cronin, 2017; Jhangiani & Biswas-Diener, 2017), it is prudent to interrogate the range of public and private boundaries endemic to educators' professional lives by mapping the distributed ecologies of social relations, resources, and settings relevant to educators and their professional agency.

In this chapter, we are interested in more open or *deprivatized* educational practices, such as elements of teaching and learning that are accessible to different publics for observation and critical review by invitation or context. We contrast open educational practices with private practices, or those practices

 | DOI: 10.1163/9789004422988_009

which are not openly shared due to cultural norms, individual choices, proximity, or other factors, such as sociopolitical contexts, security of employment, and social group membership. Notably, individual educators' practices may waver along a continuum of deprivatized (or open) and private depending on context, the nature of the practice, or lack of recognition that a continuum across public and private boundaries exists. By conceptualizing and describing educator SLEs, we assert that educators can name, access, and more purposefully navigate newly articulated open learning pathways so as to deprivatize – and more openly share – their practices. This chapter presents key concepts related to educator SLEs, offers a theoretical framework for educator SLEs, and describes how educators might use such a construct to better understand, access, and navigate public-private tensions and open their practices, becoming increasingly deprivatized.

Why are we motivated to discuss and describe educator SLEs? Consider, for example, how public and private boundaries influence educator social capital and connectedness (Bridwell-Mitchell & Cooc, 2016) as but one indicator of engagement with open educational practice. Imagine an early career educator who received her teaching license via an alternative certification program and teaches in an under-resourced urban school. Each morning, after her students arrive, she, like most teachers in the school, literally – and figuratively – closes the door to her 7th grade geometry classroom. Closing the door is partly habit and part cultural norm. The closed door allows for a quieter learning environment for students by limiting distractions from an often disruptive hallway. Yet it also places a barrier to informal observation by veteran peers. Among colleagues at school, she has forged little social capital, whereas via public social networks, like Twitter, she is able to openly share about teaching, learn about new strategies, and gather resources (Carpenter & Krutka, 2015; Rehm & Notten, 2016). She knows it is beneficial to connect students' lives and interests from outside of school with activities inside her classroom (Garcia, 2014). Through the social capital and connectedness of a digital network, this novice educator has expanded her repertoire of teaching strategies to better connect teaching and learning opportunities across formal and informal, community and classroom boundaries (Ito et al., 2013). Professional learning, for this educator, means building social capital outside the immediacy of her workplace. Indeed, she has experienced stronger connectedness with educators in her distributed social network than with colleagues down the hall.

As another scenario about open practice and professional learning, consider a different set of public and private boundaries that a team of fifth grade educators traverse as they engage in continuous improvement. These educators are focused on responsiveness to student needs and are eager to collaborate about effective instructional practices and lesson designs. These educators routinely open their classrooms to one another for informal peer observations. This requires that they make themselves vulnerable as they work through challenging situations, and that they openly admit when they have not been successful. They maintain a grade-level website for shared resources, and willingly invite their principal and building literacy coach to observe lessons and offer feedback, trusting that both understand how the team is adapting the district's curriculum to meet learner needs. With their trusted colleagues, these educators confidently open their classrooms. However, they also close their doors, take fewer risks, and superficially adhere to district-produced curricula and pacing documents when district or state administrators enter the building or request student achievement data. Years of experience, as well as a steadfast commitment to meet their students' needs and protect aspects of their students' privacy, lead these educators to share only what they believe outside leaders want to see. Thus, in response to the political context of their school district, they do not openly discuss efforts to innovate beyond their school walls.

These hypothetical examples illustrate tensions and opportunities of open educational practices within real-world constraints; as educators move across a continuum of public and private boundaries, where, with whom, and how do they open their practice in service of both professional and student learning? As professionals cross and blur boundaries, they encounter unfamiliar territory, engage in fluid identity construction, and synthesize 'ideas, concepts, and instruments from seemingly unrelated domains into the domain of focal inquiry' (Engestrom, Engestrom, & Karkkainen, 1995, p. 321; see also Akkerman & Bakker, 2011; Trent, 2013). While educators, like those in the previous two scenarios, can be proactive in finding needed ideas and supports in different contexts, like face-to-face and digital communities (Vescio, Ross, & Adams, 2008), the fluidity, conflict, and risk endemic to both situations is neither uncommon nor unrealistic. Norms of privacy in schools often do not support educators in reaching out to peers for substantive conversation (Coburn, Mata, & Choi, 2013). Privatized educational practice – or a closed stance toward openly sharing aspects of professional knowledge and knowhow – can, in part, be traced to the compartmentalized nature of the school itself (Boreen & Niday, 2000), and a longstanding norm of educator isolation coupled with high degrees of autonomy and limited opportunities for collaboration (Mawhinney, 2008). Historically, educators have struggled to share their expertise and challenges with peers, and are seldom fully aware of their colleagues' strengths, areas for growth, and beliefs about teaching and learning. Information about colleagues' teaching practice is often gathered second-hand and is typically incomplete, filtered, and presented in such a way as to not expose vulnerabilities. Given the choice between working in isolation, as with a closed-door policy inside school, or engaging in more public and open collaboration with a (distributed) peer network, it is understandable that educators who crave a more open learning environment may look beyond their immediate school colleagues for professional learning networks across settings (e.g., Duncan-Howell, 2010; Krutka, Carpenter, & Trust, 2016). At the same time, shifting public and private boundaries across both physical and digital spaces may result in educators strategically limiting access to their classrooms, students, and evidence of learning as a means to limit surveillance and maintain classroom-level decision-making, suggesting contested and complex qualities are associated with professional learning communities (Watson, 2014). Educators differentially experience tensions associated with who gets to participate – free of personal or professional risk – in certain open learning opportunities and arrangements.

These two scenarios suggest that public-private tensions associated with teaching practices, participation across professional settings, use of tools, and social relations collectively position educators in contrived and contested open configurations. Who are the publics in these scenarios – students and their families, or educators in the same school, or educators in a shared social network, or the taxpayers who fund public schools? What are the benefits of privacy in these scenarios – for student learning, for the design of learning environments, or for educator risk-taking and reflection on their teaching practice? And what are the boundaries, both known and unknown that educators traverse if inclined to open their teaching practices? Amidst the difficulty of navigating public-private tensions, educators are often forced to eschew consent – over curricula and what they teach, or over the use of certain technologies, or over the transparency of data (or lack thereof). Through no fault of their own, the limited capacity of educators to name – much less access and navigate – pathways through public-private tensions can lead to limited or superficial educator agency (Webb, 2006). As one response, we suggest there is a need to conceptualize and describe how educator SLEs can help to shape both their practices and their own professional development. This chapter advances an ecological orientation toward open education, or a perspective on openness that is responsive to the ways in which teaching practice, tool use, and personal and professional interest flow across distributed social relations and settings.

This chapter will explore theory, literature, and professional commitments associated with SLEs as a framework relevant to deprivatizing and opening educator practice. We adapt the construct and definition of a SLE from the youth development literature (Ching et al., 2014), and suggest educator SLEs are an assemblage of individuals, material resources, knowledge-building practices, technologies, and other proximal and distal supports that span multiple settings and can sustain open educational practices. First, we will interpret educational openness from an ecological perspective on learning (Barron, 2004) and educator development (Jurow, Tracy, Hotchkiss, & Kirshner, 2012), complemented by a review of literature about deprivatizing educator practice, collaboration arrangements, and educator networks. Second, we will present a theoretical framework for educator SLEs, and will describe how educators might use such a construct to map, access, and navigate public-private tensions. Key to our framework is an articulation and multiple visual representations of the ways in which teaching practice can span material and digital settings, how educators may connect with peers to support their interest-driven and professional learning, and the ways in which material, technological, and conceptual resources are accessed and utilized across public and private contexts. Finally, our chapter concludes with a discussion about the importance of defining and mapping educator SLEs, implications for the design of professional development, and the role an educator's SLE can play in navigating pathways across public and private boundaries toward more open professional practices.

1 Open as Ecological Perspectives on Teaching and Educator Learning

As Cronin (2017) suggests, 'Engaging with the complexity and contextuality of openness is vitally important if we wish to be keepers not only of openness but also of hope, equality, and justice' (p. 11). The previously described public and private boundaries crisscrossing learning environments indicate that the complexity and contextuality of openness can constrain the capacity of educators to be such equity-oriented 'keepers' for their students, colleagues, and also for broader publics. New models of – and strategies engendering – openness are necessary so as to address deeply rooted tensions in the professional lives of educators, and to also deprivatize teaching practices. As a novel contribution to ongoing developments in both open pedagogy (DeRosa & Jhangiani, 2017) and open education (Havemann, 2016), we suggest ecological learning perspectives are a promising means of engaging with the complexity and contextuality of openness in teaching and educator learning.

Ecological perspectives on learning and development, while not new (Beach, 1999; Bronfenbrenner, 1979), have recently garnered renewed interest given research suggesting connections among formal schooling and informal, out-of-school, and interest-driven learning contribute to more equitable learning environments and outcomes (Bevan, Bell, Stevens, & Razfar, 2013;

Greenhow, Robelia, & Hughes, 2009; Ito et al., 2013). Such connections emerge due to the ways in which individuals move across learning ecologies, or 'the set of contexts found in physical or virtual spaces that provide opportunities for learning' (Barron, 2006, p. 195). These settings can include a learner's home, school, community, work, and neighborhood, as well as distributed resources such as online environments and social networks. Each of these settings is also 'comprised of configurations of activities, material resources and relationships' (Barron, 2004, p. 6). From an ecological perspective, Putnam and Borko (2000) suggest educator learning may be situated amongst classroom, school, discourse, and technology-mediated settings. By emphasizing the importance of 'examin[ing] more closely the question of where to situate teachers' learning' (p. 12), they challenge educators, teacher educators, and researchers to redefine how educators learn, and what educators come to know and do when their professional learning spans settings. Our interest in open educator learning and deprivatized teaching practice is motivated by growing research about how adults, whether driven by interest or professional responsibility, pursue learning opportunities across distributed ecologies of settings that are embodied and digital, saturated with material and ideational resources, and are supported by peer relations (Garcia, 2014; Hollett & Kalir, 2017; Krutka, Carpenter, & Trust, 2016).

In embracing an ecological perspective on learning, we find that three themes in the literature about teaching and educator professional learning demonstrate the relevance of a distributed, socially situated, and technologically-mediated interpretation of educational openness. Our interest in deprivatizing practice, collaboration arrangements, and educator networking collectively glimpse ecological aspects of open education and open educator learning. We consider these trends in the literature of central importance to a fuller articulation of why ecological perspectives are necessary for opening educators' professional learning pathways.

2 Deprivatizing Practice

Historic and contemporary efforts to deprivatize – or open – teaching practice suggest an ecological perspective on open education may be generative for educators, their colleagues, and their schools. Decades of education reform, driven both from top-down mandate and bottom-up advocacy, have privileged the creation of more open learning environments across varied settings (i.e. classroom vs. school) and scales (i.e. school vs. district), through experimentation with pedagogical configurations (Fullan & Langworthy, 2014; Scott, 2015), team and collaborative teaching structures (Meehan, 1973), shared responsibility for smaller 'houses' of students within larger schools (Cotton, 1996), and the open classroom models and architecture of the 1960s and 1970s (Cuban, 2004.) More recently, efforts to support and sustain professional learning communities, defined as a team of educators who regularly engage in focused, active learning to improve their professional practice in service to student learning (Hord, 2009), have been interpreted as an effort to create more open connections among educators about their teaching practices. DuFour (2004) advocated that professional learning communities galvanize intentional efforts to deprivatize – and open – teaching and create collaborative educator and school cultures focused on student learning. Deprivatized educational practices may include shared activities related to how educators work together and conduct their classes, share lessons, or plan common projects (Kougioumtzis & Patriksson, 2009). Other examples of activities leading to deprivatized educational practices include the use of protocols for transparent and shared decision-making, and systematic record-keeping to inform colleagues about one another's work (Vescio, Ross, & Adams, 2006).

A persistent challenge to open education may be a tendency for formal schooling to reinforce the privatization or, at best, the guarded openness of teaching practices (Kougioumtzis & Patriksson, 2009; Webb, 2006). Professional learning commitments, educator collaborative practices, and even a school's built-environment can contribute to educator isolation and privatized – rather than open – practice. Boreen and Niday (2000), for instance, identified the compartmentalized nature of typical educational settings as a barrier for opening educator practice. Similarly, Mawhinney (2008) reported that educators' physical and collegial isolation results in high degrees of teacher autonomy, which may yield less teacher collaboration. Watson (2014) has also suggested that increased collaboration can actually result in the purposeful creation of boundaries in an effort to reduce oversight and surveillance, thereby intentionally privatizing some aspects of practice. Moreover, we recognize that accountability reforms promising greater transparency and accessibility, and whether oriented toward the individual or the institution, may counterproductively perpetuate a culture of surveillance and create additional barriers to open practice.

Efforts to encourage formal collaboration among educators, such as highly structured professional collaboration meetings and professional learning workshops, can also deprivatize educator practice. For example, when collaboration leads to educators developing shared values and practices, positive outcomes may include educators increasing their use of new pedagogical approaches and a renewed commitment to teaching all students. In other circumstances, an educator's open educational practice may mean fostering shared experience, vulnerability, and transparency among a group of colleagues (Little, 2002; Levine & Marcus, 2010). Research has also shown that implementing an instructional coach program, for instance, can make targeted, deprivatized discourse about pedagogy part of regular professional learning conversations, and may also serve to publicize educators' areas of expertise (Coburn et al., 2013). Yet it would be short-sighted in a discussion of collaboration to not consider the role of individual and incentivized competition as educators become increasingly open to sharing their practices. A climate focused on individual performance is frequently the rewarded norm, reflecting prominent cultural and institutional narratives about accomplishment and effectiveness. However, it stands that – in an ideal scenario – aspects of competition and collaboration may work in concert to support educator learning and deprivatized practice (Webster, 2015). Whether via reforms like professional learning communities, or through the removal of physical barriers separating classrooms, we suggest that ecological interpretations of open education evidence the potential to deprivatize teaching practice.

3 Collaboration Arrangements

Collaboration – whether formal, informal, or improvisational – has long been promoted as a primary means of facilitating educator and school improvement efforts (Levine & Marcus, 2010; Little, 2002). Collaboration can reduce the privatization of educator practice and yield more openness among educators who may benefit from these efforts to improve teaching and learning. Whether under the guise of professional learning communities, peer networks, or communities of practice (DuFour, 2004; Hord, 2009; Lave & Wenger, 1991), more formally structured approaches to educator collaboration have, in some cases, garnered a collective sense of efficacy as a result of educators working together to affect educational change (Goddard, Tschannen-Moran, & Hoy, 2001). Such mandated collaboration – despite invariable tension associated with individual and collective agency – has been embraced by many schools and districts, with some systems establishing protocols for extending collaboration across settings and linking support mechanisms to formal collaboration structures. For example, when teacher-leader support roles are identified as part of a school district's professional learning design, the individuals in those roles share resources and information within and across school settings, extending the reach of collaboration to help other educators improve their instructional practice (Coburn et al., 2013). The policies, practices, and arrangements that school systems implement in support of educators' more formal collaboration do have the potential to impact the ways in which educators interact with – and subsequently open – their practices to one another (Coburn et al., 2013). When, for instance, collaborative efforts among educators in a given school are bolstered by district-wide mechanisms that inform networking and support for one another, such collaboration can enhance educator agency and deprivatize teaching practices (Hopkins & Craig, 2011). Nonetheless, mandated collaboration arrangements and highly regulated methods of educator engagement do not guarantee openness, such as the creation of more open environments for professional learning or the deprivatization of teaching practice (Kougioumtzis & Patriksson, 2009). When formalities for working together run counter to educators' learning needs, collaboration can be deemed ineffective (Reeves, 2007). At the scale of systems, more structured collaboration models can actually yield less collaborative and open interactions among educators, compared to arrangements that provide for local decision-making (Hopkins & Craig, 2011; Kougioumtzis & Patriksson, 2009). It could be argued that systems and policies exercising significant control over the design and implementation of educator collaboration may unknowingly perpetuate more closed professional learning efforts and delimit educator agency; alternatively, those affording greater educator autonomy and decision-making may in fact support more open learning environments and opportunities for educators.

4 Educator Networking

Complimenting a brief review of educators' collaboration arrangements, ecological interpretations of open education should also consider the importance of educator networking. Given that social capital is key to developing collective educator agency (Bridwell-Mitchell & Cooc, 2016; Hargreaves & Fullan, 2012), it is not surprising that educators frequently network with their colleagues in order to advance their own professional learning. Educator efforts to build social capital through their peer network interactions is a means for opening practice, too; increased social capital facilitates knowledge sharing, individuals' willingness to openly discuss their experiences, and the ability to reach beyond one's regular working environments to access information (Rehm & Notten, 2016). Social capital – and the opportunities to interact within a network as a result of developing social capital – is explicitly grounded in trusting relationships among members of a network in their shared desire to learn (de Jong, Moolenaar, Osagie, & Phielix, 2016). Informal educator networks focused on interest-driven learning may have a greater impact on student achievement than more formal arrangements, since informal networks allow educators to seek support for their identified, immediate problems of practice in ways that are not always possible in more structured settings (Akiba & Liang, 2016).

In some cases, the relationships buoying educator networks need to be cultivated in order for open sharing to occur. Educator relationships have been found to be instrumental in advancing school change efforts, as such social networks help to create a safe climate for professional learning (Moolenaar, 2012). Educator networks have also been linked to increased self-efficacy; in turn, such networks can support educator motivation and student learning (de Jong et al., 2016). Moreover, educators' relationships with one another have been described as a lever for developing educator knowledge, changing teaching practices, and improving student engagement (Akiba & Liang, 2016; Little, 2002). For example, in an examination of protocol-use by collaborative teams, sharing was described as more open when teams were encouraged to use discussion guides that incorporated explicit depictions of classroom activity, as well as sharing of classroom struggles. Such protocols supported development of collegial relationships and opened conversations that may previously have run counter to school norms (Levine & Marcus, 2010).

Any contemporary review of educator networks would be remiss were it not to mention how educators engage in personal and professional dialogue through digital and social networks. Research about educator networking via blogs and social media platforms (i.e. Facebook, Twitter) suggests educators' interactions in these open spaces can usefully contribute to professional learning. Social media provides a pathway for educators to quickly access and evaluate multiple perspectives on a topic, and to easily interact with both novice and more experienced peers (Hart & Steinbrecher, 2011). Educators who participate in Twitter conversations can increase their social capital through such online interactions while also expanding their networks in the process (Rehm & Notten, 2016). For educators who author blogs, blogging is a well-documented means of building social capital through author-reader interactions. Posts and subsequent comments can open educational practice; such exchanges bridge public and private space, highlight network members' expertise, provide affinity around topics of shared interest, and create (potentially safe) spaces for individuals to ask questions, provide feedback, and share ideas (Luehmann & Tinelli, 2008; Risser & Bottoms, 2014). Research also indicates that educators participate in interest-driven and social media networks for varied reasons; educators can share openly both positive and negative emotions and experiences associated with their work, ask for help and admit struggles in an environment separate from workplace colleagues, relieve isolation, explore new teaching ideas, and develop a sense of community (Hur & Brush, 2009; Kelly & Antonio, 2016).

The previous review is meant to underscore how ecological perspectives on teaching and education learning appear throughout literature concerned with deprivatizing teaching practice, educator collaboration arrangements, and educator networking. With this scholarship as a foundation, this chapter asserts there exists an opportunity to focus more intentionally on how educators' collaboration and networks can be cultivated and leveraged in service of deprivatized and more open educational practices across public and private boundaries.

5 Educator Social Learning Ecologies

In their work with youth, Ching and colleagues (2014) defined a SLE as the 'assemblage of individuals that provide material, knowledge building, emotional, brokering and/or institutional forms of support for the purposes of initiating or sustaining learning' (p. 2). Their research and characterization of SLEs posited that a youth's learning ecology could be extended with targeted supports from critical individuals who provide guidance as they pursued interest-driven learning activities. In mapping youth SLEs across sixteen different support roles, Ching and colleagues found that the depth and breadth of youth SLEs, namely the redundancy and diversity of an individual's SLE, were likely to contribute to sustained engagement in interest-driven learning.

In applying the theoretical perspective and empirical findings from Ching and colleagues' (2014) study of youth to the context of adult learning, we find the concept of a SLE to be a novel model for characterizing how educators might cultivate and nurture their professional networks across public and private boundaries. Furthermore, mapping educators' SLEs has potential as a tool for articulating the ways in which educator practice spans material and digital settings, and for how educators can access and leverage relationships and resources across a continuum of public and private settings to support their interest-driven and professionally relevant learning. In this section, we conceptualize, represent, and describe educator SLEs so as to delineate necessary supports for – and pathways toward – more open teaching and educator learning opportunities.

6 Opening Educator Social Learning Ecologies

Adapted from Ching and colleagues' (2014) definition, we define an educator's SLE as *the assemblage of individuals, material resources, knowledge-building practices, and other supports that span multiple settings and can sustain educators' open educational practices.* Figure 8.1 is a visual representation of an educator's SLE, highlighting the prominence of knowledge-building practices, emotional support, resources, and brokering as four categories of support that influence how educators propel their own learning across public and private boundaries, as well as personal and professional contexts, in navigating pathways toward open educational practice. The shaded area surrounding an educator is intentional; while educators are distinctively influenced by knowledge-building practices, emotional supports, resources, and brokering, these four categories are not entirely distinct, are mutually constituted by personal and professional contexts, and collectively shape how an educator navigates public and private boundaries.

Of note in this depiction of an educator's SLE is the absence of specific people. This theoretical framework privileges relations among multiple categories of support, however those supports may be provided, rather than between an educator and multiple other individuals. Colleagues, family members, students, and others may all be part of an educator's SLE, providing resources to the educator so as to navigate personal and professional contexts. However, the focus of mapping the SLE is to identify *support types* that educators access as they become more open in their practices. Therefore, this theoretical

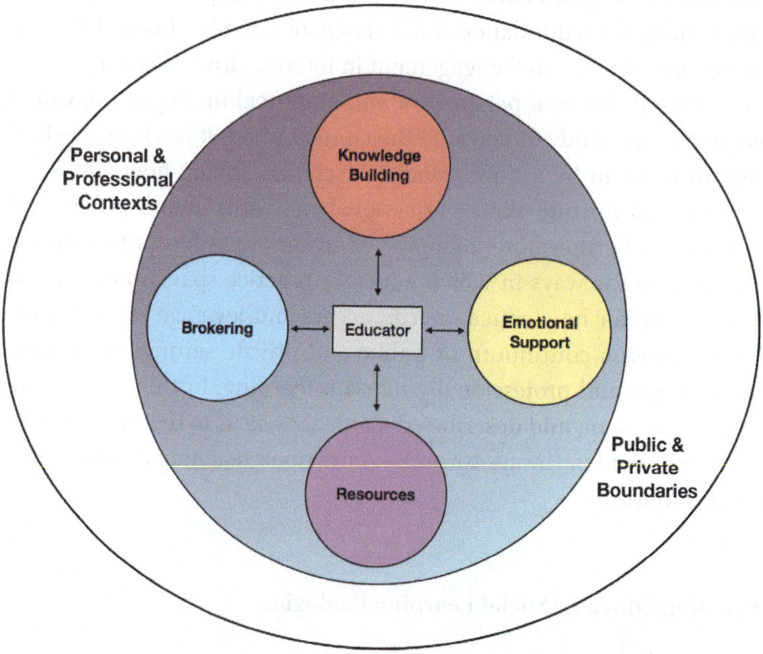

FIGURE 8.1 Educator social learning ecology illustrating interconnectedness of support categories as situated within different contexts and boundaries

framework illustrates proposed categories of support provided through both interpersonal relationships as well as supports afforded by relationships with material, ideational, and network influences.

6.1 *Knowledge-Building*

We define knowledge-building in an educator's SLE as developing competencies and skills for professional practice through social interaction. Knowledge-building practices include the ways in which educators establish knowledge and skill through their interactions with one another. These social interactions include reciprocal activities that benefit both parties, such as teaching and learning, collaborating to accomplish a task, and providing feedback, which can strengthen understanding for both the feedback provider and receiver. Knowledge-building activities also include developing a broader repertoire of teaching strategies and content, learning more about colleagues' practices, and developing content and procedural understanding to more effectively navigate the education profession.

While this definition describes educators' knowledge-building practices as they interact with other educators, such interaction is not limited to those who share similar professional expertise. Other individuals in an educator's SLE may include friends, family, and acquaintances they encounter who help them build knowledge and skills. The bookstore clerk whose brief reviews of and hearty discussion about the newest adolescent literature titles; the swim coach who models immediate and specific feedback about an athlete's performance; the long-time community member who offers insights into the shifting dynamics of the neighborhood culture – all may assist with knowledge-building practices as members of an educator's SLE.

From an ecological perspective, the knowledge-building practices of an educator's SLE can take place within school settings, as might occur when a group of educators in the same department engage in a book study about a topic of mutual interest, or when a consultant comes into a school district and provides resources for staff to learn about a new instructional approach. Such knowledge building can stretch boundaries and encourage open sharing among colleagues, as might occur when two educators decide to co-design a unit of study and, in the process, expand their shared knowledge of content and pedagogy. Other knowledge-building practices bridge public and private spaces in schools. For example, educators who observe one another teaching a lesson, in person or remotely, and then provide feedback on their observations simultaneously develop knowledge of teaching craft and lower the barriers of privatization. Knowledge-building practices can also span physical and digital spaces, as is the case when educators participate in online discussion forums or Twitter chats, learn from peers across the globe, and broaden their perspectives about teaching and learning in diverse settings.

6.2 *Emotional Support*

Emotional supports in an educator SLE are the ways in which educators are encouraged to persevere and are recognized for their accomplishments through social interaction. These emotional supports serve to create a safer environment in which individuals feel comfortable to take risks. For example, when colleagues share their successes and challenges and offer one another authentic, supportive responses, they can build a sense of collective efficacy and may feel more capable of tackling challenging situations both individually and together as a group.

Emotional support to persevere may come from family members who reinforce an educator's decision to become a principal; or from a colleague who, over coffee, openly discusses the demands of being an educator; or from a weekly video conference with colleagues from across the country during which strategies for a successful first year of teaching are shared. The emotional support given and received through one's SLE may be the catalyst needed for educators to feel safer and confident about opening their teaching practice to others, perhaps even for individuals who are working within challenging sociopolitical environments and are otherwise reluctant to share.

Likewise, when educators share successes and challenges at a faculty meeting or post examples of their work products in an online forum – their own lessons, for example, or student work samples – they are able get feedback from colleagues who may have similar experiences. As open and trusting relationships develop, educators may find that the emotional support received through their networks provides a source of optimism and encouragement. Similarly, as educators test and more fully develop their ideas by sharing blog posts or other writing on social media, the reassurance and affirmations they get in return may be support enough to encourage continued sharing – or may even spur confidence to submit their writing for publication. Through these personal interactions with SLE members, educators strengthen their social capital; in turn, this encourages continued professional learning by expanding and opening their networks.

6.3 *Resources*

Resources in an educator SLE are material, digital, and conceptual supports that educators access to advance their professional practice and learning. Resources may also include time to engage in professional learning, either in the sense that time is provided for an individual to learn, or in that others give of their own time for shared learning. Resources in an educator SLE are similar to what Akkerman and Bakker (2011) refer to as *boundary objects*, or artifacts that help to bridge activity across boundaries and may, for instance, include 'a teacher portfolio as a means by which both the mentor and the school supervisor are able to track the development of the student teacher in teacher education' (p. 133). The supports in this SLE component are frequently paired with knowledge-building practices and include both local resources and those that span boundaries.

For educators who do not have access to the same professional learning opportunities, collegial resource-sharing can be an effective way to develop knowledge and skills; moreover, resources may provide a generative platform to open discussions about pedagogy and student learning. New resources may be accessed when one member of a department attends a conference, brings back educational content, and shares new insights with the rest of the team. This also occurs, for instance, when educators on a project-based learning team initiated by a local university schedule time each week for project updates, resource sharing, and planning for each week's classroom activities. In this case, it is time, ideas, lesson plans, educational content, and pedagogical strategies that are the shared resources. Similarly, when an experienced educator shares teaching resources via social media and engages in ongoing conversation with other educators who subsequently use their materials in other classrooms, they support others in developing their knowledge of practice. Resources may also be provided by an organization, as is the case when educators are allocated professional learning days throughout the school year to meet with colleagues from across their district and discuss curriculum and instruction. Resource-sharing is a means of opening educators' practices; by offering ideas, materials, and time, educators signal an openness to learn collaboratively with one another. In this way, an educator can leverage their SLE, using new resources to build professional knowledge.

6.4 *Brokering*

Brokering describes the ways in which educators both gain and also provide access to other individuals, opportunities, or resources as mediated through SLE social interactions. Educators may serve as a learning broker or knowledge-building broker for their colleagues, or conversely may benefit from such social relations. Brokering in an educator SLE spans a range of social arrangements and professional purposes, from everyday introductions to new colleagues and their learning resources and networks, to participation in more robust and sustained learning communities over time. Social capital is often key to brokering, and through newly brokered opportunities educators can more easily expand their access to new professional learning opportunities, resources, and relationships.

Brokering in an educator SLE can be both formal and informal, with activity that occurs during a single handshake as well as throughout longer-term relationships. When a school administrator invites a novice teacher to join the school leadership team, the teacher develops knowledge about the school's shared leadership model and processes for continuous improvement that may have otherwise been inaccessible. A less formal brokering opportunity exists when a university professor introduces a group of graduate students to a network of professionals interested in similar topics, creating an open space for the students to engage in dialogue and networking. Inclusion on the school leadership team is likely a long-term commitment; taking advantage of a colleague's offer of admission to hear an author speak about a new book is a short-term commitment. A graduate student may seek to publish a paper in an academic journal with varying degrees of success and acceptance; the same student, with a brokered introduction from a faculty advisor, may be introduced to a journal editor who is willing to provide feedback and mentoring, increasing the likelihood of eventually having a paper accepted for publication. These brokered opportunities, by definition, open educator practice when they make accessible new pathways for learning that may cross boundaries and span public and private spaces.

7 Educator SLE and Mapping Learning across Public and Private Boundaries

The four proposed categories of an educator SLE are inextricably linked, and each component of the SLE contributes to that individual's learning across the continuum of public and private boundaries. Participation in knowledge-building practices can inform emotional supports, as when collegial interactions strengthen social capital and bolster confidence to apply new instructional practices. Similarly, brokering activities and relationships can be linked to emotional supports. As the different components of an educator's SLE – the people, resources, practices, and supports – interact and are accessed, the nature of any given SLE shifts. While each individual sits at the nexus of intersecting SLE components, an ecological perspective on educator learning suggests the qualities and reach of an SLE are also influenced by factors well beyond the individual scale. Learning by one member of an SLE influences the learning of others, reinforcing the dynamic and networked attributes of learning ecologies and the importance of collective activity. Further, SLEs, by definition, are also situated; SLEs are shaped by both personal and professional contexts, as well as by public and private boundaries educators routinely encounter and cross.

Understanding the dynamics of an educator's SLE – and how the SLE can be instrumental in crossing public and private boundaries of learning and educator practice – can be aided by an individual articulating specific sources of practice, support, and brokering. In this section, we present two different types of SLE 'maps' as visual representations to assist researchers, educators, and facilitators of professional learning in bridging the previously detailed conceptual framework with the practicalities of individual experience. These two SLE maps are suggested tools for detailing an educator's SLE, identifying possible pathways along and across public and private boundaries, and signaling new opportunities to create open professional learning environments, teaching practices, and educational opportunities. The first of these tools, SLE Supports Map (Figure 8.2), depicts how one educator might begin to identify and categorize sources of support in their SLE.

The process of mapping an educator SLE, as represented in Figure 8.2, can be both a generative and iterative process, and need not necessarily adopt the precise form (i.e., similar to a spreadsheet, more linear) as suggested above. The broader intention of creating a visualization tool like an SLE Supports Map is to articulate and represent the sources of support that contribute to how an educator learns and interacts with others across public and private boundaries. Such a map is useful to help identify, name, and understand how particular individuals and resources might support boundary-crossing transitions in service of more open educational practices.

The hypothetical SLE Supports Map in Figure 8.2 includes the four proposed educator SLE categories: Knowledge-building practices, emotional support, resources, and brokering. It is evident from this example that the educator has a broad SLE, as it spans the work environment, connections through a university, other educators with shared digital platform memberships, and brokered opportunities like the 'PBL Plan.' As depicted in this example, a SLE may include individuals in similar and different positions of authority; an educator's map may also include other classroom educators, as well as school and district administrators. A SLE Supports Map may identify colleagues with similar role responsibilities, such as other English educators, as well as those who work in the same school but in different roles; the English educator may point to colleagues in mathematics and the counseling department as members of their SLE. The sample SLE Supports Map also reveals redundancies in support. Every source is identified as an opportunity for learning and, in the majority of cases, the sources are learners as well. As a SLE encompasses a broader

Name/Activity	Role in SLE	Knowledge Building: Teaches me	Knowledge Building: Learns from me	Knowledge Building: Feedback	Knowledge Building: Collaboration	Emotional Support: Encouragement	Emotional Support: Follows activity	Emotional Support: Recognizes activity	Emotional Support: Socializes	Resources: Material	Resources: Time	Brokering: Opportunity	Brokering: Connection	Brokering: Advice
Sheila	School admin	X	X	X	X	X	X	X		X	X	X	X	X
Linsday	English colleague 1	X	X	X	X	X	X	X	X	X	X			
Tonia	English colleague 2	X	X	X	X	X	X	X	X	X				
Teresa	District admin	X	X	X		X	X	X		X	X	X	X	X
Richard	Content expert	X								X				X
Brock	University prof	X	X	X		X					X		X	X
Kylie	University prof	X	X	X	X	X	X	X		X	X	X	X	X
Project Team	University workgroup	X	X	X	X	X					X			
Tom	Classmate	X	X	X	X	X	X	X	X		X			
Sharon	Math teacher	X	X	X	X	X	X	X	X		X			
#Englishchat	Twitter chat group	X	X	X		X	X	X					X	
Carol	Twitter chat moderator	X		X							X	X		
Maribel	Blog author	X									X		X	
Assessment project	Work/regular	X	X									X		
PBL plan	Work/brokered	X												
PLC	Work/regular	X	X	X	X									
English 9 team	Work/regular	X	X	X	X	X	X		X	X	X			X
Students	Work/regular	X	X	X										
Kerry	Home/spouse	X	X	X		X	X	X	X		X			
Robin	Home/daughter	X	X	X		X	X	X	X		X			
Dena	Home/best friend	X	X	X		X	X	X	X					

FIGURE 8.2 SLE Supports Map illustrating how an educator can map supports associated with the four categories of support in the theoretical framework

network of supports provided by a range of individuals – university professors, classmates, contacts from online sources, friends, family members, others – the potential increases for a given educator to engage in more interconnected, expansive, and open professional learning.

To begin generating a SLE Supports Map, and whether in similar or dissimilar form to the hypothetical example, questions such as the following may be useful for educators interested in beginning the process of mapping the people, practices, and supports present in their SLE:

- Knowledge-building: Who are the people and/or what are the activities that provide useful knowledge about teaching and learning?
- Emotional support: Who are the people and/or what are the activities that provide emotional support about teaching and learning?
- Resources: Who are the people and/or what are the activities that provide resources – such as materials, time, or other supports – to encourage teaching and learning?
- Brokering: Who are the people and/or what are the activities that provide access to (new) resources and opportunities about teaching and learning?

To gain further insights into how an educator's SLE can contribute to open educational practices, we further suggest the SLE Supports Map can be extended to include the interactions among individuals, practices, and resources. A second type of visual representation, the SLE Connections Map (Figure 8.3), indicates these interactions by acknowledging how specific elements of the SLE are connected, both intentionally and by association.

This SLE Connections Map illustrates how a single educator's SLE can generate connections among SLE members, for the purposes of identifying how supports are distributed across the network. In this map, three connection types are represented by different colored symbols. Blue symbols indicate existing connections between SLE members. A green symbol reveals situations where the educator introduced one or more SLE members to one another, or where a resource or opportunity was shared across SLE members. Purple represents a third connection type – connected by association. In these situations, no direct introduction is made; however, the educator's interactions with these SLE members has been influenced by other SLE members, resources, or opportunities. Like the SLE Supports Map, the represented form of this sample SLE Connections Map is less important than the processes of visually mapping various types of connections. Similarly, the three types of connections featured in this example (existing connections, introductions, and associations) may not necessarily be useful for all educators; again, the broader impetus is to usefully categorize SLE connection types as a step toward opening educational practices.

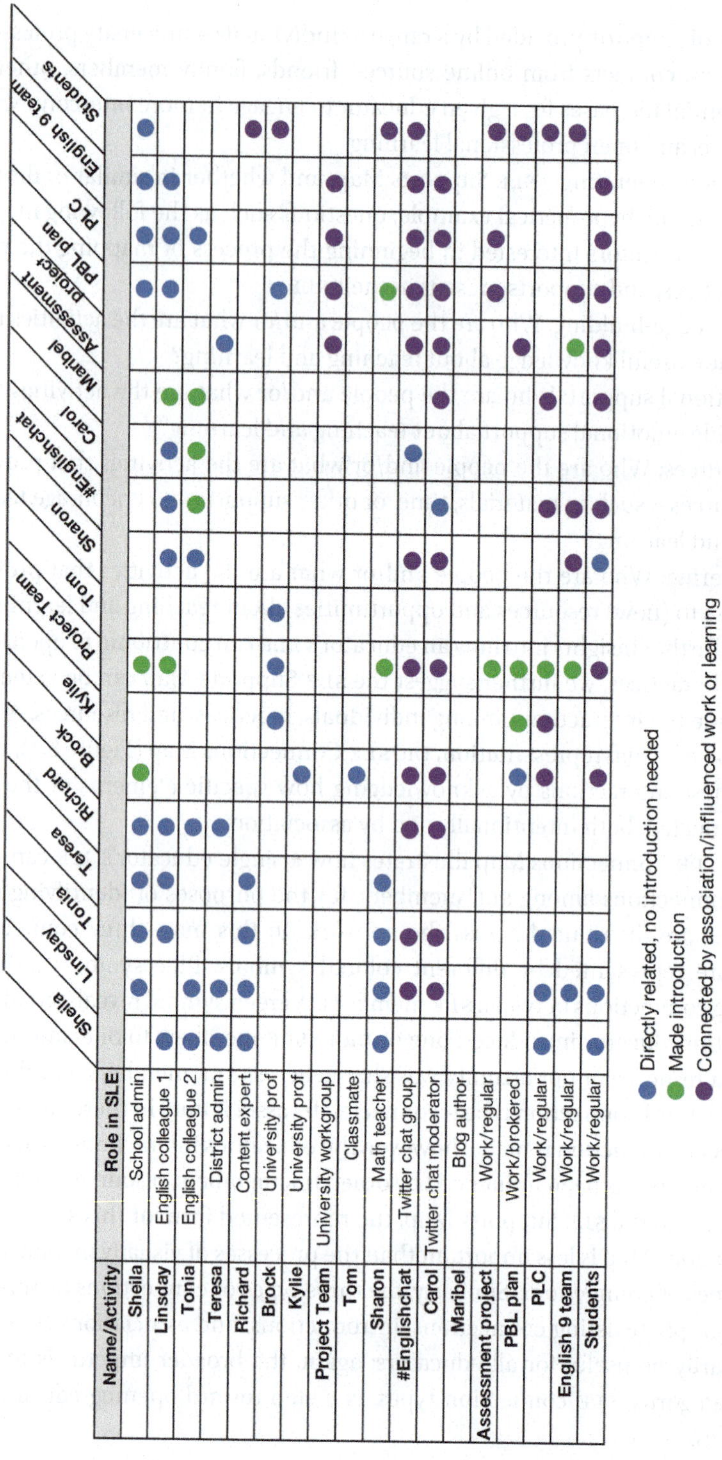

FIGURE 8.3 SLE Connections Map illustrating how the various aspects of an educator SLE are connected

A SLE Connections Map can help illustrate how the people, practices, and resources of an educator's SLE create pathways for navigating public and private boundaries with the aim of encouraging open educational practices. As an educator interacts with members of their SLE, their learning, ways of working, and knowledge of new resources can become entangled with the practices, ways of knowing, and resources of connected SLE members. When an educator leverages their SLE to make professionally-relevant connections, learning may be advanced for the collective network. Moreover, the potential for boundary-crossing is enhanced when an educator's learning involves brokering among opportunities and individuals inaccessible without an intentional introduction across SLE connections. In the sample SLE Connections Map, note connections among the brokered opportunity titled Project Team and the university professor who served as the educator's broker. This brokered opportunity contributes to the educator's learning. Furthermore, because relationships of reciprocity for professional learning exist with school administrators, the educator also shared project group activities at their school, influencing the creation of an interdisciplinary project-based learning team. While hypothetical, this example is not unrealistic (Tsui & Law, 2007); in such circumstances, an educator's SLE interactions, and the manifestations of the supports enmeshed in the SLE, cross various public and private boundaries – university and K-12 settings, research project and practitioner actions, and professional collaborations that span multiple geographic locations. Such boundary-crossing SLE interactions may help educators deprivatize their practice and open educator learning for both the individual and the shared network.

8 Discussion and Implications

In this chapter, we have asserted the value of approaching educators' professional collaboration and peer networking from an ecological perspective on learning (Barron, 2004; Bronfenbrenner, 1976). More specifically, we have adapted ecological conceptions of development (Ching et al., 2014) to forward a conceptual framework of educator SLEs as a means of encouraging more open educational practices. Accordingly, this discussion addresses three related concerns: First, the importance of defining and mapping educator SLEs; second, implications for the design of professional development; and third, the role an educator's SLE can play in navigating pathways across public and private boundaries toward more open educational practices.

8.1 *Importance of Defining and Mapping Educator Social Learning Ecologies*

We have proposed a conceptually-grounded and pragmatically-oriented means of guiding educators to define and map their SLEs as a valuable activity for navigating public and private boundaries that are endemic to teaching practices across a variety of educational settings. The relevance of an educator SLE to expanding professional networks, developing social capital, and promoting boundary-crossing activities can more seamlessly occur by intentionally naming SLE supports and memberships, identifying and understanding connections among members and learning opportunities, and by considering how to deliberately leverage various SLE components. Educators can bolster their capacity to more effectively engage in the ongoing activity of crafting more open educational practices when they leverage a distributed network that provides supports for knowledge and skill development, offers reassurance and encouragement, and brokers opportunities for further learning. Furthermore, by using visual representations such as SLE Supports and Connections Maps, educators can illustrate how generative connections can be encouraged across public and private spaces so as to further develop open educational practices among both individuals and broader networks.

Because SLE research has predominantly examined youth connected learning across boundaries (Barron, 2006; Ching, Santo, Hoadley, & Peppler, 2016), there are broad implications for the study of educator SLEs, and, specifically, how educator SLEs intersect with efforts to deprivatize and open educator practice. Future study may seek to understand the intentionality with which educators cultivate and nurture their SLE, and whether articulating a SLE and its inherent connections contributes to more open educational practice, as well how other factors such as concerns for personal and job security, issues of sociopolitical conflict, and institutional and individual competition intertwine with one's SLE and local efforts to deprivatize practice. Exploration and definition of strong and weak ties within a SLE may provide more information about how educators conceptualize their SLE. We speculate that when educators create their own representations of a SLE Supports Map and a SLE Connections Map, their understanding of its complex interactions will result in more purposeful engagement with members of the SLE, including the role of the individual educator as a broker to facilitate subsequent network interactions. Studies should also explore how educator practice changes as a result of the open environments encouraged by SLEs. In studying how educator SLEs contribute to deprivatized educator practice, we would be remiss to not also encourage researcher inquiry about connections between an educator's SLE and their students' learning. Future research should focus on the characteristics of an educator's SLE that inform specific learner outcomes, including the relationship between breadth and redundancy of SLE supports and the effectiveness of educator practices on student learning.

8.2 *Implications for the Design of Professional Learning*

Conceptualizing and mapping educator SLEs suggests implications for the design of educator professional learning. First, this chapter indicates there are likely promising opportunities associated with new professional development designs that guide educators in advancing their familiarity with the concept of a SLE and then by mapping their own SLEs. Second, such professional learning can encourage both breadth and depth of SLE interaction, assisting educators as they cultivate different perspectives and forms of expertise in service of opening their educational practices across settings, technologies, and domains. Professional learning about distributed SLE opportunities and resources may encourage educators to expand their networks, opening professional learning to span what may have previously been private spaces. Another consideration for professional learning design concerns educators' equitable access to brokered opportunities. In identifying and mapping SLEs among multiple educators, it is likely that opportunities afforded by brokers will vary from person to person. This variance is not unexpected; however, articulating who may benefit from a greater variety of learning opportunities may subsequently inform how school and district leaders provide additional supports for a range of professionals.

The implications for educator SLEs on professional learning designs are further apparent when considering how knowledge and resources may be shared within and across professional settings. It is not uncommon for schools or districts to focus professional learning and resource development in alignment with previously identified high-leverage instructional approaches (Goodwin, 2011). While this approach may have some initial merit for institutions in need of significant change, there are also promising opportunities associated with educator learning that is geared toward exploring diverse knowledge and material resources well-matched to student learning needs (Craig & Hopkins, 2011; Goodwin, Rouleau, & Lewis, 2018). When the majority of resources identified in an educator's SLE are from a limited range of sources, diversity of thought and openness to new ideas may be limited. By mapping and analyzing educator SLEs, it may be possible to identify whether resource-diversity should be amplified in professional learning design. If so, intentionally introducing or encouraging educators to access varied resources from outside their local context – that is, from across their SLE – may prompt educators to expand the boundaries of their professional learning. These insights from educator SLEs provide an opportunity for responsive professional learning design that may result in increased deprivatization of both individual educator practices and instructional systems.

8.3 *Toward Open Practice: Navigating Pathways across Public and Private Boundaries*

A goal of conceptualizing and mapping educator SLEs is to surface pathways that educators can use to navigate along and across the many public and private boundaries that characterize teaching and learning. While more connected than ever before as a result of digital advancements (Kemp, 2017), educators still experience professional isolation for a variety of reasons, including structural features of physical buildings, the programmatic designs of schools as institutions, the degree of autonomy granted to educators in some schools, and the limited time available for substantial collegial discussions (Ostovar-Nameghi & Sheikhahmadi, 2016). Given a supportive and safe context in which to do so, encouraging educators to share openly about their pedagogy, classroom challenges, student learning, and trends and advancements in educational research can help to counter isolation and establish norms of collaboration that support open teaching and learning practices.

Our educator SLE conceptual framework and hypothetical SLE maps are meant to illuminate pathways across a continuum of public and private boundaries that classroom educators encounter every day, to identify tangible entry points toward greater social connectedness, and to provide pragmatic scaffolds toward more open educational practices. In this respect, our exploration of educator SLEs is not meant to be an esoteric endeavor. Rather, we approach our work as establishing a conceptual foundation that can help characterize how educators might build and sustain their professional networks across public and private boundaries, and for both individuals and groups. An educator's SLE may present multiple pathways toward open educational practices at both the individual and collective scales. While the specifics of an educator's SLE are unique to each individual, the interactions educators have with the people, resources, and opportunities in their SLE likely intersect with and impact other educators' SLEs. The power of a SLE is in both the individual human capital that is developed, and the collective capacity that is cultivated as individuals interact and change the learning environment experienced by networked peers. The potential for individual and collective capacity-building can take a variety of forms; it can include learning of content and skills relevant to one's discipline, it may be centered on developing self- and collective-efficacy, or it may concern strengthened and affirming social interactions with SLE members. Across circumstances, both the individual and the collective can benefit. When an individual educator pursues new learning opportunities and connections, the impact on the network of SLEs may include more expansive and shared repertoires of knowledge and skills.

By mapping and leveraging their SLE, we maintain that educators can more easily navigate the public and private spaces of their profession, deepening their competence and confidence to meaningfully engage in open educational practices. In this respect, open educational practices are synonymous with the knowledge-building practices, emotional supports, resources, and brokering practices that distinguish educators' SLEs. Through the lens of ecological learning theory, we have suggested that educators can productively nurture collaborative social relationships that sustain their learning across settings and in coordination with a distributed constellation of people, resources, interactions, and supports. Educator SLEs are a promising means of both defining and expanding educator practice and relationships across settings, and for articulating how educators can access and leverage resources in service of open practices as boundary-crossing and transformative educational opportunities.

References

Akiba, M., & Liang, G. (2016). Effects of teacher professional learning activities on student achievement growth. *The Journal of Educational Research, 109*(1), 99–110.

Akkerman, S. F., & Bakker, A. (2011). Boundary crossing and boundary objects. *Review of Educational Research, 81*(2), 132–169.

Barron, B. (2004). Learning ecologies for technological fluency: Gender and experience differences. *Journal of Educational Computing Research, 31*(1), 1–36.

Barron, B. (2006). Interest and self-sustained learning as catalysts of development: A learning ecology perspective. *Human Development, 49*, 193–224.

Beach, K. (1999). Consequential transitions: A sociocultural expedition beyond transfer in education. *Review of Research in Education, 24*, 124–149.

Bevan, B., Bell, P., Stevens, R., & Razfar, A. (Eds.), (2013). *LOST opportunities: Learning in out-of-school time*. New York, NY: Springer.

Boreen, J., & Niday, D. (2000). Breaking through the isolation: Mentoring beginning teachers. *Journal of Adolescent & Adult Literacy, 44*(2), 152–163.

Bridwell-Mitchell, E. N., & Cooc, N. (2016). The ties that bind: How social capital is forged and forfeited in teacher communities. *Educational Researcher, 45*(1), 7–17.

Bronfenbrenner, U. (1976). The experimental ecology of education. *Educational Researcher, 5*(9), 5–15.

Carpenter, J. P., & Krutka, D. G. (2015). Engagement through microblogging: Educator professional development via Twitter. *Professional Development in Education, 41*(4), 707–728.

Ching, D., Santo, R., Hoadley, C., & Peppler, K. (2014). *Mapping social learning ecologies of Hive youth*. New York, NY: Hive Research Lab.

Ching, D., Santo, R., Hoadley, C., & Peppler, K. (2016). Not just a blip in someone's life: Integrating brokering practices into out-of-school programming as a means of supporting and expanding youth futures. *On the Horizon, 24*(3), 296–312.

Coburn, C. E., Mata, W. S., & Choi, L. (2013). The embeddedness of teachers' social networks: Evidence from a study of mathematics reform. *Sociology of Education, 86*(4), 311–342.

Cotton, K. (1996). *School size, school climate, and student performance: Close-up #20*. Portland, OR: Northwest Regional Educational Laboratory.

Cronin, C. (2017). Open education, open questions. *EDUCAUSE Review, 52*(6), 11–20.

Cuban, L. (2004, Spring). What ever happened to the open classroom? *Education Next, 2004* (Spring). Retrieved from http://educationnext.org/files/ednext20042_68.pdf

de Jong, K. J., Moolenaar, N. M., Osagie, E., & Phielix, C. (2016). Valuable connections: A social capital perspective on teachers' social networks, commitment and self-efficacy. *Pedagogía Social, 28*, 71–83.

DeRosa, R., & Jhangiani, R. (2017). Open pedagogy. In E. Mays (Ed.), *A guide to making open textbooks with students* (pp. 6–21). Montreal: Rebus Community.

DuFour, R. (2004). What is a professional learning community? *Educational Leadership, 61*(8), 6–11.

Duncan-Howell, J. (2010). Teachers making connections: Online communities as a source of professional learning. *British Journal of Educational Technology, 41*(2), 324–340.

Engeström, Y., Engeström, R., & Kärkkäinen, M. (1995). Polycontextuality and boundary crossing in expert cognition: Learning and problem solving in complex work activities. *Learning and Instruction, 5*(4), 319–336.

Fullan, M., & Langworthy, M. (2016). *A rich seam: How new pedagogies find deep learning*. London: Pearson.

Garcia, A. (Ed.). (2014). *Teaching in the connected learning classroom*. Irvine, CA: Digital Media and Learning Research Hub.

Goddard, R. D., Tschannen-Moran, M., & Hoy, W. K. (2001). A multilevel examination of the distribution and effects of teacher trust in students and parents in urban elementary schools. *The Elementary School Journal, 102*(1), 3–17.

Goodwin, B. (2011). *Simply better: Doing what matters most to change the odds for student success*. Alexandria, VA: ASCD.

Goodwin, B., Rouleau, K., & Lewis, D. (2018). *Curiosity works: A guidebook for moving your school from improvement to innovation*. Denver, CO: McREL International.

Greenhow, C., Robelia, B., & Hughes, J. E. (2009). Learning, teaching, and scholarship in a digital age: Web 2.0 and classroom research: What path should we take now? *Educational Researcher, 38*(4), 246–259.

Hargreaves, A., & Fullan, M. (2012). *Professional capital: Transforming teaching in every school.* New York, NY: Teachers College Press.

Hart, J. E., & Steinbrecher, T. (2011). OMG! Exploring and learning from teachers' personal and professional uses of Facebook. *Action in Teacher Education, 33*(4), 320–328.

Havemann, L. (2016). Open educational resources. In M. A. Peters (Ed.), *Encyclopedia of educational philosophy and theory.* Singapore: Springer Singapore.

Hollett, T., & Kalir, J. (2017). Mapping playgrids for learning across space, time, and scale. *TechTrends, 61*(3), 236–245.

Hopkins, D., & Craig, W. (2011). Powerful learning: Taking education reform to scale in the Northern Metropolitan Region. In D. Hopkins, J. Munro, & W. Craig (Eds.), *Powerful learning: A strategy for systemic educational improvement* (pp. 28–37). Victoria: ACER Press.

Hord, S. M. (2009). Professional learning communities. *Journal of Staff Development, 30*(1), 40–43.

Hur, J. W., & Brush, T. A. (2009). Teacher participation in online communities: Why do teachers want to participate in self-generated online communities of K–12 teachers? *Journal of Research on Technology in Education, 41*(3), 279–303.

Ito, M., Gutiérrez, K., Livingstone, S., Penuel, B., Rhodes, J., Salen, K., & Watkins, S. C. (2013). *Connected learning: An agenda for research and design.* Irvine, CA: Digital Media and Learning Research Hub.

Jhangiani, R. S., & Biswas-Diener, R. (2017). *Open: The philosophy and practices that are revolutionizing education and science.* London: Ubiquity Press.

Jurow, A., Tracy, R., Hotchkiss, J., & Kirshner, B. (2012). Designing for the future: How the learning sciences can inform the trajectories of preservice teachers. *Journal of Teacher Education, 63*(2), 147–160.

Kelly, N., & Antonio, A. (2016). Teacher peer support in social network sites. *Teaching and Teacher Education, 56*, 138–149.

Kemp. S. (2017, January 24). *Digital in 2017 global overview: A collection of internet, social media, and mobile data from around the world.* Retrieved from https://wearesocial.com/special-reports/digital-in-2017-global-overview

Kougioumtzis, K., & Patriksson, G. (2009). School-based teacher collaboration in Sweden and Greece: Formal cooperation, deprivatized practices and personalized interaction in primary and lower secondary schools. *Teachers and Teaching: Theory and Practice, 15*(1), 131–154.

Krutka, D. G., Carpenter, J. P., & Trust, T. (2016). Elements of engagement: A model of teacher interactions via professional learning networks. *Journal of Digital Learning in Teacher Education, 32*(4), 150–158.

Lave, J., & Wenger, E. (1991). *Situated learning: Legitimate peripheral participation.* Cambridge: Cambridge University Press.

Levine, T. H., & Marcus, A. S. (2010). How the structure and focus of teachers' collaborative activities facilitate and constrain teacher learning. *Teaching and Teacher Education, 26*(3), 389–398.

Little, J. W. (2002). Locating learning in teachers' communities of practice: Opening up problems of analysis in records of everyday work. *Teaching and Teacher Education, 18*(8), 917–946.

Luehmann, A. L., & Tinelli, L. (2008). Teacher professional identity development with social networking technologies: Learning reform through blogging. *Educational Media International, 45*(4), 323–333.

Mawhinney, L. (2008). Laugh so you don't cry: Teachers combating isolation in schools through humour and social support. *Ethnography and Education, 3*(2), 195–209.

Meehan, M. (1973). What about team teaching? *Educational Leadership, 30*(8), 717–720.

Moolenaar, N. M. (2012). A social network perspective on teacher collaboration in schools: Theory, methodology, and applications. *American Journal of Education, 119*(1), 7–39.

Ostovar-Nameghi, S. A., & Sheikhahmadi, M. (2016). From teacher isolation to teacher collaboration: Theoretical perspectives and empirical findings. *Modern Journal of Language Teaching Methods, 6*(1), 765.

Putnam, R. T., & Borko, H. (2000). What do new views of knowledge and thinking have to say about research on teacher learning? *Educational Researcher, 29*(1), 4–15.

Reeves, J. (2007). Inventing the chartered teacher. *British Journal of Educational Studies, 55*(1), 56–76.

Rehm, M., & Notten, A. (2016). Twitter as an informal learning space for teachers!? The role of social capital in Twitter conversations among teachers. *Teaching and Teacher Education, 60*, 215–223.

Risser, H. S., & Bottoms, S. (2014). 'Newbies' and 'celebrities': Detecting social roles in an online network of teachers via participation patterns. *International Journal of Computer-Supported Collaborative Learning, 9*(4), 433–450.

Scott, K. S., Sorokti, K. H., & Merrell, J. D. (2016). Learning 'beyond the classroom' within an enterprise social network system. *Internet and Higher Education, 29*, 75–90.

Swanson, K. (2014). Edcamp: Teachers take back professional development. *Educational Leadership, 71*(8), 36–40.

Trent, J. (2013). Becoming a teacher educator: The multiple boundary-crossing experiences of beginning teacher educators. *Journal of Teacher Education, 64*(3), 262–275.

Tsui, A. B., & Law, D. Y. (2007). Learning as boundary-crossing in school–university partnership. *Teaching and Teacher Education, 23*(8), 1289–1301.

Vescio, V., Ross, D., & Adams, A. (2008). A review of research on the impact of professional learning communities on teaching practice and student learning. *Teaching and Teacher Education, 24*(1), 80–91.

Watson, C. (2014). Effective professional learning communities? The possibilities for teachers as agents of change in schools. *British Educational Research Journal, 40*(1), 18–29.

Webb, P. T. (2006). The choreography of accountability. *Journal of Education Policy, 21*(2), 201–214.

Webster, C. (2011). Competition and collaboration in teaching and learning. *Enhancing Learning in the Social Sciences, 4*(1), 1–4.

CHAPTER 9

Openness in Context: Realizing Openness with Open Educational Resources and Prior Learning Assessment and Recognition

Lisa Marie Blaschke, Wolfgang Müskens and Olaf Zawacki-Richter

As they attempt to address many of the issues confronting higher education today – from continuously rising educational costs to changing demographics and increasing market competition – universities across the world are turning to innovative approaches for incorporating openness into their institutional strategies, through the use of open educational resources (OER) and, in some cases, prior learning assessment and recognition (PLAR). In pursuing openness in the form of OER, institutions may foresee a move to OER as a quick economic fix for reducing costs and increasing resource accessibility. However, such a transition can be accompanied by a variety of multi-layered challenges – for example, copyright and intellectual property issues, OER resource quality, relevance and applicability, resistance from faculty and the publishing industry, and institutional degrees of openness (D'Antonio & Savage, 2009; Wiley, 2010) – each of which needs to be addressed before successfully implementing a full-scale OER solution. PLAR services are another approach to introducing openness in education institutions as a way to gain competitive advantage in education markets, as well as for making education more accessible to a wider population of lifelong learners from diverse backgrounds with knowledge acquired through prior experiential and non-formal learning – such as provided by Massive Open Online Courses (MOOCs); and informal learning such as workplace training and community volunteer work (Cummins & Kunkel, 2015; Friesen & Wihak, 2013; Yin & Kawachi, 2013). Regardless of the path to openness chosen, institutions must weigh the degree of openness in which they will engage, as well as considering the advantages and disadvantages of each approach.

This chapter will present case studies and institutional practices in higher education that demonstrate openness in the form of OER and PLAR within a variety of contexts. The chapter is separated into two parts. In the first part of this chapter, case study examples examining the approaches used by open and distance learning (ODL) institutions in Canada, the United States, the United Kingdom, and Germany to define and implement OER strategic projects are

 | DOI: 10.1163/9789004422988_010

presented. In the second part of the chapter, a fifth case study explores openness in the form of PLAR and describes the services being offered by the PLAR Center at Carl von Ossietzky University in Oldenburg, Germany, as well as discusses the various openness initiatives that are developing in Germany. The chapter will also provide definitions and benefits of openness and describe strategies for and the respective challenges of implementing OER and PLAR, as well as offer best practices and approaches for achieving openness within higher education.

1 Open Educational Resources (OER)

Openness in education can exist in many forms: open access textbooks and publishing, open courseware, open source software (OSS), MOOCs, open course design, open delivery, open research, open evaluation, reflection, and scholarship, and open policy (Conole, 2010; Weller, 2014). OER occupy 'a middle ground, intersecting with open access, through open textbooks, and MOOCs, which can be seen as a subset of OER' (Weller, 2014, p. 85). Lane (2009) identifies two defining factors of openness: free accessibility using the Internet and limited restriction in using resources, which includes free access to source code, no subscription or licensing fees, and little or no restrictions to copyright and licensing. UNESCO (n.d.) offers this definition that further details types of educational resources:

> Open Educational Resources (OER) are any type of educational materials that are in the public domain or introduced with an open license. The nature of these open materials means that anyone can legally and freely copy, use, adapt and re-share them. OERs range from textbooks to curricula, syllabi, lecture notes, assignments, tests, projects, audio, video and animation. (para. 1)

2 Why an OER Strategy?

De Langen (2013) classifies institutional motives for participating in OER into three categories: the *public good motive*, the *efficiency motive*, and the *marketing motive* (p. 57). Additional categories could be the *innovation motive*, the desire of today's institution to adopt new educational and technology innovations, and the *pedagogy motive*, improvements in teaching and learning that can result from engaging with OER.

2.1 *The Public Good Motive: Altruism and Policy*

Due to its potential to provide learners with free access to knowledge and to bridge significant digital, societal, and cultural divides, OER is well aligned with academic traditions of altruism (D'Antonio & Savage, 2009; Hylén, 2009; OECD, 2007). In addition, the use of OER can reap social benefits such as 'altruistic public service,' by boosting human capital through sharing of knowledge and educational resources (Stacey, 2011). This decision to engage with OER can also be externally influenced by emerging governmental policies, such as the recent decision by the US Department of Education (2015) requiring an open license for tools that have been developed using federal grant money. A similar decision made by the European Commission (2015) required open licensing of content funded by the EC. Transitioning to OER also gives educational institutions an opportunity to 'leverage taxpayers' money' and give back the investment through the 'free sharing and reuse of resources' (OECD, 2007, pp. 11–12)

2.2 *The Efficiency Motive: Costs, ROI, Quality, and Student Retention*

One of the most commonly cited reasons for moving to OER is the desire to reduce costs, namely the textbook cost for students – although these costs can vary depending on national context (Hylén, 2009; Weller, 2014). Within the United States, for example, textbook costs are estimated to be up to 26% of the cost of a four-year degree (GAO, 2005, as cited in Weller, 2014). Some sources claim that textbook prices have skyrocketed to 'over three times the rate of inflation from January 1977 to June 2015, a 1,041 percent increase' (Popken, 2015, para. 2); the Student Public Interest Group (PIRG) estimates an increase of 812% in textbook costs since 1978 and recommends budgeting $1,200 annually for course textbooks (Senack, 2015; Weisbaum, 2016).

Senack (2015) estimates potential savings in textbook costs at $128/course in a semester and suggests that implementing OER could save US students more than a billion dollars annually, as well as generate a return on investment that is six times the initial investment. These cost savings could translate to more tuition income, a possibility supported by a study from Fischer et al. (2015), which found that students saving money using OER will use the savings to invest in a higher course load within a semester. Reduced cost and free access to educational resources can also help improve student retention, as well as lower content development costs, improve development and quality processes, and spur innovation (D'Antonio, 2009; De los Arcos et al., 2014; OECD, 2007; Pawlyshyn et al., 2013; Stacey, 2011).

2.3 *The Marketing Motive: Branding and New Sales Channels*

Adoption of OER can be a selling point for institutions, and by showcasing their OER use, institutions can better market and improve their brand and public image, as well as attract new students (D'Antonio, 2009; Hylén, 2009; OECD, 2007; Stacey, 2011; Weller, 2014). OER can also support the generation of new revenue by giving institutions an opportunity to recruit and channel students into formal education (D'Antonio, 2009; Stacey, 2011; Weller, 2014). The OER Research Hub reports that 31.5% of informal learners view OER as an opportunity to test courses with 24.2% stating that they would pay for a course after using OER (De los Arcos et al., 2014).

2.4 *The Pedagogy Motive: Student-Centered Learning and Faculty Collaboration*

Adopting OER can also lead to improved pedagogical practice and improve learning outcomes through more student-centered and personalized learning, resulting in fewer student failures, better retention, and an improved pass rate (Pawlyshyn et al., 2013; Weller, 2014). Course completion rates were also higher in courses that used open textbooks as compared to those using purchased textbooks (Fischer et al., 2015). Faculty also found that OER can 'provide a richer and more personalized learning experience than traditional print materials' (Green, 2015, para. 1), as negative consequences to learning can result from students deciding not to purchase costly textbooks; Hill (2015) reports that first generation students and those with low socio-economic status are less likely to purchase expensive textbooks.

Educators can also benefit from producing OER, for example, through quicker distribution of research results to a wider audience, thus opening up opportunities for including other colleagues in the processes of quality assurance, idea development, and problem-solving (Hylén, 2009). This inclusion of and exposure to OER further promotes collaboration amongst educators (Pawlyshyn et al., 2013; Stacey, 2011), which according to De los Arcos et al. (2014) further boosts reflection on teaching practice. Another positive result for faculty is increased 'publicity, reputation and the pleasure of sharing with peers' (D'Antonio, 2009; Hylén, 2009, para. 29).

2.5 *The Innovation Motive: Fear of Being Left Behind*

Although not yet mainstream in its adoption (Weller, 2014), OER is a rising trend, and institutions that do not engage with OER run the risk of becoming 'increasingly marginalised by market forces' (Hylén, 2009, para. 28; OECD, 2007). According to Weller (2014), a move to OER can also support experimentation and innovation within the institution. De los Arcos et al. (2014) report that '79.5% of educators use OER to get new ideas and inspiration' (p. 6).

Whatever their motivation for engaging in OER, institutions planning to use and/or create OER are well-advised to develop an OER strategy, one that identifies how and the extent to which they will use OER.

3 Strategies for Engaging in OER

In developing their OER strategies, institutions must consider the level to which they will engage with OER. Weller (2014) describes OER engagement levels as:

- *Primary OER usage:* OER are used extensively, and there is a comprehensive awareness and understanding of OER licenses. Educators are active proponents of open education.
- *Secondary OER usage:* OER are used within the institution and in practical ways and in support of innovative educational approaches; there is a general awareness of OER licensing.
- *Tertiary OER usage:* OER are used within an institution but do not play a central role; there is little awareness of licensing aspects of OER, and OER are primarily used for consumption.

In the next part of this chapter, four case studies featuring the use of OER are presented. In the first three of these cases studies (Athabasca University, University of Maryland University College, and the Open University UK), the research strove to identify potential issues and current strategic approaches from the field in managing and implementing an OER solution and used a mix of standardized open-ended interviews and conversational interviews with institutional leadership from which emerging themes and strategies were clustered and summarized. From this research then emerged a set of general best practices that could be used as a basis when considering an OER implementation. The fourth case study (Hamburg Open Online University) carried out a review of nine evaluation instruments (rubrics) for measuring the quality of the OER that are used, and consequentially developing a holistic model to support the creation of quality OER.

4 OER Case Study 1: Athabasca University (Canada)

Founded in 1972, Athabasca University (AU) is a leading online and open university located in Canada and since 2010 has been the host of UNESCO's OECD and Commonwealth of Learning Chair in OER (UNESCO, 1995–2010; Athabasca University, n.d.). AU's early involvement in OER dates back to the 1990s, when a decision was made to use openly licensed course materials for its mobile learning course offerings, in order to avoid potential legal issues due to copyright infringement of commercial content. More recently, AU has engaged more deeply with the OER movement after ACCESS Copyright, a Canadian copyright collective, increased its fees for students using its resources from $3.38 per student to $45.00 (Ives & Pringle, 2013).

Open education and OER align closely with the AU's open admissions policy and its institutional mission to make education and accessible to all as an open university (Ives & Pringle, 2013). AU has also traditionally been a proponent of open education and OER, for example, through its open access Athabasca University Press,[1] its use of open source software (Moodle), and its Open Library, which provides a listing of open and free resources (Elliott & Fabbro, 2015; Stewart & Associates, 2006)). By adopting OER, the institution also saw an opportunity to lower costs and develop and deliver courses more quickly, as well as to increase student motivation and retention rates (Ives & Pringle, 2013).

AU has not made an official decision to apply a specific strategy for implementing OER. However, executive decision-making about open access and use of open resources indicates committed and comprehensive support of OER within the institution. This commitment has been demonstrated through decisions to support the OER Chair and provide resources such as the Open Library and AUPress. The institution produces OER using 'teams of learning designers, subject matter experts, visual designers, and programmers,' who produce OER such as 'podcasts, interactive tutorials, crosswords, videos, visualization exercises, and multimedia learning objects,' most having CC BY licenses (Ives & Pringle, 2013, p. 7).

To help instructors prepare for OER, the institution provides OER examples and demonstrations as well as holding 'a series of workshops and community conversations' both online and face-to-face (Ives & Pringle, 2013, p 8). OER that have been developed – from individual learning objects to complete courses – are stored in an open repository and are assigned an open license. The success of the strategy is based on the number of OER that are used and prepared by faculty members.

Awareness and promotion of OER success stories have been critical to AU's success in using OER: 'people have done it ... Other faculty have seen it done and work ... When faculty become aware of it, for the most part, they support it quite strongly' (R. McGreal, personal communication, January 26, 2016). McGreal has also served a central role in raising awareness of OER, due to his role as UNESCO Chair in OER. In addition, the awareness campaign is carried out by champions throughout the institution, from course developers to executive management.

As a next step toward realizing OER, AU will be offering an online, first-year program – completely open – for students. At the end of the year, students can then decide whether to apply for certification of learning, which is fee-based.

McGreal's advice for institutions contemplating a transition to OER is threefold: first, institutions need to *create awareness* for OER; second, they need to *provide incentives* for faculty to adopt OER; and finally, they should *install and support champions* of OER within the organization (personal communication, January 26, 2016).

AU has realized numerous benefits from using OER, for example, reduced time for developing and producing courses and lowered costs of using commercial content: 'now we're using more and more OER ... we can adapt them and change them to our needs, and this is considered by faculty to be an important benefit of OER' (McGreal, personal communication, January 26, 2016). Another benefit cited by McGreal was that use of OER promotes faculty collaboration both within and outside of the institution, and faculty could more easily adapt content to local needs. In addition, use of OER has reduced dependency on the publishing industry and costs related to using commercial textbooks and sources. AU graduate students also benefit by developing and adapting their own OER.

Challenges in adopting OER at AU include sustainability and funding an OER approach; difficulties in adapting resources to the Canadian context; a lack of open courses (i.e., availability of the complete course package); and issues surrounding student fees and copyright. According to Ives and Pringle (2013), faculty reluctance to adopt OER has also been a challenge, as has a deficit in skills for incorporating OER into the curriculum. Another hindrance is Canadian copyright laws (Fair Dealing rights), laws which are quite open, allowing for extensive reuse of commercial content. As a result, faculty do not always see the value in using OER, since commercial content is readily available.

5 OER Case Study 2: University of Maryland University College (UMUC) Undergraduate School (USA)

In 2013, UMUC leadership made the decision to move to OER in an attempt to reduce student textbook costs – a move that strongly aligns with UMUC's mission as an open admissions institution, and one that focuses on student-centered learning and achieving specific learning outcomes aligned with industry need. As of fall 2015, all UMUC's undergraduate courses (over 700) use embedded no-cost textbooks; in fall 2016, all graduate courses transitioned 100% to OER (Klein, 2015). The resulting savings is estimated 'to be in the millions for the more than 80,000 students taking classes at UMUC annually' (Klein, 2015, para. 3). While the goal of the endeavor was to reduce textbook costs for students, the move also resulted in more learner-centered courses that in turn have helped to improve learning and performance.

In transitioning to OER, UMUC built teams that consisted of: 'a program chair, a faculty member or two, a librarian, and a member of the Design Solutions office' (Klein, 2015, para. 14). The team-based approach helped ensure that responsibility of finding OER was not placed solely on individual faculty; it also gave faculty support during the transition to OER. Librarians and faculty would search for OER – often Creative Commons resources (Klein, 2015) – which would in turn be approved by the program chair. Working together with faculty and the program chair, a gap analysis would be performed, where the team would identify missing content and then work with the library to fill those gaps. Once suitable OER were found, content would be stored in an internal database, and an instructional designer would prepare and incorporate these into courses, aligning the OER and content with learning outcomes. Program chairs would then approve the redesign.

While a shift to OER ultimately reduced textbook costs for students, it also caused a rethinking of the educational approach to be more learner-centered (Klein, 2015). The process was not a simple switch out of commercial textbooks for OER but was also a move toward creating learning journeys for students, based on specific learning outcomes.

The success of the strategy has been measured based on factors such as student satisfaction, student performance in terms of grades, and completion rates; OER were not found to have a negative impact on these factors. The next phase in the project will be a focus on improving the measurement of student achievement of specific competencies and content effectiveness in supporting learning objectives.

Factors contributing to the project's success were strong institutional leadership and management and stakeholder support at all institutional levels. As a result of its OER effort, UMUC was recognized by the Open Education Consortium (OEC), receiving the 2015 OEC President's Award (Ludwig, 2015). The UMUC interviewee's[2] (2016) advice for institutions considering OER is to *involve faculty* and to *align the initiative with improving the student learning experience*.

A major benefit of the transition to OER was substantial cost savings for UMUC students. OER has also been found to better support student learning (Green, 2015; Pawlyshyn et al., 2013; Weller, 2014). Prior to using OER, UMUC found that students would often receive their commercial textbooks long after a course began, or they would choose not to purchase the textbook at all. Other benefits of the transition were more flexibility in 'switching out' resources, more sharing of resources; and a stronger focus on practical, competency-based learning outcomes that better align with workforce needs. Another benefit has been student involvement in helping to find OER for courses.

On the other hand, one of the major challenges was 'to find materials that were at least as effective as the interactive material provided by the textbook'

(Klein, 2015, para. 20). UMUC also had no existing model to follow in making the transition. Initially, teams focused on searching for open textbooks, but found that this approach limited them in their ability to provide course content focused on learning outcomes; the focus quickly shifted to smaller chunks of OER. Also, a large portion of the student population required offline/downloadable access to OER, which was not an option with many of the open textbook offerings. It was particularly the veteran teaching staff who needed to readjust thinking about using free resources rather than UMUC's newer staff (Klein, 2015).

Issues around copyright and accessibility also arose, and these were handled first by the library, and then, as needed, by UMUC's legal department. This required that UMUC develop a feedback loop in resolving issues as they emerged. Project costs, mostly operational, also landed squarely on the institution. These costs were related in part for searching for OER but also for developing new content, for example, when incorporating specific contextual information and for maintaining OER, for example, ensuring that web links are current.

6 OER Case Study 3: The Open University United Kingdom (OUUK) (UK)

The Open University (OUUK) is one of the largest providers of online education in the world and the foremost model of open learning institutions within open and distance learning; and is prominently positioned as a leader within open education and OER. Shortly after MIT introduced its Open CourseWare project, the OUUK was approached by the Hewlett Foundation with an intriguing proposition: would they like to produce OER? Openness and access to education have always been critical to the OUUK mission from both a social and business standpoint, so providing OER was seen as contributing to the overall charter of the institution. Leadership also saw an opportunity to achieve scale by expanding OUUK market reach, as well as to participate in a potentially disruptive innovation. Having received substantial funding from Hewlett for the OER project, the institution made a strategic decision to set out on a journey to expand OER production and distribution and to more prominently position OER both within the institution and the field of online learning.

The Open Media Unit at the OUUK oversees a number of initiatives in support of open learning. Two of these are OpenLearn, which is the OUUK web portal to OER; and FutureLearn, which is the OUUK's open platform for delivering open online courses and supporting MOOC development and delivery.

Content is provided using open source software (such as Moodle and Drupal) and platforms (such as Google Play, AudioBoom, Bibblio, and FutureLearn, an OU MOOC host).

In implementing its OER strategy, the most senior support has been involved, as well as academics, production, IT, the strategy development unit, business development units (BDU), marketing, and the technology enhanced learning (TEL) unit. Stakeholder groups have played a critical role in contributing to the development and evaluation of the program; and, for example, in considering new pedagogical approaches, business models, market strategies, and uses of technology.

As the OER project evolved, management saw the need for a policy that would define how OER would be positioned and used. The current policy[3] defines the purpose and types of educational media with the context of OU: guidelines for channels (OU and third-party channels) and for licensing; key performance indicators (KPIs); operating guidelines (how content should be licensed); and guidelines for partnership and research projects (Open Educational Media Operating Policy, 2018). KPIs play a central role in measuring the success of the OUUK strategy and include measurement of factors such as conversion (number of informal learners becoming formal learners based on enquiries and registrations); brand impact (level of awareness and reach of the OUUK brand, as measured through channel views; unique hits; time and engagement on site; comments/rating) assets (level of media asset use in learning and teaching and their value contribution); and income (revenue income from media sales). Monetary value is then attached to each of these measurements, thus allowing management to measure the impact of the OER project on revenue and operations. This focus on aligning KPIs with institutional mission and strategy and measuring these meticulously against the institutional strategy and assets and value of the brand, and then being able to coherently describe these has largely contributed to the project's successful sustainability.

Through its OER initiative, the OUUK has strongly positioned itself as a leader within the OER playing field: the MoocLab recently placed OpenLearn in first place in its international open courseware provider league table (2016). Andrew Law (2016) attributes this achievement to OpenLearn's fundamental principles, that learning is immediate, flexible, relevant, convenient, free, reusable, and adaptable.

In realizing an OER project, the OUUK Interviewee identifies critical success factors such as *strategically aligning the project with overall institutional strategy, building on institutional strengths and capacity, incorporating levers for motivation* at all organizational levels, *identifying clear values for measurement* that are aligned with strategy, and *engaging senior-level and faculty support.*

A variety of benefits emerged as the OUUK embarked on its OER project in terms of improvement of the OUUK brand and reputation, expanded reach to new audiences (with 5 million visitors to its websites each year), increased access, e.g., to those with disabilities (De los Arcos et al., 2014), growing use of media assets through re-use of content and new technology enhancements, more partnerships, new business and process models, and growth of academic and business research opportunities. More informal learners are also being channeled into formal learning programs at an estimated 1,000 learners annually, thus increasing OUUK revenue. Revenues have also been achieved through the resale of courses to businesses who then repurpose them for individual use, as well as through a Google grant that 'complements a commercial marketing budget' (OUUK interviewee,[4] 2016).

Development of new, synergistic partnerships (such as training programs in Africa) and revaluation of established partnerships (such as delivery over the BBC) was one of the benefits that the OUUK had originally anticipated – and has led to new partnerships and business models. The partnerships have given the OUUK competitive advantage through expanded brand awareness and recognition, while the new business models focus less on content and more on business processes. Research opportunities have also excelled within both academic and business realms. Competitive advantage has also been realized by monetizing on the OER content by offering MOOCs through FutureLearn. A further benefit has been a reimaging of the institutional brand as digitally savvy and 'an innovator in the field' (OUUK interviewee, 2016).

A major challenge for the project has been in the provision of free OER and how that content would be licensed; with these issues, the OUUK benefited from its existing institutional structure for addressing intellectual property and licensing issues. To limit commercial use of content, OER are offered under a Creative Commons CC BY-NC-SA 4.0. Another initial challenge was the lack of an operational policy, which had the possibility of endangering sustainability of the project. This policy emerged as the project developed.

7 OER Case Study 4: The Hamburg Open Online University (Germany)

The Hamburg Open Online University[5] (HOOU) is a consortium of seven higher education institutions in the city of Hamburg in Northern Germany, established in 2014 (Bessenrodt-Weberpals et al., 2017). A major goal of the HOOU is to establish a repository in which OER can be published, freely shared and reused. At the HOOU, openness and OER are conceptualized as follows (Bessenrodt-Weberpals et al., p. 10):

> The HOOU is based on the idea of open education. It consistently aims to ensure that learning materials are available as Open Educational Resources (OER) through the HOOU, which can be revised and shared. OER come in varying degrees of structure and purpose, for example as collaborative learning objects in repositories for further use [...]. In addition, the HOOU promotes the idea of openness through the use of primarily open source software, legal openness through the use of open licenses, social openness, as well as open learning spaces through open pedagogical design of various learning scenarios. Openness is also expressed through access to materials and interactions that offer the greatest possible accessibility for students with disabilities. Last but not least, openness also includes the promotion of a learning and teaching culture in the sense of an Open Educational Practice (OEP). (translated by the authors)

A major challenge in the project is to convince faculty members to contribute and share their learning materials. As Jung et al. (2016) state, lack of confidence in the quality of learning objects is one of the main barriers to the adoption of OER practices. Therefore, it was seen as essential that a quality assurance system for OER be introduced – a system that would support faculty members in creating and publishing high quality learning materials.

Although various evaluation instruments for learning materials have been developed since 2000 (see Yuan & Recker, 2015), a widely accepted instrument for the evaluation of OER does not exist (Mayrberger & Zawacki-Richter, 2017). Therefore, in a review of evaluation instruments in which nine different rubrics where analysed, Zawacki-Richter and Mayrberger (2017) revealed a complex picture and heterogeneity in the various dimensions and criteria to measure the quality of OER. Based on a qualitative analysis of over 160 different criteria identified in the review, a holistic model was developed. In order to find an appropriate balance between a solid scientific foundation and efficient applicability, the various dimensions and subscales of the original model were reduced and adopted to the German HOOU context without losing relevant information (see Figure 9.1).

Another issue involves Creative Commons (CC) licensing. A considerable number of faculty members would prefer not to allow commercial use of their learning materials. They argue that their salaries as professors at public higher

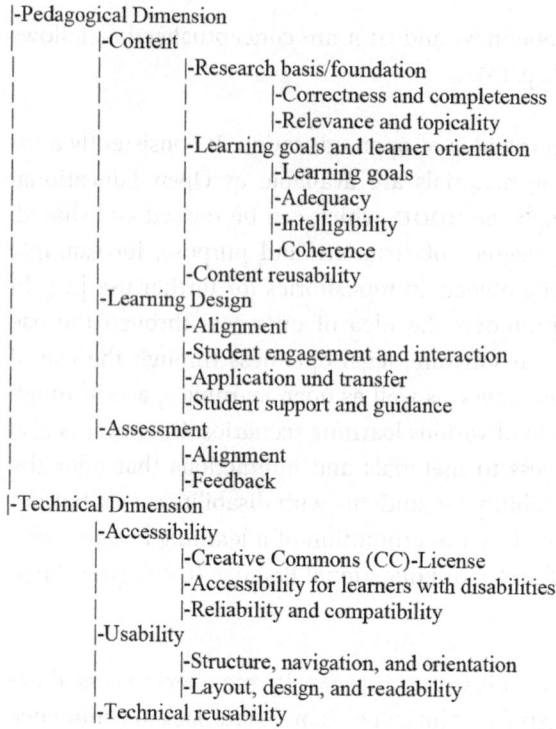

|-Pedagogical Dimension
| |-Content
| | |-Research basis/foundation
| | | |-Correctness and completeness
| | | |-Relevance and topicality
| | |-Learning goals and learner orientation
| | | |-Learning goals
| | | |-Adequacy
| | | |-Intelligibility
| | | |-Coherence
| | |-Content reusability
| |-Learning Design
| | |-Alignment
| | |-Student engagement and interaction
| | |-Application und transfer
| | |-Student support and guidance
| |-Assessment
| | |-Alignment
| | |-Feedback
|-Technical Dimension
| |-Accessibility
| | |-Creative Commons (CC)-License
| | |-Accessibility for learners with disabilities
| | |-Reliability and compatibility
| |-Usability
| | |-Structure, navigation, and orientation
| | |-Layout, design, and readability
| |-Technical reusability

FIGURE 9.1 Quality dimensions for learning materials/OER (based on Zawacki-Richter & Mayrberger, 2017)

education institutions are paid by taxpayers. Thus, the content that they produce should be available to the public for non-commercial use only. However, this view is not in line with the current UNESCO definition of OER in which commercial use is not restricted, where 'anyone can legally and freely copy, use, adapt and re-share them' (para. 1). Therefore, the steering board of the HOOU decided to distinguish between different degrees of openness of OER or learning materials in general when they are published on the HOOU portal:

- HOOU OER that are licensed in the range of CC 0, CC BY, CC BY-SA, which are 'real' OER in the sense of the UNESCO definition,
- Open Learning Materials of the HOOU that restrict commercial use (CC NC), and
- -All other leaning materials of the HOOU (CC BY-ND, CC BY-ND-NC).

8 Elements in an OER Strategy

Before embarking on an OER strategy, an institution must assess its capacity for adopting OER, as well as decide upon its level of OER engagement and openness (Pawlyshyn et al., 2013; Weller, 2014). This section provides guidance in building an OER strategy, by focusing on measurements of strategy effectiveness, critical success factors, and best practices that emerged from the OER case studies presented here.

The institutions profiled here chose different means for measuring the success of their OER projects. At AU, the success of the initiative was based on the number of OER that were used and prepared by faculty members, while UMUC placed a stronger emphasis on student satisfaction, student performance (grades), and completion rates, as it moves toward measuring the OER role in supporting achievement of competencies and learning outcomes. Measurements implemented by the OUUK centered on the conversion of informal learners to formal learners, brand impact, use and value of assets, and revenue income. As demonstrated in the research studies, the measurement used can differ based on the institutional context and approach to adopting OER.

In the first three case studies presented here, critical success factors in an OER project also emerged. *Executive management leadership and support* were identified as significant factors contributing to OER success (Weller, 2014; Wiley, 2010). *Alignment of the OER strategy with overall institutional mission and strategy* was also evident (D'Antonio, 2009). Additionally, *support and promotion of champions* of OER at all institutional levels was seen as important in increasing OER awareness and acceptance (D'Antonio, 2009; Friesen, 2009)). *Sustainability of the strategy*, for example by defining policy in handling OER and in identifying clear values for measurement, was also cited (D'Antonio, 2009; Downes, 2007; Yuan, MacNeil, & Kraan, 2007). *Incentives and motivational measures* can also contribute to the success and sustainability of OER, for example, by incorporating OER development into the tenure process and giving faculty control of intellectual property (Jacobs, 2014; Stacey, 2011; Wiley, 2007).

Best practices or guidelines found within this research – and supported by current literature – include:

- Promoting awareness for OER within the organization, for example, through testimonials;
- Providing incentives for faculty to adopt OER, for example, by supporting attendance at OER conferences;
- Installing and supporting champions of OER within the organization;
- Using design teams for identifying and incorporating OER;
- Involving faculty in the process;
- Linking the OER initiative to improving the student learning experience;
- Aligning the project with overall institutional mission and strategy;
- Identifying institutional strengths that can contribute to the transition;

- Utilizing available resources such as existing frameworks and the library in finding and assessing OER content (De Langen, 2013; Jung, Sasake, & Latchem, 2016; Friesen, 2009; D'Antonio, 2009).

9 Benefits of Using OER

Benefits of using OER were diverse and dependent upon institutional context. One benefit cited in all case studies was the *increased opportunities for collaboration and sharing of resources*, whether that occurred within (faculty) or outside the institution (other faculty and institutions, businesses, research organizations) (De los Arcos et al., 2014; Hylén, 2009; Pawlyshyn et al., 2013; Stacey, 2011). AU and UMUC both cited a *reduction in costs* related to use of commercial textbooks and resources, as well as lowered dependency on the publishing industry (Fischer et al., 2015; Hylén, 2009; Senack, 2015; Weller, 2014). OER also provided *added flexibility* in adapting content to individual needs (Weller, 2014). Both AU and UMUC also identified areas for *student involvement*, either in finding OER (UMUC) or in developing and adapting their own OER (AU), an aspect not identified as a benefit in the literature. A benefit that was unique to UMUC was improved pedagogy through a *focus on practical, competency-based learning outcomes* that better aligned with workforce needs (Caraher, 2016; Green, 2015; Pawlyshyn et al., 2013; Weller, 2014). Significant savings in textbook costs were only evident in the UMUC case, which can be attributed to the institutional context (based in the US, where textbook costs are substantial) (Hylén, 2009; Senack, 2015; Weller, 2014). At AU, a benefit not mentioned in the other case studies was the *reduced time for developing and producing courses* (D'Antonio, 2009; OECD, 2007; Pawlyshyn et al., 2013; Stacey, 2011). The OUUK had its own set of individual benefits that were exclusive to the institution, related to *expanding its brand, reputation, and reach, increasing accessibility and use of media assets, more partnerships and research collaboration*, and *new business and process models* (D'Antonio, 2009; De los Arcos et al., 2014; Hylén, 2009; OECD, 2007; Stacey, 2011; Weller, 2014).

10 Challenges in Implementing OER

Challenges faced by the institutions in these case studies varied, depending on context, and were issues surrounding *sustainability, project funding and costs, intellectual property and copyright*, and *faculty resistance* to adopting OER (Allen & Seaman, 2014; D'Antonio & Savage, 2009; Hylén, 2009; Kortemeyer,

2013; OECD, 2007; Wiley, 2007). AU and UMUC reported on *difficulties in finding, adapting, and localizing content* and a *deficit in faculty skills* for incorporating OER (Allen & Seaman, 2014; Jacobs, 2014; Pawlyshyn et al., 2013). The OUUK, HOOU, and UMUC all reported on the *lack of an existing model* to follow in making the transition and in evaluating quality of OER (e.g., HOOU), an aspect not identified in the literature.

Context-specific issues for AU were those surrounding *student fees and copyright*, as well as issues emerging from dependency on commercial assets (Senack, 2015; Wiley, 2016). UMUC, on the other hand, dealt with *accessibility issues* and the need to rethink *strategies for teaching using OER* and to have *downloadable OER* (rather than open textbooks) (Downes, 2007), the former two aspects not arising as challenges in the literature. Another issue that was specific to the OUUK, but which could also become an issue for UMUC and AU, was the *lack of an operational policy* that contributes to project sustainability (Downes, 2007). For HOOU, making the OER available for commercial purposes was an issue, i.e., in deciding upon the appropriate CC license.

11 Deciding on an OER Project

In defining an OER project, institutional leadership should consider the following questions:

- What level of engagement will the institution use in OER? Primary, secondary, or tertiary (Weller, 2014)?
- How does the OER initiative align with the overall institutional mission and strategies? What factors are specific to the institutional context?
- What are institutional strengths and how can these be leveraged through OER? Are infrastructures in place to support the transition?
- What institutional policy will be developed and applied in using and distributing OER? How will needs/requirements of faculty be met?
- What are the potential costs of the OER project? How can ROI be achieved?
- Is the OER project sustainable? What factors will be used to measure the project success?

Choosing to use OER can be an initial first step toward openness, and this section has discussed how institutions can move forward in creating a strategy for using OER in their organizations. As an institution engages further in openness, it may also choose to explore additional forms of 'open,' such as prior learning assessment and recognition (PLAR), as part of its strategy. In the next section of this chapter, the case study presented is an example of how a university in Germany has established PLAR services that recognize students' prior vocational and informal learning, thereby 'opening' their learning journeys.

12 Prior Learning Assessment and Recognition (PLAR)

Prior Learning Assessment and Recognition is connected in many ways with the concept of 'openness.' Firstly, PLAR contributes to opening the university to non-traditional students by recognising professionally acquired skills. Secondly, PLAR enables the recognition of learning outcomes from 'open educational activities,' such as those described by Friesen and Wihak (2013). Thirdly, PLAR is based on an open understanding of education that includes non-formal and informal learning and does not designate a specific learning context. In the second part of this chapter, we explore PLAR with a case study from Germany that describes how PLAR has been realized at the Carl von Ossietzky University of Oldenburg.

PLAR is commonly understood as a branch of the more comprehensive term Recognition of Prior Learning (RPL):

> Prior learning assessment and recognition is itself an arm of the larger umbrella term, recognizing prior learning (RPL). Under the aegis of the latter is contained, in addition to PLAR, the related (but different) processes of credit transfer. (Conrad, 2006, p. 2)

In a more recent publication, Conrad (2008) proposes a more detailed typology of these terms, which describes RPL as a generic term that includes PLAR, credit transfer (CT), and qualification recognition (QR). The difference between QR and PLAR lies in how the evidence of competence is demonstrated: Whereas QR is based on the learning outcomes of a formal qualification that is acquired by all successful learners, PLAR focuses on individual learning outcomes, which must be proven separately for each learner. Within the context of recognizing vocational learning outcomes for the purpose of exempting higher education study modules, the individual RPL of personal learning outcomes (i.e. skills and competencies) is referred to as PLAR. In contrast, individual RPL of a vocational qualification in curricular content is called QR according to this definition. A substantial difference between PLAR and QR lies in how the evidence is utilized in equivalency assessment: QR is mostly based on curricula, module descriptions, and syllabi (i.e. qualification-related learning outcome descriptions), while PLAR is based on individual evidence of skills, which is usually collected by means of a portfolio.

The term PLAR is related closely to the portfolio method, so much so that PLAR sometimes is equated with portfolio-based RPL. Conrad (2008) complains about this practice: 'There is also a tendency in Canada for PLAR to be understood synonymously with the use of portfolios as an assessment methodology' (p. 91). In principle, however, PLAR isn't restricted to portfolio assessment, and other methods of competence assessment can be used in PLAR. For example, the Ohio Department of Education (2016) lists several assessment methods as a PLAR guideline:

> In PLA, students can be assessed using a variety of methods, such as portfolio-based assessments, standardized exams [...] faculty-created departmental 'challenge exams', or evaluations of standardized training (e.g. apprenticeship, military training). (p. 14)

13 Case Study 5: PLAR Service at University of Oldenburg

Carl von Ossietzky University in Oldenburg was one of the first universities in Germany to engage in recognition of prior vocational and informal learning (RPL-IV). As part of the project 'Qualifikationsverbund Nord-West' (Qualification Group North-West), the university began exploring PLAR when it participated in the federal ministry's initiative called Accreditation of Vocational Competences in Higher Education Programs (ANKOM) (Hartmann & Stamm-Riemer, 2006).

Since that time, the University of Oldenburg has been continuously involved in model initiatives and pilot projects related to the recognition of prior learning and its use and application within vocational and higher education. The majority of projects have focused on continuing education master's programs (part-time) and bachelor programs, where students study as they work. Recognition in these projects relates to learning outcomes of vocational qualifications like business specialists or certified technicians. Usually, RPL-IV uses methods of curriculum analysis based on formal vocational qualifications. This kind of RPL matches the definition of QR, whereas RPL-based on individual learning (PLAR) – has been practically unknown in Germany until recently.

In 2010, changes to examination regulations at the University of Oldenburg allowed for recognition of vocational and informal prior learning (RPL-IV), which was then formally implemented for all full-time programs. However, up until 2015 only approximately 50 students took advantage of this new possibility of RPL in full-time programs, resulting in an average of only 10 completed RPL-IV cases per year. These numbers were deemed too low.

14 The PLARnet Project at University of Oldenburg (Open University Task Force)

Upon recognition of the insufficient utilization of RPL-IV, the University of Oldenburg established an 'Open University' task force in the summer of 2015, with the purpose of working on a more practical implementation of prior learning recognition. The department of the Vice-president for Study and Teaching, the Center for Lifelong Learning, the Faculty of Education, and the department for Student and Academic Affairs participated in this task force, which worked together to develop a concept for university-wide RPL-IV counselling. This project supported students seeking RPL-IV, as well as lecturers who reviewed and approved the RPL-IV applications. A further aim of the project was the development of RPL-IV standards and guidelines for the whole university.

The 'Open University' task force in Oldenburg prepared a project proposal based on PLAR principles. This proposal was accepted by the Ministry of Science and Culture in Lower Saxony within the 'Opening of Universities' program, and in February 2017, the central PLAR service at the University of Oldenburg was established. As part of the PLARnet project, the PLAR service is funded by the federal state of Lower Saxony and the European Union.

15 PLAR Strategy at the University of Oldenburg

While PLAR at Oldenburg is modelled on Athabasca University's PLAR model, it differs from Athabasca University on two central points. Firstly, University of Oldenburg does not charge fees for full-time bachelor and master's programs. As a consequence, the staff of the PLAR service cannot be financed by students' fees, and financing of PLAR staff must be handled through other means (e.g., project funding). Secondly, online. Correspondingly, PLAR counselling and support uses online platforms. In comparison, the PLAR Service at University of Oldenburg only supports students in on-campus study programs. These students expect face-to-face counselling as part of the PLAR service.

During the concept development phase of the PLAR service, these general conditions and the appropriate measures and design approaches were implemented to recognize the special circumstances at the University of Oldenburg. Because of the comparatively limited resources and staff of the PLARnet project, an attempt was made to reduce PLAR staff workloads by involving students actively in the PLAR process. For example, a student seeking recognition of vocational or informally-acquired competencies is required to independently compile a PLAR portfolio. Part of the portfolio is used to compare learning outcomes of the study modules with the student's acquired skills and competences. In this way, the students themselves – to some extent – carry out the equivalence check, with the lecturer (as an assessor) then validating this equivalence check. The task of the PLAR service is then restricted to counselling and support in the context of the portfolio compilation. This adaptation, based on logistics, at the same time incorporates a new degree of 'openness' into the process.

The 'new' PLAR has been a great success at the University of Oldenburg. Within the first year of the PLAR service more than 100 students attended the joint consultation hour; more than 40 portfolios were successful completed, so that one or more study modules were accredited. In addition, approximately 50 portfolios were still being processed in January 2018. This data demonstrates that, as a direct result of the implementation of the PLAR service, the number of RPL-IV cases has increased significantly as compared to 2015. A further increase in the number of RPL-IV cases is expected in the next year, as students will be informed about the possibility of PLAR immediately upon enrolling at the University of Oldenburg.

16 Conclusion

The research presented here demonstrates diverse benefits for institutions that transition to enhanced openness using OER and PLAR: reduced costs, greater accessibility to education, and improved learner outcomes – findings that are also supported by Conrad (2013) and Friesen and Wihak (2013). Through the use of OER, institutions have an opportunity to provide more learner-centered instruction, as well as make resources more accessible to learners. PLAR services, a further extension of openness, recognizes prior knowledge, competencies, and skills as well as that gained through OER, making certification of informal education more accessible and officially recognized.

At the same time, the research also reveals real challenges faced by institutions when venturing into openness, primarily when deciding upon the models and approaches to adopt. A decision for or against increased openness, whether through OER or PLAR, is highly contextual and influenced by factors such as the overall institutional mission, values, and strategy, capacity and core strengths of the institution, external and internal forces (such as state policy), and institutional motivation. Within both OER and PLAR constructs, faculty and staff who practice openness must possess or be trained in the appropriate skill set in order to ensure quality within the models, strategies, and frameworks. The success and sustainability of an initiative toward more openness can be influenced by these factors, as well as by the degree of executive commitment and support and the existence of institutional policy on openness. Each of these case studies, however, is a manifestation of how moving toward openness can provide unique opportunities for meeting student needs and optimizing business models, processes, and content according to individual institutional context and which can result in measurable benefits and value for the organization.

Notes

1 See http://www.aupress.ca
2 The interviewee preferred to remain anonymous.
3 See http://www.open.ac.uk/about/open-educational-resources/home/open-educational-media-operating-policy
4 The interviewee preferred to remain anonymous.
5 See http://www.hoou.de

References

Allen, I. E., & Seaman, J. (2014). *Opening the curriculum: OER in US higher education, 2014*. Babson Survey Research Group. Retrieved from http://www.onlinelearningsurvey.com/reports/openingthecurriculum2014.pdf

Athabasca University. (n.d.). *Brochure*. Retrieved from http://www.athabascau.ca/content/aboutau/media/documents/AUbrochure.pdf

Athabasca University: Mission and Mandate. (n.d.). Athabasca University. Retrieved from http://www.athabascau.ca/aboutau/mission.php

Athabasca University: Open Courseware. (n.d.). Athabasca University. Retrieved from http://ocw.lms.athabascau.ca/

Bessenrodt-Weberpals, M., Göcks, M., Knutzen, S., & Mayrberger, K. (2017). Hamburg Open Online University (HOOU) Rückblick Vorprojekt – Ausblick Projekt [Looking back – Looking forward: Project history and outlook]. In HOOU (Eds.), *HOOU Content Projekte der Vorprojektphase 2015/16 der Hamburg Open Online University* [Content project in the early project phases at HOOU 2015/16] (pp. 8–24). Hamburg: Hamburg Open Online University. Retrieved from https://www.synergie.uni-hamburg.de/media/sonderbaende/hoou-content-projekte-2015-2016.pdf

Conole, G., & Weller, M. (2010). Grainne Conole discusses open education with Martin Weller (3/4) [YouTube video]. *The OU on YouTube*. Retrieved from https://www.youtube.com/watch?v=A4Uoa9OqoAo

Conrad, D. (2006). *E-portfolios as new learning spaces? Portfolios, paradigms, and pedagogy.* Paper presented at EDEN-Conference, Vienna. Retrieved November 31, 2017, from http://priorlearning.athabascau.ca/documents/e-portfolios-EDEN-feb-1.doc

Conrad, D. (2008). Revisiting the Recognition of Prior Learning (RPL): A reflective inquiry into RPL practice in Canada. *Canadian Journal of University Continuing Education, 34*(2), 89–110.

Cummins, P. A., & Kunkel, S. R. (2015). A global examination of policies and practices for lifelong learning. *New Horizons in Adult Education and Human Resource Development, 27*(3), 3–17. doi:10.1002/nha3.20107

D'Antonio, S. (2009). OER: Reviewing initiatives and issues. *Open Learning: The Journal of Open, Distance and e-Learning, 24*(1), 3–10. Retrieved from http://www.tandfonline.com/doi/abs/10.1080/02680510802625443

D'Antonio, S., & Savage, C. (2009). *OER: Conversations in cyberspace.* Paris: UNESCO. Retrieved from http://unesdoc.unesco.org/images/0018/001816/181682e.pdf

De Langen, F. H. T. (2013). Strategies for sustainable business models for OER. *The International Review of Research in Open and Distributed Learning, 14*(2), 53–66. Retrieved from http://www.irrodl.org/index.php/irrodl/article/view/1533/2485

De los Arcos, B., Farrow, R., Perryman, L.-A., Pitt, R., & Weller, M. (2014). OER evidence report 2013–2014. *OER Research Hub.* Retrieved from http://oerresearchhub.org/2014/11/19/oer-evidence-report-2013-2014/

Downes, S. (2007). Models for sustainable OER. *Interdisciplinary Journal of Knowledge and Learning Objects, 3*(1), 29–44.

Elliott, C., & Fabbro, E. (2015). The open library at AU (Athabasca University): Supporting open access and OER. *Open Praxis, 7*(2), 133–140. Retrieved from http://www.openpraxis.org/index.php/OpenPraxis/article/view/196/150

European Commission. (2015). *Adult learners in digital learning environments (EAC-2013-0563): Final report.* Luxembourg: Publications Office of the European Union. Retrieved from http://ec.europa.eu/social/main.jsp?catId=738&langId=&pubId=7820&type=2&furtherPubs=yes

Fischer, L., Hilton, III, J., Robinson, T. J., & Wiley, D. A. (2015). A multi-institutional study of the impact of open textbook adoption on the learning outcomes of post-secondary students. *Journal of Computing in Higher Education, 27*(3), 159–172.

Friesen, N. (2009). OER: New possibilities for change and sustainability. *The International Review of Research in Open and Distributed Learning, 10*(5). Retrieved from http://www.irrodl.org/index.php/irrodl/article/view/664/1388

Friesen, N., & Wihak, C. (2013). From OER to PLAR: Credentialing for open education. *Open Praxis, 5*(1), 49–58.

Green, K. C. (2015). Great faith in the instructional benefits of digital technologies: Great expectations for the rising use of OER. *The Campus Computing Project.* Retrieved from http://www.campuscomputing.net/new.html

Hartmann, E. A., & Stamm-Riemer, I. (2006). Die BMBF-Initiative „Anrechnung beruflicher Kompetenzen auf Hochschulstudiengänge' – ein Beitrag zur Durchlässigkeit des deutschen Bildungssystem und zum lebenlangen Lernen [The BMBF initiative: Calculating professional competencies for a higher education program: A commentary on the flexibility of the German education system and lifelong learning]. *Hochschule & Weiterbildung, 1*, 52–60.

Hewlett. (n.d.). *OER defined*. Retrieved from http://www.hewlett.org/programs/education/open-educational-resources

Hill, P. (2015). Asking what students spend on textbooks is very important but not sufficient [Blog post]. *e-Literate*. Retrieved from http://mfeldstein.com/asking-what-students-spend-on-textbooks-is-very-important-but-insufficient/

Hylén, J. (2005). *OER: Opportunities and challenges*. Paris: OECD. Retrieved from http://www.oecd.org/edu/ceri/37351085.pdf

Ives, C., & Pringle, M. (2013). Moving to OER at Athabasca University: A case study. *The International Review of Research in Open and Distributed Learning, 14*(2), 1–13. Retrieved from http://www.irrodl.org/index.php/irrodl/article/view/1534/2486

Jacobs, B. (2014). OER movement needs to move beyond voluntarism (essay). *Inside Higher Ed*. Retrieved from https://www.insidehighered.com/views/2014/08/28/open-educational-resources-movement-needs-move-beyond-voluntarism-essay

Jung, I., Sasaki, T., & Latchem, C. (2016). A framework for assessing fitness for purpose in OER. *International Journal of Educational Technology in Higher Education, 13*(3). doi:10.1186/s41239-016-0002-5

Klein, G. (2015, August 27). *Embedded digital resources are in, traditional texts out at UMUC*. University of Maryland University College. Retrieved from http://www.umuc.edu/globalmedia/embedded-digital-resources.cfm

Kortemeyer, G. (2013). Ten years later: Why OER have not noticeably affected higher education, and why we should care. *Educause Review*. Retrieved from http://er.educause.edu/articles/2013/2/ten-years-later-why-open-educational-resources-have-not-noticeably-affected-higher-education-and-why-we-should-care

Lane, A. (2009). The impact of openness on bridging educational digital divides. *International Review of Research in Open and Dstributed Learning, 10*(5). Retrieved from http://www.irrodl.org/index.php/irrodl/article/viewFile/637/1408

Law, A. (2016, January 29). OpenLearn is number 1 [Blog]. *Open Media*. Retrieved from http://www.open.ac.uk/blogs/OpenMedia/?p=1378

Ludwig, R. (2015, April 24). *UMUC receives top Honor from open education consortium*. University of Maryland University College. Retrieved from http://www.umuc.edu/globalmedia/open-education-consortium.cfm

Müskens, W. (2016). *Studierende mit beruflichen Kompetenzen an der Carl von Ossietzky Universität Oldenburg* [Professional competencies of students at Carl von Ossietzky University of Oldenburg]. Retrieved August 2, 2016 from https://www.uni-oldenburg.de/fileadmin/user_upload/anrechnungsprojekte/download/NTS_OHO_19_01_16.pdf

Nesbit, J., Belfer, K., & Leacock, T. (2007). *Learning Object Review Instrument (LORI) – User manual.* Retrieved from http://www.transplantedgoose.net/gradstudies/educ892/LORI1.5.pdf

OECD. (2007). *Giving knowledge for free: The emergence of OER.* Centre for Educational Research and Innovation (CERI). Retrieved from http://www.oecd.org/edu/ceri/38654317.pdf

Ohio Department of Higher Education. (2016). Competency-based education – 9th report on the Condition of Higher Education in Ohio. Retrieved August 19, 2017 from https://www.ohiohighered.org/sites/ohiohighered.org/files/uploads/board/condition-report/2016-Conditions-Report_FINAL.pdf

Open Courseware Provider League Table. (2016). *MoocLab.* Retrieved from http://www.mooclab.club/pages/ocw_league_table/

Open Educational Media Operating Policy. (2018). *The Open University.* Retrieved September 11, 2018, from http://www.open.ac.uk/about/open-educational-resources/home/open-educational-media-operating-policy

Open Media Unit. (2016). *The Open University.* Retrieved from http://www.open.ac.uk/about/open-educational-resources/what-we-do/open-medhttp://www.open.ac.uk/about/open-educational-resources/openlearn

Orr, D., Rimini, M., & van Damme. (2015). *'Executive summary' in OER: A catalyst for innovation.* Paris: OECD Publishing.

The OU Mission. (2016). *The Open University.* Retrieved from http://www.open.ac.uk/about/main/mission

The OU Story. (2016). *The Open University.* Retrieved from http://www.open.ac.uk/about/main/strategy/ou-story

Pawlyshyn, N., Braddlee, D., Casper, L., & Miller, H. (2013). Adopting OER: A case study of cross-institutional collaboration and innovation. *Educause Review.* Retrieved from http://er.educause.edu/articles/2013/11/adopting-oer-a-case-study-of-crossinstitutional-collaboration-and-innovation

Popken, B. (2015, August 6). College textbook prices have risen 1,041 percent since 1977. *NBC News.* Retrieved from http://www.nbcnews.com/feature/freshman-year/college-textbook-prices-have-risen-812-percent-1978-n399926

Recommendations of the EU. (2012). Council recommendation from December 20, 2012 for validating non-formal and informal learning. Retrieved from https://eur-lex.europa.eu/legal-content/EN/TXT/PDF/?uri=CELEX:32012H1222(01)&from=EN

Senack, E. (2015). *Open textbooks: The billion-dollar solution.* The Student Public Interest Research Groups. Retrieved from http://www.studentpirgs.org/reports/sp/open-textbooks-billion-dollar-solution

Stacey, P. (2011). Evolution of an OER initiative: An eight year retrospective [Blog post]. *Musings on the Edtech Frontier.* Retrieved from http://edtechfrontier.com/2011/02/28/evolution-of-an-oer-initiative-an-eight-year-retrospective/

Straumsheim, C. (2016, February 22). Study: Faculty members skeptical of digital course materials, unfamiliar with OER. *Inside Higher Ed.* Retrieved from https://www.insidehighered.com/news/2016/02/22/study-faculty-members-skeptical-digital-course-materials-unfamiliar-oer

Stewart, W., & Associates. (2006). *Athabasca University: A case study in OER production and use in higher education in Canada.* Canadian Council of Learning/OECD-CERI. Retrieved from http://www.oecd.org/edu/ceri/37647739.pdf

UMUC at a Glance. (2015). University of Maryland University College. Retrieved from http://www.umuc.edu/visitors/about/ipra/glance.cfm

UMUC's Mission and Core Values. (2016). University of Maryland University College. Retrieved from http://www.umuc.edu/visitors/about/mission.cfm

UNESCO. (1995–2010). UNESCO-COL Chair in OER (903), established in 2010 at Athabasca University (Canada). Retrieved from http://www.unesco.org/en/university-twinning-and-networking/access-by-region/europe-and-north-america/canada/unesco-col-chair-in-open-educational-resources-903/

UNESCO. (n.d.). *What are open educational resources (OERs)?* Retrieved May, 2017, from http://www.unesco.org/new/en/communication-and-information/access-to-knowledge/open-educational-resources/what-are-open-educational-resources-oers/

Weisbaum, H. (2016, February 10). Students are still saddled with soaring textbook costs, report says. *NBC News.* Retrieved from http://www.nbcnews.com/business/business-news/students-are-still-saddled-soaring-textbook-costs-report-says-n516011

Weller, M. (2014). *The battle for open: How openness won and why it doesn't feel like victory.* London: Ubiquity Press.

Weller, M. (2015, September 7). The ROI on open education [Blog post]. *The Ed Techie.* Retrieved from http://blog.edtechie.net/oer/the-roi-on-open-education/

Wiley, D. (2007). *On the sustainability of open education resource initiatives in higher education. OECD Centre for Educational Research and Innovation (CERI) for the project on OER.* Retrieved from http://www.oecd.org/edu/ceri/38645447.pdf

Wiley, D. (2010). Open education resources: Moving from sharing to adopting. *OpenSource.com.* Retrieved from https://opensource.com/education/10/10/open-education-resources-moving-sharing-adopting

Wiley, D. (2016, February 12). Slow or sophisticated? Squandered or sustainable? [Blog post]. *Iterating toward openness.* Retrieved from http://opencontent.org/blog/

Yin, S., & Kawachi, P. (2013). Improving open access through prior learning assessment. *Open Praxis, 5*(1), 59–65.

Yuan, L., MacNeil, S., & Kraan, W. (2007). OER: Opportunities and challenges for higher education [Briefing paper]. *JISC CETIS*. Retrieved from http://wiki.cetis.ac.uk/images/0/0b/OER_Briefing_Paper.pdf

Yuan, M., & Recker, M. (2015). Not all rubrics are equal: A review of rubrics for evaluating the quality of open educational resources. *International Review of Research in Open and Distributed Learning, 16*(5), 16–38.

Zawacki-Richter, O., & Mayrberger, K. (2017). *Qualität von OER: Internationale Bestandsaufnahme von Instrumenten zur Qualitätssicherung von Open Educational Resources (OER) – Schritte zu einem deutschen Modell am Beispiel der Hamburg Open Online University* [OER quality: International review of quality assurance instruments for OER]. Hamburg: Hamburg Open Online University. Retrieved from https://www.synergie.uni-hamburg.de/media/sonderbaende/qualitaet-von-oer-2017.pdf

CHAPTER 10

Fostering a Culture of Openness in Open Universities, with a Focus on India

Sujata Santosh

The idea of openness has been entwined with the ideals of education for a long time, and with today's open access and open education movements, it has become all the more crucial. There is increased emphasis on the adoption of open practices and the use of open educational resources (OER) to provide educational opportunities to the masses. Educational institutions are realizing the need to share, collaborate and exchange ideas and knowledge. Openness is a complex phenomenon, which is technical, social, cultural and economic in nature (Cronin, 2017). The emergence and use of OER and MOOCs on the educational landscape has enlarged the open landscape. Though openness is largely discussed in terms of OER, the idea has expanded to include open pedagogies, open research and open data. As mentioned by Lane (2009), this diversity of openness reflects the variety of provisions and modes of study that are emerging. Wiley and Hilton III (2009) posit that 'Openness is a fundamental value underlying significant changes in society and is a prerequisite to changes institutions of higher education need to make in order to remain relevant to the society in which they exist' (p. 1). The movement stresses the need for unrestricted access to educational materials and removal of geographic and economic barriers (Knox, 2013a, 2013b). In the face of 'open,' distance education institutions are revisiting their policies to face the challenges of global competition, changing educational needs, shrinking resources, and rising costs (Panda & Santosh, 2017), resulting in change at institutional, pedagogical and individual levels. However, it remains challenging to nurture openness as a core value in academic institutions.

This chapter explores the different notions and degrees of openness in the context of open universities, both in principle and in practice. It discusses the need for fostering a culture of openness in higher education institutions, especially open universities. The chapter highlights the different strategies that can be adopted at the policy level and also at organizational and technical levels, in academic institutions in a developing country such as India. It also reflects on the various existing conflicts, tensions and the challenges related to introducing openness in open universities, again, especially in India.

 | DOI: 10.1163/9789004422988_011

1 Defining Openness

The term *open* is an umbrella term that refers to 'resources (the artefacts themselves as well as access to and usage of them), learning and teaching practices, institutional practices, the use of educational technologies, and the values underlying educational endeavours' (Cronin, 2017; Weller, 2014).

The open education movement gained prominence with MIT's OCW initiative in 2001, undertaken to

> share the core academic materials – including syllabi, lecture notes, assignments and exams – from all of its courses freely and openly on the web, providing resources that educators and learners could use to improve a wide variety of formal and informal educational experiences. (OCW website, 2011, para. 2)

There were many such initiatives by other large universities including Stanford, University of Pennsylvania, University of Michigan, Utah State University (Conrad, 2013). However, it must be kept in mind that 'openness' is also mandated – and restricted – by national regulatory and funding frameworks. The University of South Africa (UNISA) is such an example, demonstrating that openness must be considered in context.

In the context of open education resources, openness refers to the 'ability to modify and use materials, information and networks so education can be personalized to individual users or woven together in new ways for large and diverse audiences' (Open Education Consortium, n.d., para. 6). Universities worldwide have introduced initiatives such as Open Learn by UKOU, Open Learning Initiative by Carnegie Mellon University, Connexions, Creative Commons and Internet Archive, Peer to Peer University (P2PU), Udacity, Coursera, Wikieducator, and OpenStudy.

Jenkins (2006) highlights that the opening of knowledge requires inculcating a set of ideas that includes inquiry, co-creation, connection, sharing, reuse, and reliability. There is a need for policies and practices that encourage and reward openness, and also for programs that support diversity and monitoring quality (Iiyoshi & Kumar, 2008). Freedom and transparency enable sharing, collaboration, control over the learning process, ownership of ideas and content, self-direction and a culture of openness (Baker III, 2017). Universities are taking initiatives such as making some or all of their educational resources available under open licenses as well as open access publishing of research papers and reports (Lane, 2009). In view of these developments, it becomes extremely important for open universities, especially in developing countries such as India, to keep pace with the changing times and to meet the rising educational requirements.

2 Applying a Theoretical Framework

This chapter explores the 'openness' of open universities in a wider social and cultural context. The underlying thematic focus is on the 'processes by which structures, including schemas, rules, norms and routines, become established as authoritative guidelines for social behaviour' (Amis & Aïssaoui, 2013, p. 73). Toward this end, openness is analyzed by examining the institutional environment that shapes the change process, the role of agency in institutional change, and the interplay between the institution and its actors. Institutional theory posits that individuals do not act or think in a vacuum; but they are embedded in a web of interactions shaping their behaviour (Selznick, 1996). The use of an institutional approach provides a useful framework to assess the adoption of open educational resources and open educational practices at the organizational level and also permits exploration of how learners' individual and cognitive processes related to openness are shaped by various contextual factors and the broader institutional environment (Scott, 2008).

In 2001, Scott identified three elemental pillars on which institutions are based – regulative, normative and cognitive. The regulative element signifies the rules or laws of the institutional environment that structure social interaction and condition actors' behaviours including those determined by government policies and regulations (Scott, 2001). The normative pillar includes values, norms, roles, rules, and established practices. The cultural-cognitive element refers to the shared beliefs that constitute 'the nature of social reality and the frames through which reality is made' (Scott, 2001, p. 57).

Drawing from this theoretical framework, and keeping the caveat around 'openness' in mind, this chapter discusses openness in open universities in terms of a frameworks at various levels; structures (including policies, guidelines, operational mechanisms); and awareness and attitudes of stakeholders.

3 Open Universities and Openness

Open universities are a representation of the earliest efforts towards democratization of education and increasing participation in education (Deimann & Sloep, 2013). The initial foundations of the open universities, considered as models of open learning or open education, are centred on the concept of 'learning anytime, anywhere, open entry and alternative exit points' (Stagg &

Bossu, 2016) and were first implemented in the form of the Open University (OU) in the United Kingdom in 1969 (Deimann & Sloep, 2013). The OU's aim was to provide opportunity, against geographical, social, economic and time constraints, to those who were 'unfairly excluded' (Harris, 1987, p. 3). The model was widely emulated world over by the establishment of similar open universities in Germany (1974), Netherlands (1984), India (1982), among others.

An open university, therefore, is an autonomous higher education institution (HEI) that grants academic degrees and is based on the notions of openness of access and flexibility, subject to existing regulatory frameworks (Lockwood, 1998; Sampson, 2003; Villamejor-Mendoza, 2013). Openness of access in open university systems is realized in terms of entry requirements; freedom of time, place and pace; and curriculum design (Agbu, Mulder, de Vries, Tenebe, & Caine, 2016). Tait (2008) suggests that, as open universities are institutions that are sharply exposed to change depending on developmental requirements of the time, 'openness in an open university is an ongoing dialogue between political objectives (often expressed via the state), pedagogic practices (embedded in the institution), and the available technologies' (Jones, 2015). Tait (2008) explains that though open universities uphold the ideals of openness in higher education, these institutions are 'deeply embedded in the political and social fabric of their societies' (p. 89), and, as such, serve the functions of national development, capacity building, widening access, and encouraging change in the higher education system in the country.

4 Interpretations and Dimensions of Openness in Open Universities

The literature presents us with many lenses through which to consider open learning in institutions of higher learning. The phenomenon of openness in education is a complex one with 'heterogeneous philosophical roots' (Deimann & Sloep, 2013, p. 2) that are deeply embedded in the higher education's structure, the institutionalization of society and the institutionalization of education, technological advancements and their use in education, and developments in the field of distance education (Deimann & Sloep, 2013). And, as Edwards (2015) explains,

> openness itself is not the opposite of closed-ness, nor is there simply a continuum between the two. … An important question therefore becomes not simply whether education is more or less open, but what forms of openness are worthwhile and for whom; openness alone is not an educational virtue. (p. 253)

Researchers have sought to explain the phenomenon of openness in a variety of ways, creating typologies that attempt understanding at various levels. Hill (1975), for example, considered openness broadly in an era where openness in education as a concept was new, very vague and still in the process of being defined. He identified *procedural* openness which allows freedom in terms of spatial and temporal elements such as attendance and curriculum; and *normative* openness which signifies radical freedom regarding what learners study and how their learning will be assessed. Hill (1975) saw *revolutionary* openness as an extreme state of change from that era's status quo, and even foresaw the social change that characterizes current society.

Rossetti (1989) defined six major characteristics of open learning: open entry, individualized learning, self-assessment, learner support, self-pacing, and many start dates. Similarly, Alfonso and Garcia (2015) saw openness in higher education institutions existing as

> openness in admission policies; openness in credit recognition and accreditation; openness in delivery modes; openness in cost and affordability (some are free); openness in choosing educational track through multiple bridges and pathways, exits and entrances; openness in course design and evaluation; openness in strengthening digital literacies and e-pedagogies, and emerging e-research paradigms. (p. 1)

The openness in open universities is, therefore, marked by flexible organizational structures, delivery and communication patterns and a set of common characteristics that aim to provide opportunity for higher education to learners regardless of age, status, location and other such barriers by providing structures, processes and services to assist learners in overcoming these barriers (UNESCO, 2002).

Distance education pioneer Otto Peters (2001) outlined four distinct criteria of openness in open universities: extended accessibility to more students, independence of the institution's location, methodological flexibility, and openness to new ideas. Peters (2008) also noted that the idea of openness in education is closely intertwined with the democratic values of freedom, equality and creativity.

5 'Degrees of Openness' and Their Institutional Conditions

When is 'open not really open' … or not as open as others? As open universities vary considerably in form and structure, some are more open than others

(Paul, 1993), representing variations in the interpretation of openness and also reflecting certain inherent limitations. The notion of openness – in addition to the aforementioned and historical issues of access, choice, and no cost or low-cost access – also features various contributing and determining conditions of openness that are institutional, pedagogical, technical, and socio-economic (Panda & Santosh, 2017). These conditions are described below.

Institutional. An important aspect of openness entails issues of institutional or organizational structures and processes; accompanied by intellectual property policies, Internet speed or usage rules, funding, capacity building programs, incentives or reward mechanisms and effective marketing strategies (dos Santos, Punie & Munoz, 2016; Lesko, 2013; Torres, 2013). These institutional aspects of openness centre around the institution's strategy and vision for open and quality education intertwined with the strands of leadership (to enforce change and shaping and reinforcing culture); commitment (towards expanding learning opportunities); and practices (that include various policies and measures) (Leichsenring, Noe, & Brandenburg, 2012).

Pedagogical. A major variable of openness is the extent to which learners control the learning process – the educational content, how it is learned (organization of materials, various media and teaching methods), where it is learned, when it is learned, and how it is assessed (Paul, 1993). Dalsgaard and Thestrup (2015) provide three pedagogical dimensions of openness: transparency, communication, and engagement. According to them, transparency calls for opening up the work and activities of learners to enable input and inspiration from peers; communication enables the learners to connect with the outside world and situates their educational activities in the social context; and engagement aims at collaborative relationship between educational institutions and external practices (Dalsgaard &Thestrup, 2015).

Technical. Openness is intertwined with Internet technologies, and digital technologies are integral to open educational initiatives (Edwards, 2015; Tuomi, 2013). How and what is opened to learners is largely determined by institutional technical interoperability and functionality, use of open standards and formats, technical skills and resources, and accessibility and discoverability of the resource (Hodgkinson-Williams & Gray, 2009; Tuomi, 2013; Tuomi, 2006).

Socio-economic. Open provision is closely associated with social conditions, social practices, national politics, economics and law (Edwards, 2015; Jones, 2015; Paul, 1993). Socio-economic conditions underlie most learners' access and opportunity occasions, their cultural perceptions towards sharing of resources and their attitudes towards using the resources created by others. Similarly, the importance of and value connected to costs of sustaining open initiatives, including the costs of staff time required to maintain 'openness,' are all related to socio-economic conditions (Hodgkinson-Williams & Gray, 2009; Oliver, 2015; Tuomi, 2006, 2013).

6 Facets of 'Open' within Universities

Within open universities, openness, termed 'classical' openness by Mulder and Jansen (2013), features many facets associated with accessibility, flexibility, learner control over content and structure, choice of delivery systems, and accreditation (Alfonso & Garcia, 2015; Paul, 1993; Villamejor-Mendoza, 2013). The various facets of openness within open universities are discussed briefly below.

6.1 *Access and Admission*

One of the most promising dimensions of openness is that educational opportunities are made accessible to all, regardless of physical location, age, gender, socio-economic background, and economic status. McGreal (2013) states that the principle of openness is at the forefront the principle of accessibility. As mentioned by dos Santos et al (2016), universal access should signify 'lowering of economic, technological, geographical and institutional barriers which obstruct the doorway to knowledge.' However, there remains contention on this issue as regards the extent to which open education will address the world's access problems (Daniel, 2009; McGreal, 2017).

Only some of the open universities (such as UK's Open University, the Dutch Open University, and the Open University of Israel) have an open admission policy with no entry requirements (Guri-Rosenblit, 2009). In India, with its many open universities, the University of Mysore and the Andhra University were the first universities to adopt an open admission policy in the early 1970s (Hogan, 2012). India's national open university, Indira Gandhi National Open University, offers admissions to its various programmes on the basis of flexible entry requirements.

6.2 *Curricula or Content*

This dimension offers learners the freedom to choose their courses within a programme of study. Open curricula empower learners to be the creators and curators of knowledge as they govern their learning process; open curricula determine the order in which the topics are approached and also how they are to be assessed (Paul, 1993). Some open universities have attempted new multi-disciplinary curricul; however, as is the case of University of the Philippines Open University (UPOU), academic offerings are institution-prescribed and system regulated; and opportunity for students to designate their own learning plan is not yet present (Villamejor-Mendoza, 2013).

Educational content in the form of OER, enabled by open licensing and new digital technologies, creates new possibilities for teaching and learning, although OER are restricted in some learning environments based on the rights granted to the user of the content as regards the 5R's – reuse, revise, remix, redistribute and retain (Wiley, 2009, 2014). Openness with OER has evolved from open provision (without any requirements) to one framed by Intellectual Property Rights (IPR), thus signifying free-yet-copyright-protected resources (Deimann & Sloep, 2013). Lane (2009) equates the openness of OER with freedom, but degrees of freedom can vary (as with open licenses) and can be influenced by many factors such as institutional willingness to make the materials available; preparedness of institution, faculty, and learners to adapt; policy directives within the universities; freedom for faculty and students to use, create and share educational resources; use of interoperable standards; need for user registration to access the content, and the degree of freedom with which people can use the resource without a prior license or permission; and related costs on the part of the user or institution (Hodgkinson-Williams & Gray, 2009; Jones, 2015; Lane, 2009; Pete, Mulder, & Oliveira Neto, 2017).

6.3 *Pedagogy*

The issue of pedagogy spans content and curriculum; one cannot talk about one without talking about the others. The introduction of open content such as OER, videos, podcasts, etc., and social media must coalese effectively with appropriate teaching approaches and strategies. Based on the adoption of appropriate philosophical foundations, for example, constructivism, instructors can ensure active participation among learners that strengthens pedagogical design and content (Conrad & Openo, 2018; DeRosa & Robison, 2015; Hegarty, 2015; Rosen & Smale, 2015; Weller, 2014).

6.4 *Flexibility*

Theoretically, increased flexibility is a facet of the open university, subject to regulatory and funding frameworks, providing the ability for learners to study and learn at anytime, anywhere, and at any pace. Theoretically, learners have the flexibility to choose the mode, medium, time, place and pace of study as per their individual learning needs and interest. 'Pace' is often a disputed and/or misunderstood term as deadlines and due dates are still features of many courses even within an open structure. That is to say: restrictions still exist within the open framework in some institutions.

6.5 *Recognition or Accreditation*

Another hotly disputed facet of openness concerns the recognition, certification, and accreditation of learners who engage in some open affordances, specifically MOOCs. The recognition and accreditation of MOOC-learning has been a hurdle and, to some, a contentious issue since their inception. Various solutions have been sought, including 'two-tiered' MOOCS where some learners complete assessment protocols in order to receive accreditation for their MOOC, whereas others simply receive a certificate of completion or perhaps nothing at all. MOOC recognition, at the time of writing, is still very much under discussion (Mackintosh, McGreal, & Taylor, 2011; McGreal, Conrad, Murphy, Witthaus, & Mackintosh, 2014).

7 Fostering a Culture of Openness: The Need for Change

In India, as well as elsewhere, open universities must be viewed as open systems in a wider context or environment (Scott, 2001). Various institutional pressures (internal and external), the actors (and their behaviours) and the need for change are discussed here in terms of three levels: inter-organizational (in terms of external environment), organizational (in terms of culture) and individual (in terms of norms and practices) (Oliver, 1997).

7.1 *Change at the Inter-Organizational Level*

Higher education's complex and dynamic system is embedded in the super system of human society, marked throughout history – and recently – by radical changes caused by technological innovation. According to Wiley and Hilton III (2009), since openness is a 'critical attribute of the super system in which higher education is positioned ... higher education must therefore become more open to remain relevant to the society in which it exists' (p. 11). While the range of educational offerings is changing and becoming even more diversified due to a range of social, demographic, and economic pressures (Lynch, 2008), universities are facing challenges of shrinking resources and rising costs (Santosh & Panda, 2016a). Traditional universities also face limitations in accessing educational resources because of various technological, regulatory or participatory barriers, as outlined earlier (Lane, 2009). But, as highlighted by UNESCO,

> It is clear that openness is here to stay and is changing the nature of higher education and therefore it is essential for institutions to engage with openness as a potential core organizational value if they wish to remain relevant and contribute to the positive advancement of the field of higher education. (2014, p. 9)

Openness is, therefore, considered as the next step to bring the required change in educational systems, demonstrated by an increased emphasis on enhanced quality and transparency in education and research (Ossiannilsson & Creelman, 2012). Institutions that are reluctant to openness may face the risk of becoming obsolete (Torres, 2013). Wiley and Hilton III (2009) posited that for educational transformation, increases in connectedness, personalization, participation, and openness are needed. They further proposed that of these, openness should be a priority, as a culture of openness is a prerequisite to progress in the other three areas.

7.2 *Change at the Organizational Level*

van der Merwe (2015) stresses the need for an environment where 'the culture of openness is recognized, valued and promoted as a central pillar of the education system.' Camilleri, Ehlers, and Pawlowski (2014) emphasize the need for opening up the learning architectures within formal systems of education, which would involve processes of course design, teaching, learning, assessment, and recognition with the introduction of new types of learning such as that made possible by MOOCs. Education has always been treated as a system that should be tightly controlled; therefore, open approaches are required to instill transparency and freedom in the system, releasing some control to the users (Baker III, 2017). A culture of openness in higher education institutions, especially distance education institutions and open universities, can encourage practices that support innovation, the use and production of open education resources, innovative pedagogical models, and the empowering of learners as co-producers on their lifelong learning path (de Hart, Chetty & Archer, 2015; Ehlers, 2011; OPAL, 2011). As Ehlers suggests,

> a combination of open resources use and open learning architectures … could transform learning into 21st century learning environments in which universities, adult learners, and citizens are provided with opportunities to shape their lifelong learning pathways in an autonomous and self-guided way. (2011, p. 3)

7.3 *Change at the Individual Level*

For learners, openness should offer the potential of effectively-designed learning environments; access to common intellectual capital; the potential of collaboration to improve quality; and the ease of adaptation to and contextualization of materials (Butcher, 2011). As opposed to traditional closed, top-down and exam-focused learning environments that have created restrictive forms of learning (Camilleri, Ehlers, & Pawlowski, 2014; Ehlers, 2011), change should result in collaborative practices where learners are not just passive consumers of content but are also involved in content creation. Openness along with resources of value and examples of practice may offer a route to learning that aligns with other 'changes in society and reduces the dependence on ingrained institutions and approaches' (McAndrew, 2011, p. 7). Previous research (Cronin, 2017; de Hart et al., 2015; Rolfe, 2012) has highlighted the reluctance to openness among some teaching staff due to concerns of quality, privacy, intellectual property rights, and their own lack of capacity. Researchers (Cronin, 2017; de Hart et al., 2015; Kursun, Cagiltay, & Can, 2014; Panda & Santosh, 2017) have emphasized the need for institutions to build teaching staff capacity in terms of digital capability, awareness of copyright issues, open licensing and recognition of the potential role of educators in an open and networked society.

8 Strategies for Fostering Openness

Open educational practices (OEP) is a broad term that encompasses a range of strategies and techniques that embrace the notion of 'open' (Deimann & Farrow, 2013). To enact OEP, systematic efforts include investments in improved curricula, improved course design, well-planned contact sessions, development and procurement of quality teaching and learning materials, and effective assessment strategies (Butcher, 2011). Institutions must undertake a systematic analysis of various aspects of their teaching-learning processes such as curriculum frameworks, student support, assessment and accreditation systems, and mechanisms to recognize prior learning in order to examine the level of openness possible. Butcher (2011) enumerated these key principles of open education:
- lifelong learning opportunities
- learning process centred on the learner
- flexible learning provision
- recognition of prior learning, prior experience and demonstrated competencies
- credit accumulation from different learning contexts
- fair chance of learner success

In order to attain and imbed OEP, initiatives are required at several levels. Cox and Trotter (2016) argue for a 'nuanced, tailored and often multi-pronged approach' (p. 160), elements of which are outlined below.

8.1 *Policy Frameworks at National Levels*

New policies and practices are required in higher education to address various issues related to openness and open educational resources (McAndrew, Farrow, Law, & Elliot-Cirigottis, 2012; Lane, 2009). Policies that change objectives, goals and metrics have a scaling effect on the functioning of the institution; and policies and strategies at the national level especially have a significant impact on the integration of OER in teaching and learning practices by providing the fluid and flexible frameworks that support innovation of OEP (McNamara, 2012; Nikoi, Rowlett, Armellini, & Witthaus, 2011).

8.2 *Structures at Institutional Levels*

The UNESCO-COL guidelines (2011) suggest that institutions should formulate institutional strategies for the integration of OER and OEP by making investment toward proper infrastructure for enabling use and reuse of OER and moving toward OEP (de Hart et al., 2015; McAndrew et al., 2012). Attitudes and behaviours, influenced by institutional policy structures and the social, departmental, and disciplinary norms and expectations that form the culture of the organization should support strategies to empower and support teachers to adopt open approaches in the creation of effective and innovative learning environments (Cox & Trotter, 2016). The provision of ongoing opportunities for professional and technical skill development is essential to achieving this goal (Nascimbeni & Burgos, 2016).

8.3 *Technical Structures*

Paskevicius (2017) suggests that digital technologies present innumerable opportunities for innovative usage in the educational context; however, their effective application and optimal usage remains a challenge. To develop teachers and learners' technical skills and capabilities, focus should be placed on the 'combination of open resource use and open learning' (Camilleri & Ehlers, 2011, p. 6). Technological solutions such as repositories and authoring systems, tools for finding and using content, platforms for running courses, and social tools for sharing content to support the use of OER in teaching learning are available to support these goals (Judith & Bull, 2016; MacAndrew et al., 2012). Other strategic drivers for promoting a positive climate toward creating open practices involve the appreciation of intellectual property rights and leveraging open access publishing (Hoosen & Butcher, 2012; Mackintosh, 2012; Masterman, 2016). As institution-wide strategies involve considerable financial investments and costs, continual research will help to monitor their effectiveness (Lane & McAndrew, 2010; UNESCO-COL, 2011).

8.4 *Awareness and Use at Pedagogical Levels*

Strategies for fostering openness in open universities will necessarily include raising awareness of users – of teachers and learners – of their capacity to create, use, and re-use OER. Strategies aimed at fostering a pedagogical culture of openness in open universities could involve the following:

- Encouraging and supporting the use and production of open educational resources by teachers and learners.
- Implementing rigorous quality assurance process to ensure the quality of educational materials being made available as OER.
- Ensuring that robust, enforceable IPR, copyright and privacy policies are in place.
- Academics should be encouraged to use open (Creative Commons) licenses when publishing their resources.
- Undertaking awareness-raising and capacity building activities for ensuring effective use of OER.
- Providing required ICT infrastructure, hardware, software and Internet connecting for accessing, adapting, and creating educational resources.
- Developing an institutional repository for storing, managing and sharing educational materials. These repositories should use open formats and open standards.
- Provision of professional development and support for using the repositories to ensure that the teachers and students build on the institutional knowledge.
- Encouraging teachers to publish and share their materials for use by other academics and researchers within the institution as a good practice.
- Incentivizing the teachers through recognition and rewards for development, acquisition, adaptation and use of open educational resources, and for using innovative pedagogic approaches.
- Networking and collaboration with other institutions for developing and sharing of educational resources (Butcher, 2011; Masterman & Chan, 2015; UNESCO-COL, 2011).

9 Open Universities in India

The demand for education, especially higher education, has grown rapidly in countries marked by high economic development such as India. To meet this need, the Open University system in India was designed 'as an instrument of democratizing education' and augmenting opportunities for quality higher education to diverse population (NPE, Govt. of India, 1986, p. 15). The objective, in seeking to augment opportunities for higher education, was to 'reach the unreached and also to make it a lifelong process with no restriction of age at the time of enrolment, prior educational attainments or pace and place of study' (Srivastava, 2016).

In India, the first state level open university, the Andhra Pradesh Open University (renamed Dr. B.R. Ambedkar Open University i.e. BRAOU in 1991) was established in the year 1982. The National Open University, also known as Indira Gandhi National Open University (IGNOU), was set up in 1985, by an act of Parliament, for promotion and coordination of distance education system in the country. Though the implementation took over a decade, the idea behind the genesis, as stated (in 1975) by the working group that examined the feasibility of initiating another an Open University in India, was explained in this way:

> In a situation of this type, where the expansion of enrolments in higher education has to continue at a terrific pace and where available resources in terms of men and money are limited, the obvious solution, if proper standards are to be maintained and the demand for higher education from different sections of the people is to be met, is to adopt the Open University system with its provision of higher education of part-time or own time basis. (Srivastava, 2016, p. 14)

The Government of India recognized the need and supported several state open universities to meet regional educational requirements, in view of the multiplicity of languages, cultural, diversity and the vast numbers of potential learners to be catered to. The Central Advisory Board of Education (CABE), the highest advisory body to advise the central and state governments in the field of education, recommended in 1992 that each major state should have an open university. In India there are 29 states and six Union Territories and, following this, 13 states established their own open universities. At present, there are 14 open universities – one national university and 13 state open universities in the country, thus forming one of the largest networks of open universities in the world. In addition, India also has about 118 dual-mode universities and institutions recognized by the University Grants Commission (UGC) for providing higher education through open and distance learning programmes. The UGC is a statutory body for determination and maintenance of standards of higher education in India. Gross Enrolment Ratio (GER) in higher education in India is 24.5% with distance enrolment constituting about 11.05% of the total enrolment in higher education (MHRD, 2016). The Indira Gandhi National Open University (IGNOU) has a cumulative student enrolment of three million learners in 225 programmes.

As the UK Open University was built on the notion that learning was not just the acquisition of knowledge but a process of ubiquitous participation in knowledge construction (Weinbren, 2014), so too open universities in India, just as their counterparts in other parts of the world, have played a vital role in widening participation, lowering costs, creating possibilities for enhancing the quality of teaching-learning, and complementing the conventional systems of education. From the beginning, the emphasis was on ensuring quality education for all, based on an academic standard comparable to conventional universities. To achieve this, open universities have consistently adapted and utilized the latest enabling technologies from print to audio-video programmes, broadcasting, interactive radio counselling, teleconferencing, CD-ROMs, and Web-based content delivery. IGNOU has set many educational precedents in the country such as the use of the multimedia approach for programme delivery, the use of electronic and broadcast media for instruction, and use of a credit-based system, as opposed to marks or percentage-based evaluation systems followed in the majority of higher education institutions in India. Dedicated educational channels on TV (such as GyanDarshan) and on the radio (such as Gyanvani) deliver innovative educational content to distance learners.

The National Open University also functions as an apex body, responsible for development and coordination of open and distance education systems in the country, as the Distance Education Council (DEC), a statutory body for determination of standards of the distance education system and accreditation of distance education programmes, was housed in IGNOU. In 2012, DEC was dissolved and a new statutory body, the Distance Education Bureau, was set up under the University Grants Commission for regulation of distance education in India. This also led to the revision of the distance education policy and regulations in the country. The University Grants Commission (Open and Distance Learning) Regulations of 2017 paved the way for online delivery of courses and credit transfer that enabled students to opt for online courses offered by various universities and institutions across the country, although universities offering distance education programmes were required to seek fresh approval for offering their programmes. Students may take up to 20% of the total courses being offered in a particular programme in a semester through online courses or MOOCs as per UGC (Credit Framework for Online Learning Courses through SWAYAM) Regulations, 2016. In 2018, most recently, the UGC (Online Courses) Regulations dictate that higher educational institutions can now offer certificate, diploma and degree programmes in full-fledged online mode in line with their regular programmes, except for programmes requiring practical/laboratory courses.

10 Challenges to Making Open Universities More Open

While openness has historically been closely related to free availability of resources and licensing options, policy, pedagogy, rights, and technology (Harishankar, Balaji, & Ganapuram, 2013), the concept of openness and OER in India raises many issues and challenges, even within open universities (Nikoi et al., 2011; Santosh & Panda, 2016a) These issues, described below, relate to the operational and socio-cultural aspects of openness and OER.

10.1 *Promotion of a Culture of Academic Collaboration and Sharing to Encourage OEP*

Openness and OER are altruistic notions that are aligned with academic traditions of sharing and expanding knowledge (de Hart et al., 2015; McNamara, 2012; OECD, 2007). However, the extent to which institutional sharing is influenced by these traditional values is not clear (Bernstein, 2015) and, as Geser (2007) states, 'the established culture of academic and higher education institutions does not particularly foster the creation, sharing and re-use of Open Educational Resources' (p. 65). Therefore, not only external barriers but also internal challenges to the processes of introducing a culture of openness to educational institutions create difficulties for universities in India (Kumar, 2009; McGrath, 2008). Santosh and Panda (2016b) also reported an absence of an organizational culture of knowledge-sharing within institutions and a lack of official recognition and reward system for open practices in the National Open University in India.

10.2 *Lack of Awareness and Acceptance of OER among Stakeholders: Policy Makers, Educators and Distance Learners*

While India's open universities are in the process of setting up of institutional OER repositories, it is important for them to ensure that the content is available openly for use. As mentioned by Kumar (2009), 'design and technology considerations often limit the productive use and adoption of OER, rendering tools incompatible with infrastructure, content to be trapped in repositories, and ultimately limiting adaptation and adoption as well as sustainability' (p. 81). As Brent, Gibbs and Gruszczynska (2012) reported on universities in the UK, often these resources are hidden behind password protected institutional virtual learning environments, rendering them useless to the external users. It has been found that the inertia inherent in established systems of education does not permit change, and the greatest challenge is to break the aversion to openness (Torres, 2013). Torres also suggests that institutions do not embrace openness for fear of losing their competitive edge; and notes that keeping educational content closed, today, signals a lack of innovation and quality.

Similarly, research suggests that the 'risk of misuse by other institutions and unethical competition' is a major barrier to the sharing of educational materials and content (OECD, 2007, p. 60). The president of Athabasca University in Canada argued that he was unwilling to openly release university resources as he was unable to prevent for-profit organizations from profiting from the content (OECD, 2007; Stewart, 2006). This is also true in India. Initially, the National Open University of India, i.e. Indira Gandhi National Open University, viewed resource sharing with society, especially with students and faculty, as a progressive and democratic step. The first national knowledge repository (E-Gyankosh) was developed in 2005 to provide online access to around 3,000 IGNOU courses and 2,000 video lectures (Kanjilal, 2013). However, the university's inability to stop unethical use by profit-making institutions forced it to abandon open sharing (Santosh & Panda, 2016a, 2016b). As the content in the repository was bound by copyright rules and non-reusable, IGNOU proposed to offer these materials as OER with an open-licensed policy (Kanjilal, 2013). However, that gesture was withheld due to a change in the university stance on open licensing and copyright. At this time, the IPR and OER policies of IGNOU are still under review and consideration.

10.3 *Inadequate Infrastructure*

The recommendations of the National Knowledge Commission (in 2007) gave considerable impetus to open access and OER initiatives in India. One of the suggestions was the creation of the National Knowledge Network (NKN), a dedicated digital broadband network, interconnecting all research and education institutions for ensuring better access. As a result, with the NKN, the bandwidth in Indian colleges and universities is not a current concern; however, there is a lack of adequate infrastructure for sharing of resources (Santosh & Panda, 2016a).

10.4 *Institutional Policies on OER and Copyright*

Open universities in India have a hierarchical power structure, with policies and regulations aligned with the institutional vision and mission. To promote faculty engagement with OER, institutional policies on open access and OER are essential (Cox & Trotter, 2017). In case of Intellectual Property (IP) rights, however, copyright of teaching resources and instructional materials developed by faculty members is vested in the institution, and therefore institutions retain the copyright. The faculty cannot share them as OER.

The lack of awareness about OER and faculty concerns about copyright and intellectual property rights (IPR) combined with a conservative and protective mindset and 'latent fear of external scrutiny' (Santosh & Panda, 2016b, p. 260) are other factors inhibiting openness in India's open universities. Kursun et al. (2014) point out a paradox in academia where faculty members express a strong support for open sharing but, at the same time, demonstrate an 'unresponsive attitude towards sharing or using educational resources developed by someone else' (p. 25), also known as 'not-invented-here' syndrome.'

However, research indicates that the faculty in National Open University is positively inclined towards using resources made available by others, although they too have concerns about copyright and IPR permissions to use the content (Panda & Santosh, 2017; Santosh & Panda, 2016b).

Nevertheless, and however slowly, the move towards openness in open universities in India is perceptible. There is a need for a culture of openness, for effective institutional systems, and for the provision for OER and sharing of resources (Panda & Santosh, 2017). So far, at the time of writing, seven open universities have developed OER policy with the help from Commonwealth Media Centre for Asia (CEMCA). These open universities include Central University of Himachal Pradesh (CUHP) (dual mode university); Netaji Subhash Open University (NSOU), Kolkata; Uttarakhand Open University (UOU) Haldwani; Odisha State Open University (OSOU), Sambhalpur; Krishna Kanta Handique Open University (KKHSOU), Guwahati; U. P. Rajshri Tandon Open University, Allahabad; and Vardhaman Mahaveer Open University, Kota.

11 Conclusion

Torres (2013) suggests that the mindset of a majority of institutions is fixed on a culture of 'not open' rather than open, and that changing the mindset is not easy. Both tradition and administrative ease permit the commonly held belief that education can be tightly controlled (Baker III, 2017). For nurturing a culture of openness and embedding OER into teaching and learning practices, higher education institutions, especially open universities in India, must adopt an approach of transparency and freedom in their teaching and learning processes. Thakran and Sharma (2016) note that all stakeholders, including policy makers, should be made aware of the potential of OER to support equitable access to education in India. As part of the openness agenda, open universities should develop open repositories, offer free courses, and willingly collaborate with other institutions. A slow and steady change, coming from within, will ensure that the shift toward openness is sustainable.

References

Agbu, O. J., Mulder, F., De Vries, F., Tenebe, A. V., & Cane, A. (2016). The best of two open worlds at the National Open University of Nigeria. *Open Praxis, 8*(2), 111–121. http://dx.doi.org/10.5944/openpraxis.8.2.279

Alfonso, G. J., & Garcia, P. G. (2015). Open and distance elearning: New dimensions in teaching, learning, research, and extension for higher education institutions. *International Journal on Open and Distance e-Learning, 1*(1 & 2). Retrieved from http://ijodel.com/journal/index.php/ijodel/article/view/12/5

Amis, J. M., & Aïssaoui, R. (2013). Readiness for change: An institutional perspective. *Journal of Change Management, 13*(1), 69–95. doi:10.1080/14697017.2013.768435

Baker III, F. W. (2017). An alternative approach: Openness in education over the last 100 years. *TechTrends, 2*, 130–140. https://doi.org/10.1007/s11528-016-0095-7

Bernstein, S. (2015). OER and the value of openness: Implications for the knowledge economy. *Globalisation, Societies and Education, 13*(4), 471–486. http://dx.doi.org/10.1080/14767724.2014.965012

Brent, I., Gibbs, G. R., & Gruszczynska, A. K. (2012). Defining openness: Updating the concept of 'open' for a connected world. *JIME*. Retrieved from http://jime.open.ac.uk/2012/05

Butcher, N. (2011). *A basic guide to Open Educational Resources (OER)*. Vancouver: UNESCO & COL. Retrieved from http://www.col.org/PublicationDocuments/Basic-Guide-To-OER.pdf

Camilleri, A. F., & Ehlers, U. D. (2011). *Mainstreaming open educational practice: Recommendations for policy*. Retrieved from http://efquel.org/wp-content/uploads/2012/03/Policy_Support_OEP.pdf

Camilleri, A. F., Ehlers, U. D., & Pawlowski, J. (2014). *State of the art review of quality issues related to Open Educational Resources (OER)*. Luxembourg: Publications Office of the European Union.

Conrad, D. (2013). Assessment challenges in open learning: Way-finding, fork in the road, or end of the line? *Open Praxis, 5*(1), 41–47.

Conrad, D., & Openo, J. (2018). *Assessment strategies for online learning: Engagement and authenticity*. Edmonton: Athabasca University Press.

Cox, G., & Trotter, H. (2016). Institutional culture and OER policy: How structure, culture, and agency mediate OER policy potential in South African Universities. *The International Review of Research in Open and Distributed Learning, 17*(5). http://dx.doi.org/10.19173/irrodl.v17i5.2523

Cronin, C. (2017). Openness and praxis: Exploring the use of open educational practices in higher education. *International Review of Research in Open and Distance Learning, 10*(5), 15–34.

Dalsgaard, C., & Thestrup, K. (2015). Dimensions of openness: Beyond the course as an open format in online education. *The International Review of Research in Open and Distributed Learning, 16*(6), 78–97. Retrieved from http://www.irrodl.org/index.php/irrodl/article/view/2146/3555

Daniel, J. (2009). *Breaking higher education's iron triangle: Access, cost, and quality*. Retrieved from http://oasis.col.org/handle/11599/1442

de Hart, K., Chetty, Y., & Archer, E. (2015). Uptake of OER by staff in distance education in South Africa. *International Review of Research in Open and Distributed Learning, 16*(2). Retrieved from http://www.irrodl.org/index.php/irrodl/article/view/2047

Deimann, M., & Farrow, R. (2013). Rethinking OER and their use: Open education as Bildung. *The International Review of Research in Open and Distributed Learning, 14*(3), 344–360. http://dx.doi.org/10.19173/irrodl.v14i3.1370

Deimann, M., & Sloep, P. (2013). How does open education work? In A. Meiszner & L. Squires (Eds.), *Openness and education: Advances in digital education and lifelong learning* (pp. 1–23). London: Emerald.

DeRosa, R., & Robison, S. (2015). Pedagogy, technology, and the example of open educational resources. *Educause Review*. Retrieved from http://er.educause.edu/articles/2015/11/pedagogytechnology-and-the-example-of-open-educational-resources

dos Santos, A. I., Punie, Y., & Castaño-Muñoz, J. (2016). Opening up education: A support framework for higher education institutions. *JRC Science for Policy Report*. Retrieved from http://publications.jrc.ec.europa.eu/repository/bitstream/JRC101436/jrc101436.pdf

Edwards, R. (2015). Knowledge infrastructures and the inscrutability of openness in education. *Learning, Media and Technology, 40*(3), 251–264. https://doi.org/10.1080/17439884.2015.1006131

Ehlers, U. D. (2011). From open educational resources to open educational practices. *eLearning Papers, 23*. Retrieved from http://elearningpapers.eu/en/download/file/fid/22240

Geser, G. (2007). *Open educational practices and resources OLCOS Roadmap 2012*. Austria: OLCOS Project. Retrieved from http://www.olcos.org/cms/upload/docs/olcos_roadmap.pdf

Government of India. (1986). *National policy on education*. New Delhi: Ministry of Human Resource Development, Government of India.

Guri-Rosenblit, S. (2009). Openness dimensions of distance teaching universities. In P. Rogers, G. Berg, J. Boettcher, C. Howard, L. Justice, & K. Schenk (Eds.), *Encyclopedia of distance learning* (Information Science Reference, Vol. III, pp. 1557–1563). New York, NY: Hershey.

Harishankar, V., Balaji, V., & Ganapuram, S. (2013). An assessment of individual and institutional readiness to embrace open educational resources in India. In G. Dhanarajan & D. Porter (Eds.), *Open educational resources: An Asian perspective* (pp. 53–72). Vancouver: COL and OER Asia.

Harris, D. (1987). *Openness and closure in distance education*. New York, NY: Falmer Press.

Hegarty, B. (2015). Attributes of open pedagogy: A model for using open educational resources. *Educational Technology*. Retrieved from https://www.scribd.com/doc/276569994/Attributes-of-Open-Pedagogy-A-Model-for-Using-Open-Educational-Resources

Hill, B. V. (1975). What's 'open' about open education? In D. A. Nyberg (Ed.), *The philosophy of open education* (pp. 3–13). London: Routledge & Kegan.

Hodgkinson-Williams, C., & Gray, E. (2009). Degrees of openness: The emergence of open educational resources at the University of Cape Town. *International Journal of Education and Development Using Information and Communication Technology, 5*(5), 101–116.

Hogan, R. (2012). Transnational distance learning and building new markets for universities. In *Proceedings of global TIME -online conference on technology, innovation, media & education* (pp. 116–121). Association for the Advancement of Computing in Education (AACE). Retrieved February 2012, from https://www.learntechlib.org/p/39408/

Hoosen, S., & Butcher, N. (2012). Experiences of developing OER-amenable policies. In J. Glennie, K. Harley, N. Butcher, & T. van Wyk (Eds.), *Open educational resources and change in higher education: Reflections from practice* (pp. 217–240). Vancouver: Commonwealth of Learning and Athabasca University.

Iiyoshi, T., & Vijay Kumar, M. S. (Eds.). (2008). *Opening up education: The collective advancement of education through open technology, open content, and open knowledge.* Cambridge, MA: The MIT Press.

Jenkins, H. (2006). *Confronting the challenges of participatory culture: Media education for the 21st century* (Occasional paper). Chicago, IL: MacArthur Foundation.

Jones, C. (2015). Openness, technologies, business models and austerity. *Learning, Media and Technology, 40*(3), 328–349.

Judith, K., & Bull, D. (2016). Assessing the potential for openness: A framework for examining course-level OER implementation in higher education. *Education Policy Analysis Archives, 24*(42). http://dx.doi.org/10.14507/epaa.24.1931

Kanjilal, U. (2013). Digital repository to open educational resource repository: IGNOU's eGyankosh. In G. Dhanrajan & D. Porter (Eds.), *Open educational resources: An Asian perspective* (pp. 221–230). Vancover: CEMCA.

Knox, J. (2013a). The limitations of access alone: Moving towards open processes in education technology. *Open Praxis, 5*(1), 21–29.

Knox, J. (2013b). Five critiques of the open educational resources movement. *Teaching in Higher Education, 18*(8), 821–832.

Kumar, M. S. V. (2009). Open educational resources in India's national development. *Open Learning, 24*(1), 77–84. http://dx.doi.org/10.1080/02680510802627860

Kursun, E., Cagiltay, K., & Can, G. (2014). An investigation of faculty perspectives on barriers, incentives, and benefits of the OER movement in Turkey. *International Review of Research in Open and Distributed Learning, 16*(6), 15–32. Retrieved from http://www.irrodl.org/index.php/irrodl/article/view/1914

Lane, A. (2009). The impact of openness on bridging educational digital divides. *International Review of Research in Open and Distance Learning, 10*(5). Retrieved from http://www.irrodl.org/index.php/irrodl/article/view/637/1396

Lane, A., & McAndrew, P. (2010). Are open educational resources systematic or systemic change agents for teaching practice? *British Journal of Educational Technology, 41*(6), 952–962.

Leichsenring, H., Noe, S., & Brandenburg, U. (2012, November 21–22). *Towards a culture of openness: Cultural change of the institution and the impact of widening access measures*. Paper presented at ExpandO Workshop: Peer Learning in Expanding Opportunities in Higher Education in Ghent.

Lesko, I. (2013). The use and production of OER & OCW in teaching in South African higher education institutions. *Open Praxis, 5*(2), 103–121. http://dx.doi.org/10.5944/openpraxis.5.2.52

Lockwood, F. (1998). *The design and production of self-instructional materials*. London: Kogan Page.

Lynch, C. (2008). Digital libraries, learning communities and open education. In T. Iiyoshi & M. V. Kumar (Eds.), *Opening up education: The collective advancement of education through open technology, open content, and open knowledge* (pp. 105–118). Cambridge, MA: MIT Press.

Mackintosh, W. (2012). Opening education in New Zealand: A snapshot of a rapidly evolving OER ecosystem. In J. Glennie, K. Harley, N. Butcher, & T. van Wyk (Eds.), *Open educational resources and change in higher education: Reflections from practice* (pp. 263–281). Vancouver: Commonwealth of Learning and Athabasca University.

Mackintosh, W., McGreal, R., & Taylor, J. (2011). *Open Education Resources (OER) for assessment and credit for students' projects: Towards a logic model and plan for action*. Retrieved from http://hdl.handle.net/2149/3039

Masterman, E. (2016). Bringing open educational practice to a research-intensive university: Prospects and challenges. *The Electronic Journal of e-Learning, 14*(1), 31–42. Retrieved from http://www.ejel.org/issue/download.html?idArticle=483

Masterman, L., & Chan, J. (2015). *Openness in teaching and learning: An exploration of principles and practices at the University of Oxford* (Research report). Academic IT Group, IT Services, University of Oxford. Retrieved from https://weblearn.ox.ac.uk/x/nNvkjt

McAndrew, P. (2011). Inspiring creativity in organisations, teachers and learners through open educational resources. *European Journal of Open, Distance and E-Learning*, 1–9. Retrieved from http://www.eurodl.org/materials/special/2011/McAndrew.pdf

McAndrew, P., Farrow, R., Law, P., & Elliot-Cirigottis, G. (2012). Learning the lessons of openness. Journal of Interactive Media in Education, *2012*(2), 10. Retrieved from http://jime.open.ac.uk/2012/10

McGrath, O. (2008). Open educational technology: Tempered aspirations. In T. Iiyoshi & M. V. Kumar (Eds.), *Opening up education: The collective advancement of education through open technology, open content, and open knowledge* (pp. 105–118). Cambridge, MA: MIT Press.

McGreal, R. (2013). Introduction: The need for open educational resources. In R. McGreal, W. Kinuthia, S. Marshall, & T. McNamara (Eds.), *Perspectives on open and distance learning: Open educational resources: Innovation, research and practice*. Vancouver: Commonwealth of Learning and Athabasca University.

McGreal, R. (2017). Special report on the role of open educational resources in supporting the sustainable development goal 4: Quality education challenges and opportunities. *The International Review of Research in Open and Distributed Learning, 18*(7). http://dx.doi.org/10.19173/irrodl.v18i7.3541

McGreal, R., Conrad, D., Murphy, A., Witthaus, G., & Mackintosh, W. (2014). Formalising informal learning: Assessment and accreditation challenges within disaggregated systems. *Open Praxis, 6*(2), 125–133. http://dx.doi.org/10.5944/openpraxis.6.2.114

McNamara, T. (2012). *Open education: Emergence and identity.* Retrieved from http://oh-institute.org/external_resources/pub/McNamara-OpenEd_Emergence_Identity-CC-by.pdf

MHRD. (2016). *All India survey on higher education.* New Delhi: Government of India.

Mulder, F., & Janssen, B. (2013). Opening up education. In R. Jacobi, H. Jelgerhuis, & N. van der Woert (Eds.), *Trend report: Open educational resources 2013* (pp. 36–42). Utrecht: SURF SIG OER.

Nascimbeni, F., & Burgos, D. (2016). In search for the open educator: Proposal of a definition and a framework to increase openness adoption among university educators. *The International Review of Research in Open and Distributed Learning, 17*(6). http://dx.doi.org/10.19173/irrodl.v17i6.2736

Nikoi, S. K., Rowlett, T., Armellini, A., & Witthaus, G. (2011). CORRE: a framework for evaluating and transforming teaching materials into open educational resources. *Open Learning: The Journal of Open, Distance and e-Learning, 26*(3), 191–207. http://dx.doi.org/10.1080/02680513.2011.611681

NKC. (2007). *National knowledge commission: Report to the Nation 2007.* Government of India. Retrieved from http://www.knowledgecommission.gov.in/recommendations/oer.asp

OECD. (2007). *Giving knowledge for free: The emergence of open educational resources.* Paris: OECD. Retrieved from http://www.oecd.org/edu/ceri/38654317.pdf

Oliver, C. (1997). Sustainable competitive advantage: Combining institutional and resource-based views. *Strategic Management Journal, 18*(9), 697–713.

Oliver, M. (2015). From openness to permeability: Reframing open education in terms of positive liberty in the enactment of academic practices. *Learning, Media and Technology, 40*(3), 365–384.

OPAL. (2011). *Beyond OER: Shifting focus to open educational practices.* Retrieved from https://oerknowledgecloud.org/sites/oerknowledgecloud.org/files/OPAL2011.pdf

OpenCourseWare. (2011). *MIT OpenCourseWare celebrates 10th anniversary.* Retrieved from https://ocw.mit.edu/about/media-coverage/press-releases/tenth-anniversary/

Open Education Consortium. (n.d). *About the open education consortium.* Retrieved from http://www.oeconsortium.org/about-oec/

Ossiannilsson, E. S. I., & Creelman, A. M. (2012). OER, resources for learning–Experiences from an OER project in Sweden. *European Journal of Open, Distance and E-Learning, 1*. Retrieved fromhttp://www.eurodl.org/materials/contrib/2012/Ossiannilsson_Creelman.pdf

Panda, S., & Santosh, S. (2017). Faculty perception of openness and attitude to open sharing at the Indian National Open University. *International Review of Research in Open and Distance Learning, 18*(7), 89–111. Retrieved from http://www.irrodl.org/index.php/irrodl/article/view/2942/4463

Paskevicius, M. (2017). Conceptualizing open educational practices through the lens of constructive alignment. *Open Praxis, 9*(2), 125–140. http://dx.doi.org/10.5944/openpraxis.9.2.519

Paul, R. (1993). Open Universities – The test of all models. In K. Hurry, M. John, & D. Keegan (Eds.), *Distance education: New perspectives*. London: Routledge.

Pete, J., Mulder, F., & Oliveira Neto, J. D. (2017). Differentiation in access to, and the use and sharing of (Open) educational resources among students and lecturers at Kenyan Universities. *Open Praxis, 9*(2), 173–194. http://dx.doi.org/10.5944/openpraxis.9.2.574

Peters, M. A. (2008). The history and emergent paradigm of open education. In M. A. Peters & R. Britez (Eds.), *Open education and education for openness* (pp. 3–16). Rotterdam, The Netherlands: Sense Publishers.

Peters, O. (2001). *Learning and teaching in distance education – Analyses and interpretations from an international perspective*. London: Kogan Page.

Rolfe, V. (2012). Open educational resources: Staff attitudes and awareness. *Research in Learning Technology, 20*, 1–13. doi:10.3402/rlt.v20i0/14395

Rosen, J. R., & Smale, M. A. (2015). Open digital pedagogy = Critical pedagogy. *Hybrid Pedagogy*. http://www.digitalpedagogylab.com/hybridped/open-digital-pedagogy-critical-pedagogy/

Rossetti, R. (1989). Student and parent images of vocational education offerings: Declining enrollment in vocational education. *Eric, 8*.

Sampson, N. (2003). Meeting the needs of distance learners. *Language Learning and Technology, 7*(3), 103–118.

Santosh, S., & Panda, S. (2016a). Use of open educational resources in distance education – Opportunities and challenges in Indian scenario. *Staff and Educational Development International, 20*(1), 39–54.

Santosh, S., & Panda, S. (2016b). Sharing of knowledge among faculty in a Mega Open University. *Open Praxis, 8*(3), 247–264. Retrieved from https://openpraxis.org/index.php/OpenPraxis/article/view/317/221

Scott, R. W. (2001). *Institutions and organisations*. Thousand Oaks, CA: Sage.

Scott, W. R. (2008). *Institutions and organizations: Ideas and interests* (3rd ed.). Thousand Oaks, CA: Sage.

Selznick, P. (1996). Institutionalism 'old' and 'new'. *Administrative Science Quarterly, 41*, 270–277.

Srivastava, M. (2016). *Status of the state open universities in India – Report.* New Delhi: CEMCA.

Stagg, A., & Bossu, C. (2016). Educational policy and open educational practice in Australian higher education. In P. Blessinger & T. Bliss (Eds.), *Open education: International perspectives in higher education* (pp. 115–136). Cambridge: Open Book. Retrieved from http://www.jstor.org/stable/j.ctt1sq5v9n.11

Stewart, W. (2006). *Athabasca University – A case study in open educational resources production and use in Canada.* Toronto: OECD.

Tait, A. (2008). What are open universities for? *Open Learning, 23*(2), 85–93. https://doi.org/10.1080/02680510802051871

Thakran, A., & Sharma, R. C. (2016). Meeting the challenges of higher education in India through open educational resources: Policies, practices, and implications. *Education Policy Analysis Archives, 24*(37). http://dx.doi.org/10.14507/epaa.24.1816

Torres, N. P. M. (2013). Embracing openness: The challenges of OER in Latin American education. *Open Praxis, 5*(1), 81–89. Retrieved from http://openpraxis.org/index.php/OpenPraxis/article/view/33

Tuomi, I. (2006). *Open educational resources: What they are and why do they matter* (Report prepared for the OECD). Retrieved from http://www.meaningprocessing.com/personalPages/tuomi/articles/OpenEducationalResources_OECDreport.pdf

Tuomi, I. (2013). Open educational resources and the transformation of education. *European Journal of Education, 48*(1). Retrieved from http://onlinelibrary.wiley.com/doi/10.1111/ejed.12019/full

UNESCO. (2002). *Open and distance learning: Trends, policy and strategy considerations.* Paris: UNESCO. Retrieved from http://unesdoc.unesco.org/images/0012/001284/128463e.pdf

UNESCO. (2014). *How openness impacts on higher education: Policy brief.* Retrieved from http://iite.unesco.org/pics/publications/en/files/3214734.pdf

UNESCO-COL. (2011). *Guidelines for Open Educational Resources (OER) in higher education.* Paris: UNESCO. Retrieved from http://www.col.org/PublicationDocuments/Guidelines_OER_HE.pdf

van der Merwe, A. D. (2015). *The attitudes of high school teachers to open education resources: A case study of selected South African schools* (OE Global Conference 2015). Retrieved from http://conference.oeconsortium.org/2015/wp-content/uploads/2015/01/Alex-van-der-MerweOpen-education-conference-paper.pdf

Villamejor-Mendoza, M. F. (2013). The openness of the university of the Philippines Open University: Issues and prospects. *Open Praxis, 5*(2), 135–150. Retrieved from http://openpraxis.org/index.php/OpenPraxis/article/view/26

Weinbren, D. (2014). *The Open University: A history.* Manchester: Manchester University Press.

Weller, M. (2014). *The battle for open: How openness won and why it doesn't feel like victory.* London: Ubiquity Press.

Wiley, D. (2009). Defining 'open' [Blog post]. Retrieved from http://opencontent.org/blog/archives/1123

Wiley, D. (2014). The access compromise and the 5th R [Blog post]. Retrieved from http://opencontent.org/blog/archives/3221

Wiley, D., & Hilton III, J. (2009). Openness, dynamic specialization, and the disaggregated future of higher education. *International Review of Research in Open and Distance Learning, 10*(5) 1–17. Retrieved from http://www.irrodl.org/index.php/irrodl/article/view/768/1415

PART 3

Open in Application

CHAPTER 11

Breaking Boundaries and Building Bridges across Knowledge-Sharing Communities: OpenMed

Katherine Wimpenny, Cristina Stefanelli, Saida Affouneh, Ahmed Almakari, Adiy Tweissi, Heba Abdel Naby and Seddik Tawfik

The idea of breaking boundaries and building bridges that expand the opportunities for any citizen to benefit from universities as a source of knowledge, without having to become a fee-paying student, has been a core element of Open Education Practices (OEP) in the context of OpenMed; Opening up education in South-Mediterranean countries.[1] This international cooperation project[2] involved five partners from Europe and nine from the South-Mediterranean (S-M) region (Morocco, Palestine, Egypt and Jordan). It focused on how universities from the designated countries, and other S-M countries, can join as community partners in the adoption of strategies and channels that embrace the principles of openness and reusability within the context of higher education (HE).

OEP's two fundamental concepts are that learners (i) have free and open access to knowledge; and (ii) can adapt and re-use existing teaching and learning resources, which are in the public domain, or have been released under an intellectual property license, allowing free reuse or adaptation by others (Weller, 2014).

Using openly available teaching resources enables educators to introduce learners to new forms of learning where they can also be involved in collaborating on compiling course material and resources (Petrovic-Dzerdz & Trepanier, 2018). In addition, learners can benefit through skill development in digital fluency, pedagogies for participative-teaching techniques, the understanding of processes for appropriate licensing of OER and where to house them, and in the strengthening of international collaboration and connectivity (Affouneh et al., 2018; El Hassan, 2013).

It follows then, that, openness in HE teaching and learning should be commonplace practice for the equal and democratic access to knowledge. Such openness includes the responsibility of universities to expand their social function and role as knowledge-sharing communities. Whilst Massive Open Online Courses (MOOCs) have enabled access to courses from institutions, including elite universities, to the world (considering international language

 | DOI: 10.1163/9789004422988_012

proficiency, digital skills and internet connectivity); and Open Educational Resources (OER) and OEP are widely documented as means of opening up access to education at a more intimate level in fostering and democratizing access to education (Wiley, 2006; Beetham, Falconer, McGill, & Littlejohn, 2012); there is a lack of substantive evidence on how such practices, and the use of technologies, in particular, can promote accessibility in relation to geographical access, minority access and reduction of access barriers (Fichten Asuncion & Scapin, 2014; Navarrete & Luján-Mora, 2013; Lane, 2012). Further, there is limited literature on OER usage from the perspective of academics and students in non-Western countries, who are often projected as the recipients and beneficiaries of OER (Hu et al., 2015). Indeed, there is limited evidence of how OER are localized and integrated into actual teaching and learning practices (Butcher & Hoosen, 2014), and despite the potential of OEP in helping strengthen intellectual, cultural, scientific and technological exchange for an increasingly global and knowledge-based economy, OEP and OER originating, specifically, from the S-M region are rare. As Zualkernan, Allert and Qadah (2006) contend, those advocating for open education are seeking to widen engagement, but the diffusion of OER requires more thoughtful consideration and understanding regarding the applicability and usability of these resources in different cultural settings. For example, in his seminal work, *Pedagogy of the Oppressed*, Paulo Freire (1970) described a misperception that may be an obstacle to the establishment of a successful open education learning environment. In this vision, education was conceptualised to that of a 'banking' type structure, where the teacher (in this case, the means by which information is transmitted, i.e. the Internet) is the depository (of information) and the student is the beneficiary. A teaching environment that is created without space for interaction or, as Freire described, a climate in which problems are articulated, where the transmission of knowledge is multidirectional rather than asynchronous, cannot be considered as a teaching framework; rather, it becomes a vehicle of indoctrination. Therefore, instead of emancipating oneself, the learner remains oppressed.

A similar view can be taken of the nascent movement of OER, where information (in the form of OER) may have mistakenly assumed the role of 'educator.' Some have even claimed that the movement has taken on another meaning – where benevolent 'suppliers' of OER, from developed countries, are in the presence of passive users in developing countries. As earlier stated, such projects position 'users' as recipients and beneficiaries of OER. If these knowledge transfer concerns are not critically considered, the risk is in creating an information society that looks like the map of the world in the 16th century, made up of those who colonize and those who are colonized. Therefore, whilst the open sharing of resources must be encouraged, if universities really want to invest in better teaching and research, the promise of OER lies not only in the accessibility of digitized information, but in the development of methodological approaches and mechanisms to manage and make sense of this information in a variety of dynamic teaching contexts.

In terms of the S-M context, it is evident that there have been significant education challenges in the region over the past 10 years in relation to access, accountability, quality and productivity. This can be seen in terms of the high demand for learners to access HE due to growth in the youth population (El Hassan, 2013; Heyneman, 1997), and the shift to massification (Guri-Rosenbilt, Sebkova, & Teichler, 2007) that is expected by governments determining the future of public institutions (UNESCO, 2010). We suggest here, that a change in attitude towards OEP is required, including new perspectives defining 'open education,' with new attitudes developed towards collaboration and (digital) literacy. For example, in the S-M region, the term 'open education' has been typically aligned with 'online education,' a term often synonymous with lower quality education, with graduates awarded 'open education' degrees not being viewed as having equal status within the labour market to peers holding traditional degree awards (Bouhlila, 2015; Elshamy, 2016; European Commission: Egypt, 2017; The World Bank, 2010). Further, the resistance to embrace institutional change, the mistrust of exchanging educational content and syllabi, and/or the poor adoption of new learning environments are also major constraints in higher education institutions in S–M countries (Commonwealth of Learning & UNESCO, 2012). Most universities are still locked into conventional strategies, and the evolution of tertiary education systems raises questions about the equity of access and outcomes (Cilliers, 2014). The mismatch between the current knowledge-based society, language, issues of cultural diversity, and inflexible teaching practices demands an entirely new *modus operandi* regarding how content is created, combined, updated and delivered. In parallel, the S-M is replete with learners who are very exposed to the Internet and social media and receptive to digitised content (Harbi, 2016). As Harbi argues, this population is a window of opportunity that would underpin the use of OER.

In the context of the above, the top-down governing systems of universities in S-M countries is viewed as one of the key factors viewed as hindering engagement with OEP at institutions within the region. Favouring a *bottom-up* and top-down approach, OpenMed aimed to ensure that the Mediterranean university systems are better integrated into global academic and scientific cooperation networks, which is an essential factor in the integration of Mediterranean communities and economies (Scalisi, 2016).

In this chapter, the authors will share how OpenMed focused on nurturing a culture of openness across the partner higher education institutions. Findings from across the three main project phases will be presented. They included a review of open education initiatives, widening participation in OEP, and capacity-building opportunities for lecturers and other HE professionals. The chapter begins with a preliminary focus on the aims of OpenMed and the initial research phase which focused on the review of open education initiatives globally, and in the S-M in particular. Following this, the strategies used within the project, which sought to widen engagement in OEP in the partner region – addressing issues of policy, institutional change and capacity-building of academics in open education – are shared. The development of the OpenMed capacity-building course, 'Open Education: fundamentals and approaches' will then be presented. As one of the first attempts to train university professors and PhD students in the field of open education in the Mediterranean region, the course was designed, developed and tested in a fully collaborative way among the OpenMed partners, representing a genuine experience of multicultural open education development (Wimpenny, Nascimbeni, Affouneh, Almakari, Mayo, & Aymen, 2019). The chapter will conclude with key findings about intercultural learning in promoting bottom-up and top-down approaches to the sustainable integration of OEP, where concepts, approaches and methodologies have resulted from discussions and negotiations among experts with different national, linguistic and cultural backgrounds.

1 The OpenMed Project

OpenMed adopted the 2012 UNESCO definition as a desirable end-point for a journey towards openness in education:

> Teaching, learning and research materials in any medium, digital or otherwise, that reside in the public domain or have been released under an open license that permits no–cost access, use, adaptation and redistribution by others with no or limited restrictions. (UNESCO, 2012)[3]

In addition, apart from the creation and use of content, open pedagogic approaches that place 'an emphasis in the network and the learner's connections within this' (Weller, 2014, p. 10), were key to OpenMed's definition for OEP. However, whilst OpenMed sought as an aspirational goal that stipulates, as part of its service mission, that HE professionals and institutions engage in the creation and use of educational resources that fully fit UNESCO's definition, the OpenMed partners also acknowledge that the uptake of OEP may also start with less ambitious goals, for example, by making copyrighted content publicly available on the Internet.

The overarching goal of OpenMed, therefore, was to raise awareness and facilitate the adoption of OEP and OER in the S-M countries, with a particular focus on HE in Morocco, Palestine, Egypt and Jordan.[4] OpenMed fostered the role of universities as knowledge providers not only to their on-campus students but also beyond the walls of institutions, especially towards disadvantaged groups (i.e. low-income peoples, gender equality, learners who are disabled, special needs education, people living in rural areas, learners at risk of low achievement, and refugees).

Five specific aims of the project were to (1) raise awareness and widen HEI participation in OEP and OER; (2) define the agenda for the re-use of OER at HEI level; (3) define mid-term strategic roadmaps for the implementation of the OER agenda at local-institutional level, according to the local, cultural and institutional needs and strategies; (4) instruct university teachers about how to use and repurpose OER in a pedagogically-rich context and improve their digital competences; (5) pilot a start-up OEP and offer students flexible and up-to-date open contents and learning paths, with a link to the international community and the needs of the job market.

OpenMed was focused on questioning how OEP can co-exist in HEI strategies and instructional materials in the S-M region. This included how universities rethink their mission, cost structure, international partnerships, and learning experiences. An important first phase of the OpenMed project was, therefore, to gather and analyse data about OEP globally and in the S-M region, in order to inform the subsequent work packages of the project and to facilitate the adoption of OEP at the partner institutions in the S-M region, at other universities in each of their respective countries, and at other HEI more widely. The overall aim of the review was to provide inspiration and insight into the current practices around OEP and to promote reflection and discussion about priorities for change for OpenMed.

2 A Review of Open Education Practices

While there are a few studies on the use of information communication technologies for enhancing education in the Arab countries (see for example, Jemni, 2014; Regional Focus Issues – Learning Technologies in the Middle East, *IRRODL*, 2009; Rhema, 2010; Tubaishat, Bhatti, & El-Qawasmeh, 2006), the amount of research on OEP initiatives in the S-M region published at the time when the project started, in early 2016, was minimal. As such, the research stage drew on multiple sources and types of data, gathered and analysed with the aim of offering an overview of the state-of-the-art of OEP within the HEIS of the S-M partners of the project, and the region at large. In addition, a number of initiatives and insights from other areas of the globe were incorporated with the aim of sharing expertise and good practices. Special attention was paid to previous experiences that, for different reasons, could be transferable to the target region.

Country reports from Morocco, Palestine, Egypt and Jordan were included, providing demographic details as well as detail about issues regarding connectivity, governance and the legal framework of higher education within the region. A survey was also used to capture the level of participation in OEP within the partner institutions at the time of completion (early 2016), and also to identify the future goals of the participating institutions. The data gathered indicated the differences between the four countries in terms of the concept, definition, and practices of open education. Levels of involvement were different, and in some cases. the emphasis was more on showcasing examples of blended and eLearning.

Eleven case study initiatives of current practices in open education globally, and particularly in the S–M region, were included in the Compendium[5] (available in Arabic, French as well as English) including examples of learning platforms, repositories, open access publication networks and MOOCS.

Experts in OEP, identified by the OpenMed partners, from the S–M region, Europe, and from the wider international open education community, were approached to comment on what they considered to be some of the key issues worthy of consideration regarding OEP and the S-M region, as well as more general insights into good practices.[6]

Five key themes were identified as a result of the review of the case studies gathered and interviews conducted, and a number of recommendations were proposed. These initial findings identified key endorsements from which the subsequent phases of OpenMed have developed. In brief, they included the importance of clarity about the justification for the provision of high-quality OEP and OER in HEIS; the necessary investment in infrastructure to ease process development and ways to transition materials and programmes; course accreditation schemes through institutions as a means of promoting OEP as a reputable form of learning; the need for resources to support the upskilling of staff; the importance of adopting a collaborative approach to the creation of OER; incentives to engage staff and students as co-creators of OER; understanding about how computer-mediated communication works, including how learners and teachers connect with one another, and build trust within networks; and finally, understanding licensing approaches and ways to formulate guidelines for other OER creators.

Based on this work, OpenMed fostered a regional debate with partners in the S-M region on the best strategies to embed OEP in universities, and the OpenMed OER Regional Agenda was developed. This document, starting from an understanding of the long-term challenges and priorities which are necessary for opening up higher education in the S-M countries, was brought together, presenting a set of strategic actions aimed at maximising the benefits of OER and OEP to increase the access, quality and the equity of HE in the region.[7]

3 Widening Engagement in Open Education Practices in the Partner Regions

OpenMed appreciated the necessity to embrace integral and also inclusive actions that would be meaningful and relevant for the local beneficiaries, thus avoiding fragmentation of interventions. That is why the project envisioned a multilevel and organic intervention which articulated three key dimensions: contents, platforms and cultural aspects, briefly described as follows:

- Contents: understood as educational resources or pedagogic practices which are openly and freely shared, promoting their continuing remix (re-usability), updating and sharing.
- Platforms: hardware and software designed to simplify the interoperability of the resources, facilitating semantic structures (improving their findability) and the use of open standards and open source software that decrease costs and can trigger adoption practices.
- Cultural aspects: promoting the awareness and explaining the value of 'openness,' describing the educational and also the inter-institutional benefits, and not only identifying best practices, but implementing the required incentives to foster these practices in a variety of teaching-learning environments.

Utilising a top-down approach (with recognition of the bottom-up or grass roots consequences), four OER National Strategy Forums took place between November 2016 and April 2017 in Morocco, Palestine, Egypt and Jordan, gathering educators, managers and decision makers from HEIs in the S-M countries. The objective of these events was to give the S-M higher education stakeholders opportunity to discuss, revise, and validate the OpenMed OER Regional Agenda as a long-term plan presenting challenges and priorities for strategic actions aimed at maximizing the benefits of OEP and the use, reuse and remix of OER for university course development, thus facilitating equity, access to and democratisation of HE. These events were also intended to widen participation in OEP, by showcasing outstanding cases of OER adoption and fostering networking among policy makers, university leaders, educators and OER experts from Europe and the S-M countries.

In terms of impact, the forums offered scope to build consensus within the academic communities on open education principles that will benefit HE in the S-M countries. As part of their work, 'Institutional Roadmaps,' for the adoption of OEP at an institutional level, suitable for the S-M countries, were defined to inspire commitment for immediate implementation of the long-term strategic plan at universities managerial level. In the following section, the ways in which the partners have been engaging and promoting the development and adoption of OEP, addressing both top-down and bottom-up approaches, is shared.

3.1 *Palestine*

With the stark reality of living under Israeli occupation for more than 50 years, the opportunity for opening up education in Palestine is viewed as an essential requirement to advancing scientific research being developed-in country on a global level, whilst also meeting the local community's needs by considering accessible, sustainable, economic, technical and human development (Affouneh et al., 2018.)

An early example of a move to OEP in Palestine can be traced to the beginning of the 1990s, when The Palestinian Liberation Organization (PLO) established Al Quds Open University, which started operating in 1991, in order to ensure education for Palestinians inside Palestine and to overcome all the difficulties of the Israeli occupation including the closure of many existing universities, financial restrictions and border control enforcements preventing Palestinians from studying abroad. The university's use of distance learning as a pedagogical approach enabled students to be able to study 25% of the time with their teachers, and otherwise to use online textbooks that were introduced as provided as self-learning guides.[8]

In Palestine, there are now 14 conventional universities in addition to Al Quds Open University (RecoNow, 2016). All of these institutions are enhancing technologies into their learning and teaching in different ways and whilst there is no formal policy for open education per se in Palestine, efforts are underway to draft a suggested policy. As an example, at An Najah National University (ANNU) Palestine, open education is defined as 'learning without boundaries,' where education should be offered to people without conditions

Two HEIs from Palestine, ANNU and Birzeit University, are partners in OpenMed. Both have had involvement in OEP and could be considered as leaders in their country. At ANNU, staff members engage in steps towards OER through producing online materials, either as recorded lectures or as open courses. In 2010, the university established two studios in order to produce video-based learning through recorded lectures that are broadcasted asynchronously through the university websites.[9] Through the studios, more than 260 courses were developed and more than 10 million viewers, across 45 countries, accessed their content (Affouneh & Amin Awad Raba, 2017).

In 2012, the E-Learning Centre (ELC) at ANNU was established in order to lead the process of building on the university's online offerings, including the design of blended courses. The team led academic staff through many phases including capacity-building, piloting of new modules, infrastructure development and course development. To date, more than 800 courses are available at ANNU, with 55 of them defined as 'Open Courses' (meaning that anyone can access the course content, although to be accredited as having completed the course, there is a payment fee for assessment.)

In 2015, the ELC produced the first MOOC in Palestine called 'Discover Palestine,' with 265 participants engaged over the first three cycles (with an average of 53 learners per cycle). Course distribution by participant was captured as 6.5% PhD; 34.8% BA/BSc; 32.6% MA/MSc; 15.2% Diploma and 10.9% Other. Learner distribution by gender was 54.3% female to 45.7% male, with a geographical reach of participants accessing the MOOC identified at 25 countries. What came as more of a surprise was that whilst the main thrust of the course was about sharing new narratives of Palestine to educate and inform a wide and more internationally diverse audience about Palestinian history, culture, architect, art, and culture, many Palestinians in exile and also local people from Palestine participated.

As such, the Discover Palestine team evidenced how, through the open discussion of learning experiences, an important opportunity was made possible for communities of learners, both local and global, to take part in the sharing of historical facts and cultural practices. Indeed, many of the MOOC students reported that the course was better than anything available at the 'brick-and-mortar campuses' to which they had access (Affouneh et al., 2018, p. 11). Further, the team now have the confidence to promote MOOCs for Arab learners as well as MOOCs for international learning communities. Alongside this they have decreased the previously required reading materials and instead added more content and links through generative learning resources. With a decreased number of assignments and with emphasis on socially-intensive and interactive learning experiences, the team has shifted its role to being less instructor-led and more as interlocutor/facilitator. Further, in producing more open courses, with licensed content, strategic level leads as well as university lecturers have increased understandings on the meaning and contribution of OEP and OER.

ANNU has therefore been developing its own institutional road map, based on the regional agenda, to consider how open education can be formally recognised as part of ANNU's educational policies. The road map has instigated a series of activities aimed to empower academic staff as part of the university's strategic education plan, including: developing the university's infrastructure in order to transfer the university's campus into a smart campus; designing MOOCs promoting ANNUs courses as a tool to provide learning (translated into Arabic and English) to reach learners everywhere; offering academic development workshops to build the capacity of the faculty members in what is meant by open education and how to practice it; and, co-financing the establishment of a new centre for creativity in open education.[10]

The university strategic plan will continue to be reviewed in order to continually enhance OEP locally.

3.2 *Morocco*

The diffusion of open education in Moroccan universities is closely linked to that of digital educational resources in general. As the use of these resources to date remains quite limited, one might suggest the uptake of OER is gaining traction but has yet to make its impact. Yet, in the context of the limited resources of Moroccan (and African) HE and training institutions, the OER movement has considerable potential.

The University Cadi Ayyad of Marrakech and Ibn Zohr University of Agadir are two partner HEIs in OpenMed. During the project, both have been examining how strategies and decisions for the integration of open education at the institutional level need to consider the importance of defining an appropriate framework in respect of each partner institution-teacher-student, which also represents the civil society. The added value being articulated, is to formalize and concretize the idea of quality education for all. Two considerations guide this statement. First, open education can expand access to education, knowledge transfer, social inclusion and the creation of collaboration and sharing culture. Secondly, there is a strong economic case for open education: the liberalization of publicly funded educational resources under open licenses, represents a return on public expenditure investment. This includes the development of OERs, as well as open frameworks for technology-enhanced learning and Open and Massive Online Courses (MOOCs). Additionally, it includes prior learning validation and creativity in open educational practices.

As an example, Ibn Zohr University (UIZ), believes that the best way to achieve this is through collaboration and through partnerships that focus on the four cornerstones of the evolving OER process: the creation, organization, dissemination and use of OER. The strategic combination of these elements within what the UIZ calls the 'UIZ OER Architecture,' will lead to the development of a dynamic, meaningful, rational and comprehensive OER strategy for education institutions in Morocco. As changes take effect and transform the university culture, it is expected that staff, departmental services (ICT department, quality assurance services, students, etc.) perceive the effects on students and the community as a whole. Supporting stakeholder dialogue and building the capacity of educators would ensure that the infrastructure needed for Open Education is taken into account and has sufficient resources, within the institution's strategic framework and long-term goals. Therefore, negotiation and development of such an infrastructure would also increase the virtual mobility volume in the Mediterranean countries, opening up new, flexible and educational paths, which expose students to international approaches and dialogues, with benefits to large scale in social and citizenship learners' issues. OpenMed is therefore an example of collaborative strategy adopted by the UIZ, which enables the institution to be meaningfully situated in relation to the other countries of the S-M and of Europe in general.

3.3 *Jordan*

The movement of OEP in Jordan can be traced back to the late 1990s, when the University of Jordan provided free and open e-learning courses, offered to learners, without the need for them to log into their Moodle e-learning platform. In 2010, the Jordan Open Source Association successfully proposed an Arab open education resources platform, which was originally due to be launched in June 2011. Following this, a MOOC platform was launched in November 2013, as part of Queen Rania Al Abdullah's initiatives under The Queen Rania Foundation, which now operates under the name 'Edraak.'[11] The Edraak platform presents the Arab world with unique and vital opportunities to be part of the necessary revolution in online, open, education and learning. The vision of open education in Jordan was based upon the notion that OER offer opportunities for systemic change in teaching and learning through accessible content. Through a blended model of teacher-led knowledge and student-centered sharing processes, most Jordanian universities began to develop structures for sharing, accessing and bringing participants together, with the aim of providing more equitable access, as well as levels of learning.

Regulations and instructions on an institutional and national level have been continuously changing. The Ministry of Higher Education and Scientific

Research (MOHESR) approved the blended model within 25% of programmes. Further, an alliance of three or more Jordanian universities can establish a fully online programme as well. However, MOHESR has expressed some constraints regarding quality assurance including the way exams are conducted, how learning outcomes are measured, and, how course funding and cultural perceptions are considered.

Challenges in the open education methodology, therefore, still exist in the academic medium in Jordan, where three main issues are of particular note: the governmental policies instructed by Ministry of Higher Education and Scientific Research; the alignment of these policies with regulations published by Jordanian accreditation institutes; and the cultural acceptability of open education and distance learning in general. Overall, students, instructors and policy-makers are gradually moving towards an increased acceptance of new methods of education systems, especially in the e-learning process. The following is an example from Princess Sumaya University for Technology (PSUT) and their E-Learning Centre (ELC) that represents the national goals and objectives of the Jordanian higher education system in open courses.

Since its establishment in 2016, the ELC at Princess Sumaya University for Technology (PSUT) has been operating as the core of distance learning, online courses and open educational resources. The ELC is one of the main operating units in the university and is connected to the president in the PSUT organizational system. The key ELC goals include the following, to (1) create a basis of multiple e-learning platforms and services to students, professors and staff; (2) promote and improve the methods of e-learning among youth and adult learners; (3) enable the opportunities of research and innovation the in e-learning field, and (4) provide professional training in e-learning to strengthen the overall learning outcomes and teaching techniques. The ELC staff install and operate e-learning's latest trends and technologies. The ELC will also be offering e-learning solutions such as: augmented reality applications, virtual reality station for game-based learning, workstations to take online courses designed by PSUT departments, and access for open resources. The ELC will continue to provide training sessions on how to use e-learning for maximum learning benefits and outcomes. In fact, this represents the whole ambition of open education in Jordan.

The ELC is viewed as a venue for learning solutions, and a space and place to add significant value to PSUT as an information and communication technology (ICT) institute in general, and to students and scholars specifically. This is through incorporating activities focused on enhancing collaboration and an 'active team study experience,' and establishment of research groups within universities (i.e. open education consortiums). The ELC is aimed to provide a unique experience for the public, undergraduate and graduate students in Jordan.

In summary, OEP in Jordan are arguably still in the early stages, but with all the efforts both top-down and at grassroot levels, from policy makers to instructors, and in being partners in projects with a high profile such as OpenMed, progress can accelerate in the right direction.

3.4 *Egypt*

The first initiative in open education in Egypt was in 1991 with a focus on making education and learning available to those who missed the opportunity to get into the conventional HE system, and to those who wished to pursue HE in order to enhance their careers. The definition of *open* at that time related to access to online only course offerings. With rapid advances in ICT, and recent changes in teaching and learning strategies, the Ministry of Higher Education initiated the Distance Learning Project (2010) with the objective to enhance the quality of open learning in Egypt. The project was based on adopting a blended learning approach, combining e-learning with face-to-face and virtual classes, as well as video-streaming and satellite transmission. Building on the favourable outcomes of this project, the Supreme Council of Universities (SCU) (2016) decided to make a major overhaul of the existing open learning system. Changes were based on the need for a comprehensive evaluation of existing practices and the recent trends in OEP in different countries. The SCU has since established a set of guidelines for universities to develop and run blended learning programmes. As set in these guidelines, the main objective is to make education and learning available to everyone, any time, and at any location. Flexibility is also maintained since the newly adopted system is a credit-hour system that allows students to choose from elective courses. Programmes are carefully linked to the needs of the job market and the strategic goal of sustainable development, and learning objectives have to be clearly defined.

Since the newly adopted system has an e-learning component, the SCU has continued to develop its profile in online education, through the establishment of open education centres in several of its universities, as a service provider. The role of these e-learning education centres is to help in producing online interactive courses to train faculty members in using learning management systems, and training administrators on issues related to registration, evaluation, advisement, and other administrative issues. E-learning education centres also offer incentives to encourage professors to participate in producing the e-content of the courses. In the existing system, students have to register for a programme and pay tuition fees.

The SCU initiative is built on a number of factors that aim to contribute to its success. Such factors include the readiness of faculty members to improve teaching methods and develop learning materials, the availability of supporting technologies to produce the courses, and the willingness of students to use technology as a tool for learning.

What is evident is that OEP and programmes offered by the Egyptian governmental universities vary in their definition of 'open' and reflect the character of each university, and ways to meet the needs of the surrounding locale. Participating in OpenMed, Cairo University and Alexandria University are taking the lead on re-defining the concept of open in line with the UNESCO definition, and are focused on spreading awareness of OEP and OER and taking direct action to model such practices. Key steps taken to date have focused on raising awareness about the importance of OER and its benefits among the academic community (faculty members, administration, students); establishing a lab in each university to produce OER (one of the intended outcomes of the project); providing the technical support by training technical staff in the labs; training faculty members to produce OER; emphasizing its importance in enhancing the teaching/learning environment; and, adopting policies to evaluate the current and upcoming development of OER in the short-term, in order to give feedback to the designers/creators, and as necessary to make any quality changes recommended in order to develop them. A further example of change in practices is at Cairo University, which does not currently have a formal policy or strategy on OEP; however, the university is pursuing the development and expansion of OER through co-operation with the Egyptian Knowledge Bank and is aiming to develop an institutional repository from which it can release educational content under open licenses. Alexandria University also showed another example of adoption of the new concept of open education through being connected to a group of African institutions via the Pan-African Network. The unusual practice enables educators from Alexandria University, and of course the other partners, to broadcast their lectures and exchange ideas across borders. The informal policy of open education supports the release of OER on the university website. As will be explained in the following section of the chapter, academics from both Cairo and Alexandria University are actively participating as members of 'local learning circles,' as part of the OpenMed online course collaboratively designed and delivered by OpenMed partners. The members of these learning circles will then cascade what they have ascertained and act as trainers and transmitters of knowledge to colleagues in their universities and other universities, thus creating a sustainable model for the continuing development of staff working with OER and OEP in Egypt.

4 OpenMed Capacity-building Course: 'Open Education: Fundamentals and Approaches'

The OpenMed course 'Open Education: Fundamentals and Approaches' was designed as part of the third project phase. The course ran as a pilot from September 2017 to March 2018, involving 70 teachers from across the partner HEIs. Following this pilot phase, the course was been revised, based on the feedback received by learners and facilitators.

From a pedagogical perspective, the course adopted Fink's (2003) integrated approach to course design. Whilst a Western taxonomy, it was adopted through its focus beyond rote learning, or straightforward application of skills, towards the development of more creative, engaging and reflective 'significant' learning experiences as both process and outcome. As such, the course adopted an active learning approach, composed of three phases. Phase one dealt with an intense face-to-face element, bringing together the learners participating in the pilot phase of the course, with the aim of creating a learning community, including the introduction of the learning activities. During phase two, learners worked through a number of online learning activities, during which they were expected to take a number of course modules and complete assessment tasks proposed. This phase operated through Local Learning Circles (P2P University, 2015), whereby groups of learners met face to face to collaboratively work through the online activities. Each learning circle was coordinated by a team of local facilitators, who were in charge of organising meetings, supporting learners, assessing activities, and reporting back to the wider OpenMed partner community.

In terms of content, the training programme covered the following five modules/learning units: Introducing Openness in Education; Open Licensing and Copyright; Creating and Reusing OER; Localising OER and MOOCs; and Open educational Practices. In phase three, following the online learning experience, learners were expected to apply the skills they had acquired to develop a *final project work* aimed at opening up their teaching. The project work was fully integrated with the online phase and built upon five steps that were taken at the end of each module:

Step 1. Pledge to open up a course/or teaching;
Step 2. Identify open licenses to be applied to teaching courses,
Step 3. Use OER in teaching,
Step 4. Localize OER to a specific course/context, and
Step 5. Develop an open teaching plan and share it with a learning community.

Project work resulted in the creation of some type of OER, formally licensed and complemented by a tailored, open teaching strategy. The intention being that these resources and contents would be used thereafter by the learners who produced them – as well as by other educators – within their teaching activities.

5 Intercultural Learning and Promoting Bottom-Up and Top-Down Approaches to the Sustainable Integration of OEP

In responding to the need to break boundaries and build bridges across knowledge-sharing communities, OpenMed has supported positive action amongst academics working across both shores of the Mediterranean in promoting cooperation networks, necessary for the integration of Mediterranean communities and economies (Scalisi, 2016). This has included ways to support academic capacity-building in appreciating the value of adopting OEP in terms of building skills in digital fluency and engaging in the use and creation of OER as a means of sharing, combining and updating teaching and learning content (Weller, 2014; Wiley, 2006). In particular, a focus has been on ways to consider the influence of cultural diversity when considering the exchange of educational content as a means to democratise access to education (Butcher & Hoosen, 2014; Maya Jariego, 2017). Following Aman (2017) and Patel (2017), this has included an active decolonization approach which embraces diverse knowledges and languages as reciprocal exchanges of cultural wealth.

The OpenMed course is an example of an open and intercultural learning experience in a number of ways. For example, it was based on a pedagogical approach that privileges collaboration and reflection for individual learning, leaving space for co-creation among learners from different cultural backgrounds. In adopting Fink's (2003) integrated approach to course design, the OpenMed course aimed to create a significant learning experience for those involved, building upon the different cultural and contextual backgrounds of participants, and enhancing social interactions with others (Herbert, 2006). The course was designed and produced in a fully collaborative fashion by a multi-national team composed of experts across a range of participating HEIs from Europe, the Middle East and North Africa, taking into account, as much as possible, the features and needs of the target population and the learning habits of each involved community. As Forsman (2012) contends this is key to providing experiences that allow awareness of cultural diversity that can, in turn, contribute to academic development. In addition, the course contained a module on adaptation of OER and MOOCs to the specificities of the involved target communities. This module develops the competences to adapt OER to the local contexts of the Middle East and the Maghreb, as well as to address an international audience, in this way, a more thoughtful consideration and understanding regarding the applicability and usability of these resources in different cultural settings is enabled (Zualkernan, Allert & Qadah, 2006). Furthermore, the course was based on collaborative local learning circles, where learners had the possibility to customize and localize the course to their needs, encouraging the application of course content to real-life problems. This included having facilitators who care about the subject of OEP and who desire to engage with learners, and who have good systems in place for feedback and assessment (Fink, 2003). Through the course discussion forum, the learning circles offered a space within which to discuss course themes, through intercultural and peer-to-peer learning experiences, allowing for the exchange of views, practices, and ideas among colleagues coming from different universities, countries and cultural settings (Gervedink Nijhuis et al., 2013). As noted by Deardorff (2009), an important focus for fostering intercultural learning concerns the ways in which the content is delivered and how it engages learners in the process and through a pedagogy which values the intercultural resources learners themselves bring. The active learning approach adopted by the course and underpinned by Fink's (2003) experiential and constructivist pedagogy, provided a very practical approach towards open education, with the idea that, after having taken the course, academics/teachers should be able to use OER and implement open teaching practices in their daily work. Further, the course adopted a strong contextualisation approach, starting from the fact that many resources and courseware of good quality exist that could be shared and adapted to the needs of the learning communities (Wimpenny et al., submitted).

OpenMed has stimulated transition and transformation in how reconfiguring an open education learning space (within a networked context) has facilitated partners' own learning, as well as institutional, formal and informal, experiential, interactive, online and social learning (Oblinger, 2006), while embracing a top-down and bottom-up approach to educational change. Together, with project partners and wider educational community networks, change has been mobilized by influencing senior management through the Educational Resources (OER) Regional Agenda,[12] the development of Institutional Roadmaps, and by training opportunities, to inspire educators themselves to embrace and adopt OEP. The alignment of all these strategies ensure an inclusive and equitable access to quality HE in the Mediterranean region.

Whilst the partners were working to a closer resemblance of the UNESCO (2012) definition of OER to appropriately target and mobilise their institutional practices, as well as influence national and regional agendas and education and policy strategies, work on this continues, as does the cultural acceptability of open education and distance learning in the S-M in general (Elshamy, 2016). Nonetheless, findings about the collaboration and learning dynamics experienced in the pilot run of the OpenMed Open course were largely positive, based on qualitative feedback mainly provided by the learning circle facilitators, and on the analytics gathered from the course platform (Sakai.)[13] Information sharing and collaborative learning took place, not only within the local learning circles within institutions – but also within and across the countries participating in the pilot. This was an encouraging finding that indicates the collaboration readiness of universities from the S-M to engage in regional dialogues, learn from one another's experiences and display a willingness to discuss common challenges and innovative solutions, as advocated by Fink (2003). Further, a wide range of useful project works have been developed, both based on the work of individual learners and of small teams from the same learning circles. This encouraging evidence suggests that the OpenMed course has not only offered a meaningful learning experience to participants (Falconer & Littlejohn, 2007), but has also resulted in the creation of a set of artefacts (i.e. OER, new curricula, new teaching strategies, etc.) that will represent an important knowledge bank for open education in the S-M region.

While OpenMed has been making great strides in its efforts to mobilise change in widening participation in OEP and use of OER, and moving from theoretical goals to actual practices, the move from institutional level practices to national levels of impact for each partner, while not straightforward, *is* ongoing. Alongside the National OER Strategy Forums,[14] which provided opportunities for the S-M higher education stakeholders to discuss, revise, and validate the open educational Resources (OER) regional agenda developed by OpenMed, partners in Morocco have developed and published a National Declaration.[15] This Declaration is addressed to the Moroccan and International authorities, educational institutions; primary and secondary schools, private and public universities, as well as all organizations and individuals involved in education and training – including galleries, libraries, archives centers and museums. As such it is intended to further support, enhance and develop OER and OEP in the country, with academics from Cadi Ayyad University in Marrakesh and Ibn Zohr University in Agadir leading the project. The Declaration, published in French and English, is now serving as a petition, requesting international endorsement from the open education global community, before being presented to the Moroccan Educational Authorities at governmental level, and other dignitaries such as rectors and deans. The Declaration is gathering widespread support and is almost at its target of collecting over 85 signatures out of the initial 100 requested.

A key challenge remains in changing perspectives across all levels of education policy, development and practice, and in developing and re-positioning open education within the respective regions as valid and significant. Managing this transition will take time and requires a focus at all levels of education not only in providing the necessary leadership and resources required to develop strategic planning and academic development, but in working with academic champions locally and in direct engagement with students.

6 Conclusion

Open education is not only about learning and practice, it is also about giving and sharing in order to produce knowledge to the digital community. Knowledge must be shared and spread, teachers encouraged to network and collaborate on course development, and institutions discouraged from fragmentation and the production of their own slight variations on the same course (Weller, 2014). As project partners, OpenMed has stimulated transition and transformation in how reconfiguring an open education learning space (within a networked context) has facilitated partners' own, and others' formal and informal, experiential, interactive, online and social learning (Oblinger, 2006). From the start, the partners were encouraged to consider their own cultural practices and expectations of one another and have been challenged to embrace a range of OEP whilst striving to adhere to UNESCO's definition. The project partners continued to find ways to navigate a way through their similarities and differences in terms of demographic, cultural and institutional characteristics during partner meetings and in developing project frameworks and outputs to cascade onto others.

Acknowledgments

The OpenMed project is funded by the European Union Erasmus+ Programme, and involves the work of a number of institutions, namely: UNIMED, Mediterranean Universities Union, Italy (coordinator), Politecnico di Torino, Italy, Universidad Internacional de La Rioja, Spain, University of Seville, Spain, Coventry University, UK, Cairo University, Egypt, Alexandria University, Egypt, Cadi Ayyad University, Morocco, Université Ibn Zohr, Morocco, Birzeit University, Palestine, An-Najah National University, Palestine, Association of Arab

Universities, Jordan, German Jordanian University, Jordan, Princess Sumaya University for Technology, Jordan.

This chapter has also drawn on content developed from a wide range of contributions over the project time period by the OpenMed partners.

Notes

1 See https://openmedproject.eu
2 OpenMed is co-funded by the *Erasmus+ Capacity-building in Higher Education programme* of the European Union (October 2015–October 2018).
3 http://www.unesco.org/new/fileadmin/MULTIMEDIA/HQ/CI/WPFD2009/English_Declaration.html
4 https://openmedproject.eu/home/
5 https://openmedproject.eu/results/compendium/
6 https://openmedproject.eu/category/experts/
7 https://openmedproject.eu/results/oer-regional-agenda/,
8 www.qou.edu
9 See videos Najah.edu
10 Whilst OpenMed funded the establishment of the new Creativity in Open Education Centre to support the university to develop open resources, the cost of the equipment was more than the existing budget allowed, and so ANNU contributed an additional 10,000 Euros.
11 https://www.edraak.org/en/
12 Starting from an understanding of the long-term challenges and priorities which are necessary for opening up HE in the S-M countries, the Educational Resources (OER) Regional Agenda presents a set of strategic actions aimed at maximising the benefits of OER and OEP to increase the access, the quality and the equity of HE in the region.
13 Sakai Platform, Digital Open Learning Platform https://www.sakaiproject.org
14 https://openmedproject.eu/results/national-oer-strategy-forums/
15 https://openmedproject.eu/oer-morocco-declaration/

References

Affouneh, S. J., & Amin Awad Raba, A. (2017). An emerging model of e-learning in Palestine: The case of An-Najah National University. *Creative Education, 8*, 189–201.

Affouneh, S. J., Wimpenny, K., Ra'Fat Ghodieh, A., Alsaud, L., & Obaid, A. (2018). Reflection on MOOC design in Palestine: A MOOC as a tool for nationality building. *The International Review of Research in Open and Distributed Learning, 19*(2). http://www.irrodl.org/index.php/irrodl/article/view/3469/4610

Aman, R. (2017). *Decolonising intercultural education: Colonial differences, the geopolitics of knowledge, and inter-epistemic dialogue*. London: Routledge.

Beetham, H., Falconer, I., McGill, L., & Littlejohn, A. (2012). Open practices: A briefing paper. *JISC*, 1–12. https://oersynth.pbworks.com/w/page/51668352/OpenPracticesBriefing

Bouhlila, D. S. (2015). The Heyneman–Loxley effect revisited in the Middle East and North Africa: Analysis using TIMSS 2007 database. *International Journal of Educational Development, 42*, 85–95.

Butcher, N., & Hoosen, S. (2014). Harnessing OER to drive systematic educational change in secondary schooling. *Journal of Learning for development, 3*(1). Retrieved from http://jl4d.org/index.php/ejl4d/article/view/68/48

Cilliers, L. (2014). *A marriage of convenience: Massification of higher education and a learner management system*. Paper presented at ICERI2014 Conference, Seville, Spain. Retrieved from https://www.researchgate.net/publication/286167383_A_Marriage_of_convenience_Massification_of_Higher_Education_and_a_Learner_Management_System

Commonwealth of Learning and UNESCO. (2012, June). *Survey on governments' Open Educational Resources (OER) policies*. Paper presented at the World OER Congress, by Sarah Hoosen of Neil Butcher & Associates for the Commonwealth of Learning and UNESCO. Retrieved from http://www.unesco.org/fileadmin/MULTIMEDIA/HQ/CI/CI/pdf/themes/Survey_On_Government_OER_Policies.pdf

Deardoff, D. (2009). *The Sage handbook of intercultural competence*. Thousand Oaks, CA: Sage.

El Hassan, K. (2013). Quality assurance in higher eduaction in 20 MENA ecnomies. *Higher Education Management and Policy, 24*(2), 73–84.

Elshamy, A. (2016). *Egypt reconsiders 'open learning'*. Al-Fanar Media, News and Opinion about Higher Education. Retrieved from https://www.al-fanarmedia.org/2016/01/egypt-reconsiders-open-learning/

Eshet-Alkalai, Y., & Aydin, C. H. (Eds.). (2009). Regional focus issues: Learning technologies in the middle east. *IRRODL, 10*(2). Retrieved from http://www.irrodl.org/index.php/irrodl/article/view/1103

European Commission. (2017). *Overview of the higher education system: Egypt*. https://eacea.ec.europa.eu/sites/eacea-site/files/countryfiches_egypt_2017.pdf

Falconer, I., & Littlejohn, A. (2007). Designing for blended learning, sharing and reuse. *Journal of Further and Higher Education, 31*(1), 41–52.

Fink, L. D. (2003). *Creating significant learning experiences*. San Francisco, CA: John Wiley & Sons.

Fichten, C. S., Asuncion, J., & Scapin, R. (2014). Digital technology, learning, and post-secondary students with disabilities: Where we've been and where we're going. *Journal of Postsecondary Education and Disability, 27*(4), 369–379.

Forsman, L. (2012). Investigating the cultural dimension in foreign language education – From transmission of facts to dialogical uptake. *Educational Action Research, 20*(4), 483–496.

Freire, P. (1970). *Pedagogy of the oppressed.* New York, NY: Penguin Books.

Gervedink Nijhuis, C. J., Pieters, J. M., & Vogt, J. M. (2013). Influence of culture on curriculum development in Ghana: An undervalued factor? *Journal of Curriculum Studies, 45*(2), 225–250.

Guri-Rosenbilt, S., Sebkova, H., & Teichler, U. (2007). Massification and diversity of higher education systems: Interplay of complex systems. *Higher Education Policy, 20*(4), 373–389.

Harbi, S. E. (2016). The opportunities and challenges of OER in the MENA region. In K. Wimpenny, S. Merry, G. Tombs, & D. Villar-Onrubia (Eds.), *OpenMed: Opening up education in South Mediterranean Countries* (p. 41). Retrieved from https://openmedproject.eu/results/compendium/

Heyneman, S. P. (1997). The quality of education in the Middle East and North Africa (MENA). *International Journal of Educational Development, 17*(4), 449–466.

Hu, E., Li, Y., Li, J., & Huang, W.-H. (2015). Open Educational Resources (OER) usage and barriers: A study from Zhejiang University, China. *Education Technology Research Development, 63*, 957–974. doi:10.1007/s11423-015-9398-1

Jemni, M., & Koutheair Khribi, M. (2016.) Toward empowering open and online education in the Arab World through OER and MOOCs. In M. Jemni & K. M. Khribi (Eds.), *Open education: From OERs to MOOCs* (Lecture Notes in Educational Technology). Springer, Berlin, Heidelberg.

Lane, A. (2012). Widening participation in higher education through open educational resources. In A. Okada, T. Connolly, & P. J. Scott (Eds.), *Collaborative learning 2.0: Open educational resources* (pp. 1–15). Hershey, PA: IGI Global.

Maya Jariego, I. (2017). Localising open educational resources and massive open online coursecourses. In F. Nascimbeni, D. Burgos, A. Vetrò, E. Bassi, D. Villar-Onrubia, K. Winpenny, Maya Jariego, O. Mimi, R. Qasim, & C. Stefanelli (Eds.), *Open education: Fundamentals and approaches. A learning journey opening up teaching in higher education.* Erasmus+ Programme of the European Union.

Navarrete, R., & Luján-Mora, S. (2013). Accessibility considerations in learning objects and open educational resources. In *Proceedings of the 6th International Conference of Education, Research and Innovation* (pp. 521–530).

Oblinger, D. (2006). Space as a change agent. In D. Oblinger (Ed.), *Learning spaces, educase e-book* (Chapter 1). Retrieved from https://net.educause.edu/ir/library/pdf/pub7102a.pdf

P2P University. (2015). *Learning circles.* Retrieved from https://learningcircles.p2pu.org/en/

Patel, F. (2017). Deconstructing internationalization: Advocating glocalization in international higher education. *Journal of International and Global Studies, 8*(2) 64–82. http://www.lindenwood.edu/files/resources/64-82-deconstructing-internationlization.pdf

Petrovic-Dzerdz, M., & Trepanier, A. (2018). Online hunting, gathering and sharing – A return to experiential learning in a digital age. *The International Review of Research in Open and Distributed Learning, 19*(2). http://dx.doi.org/10.19173/irrodl.v19i2.3732.

RecoNow. (2016). *The higher education system in Palestine: National report.* Co-Funded by the Tempus Programme of the European Union. Retrieved from http://www.reconow.eu/files/fileusers/5140_National-Report-Palestine-RecoNOW.pdf

Rhema, A. (2010). Towards e-learning in higher education in Libya. *Issues Informing Science and Information Technology, 7*, 423–437.

Rolfe, V. (2017). Striving towards openness: But what do we really mean? *The International Review of Research in Open and Distributed Learning, 18*(7). Retrieved from http://www.irrodl.org/index.php/irrodl/article/view/3207/4461

Scalisi, M. (2016). Introduction to the OpenMed Project. In K. Wimpenny, S. Merry, G. Tombs, & D. Villar-Onrubia (Eds.), *OpenMed: Opening up education in South Mediterranean Countries* (pp. pp. 17–18). Compendium. https://openmedproject.eu/results/compendium/

The European Framework for the Digital Competence of Educators (DigCompEdu). (2017). Retrieved from https://ec.europa.eu/jrc/sites/jrcsh/files/digcompedu_leaflet_en-2017-10-09.pdf

The World Bank. (2010). *A review of Egypt's higher education.* Retrieved from http://www.worldbank.org/en/news/feature/2010/03/25/review-egypts-higher-education

Tubaishat, A., Bhatti, A., & El-Qawasmeh, E. (2006). ICT experiences in two different Middle Eastern Universities. *Issues Informing Science and Information Technology, 3*, 667–678.

UNESCO. (2010). *Reaching the marginalised, education for all, the EFA global monitoring report.* Retrieved from http://unesdoc.unesco.org/images/0018/001866/186606E.pdf

UNESCO. (2012). *What are open education resources?* Retrieved from http://www.unesco.org/new/en/communication-and-information/access-to-knowledge/open-educational-resources/what-are-open-educational-resources-oers/

Weller, M. (2014). *The battle for open: How openness won and why it doesn't feel like victory* [Online]. London: Ubiquity Press. http://dx.doi.org/10.5334/bam

Wiley, D. (2006). *On the sustainability of open educational resource initiatives in higher education.* Retrieved from http://opencontent.org/docs/oecd-report-wiley-fall-2006.pdf

Wimpenny, K., Mayo, I., Nascimbeni, F., Affouneh, S., Almakari, A., & Aymen, E. (2019). *Curriculum development in higher education using open education practices across the mediterranean: OpenMed.* Manuscript submitted for publication.

Wimpenny, K., Merry, S., Tombs, G., & Villar-Onrubia, D. (2016). *OpenMed: Opening up education in South Mediterranean Countries.* Compendium. https://openmedproject.eu/results/compendium/

Zualkernan, I. A., Allert, J., & Qadah, G. Z. (2006). Learning styles of computer programming students: A Middle Eastern and American comparison. *IEEE Transactions on Education, 49*(4), 443–450.

CHAPTER 12

Open Learning and Open Communities: OER for PreK-12 Educators

Jenni Hayman, Rebecca Heiser and Kristina Ishmael

> Our vision of learning is one that is social and participative. Content that we provide is a starting point for you to create and connect with others in this course. If there are voices or resources missing, we encourage you to add them.
>
> SIEMENS AND WILEY (2017a)

The quote above was taken from the first week of a six-week *Introduction to Open Education* edX MOOC (Massive Open Online Course) designed and delivered by Siemens and Wiley. The spirit of social, participatory, and connected learning embedded in the quote was very much aligned with their prior research and writing related to open teaching and learning (Siemens, 2005; Wiley, 2013). The course itself represented a relatively open model of modern professional learning for those with access to the Internet and motivation to learn more about open education as an academic topic.

To determine how such a MOOC might be an effective professional learning and community building opportunity for United States (US) PreK-12 teachers and administrators, this chapter's authors ('we') took Siemens and Wiley's invitation to heart. To satisfy our interest and curiosity, and to achieve our research aim of expanding the literature of open education practice in PreK-12, we designed a small-scale qualitative study related to the *Introduction to Open Education* MOOC. We engaged in this study and collaborative writing project to explore the professional learning and community-building needs of PreK-12 educators who were interested in learning more about OER for their practice. The questions that informed our work were, 'What do PreK-12 practitioners need to learn in order to find and use OER successfully for their teaching?' and 'What types of communities might support PreK-12 practitioners to find and use OER?'

 | DOI: 10.1163/9789004422988_013

1 OER in the PreK-12 Context

As open education advocates in our practice, we share common beliefs about the potential of open education to reduce the overall cost of high-quality learning experiences and increase high school graduation rates in the United States and in other nations and regions. We actively support creation and use of open educational resources (OER) that have the potential to localize and diversify content and flatten power hierarchies regarding who is permitted to create, adapt, and share knowledge.

To guide our work, we used the Hewlett Foundation definition of open educational resources (OER). They described OER as

> teaching, learning and research materials in any medium – digital or otherwise – that reside in the public domain or have been released under an open license that permits no-cost access, use, adaptation and redistribution by others with no or limited restrictions. (Hewlett Foundation, n.d.)

For teaching and learning in primary and secondary contexts, we felt that OER for classrooms would include analog and digital materials such as lesson plans, stories, music and art guides, games, worksheets, quizzes, exams, and small-scale learning units. In secondary classrooms, we felt resources might also include fully online open courseware and open textbook-centered curriculum.

The use of OER in post-secondary education throughout the United States has steadily grown since 2002, with measurable gains in awareness of the value of open materials for teaching and learning (Allen & Seaman, 2014; Roberts, Blomgren, Peters, & Graham, 2018). However, awareness of the value of OER in PreK-12 contexts has lagged significantly behind post-secondary education (Boston Consulting Group, 2013; de los Arcos, Farrow, Pitt, Weller, & McAndrew, 2016). In 2015, the United States Department of Education (USED) launched the #GoOpen campaign, an initiative designed to 'encourage states, school districts and educators to use openly licensed educational materials' (USED, 2015). To date, there are 20 states and 115 school districts that have joined the #GoOpen campaign (Office of Educational Technology, n.d.). While excitement about OER at the PreK-12 level has been growing, funding and support for professional learning to successfully implement OER in the classroom have been limited. In addition, research on the use and effectiveness of OER in PreK-12 settings is only beginning to emerge. With few opportunities for professional learning and very little research-based evidence of the value of

OER in US PreK-12 contexts, educators and administrators are in early stages of momentum for local OER initiatives.

Based on our collective experiences as informal online learners, we sought to determine whether or not MOOCs might represent an opportunity to increase awareness and learning about OER among #GoOpen practitioners. MOOCs appeared in 2012 as a method to engage large-scale audiences in online learning experiences (Veletsianos & Shepherdson, 2016). There is a growing body of literature on the effectiveness of MOOCs for diverse learning contexts including professional development for PreK-12 and post-secondary educators. In addition to the edX-hosted *Introduction to Open Education* MOOC that was a key focus for this chapter, edX hosted at least one other OER-themed course, mainly focused on the use of OER as part of global teacher training (edX, n.d.). Canvas.net created its own course called *(HE/K12) Making the Transition to Open: The Easy Way to Create, License, and Share Free Materials* (Canvas.net, n.d.). As part of PreK-12, in-service professional learning, Duke University developed a series of MOOCs on the Coursera platform that were accepted by the USED as continuing education units (Duke University, 2014). Though the Duke University courses were not specifically related to OER, they served as an example for us of the perceived potential of MOOCs to provide effective professional learning for PreK-12 educators.

In October 2017, an edX MOOC titled *Introduction to Open Education* was offered by the University of Texas, Arlington. We felt that this MOOC would provide an opportunity to examine the effectiveness of a MOOC on this specific topic to serve the needs of PreK-12 educators interested in learning more about OER. Focusing on the *Introduction to Open Education* MOOC, we analyzed the experiences of a PreK-12 group of educators as they participated in the six-week course. We conducted several interviews with course participants, and additional PreK-12 practitioners who did not take the course, to gain more insight into the needs and opportunities for professional learning related to OER. Using lenses of open social learning and open course design, with an emphasis on participants' voices, we explored what was present and what was missing in the course for a group of PreK-12 educators.

2 Open and PreK-12: Definitions and What We Know so Far

While the experiences, opinions, and perspectives of participants were valuable for our exploration, we sought additional contexts in the literature of PreK-12 open education, MOOC design, and digital social networks. The following articles seemed most relevant for our work.

We selected the Hewlett Foundation (n.d.) definition of OER as cited in our introduction. In addition to OER, works from the literature touched on the term open educational practices (OEP) that Cronin (2017) defined as '… practices that include the creation, use, and reuse of open educational resources (OER) as well as open pedagogies and open sharing of teaching practices' (p. 15). We felt this definition aligned accurately with the day-to-day work of many PreK-12 teachers. In their article on PreK-12 teaching communities, Trust, Kutka, and Carpenter (2016) examined the meaning of professional versus personal learning networks and felt that professional was a more relevant term in the context of PreK-12 practice. In their conclusion they defined PLNs (professional learning networks) as 'uniquely personalized, complex systems of interactions consisting of people, resources, and digital tools that support ongoing learning and professional growth' (p. 28). Additional terms and concepts were defined in our chapter in context.

3 PreK-12 and OER

A frequent finding in the literature of PreK-12 open education was that studies focused on use of OER were scarce (Boston Consulting Group, 2013; de los Arcos, Farrow, Pitt, Weller, & McAndrew, 2016; Roberts et al., 2018), and that most OER research to date had focused on post-secondary practice (Robinson, Fischer, Wiley & Hilton, 2014, Kimmons, 2015). There were some studies and articles with a PreK-12 context, and some that provided mixed post-secondary and PreK-12 findings.

In 2013, the William and Flora Hewlett Foundation funded a preliminary study by the Boston Consulting Group (BCG), whose researchers recommended that a healthy OER ecosystem would require a high quality supply of content across a spectrum of disciplines, an increase in user awareness, new skills for users to find and adapt OER, district and state-level policies that empowered the adaptation and use of OER, and clarity around the issue of intellectual property. Among the 377 survey respondents for the BCG study (308 of which were PreK-12 classroom teachers), 65% cited lack of awareness as a primary barrier, and indicated that proven efficacy (research-based findings) and trusted quality would be their main criteria for incorporating OER into their teaching (Boston Consulting Group, 2013).

Kimmons (2015) conducted an OER quality assurance study with a small group of practicing classroom teachers (n = 30). He noted several challenges with copyright-restricted textbooks for PreK-12 including PhD-level and post-secondary authors that had little understanding of PreK-12 student needs.

Kimmons' research focused on a three-day institute where teachers reviewed and compared their existing textbooks with open textbooks (adopted with no revisions), and with books that they adapted as part of the institute learning experience. Teachers rated the resources they adapted significantly higher in quality than the open-adopted resources and their copyright-restricted textbooks. While Kimmons did state that the outdated nature of the copyright-restricted textbooks teachers examined may have created bias in terms of quality, he also stated that outdated textbooks were a dominant PreK-12 reality in US schools.

As mentioned in the introduction for this chapter, the #GoOpen movement was officially initiated in October 2015. The initial press release indicated a number of partners that offered support to help launch the movement and drive the creation of high-quality repositories and professional learning. However, in 2018 these supports were still in very early stages of development (Roberts et al., 2018).

A 2016 study conducted by researchers from the Open University UK's OER Research Hub provided a more global view of PreK-12 educator perceptions of OER. Of the 657 primary and secondary respondents for this study that were actively using OER, 40% were from the United States, 12.5% from the United Kingdom, and 11.6% from South Africa. Among the teachers, adaptation of OER was high, with 85% reporting that they had adapted OER for their teaching. Creation and sharing of OER were generally lower, with only 38% of teachers creating resources and only 10% sharing them using an open license. Three main criteria for teacher selection of OER were described as relevance (how well do OER align with student needs), ease of use (how easy were the OER to find and download), and quality (was the creator of the resource perceived to be a high-quality provider) (de los Arcos et al., 2016).

Recent US PreK-12 findings related to OER were contained in the 2017 report from The Babson Group. The researchers' study, which included data from 584 US school districts, identified three primary elements in resource decision-making. These elements were content that spanned the curriculum, content that worked easily with existing technology, and content that was low cost (Allen & Seaman, 2017). They found that less affluent districts were twice as likely to choose OER as more affluent districts (p. 16).

The limited literature of PreK-12 OER indicated that teachers were using OER in many different ways, and that many of them were interested in learning more about OER, particularly related to the opportunity to personally adapt them to meet the needs of their students. From this literature, we learned that prevalent teacher concerns were ease of use, difficulty locating high quality, adaptable materials in their teaching subject, the adaptability of OER with classroom technology, and the alignment of resources to current curriculum standards. Our research participants echoed many of these findings.

4 Building Successful PreK-12 OER Communities

Moreillon (2016) described US PreK-12 communities of practice that varied in size, goals, and modes of interaction. She indicated that many traditional communities were face-to-face groups within schools or districts and were comprised of grade level and content area teams. These communities focused on topics such as student achievement and growth, social and emotional development, and even professional development as determined by the district. Online communities were described as an emerging model of PLN where educators from diverse content areas, grade levels, and types of institutions could interact. These communities focused on topics relevant to the group and building knowledge together (Moreillon, 2016).

Several articles in the literature described PreK-12 PLNs, especially online communities, as essential for building and sustaining new practices. Trust, Kutka, and Carpenter's (2016) definition of a Professional Learning Network (PLN) indicated they were 'uniquely personalized, complex systems of interactions consisting of people, resources, and digital tools that support ongoing learning and professional growth' (p. 28). Before Trust et al. arrived at this particular definition, they conducted a literature review to establish a greater sense of who was participating in these communities and how they were being used. 'PLNs have been described as 'reciprocal learning system[s]' (Powerful Learning Practice, 2012, p. 8), 'vibrant, ever-changing group[s] of connections' (Crowley, 2014, para. 4), 'network[s] of fellow educators and resources' (Catapano, n.d.), 'the sum of all social capital and connections' (Couros, 2010, p. 6), and 'online communities that allow the sharing of lesson plans, teaching strategies, and student work' (Flanigan, 2011, p. 17). This collection of ideas represented important elements to consider when building successful communities.

Beyond understanding the definition of PLNS, we felt it was important to focus on the larger context of adult learning theory in which PLNs were grounded. Common instructional design and community of practice learning theories such as behaviorism, cognitivism, and constructivism were developed before technology and online communities existed. While these theories were grounded in individual and collective knowledge-building, Siemens (2005) argued that 'technology has reorganized how we live, how we communicate, and how we learn' (para 1). In a networked and global society, Siemens pointed to the idea that humans have the ability to connect like never before. He described how new digital connections might contribute to shared learning and experiences that shifted the focus of the learning process outside of the individual. Siemens' connectivism theory, a potential new lens for PLNs was described as

> the integration of principles explored by chaos, network, and complexity and self-organization theories … Learning (defined as actionable knowledge) can reside outside of ourselves (within an organization or a database), is focused on connecting specialized information sets, and the connections that enable us to learn more are more important than our current state of knowing (Siemens, 2005).

Findings in the literature indicated that successful PreK-12 communities would continue to exist in traditional settings, but would develop and scale with the use of emerging technologies. Whether communities labelled themselves as PLNs or any other formalized nomenclature, they would be rooted in connectivism, where value was placed on what was being learned, digitally stored, and shared external to individuals. Connectivism and online PLNs seemed to be one pathway for educators that were curious about OER to connect with others that were already implementing these resources in their schools and districts.

5 The Design of Open Online Courses

In the global landscape and literature of online course design, the well-established Community of Inquiry model continued to represent a descriptive framework for connecting the needs of a learner to a community of practitioners (Garrison, Anderson & Archer, 2000). Publishing an online course was described as a complex and iterative process that required an instructional designer in partnership with a subject matter expert to develop high-quality resources and curate key design elements, align assessment to learning outcomes, and create learning spaces that enhanced social and community contexts (Nunez, Caro, & Gonzalez, 2017).

The literature also indicated that developing online learning experiences, especially MOOCs, required the support of an instructional designer to reference and incorporate student perceptions, focus on student performance and engagement, explore pedagogic possibilities in the online environment, and propose new models of assessment. Based on the learner's access, resources, and time constraints to complete an online course, instructional designers were needed to help determine the balance of synchronous and asynchronous delivery modes (Stefaniak & Baaki, 2013).

When describing foundational design practice for online courses, and new paradigms for open online courses, Nunez Caro, and Gonzalez (2017) recommended that designs continued to include clear learning objectives with aligned content and assessments to help ensure learners achieve the objectives. They indicated that flow and pacing should meet the needs of the online learner and guide the learner through a transformative, cognitive process beginning with knowledge building and ending with the creation of an artifact Kauffman (2015) recommended that before the start of the professional online learning experience, it was useful to conduct a needs assessment to determine if the learning should be teacher-centered, where the teacher is the deliverer of knowledge, or student-centered where learners construct their knowledge with the guidance of the teacher. In a MOOC context, this difference is sometimes described as an xMOOC (a teacher-centered design), versus a cMOOC (a learner-centered or even learner-driven design). Veletsianos and Shepherdson (2016) helped clarify this distinction and defined MOOCs as 'an evolving ecosystem of online learning environments featuring open enrollment, characterized by a spectrum of course designs ranging from networks of distributed online resources (cMOOCs) to structured learning pathways centralized on digital platforms (xMOOCs)' (p. 200).

When designing OER PreK-12 learning opportunities, Sergis, Sampson, and Pellicccione (2017) recommended that contextualizing professional learning for the audience was an effective approach. For example, they suggested that instructors might limit participants to the micro level of teachers, and design a different experience for district administrators. They also found that student-centered learning experiences supported improved learning outcomes, instructional quality, and engagement.

Vivian, Falkner, and Falkner (2014) suggested that online programs intended for learners to apply their knowledge and encourage critical thinking would require experiential application to problems, promotion of collaboration and collective-knowledge creation, and opportunities for personalized feedback or peer review. Evidence from a variety of articles suggested that course designers provide exemplars as part of course presentation and professionally developed design elements including video, audio, and visual graphics to engage learners and add context (Kauffman, 2015; Sergis et al., 2017; Stefaniak & Baaki, 2013). However, researchers indicated that designers needed to create an artful balance of textual content with other types of media to support diverse learning preferences and needs. In addition, when choosing, creating, and remixing media design elements for professional learning, it was suggested that modeling embedded open resources into the design was ideal (Parrish, 2009).

In summary, literature-based recommendations indicated that online learning models needed to incorporate human interaction through integrated technologies, supportive communication, and reflective exercises. Instructors might support learners best by having a visible presence in online learning spaces through course announcements, discussion spaces, timely feedback, and other integrated communication channels. Learning designers might utilize social media, especially blogging platforms, to support and develop content creation and community. Connecting learners to safe learning spaces to share their knowledge and discovery with the community might help make the online learning experience more than just a one-time event, and lead to increased lifelong learning opportunities. Blogging platforms and other social media technologies were also described as opportunities for learners to reflect in a flexible digital learning space and collaborate with peers on relevant topics. Online course design was depicted as an iterative process that empowered course designers, instructors and development teams to continuously improve and modify courses for diverse learner populations with unique needs.

6 The Nature of Open Digital Data

As we began to engage with our participants in this study, we considered the ethical implications of observing the discussion forum posts of MOOC participants without explicitly informed consent. Jones and Regner (2016) provided a helpful perspective on the issue of data collection in MOOCs. They posed critical questions regarding MOOC users' status as participants or students from the perspective of US education privacy laws. Their key conclusion was that US post-secondary institutions (the primary developers of MOOCs) are federally funded and therefore subject to FERPA (The Family Educational Rights and Privacy Act), legislation that protects learner educational records including assessments, grades, and, in the case of MOOCs, discussion forum posts (Jones & Regner, 2016).

One of our original exploration strategies was to use edX participant data from discussion forums (without seeking explicit, informed consent). However, a review of the edX Terms of Service and Privacy Policy web pages revealed some important information about this option. As part of the edX Terms of Service, users agreed to grant permission for other users to read and analyze their posts for personal learning. It was interesting to note that users were required to grant a more generous and irrevocable license to edX to use their discussion forum posts (and other content) for a wide variety of potential purposes (edX, 2018). An excerpt from the edX Privacy Policy cautioned users that they might want to consider what they chose to post in discussion forums as peers and edX had permissions to use the posts in as-yet-unimagined contexts (edX, 2014). Based on what were less-than-clear edX policies, we determined the safest path for our partnership with participants was to avoid collecting data from edX discussion forums.

On Twitter, the additional site we used to observe MOOC participants, the Twitter privacy policy began with the statement that user posts were 'public by default' (Twitter, n.d.). We chose to use edX *Introduction to Open Education* user posts for observation only (we did not use any posts as data for analysis). We followed pathways through Twitter to reach out to potential interviewees for our study, and only used data from those that agreed explicitly through informed consent.

7 Explorations and Learning

We chose a case study approach for our work to focus on the critical perspectives of PreK-12 educators as they sought to increase their knowledge and skills for finding and using OER in their practice. As a reminder, the purpose of our study was to explore and share the professional learning and community-building needs of PreK-12 practitioners in order to increase the use of OER as part of US education. We informed our work with the following questions: 'What do PreK-12 practitioners need to learn in order to find and use OER in ways that align with their contexts?' and 'What types of communities might support PreK-12 practitioners to find and use OER?'

8 Structure of the MOOC

While the timing of the *Introduction to Open Education* MOOC was convenient for our study, we felt it was a unique learning example related to large-scale OER professional learning and the #GoOpen movement. Designed and delivered by the University of Texas Arlington through the edX platform, *Introduction to Open Education* was designed as an xMOOC, where instructor videos and curated content were the central focus. There was peripheral community engagement in the course discussion forum, and in social networking spaces that participants selected. Some open features of this course included its open license as a Creative Commons CC BY attribution only resource, its full course content availability outside of the edX shell for download by any interested learner, and its emphasis on contextual, learner-driven assignments to be posted in public spaces (such as blog posts).

The course ran for a period of six weeks, with weekly topics as follows:
- Why Open Matters
- Copyright, The Public Domain, and The Commons
- The 5R Activities and the Creative Commons Licenses
- Creating, Finding, and Using OER
- Research on the Impact of OER Adoption
- The Next Battles for Openness: Data, Algorithms, and Competency Mapping (Siemens & Wiley, 2017b, course syllabus).

For PreK-12 practitioners interested in learning more about the value of open education and OER, as well as basic topics such as copyright and licensing, this weekly topic list seemed generally well-aligned with participant needs. We actively promoted the course to our social media networks and #GoOpen connections in the weeks leading up to the October 1, 2017 start date. While there were 12 participants in the MOOC that self-identified as PreK-12 practitioners, only two of them began the course as a direct result of our promotion. We therefore relied on two course participants and three non-course-participant PreK-12 educators to conduct our research.

9 MOOC Participants

By observing introductory discussion forum posts from the first and second week of the MOOC, we were able to identify 12 PreK-12 educators taking part in the professional learning. We do not know how many overall participants were active in the course over the six weeks, or how many completed all of the course assignments. Through discussion forum posts we were able to gather information about participant contexts and interest in use of open educational resources. Two of our five interview participants for this study were active in the early stages of the course, but only one fully completed course activities.

We each recruited at least one interview participant based on their ability to provide us with perspectives on PreK-12 professional development, open education, and the design of open online courses. Rebecca recruited and interviewed an instructional design colleague with PreK-12 professional learning design experience (referred to in excerpts as ID). ID agreed to review the MOOC and provide a critical analysis of its design. Kristina recruited and interviewed two PreK-12 connections in her social network. One was a colleague that supported technology, and teaching and learning at an online high school (anonymously referred to in sections below as OT for online teacher), and one that was a district level technology specialist and #GoOpen advocate in a school district (referred to as DT, for district technologist, in sections below). Jenni recruited and interviewed the two PreK-12 MOOC participants that had been most active. One was a state-level PreK-12 technology administrator (referred to as SA, for state-level administrator), and one was a high-school classroom teacher at a private school in Massachusetts referred to as HS in excerpts. We used a combination of Twitter, LinkedIn, and email to recruit participants for a 30-minute interview that was recorded and transcribed with their permission.

As part of collaborative research, we collectively developed a list of personas (the type of participant we would be interviewing), and an agreed-upon set of semi-structured questions for each participant. This enabled us to analyze and develop our narrative more cohesively. In addition to general demographic questions (where do you teach or practice, how long have you been teaching, etc.) example questions for two of the participant types were as follows:

MOOC Participant:
- What attracted you to sign up for the Introduction to Open Education MOOC?
- What were three things that you learned about open education and OER that you believe are valuable for your practice?
- What are some of the benefits you believe you achieved by taking the course?
- In what ways have you connected with new colleagues/communities in the course or through social media as a result of taking the course?
- In what ways was the course well designed for you as PK-12 practitioner?

Experienced Open Educator:
- How long have you been using OER in your practice?
- What attracted you to OER? (or was it mandated?)
- What types of PL have you engaged with related to OER and open pedagogy?
- What types of learning communities do you engage with?
- What types of PL do you engage in to keep your OER skills current?

10 What We Learned

Unexpected opportunities and challenges can occur in the course of any given study and our plan of inviting and following a group of PreK-12 educators through their *Introduction to Open Education* MOOC experience shifted slightly over time. We were able to enrich our study of MOOC participant experiences with a small, purposively selected group of US PreK-12 educators and an online instructional designer. All participants had experience and interest in advocacy for open education and use of OER. Our interviews focused specifically on the types of supports and professional learning that participants felt might be needed to expand awareness and participation in the #GoOpen movement.

Following Boeije's (2010) guidelines for coding qualitative data as part of interpretive analysis, we used the web-based coding solution Dedoose to apply open codes to our transcribed interviews and a series of blog posts from one of the participants. The following topics emerged from our analysis: the value of OER, professional learning, building community, and OER repositories.

10.1 *Participants' Perceived Value of* OER

All participants in the study were invested in the value of OER for their PreK-12 work. Each of the participants, an instructional designer (ID), an online teacher (OT), a state-level administrator (SA), a district technologist (DT), and a high school teacher (HS), expressed concerns and ideas related to four main topics that emerged from our analysis. Quotes are used throughout this section to indicate specific, relevant comments taken from transcripts.

OT (the online teacher participant) talked about sharing as the reason she got into education. She explained that in her early stages of learning about OER she recognized the materials mostly as content. As she matured in her practice, however, she realized that OER were what teaching was all about. The state-level administrator participant, SA expressed that she was invested in the power of OER as adaptable resources. She felt that OER would become more important over time as teachers begin to experience the power of the ability to easily adapt materials for the needs of their specific learners.

The district-level technology participant, DT, identified a gap in current teacher needs. Specifically, she was concerned that publishers were not meeting teacher and student needs. She felt that all US states needed to accept the value of OER as a new resource model that wasn't going to go away.

HS, a high school teacher, said he had committed the past ten years to envisioning, building, and testing a PreK-12 OER repository. As part of his MOOC-related blog, he reflected and wondered if teacher curation of OER had benefits for learners, what might be the benefits for teaching practice? HS also demonstrated a positive outlook on the growth of OER and the open movement and felt that a variety of stakeholders appeared to be building momentum toward the creation of a larger OER ecosystem.

Within the three main concepts that emerged in the analysis of participant responses, professional learning, community building, and OER repositories, two sub-concepts seemed present in participant responses, these were labelled as 'concerns' and 'ideas.' These sub-concepts were used as categories to convey participant expressions in the next three sections.

10.2 *Professional Learning: Concerns and Ideas*

A common theme in our open-ended interview questions was professional learning in its various forms–self-directed (digital or analog), online, and face-to-face. We asked participants to describe their preferences and any concerns related to design, delivery, and participation in their work-related learning experiences.

OT described herself as an experienced OER user and advocate, but indicated that when she began her current role, there was no available PreK-12 learning for OER. She stated that she learned what she needed to know from the ground up. ID focused on the course balance of videos and other types of content and felt the videos were too long. She desired a mix of reading and viewing options. One of her primary concerns was that many educators were not comfortable on camera and that long videos were a chore for learners to watch.

SA expressed concern about open education conferences, specifically OpenEd17, stating that she found it too focused on post-secondary practitioners. She began, but did not complete the *Introduction to Education* MOOC for time and personal reasons, but felt that the content and format were valuable options for teachers to learn more about OER.

HS explored the larger ideas of open education and professional learning through questioning. He wondered why teachers were not taking advantage of the large number of PreK-12 OER already available. He also raised the issue that teachers may already be using OER and not calling them OER. He felt that OER might be considered a buzzword like many other new models that teachers are asked to consider.

Throughout the interviews, participants expressed the strongest interest in ideas about the shape that PreK-12 professional learning for OER might take. Common ideas among all participants were that professional learning for OER needed to be easy, collaborative among teachers, and part of the natural cycle of personal exploration through face-to-face professional learning communities. Most expressed the idea that digital communities were a key part of OER community building and that a single PreK-12 open community had not yet emerged. The OER-experienced participant, OT, conveyed that the content-use side of OER was not the end goal and felt that student use and co-creation of OER was the ultimate goal for professional learning.

ID highlighted the advantages of participating in a MOOC for professional development. She wondered if using well-known thought leaders as instructors might be an advantage, 'learning from your idol,' she called it. She also highlighted the flexibility of taking a MOOC rather than participating in face-to-face learning.

Although SA started, but did not complete the MOOC, she felt it had value in the context of her work and her OER learning goals. Related to her role in state-level technology integration, she expressed the belief that professional learning for OER might benefit from being combined with other professional learning opportunities, such as use of technology in the classroom. In terms of professional learning and the open movement, she stated, 'it's going to be a combination of top-down and grassroots up ideas.'

DT described her professional learning as a mix of network connections and formal professional learning. She explained that she particularly enjoyed the collaborative nature of connected network learning, and stated, 'I gain a lot from blogs, and just social media. Twitter. Instagram. You know, whether it's philosophical or directly connected to a tool, a tech tool, or something.'

As the only participant to complete the *Introduction to Open Education* MOOC, HS spoke about the effectiveness of the course. He explained that the open-ended assignments in the course, while challenging in their ambiguity, provided him with opportunities to practice what he was learning in a personal context. He expressed ideas about making professional learning easy, and as jargon-free as possible for teachers, stating '… a course well designed for PreK-12 practitioners would probably be a course with a title like 'how to find free stuff online' … they don't want to know about copyright, they don't want to know about history, they want to know what's out there and how can they use it? Easily, freely.' He concluded his interview with a positive reflection stating, 'Happily, we see this more and more in education today – a cultural shift from the siloed classrooms of memory – and it aligns completely with what I have always felt to be the best professional development: teachers talking with teachers about teaching.'

10.3 *Community Building: Concerns and Ideas*

While most participants articulated that OER community building was an important element of increasing awareness and use of OER among teachers, they expressed diverse concerns and ideas about how it might be accomplished.

HS conveyed concern for community-building in simple terms. He felt that teachers did not have sufficient access to each other (in terms of time and ways to connect), and that networking was a critical factor in the success of growth in the use of OER. SA also felt there were not enough networks among state educators. At the district-level, DT said she felt that self-advocacy for community building was an important driver, but that teachers needed to be motivated to create their own connection opportunities.

The majority of ideas for community-building came from DT. As a part of a district-level OER community of practice that met regularly, she stated, 'I like to gain ideas from places like social media such as Twitter or Facebook ... but I also love opportunities to meet face to face at a conference where you get that deeper understanding.' She conveyed that within the United States, and even globally, she thought that there were many generous participants in the open community. She indicated, 'There are so many knowledgeable people out there. That we can learn from, collaborate with today's social media and technology. We should not feel like we're on an island. With anything in education.' The final reflection about community from SA focused on the role of professional organizations in PreK-12 community-building. She stated 'ISTE [International Society for Technology in Education] figures heavily as a connecting organization for country-wide considerations about the GoOpen movement.'

10.4 *OER Repositories: Concerns and Ideas*

Conversations with participants about increasing awareness and use of OER in PreK-12 naturally touched on finding, adopting, adapting, and creating the open content itself.

Among interviewees, there were common concerns about OER repositories. They indicated that there were too many repositories emerging and too much choice. HS framed the issue around quality and stated '... finding resources is actually much harder than we think it is.' He also touched on the differences and potential conflict between digital and analog resources. He felt that much of PreK-12 instruction took place in face-to-face contexts and that the OER preference for digital files was a challenge. He noted that community-building and repository creation might need to be connected concepts, places where teachers could share resources and teaching practice.

Some ideas that emerged from participants for building effective repositories included limiting the number of repositories (reducing confusion), combining resources with community learning opportunities for use of OER (pedagogy), and finding strategies (such as peer review) to examine and rate the quality of OER. OT proposed that a limit on the number of repositories might lead to better investment through grants. She identified an additional advantage in limited repositories, that teachers could 'get the most bang for their buck, which for them means their time.'

SA said she felt that a good repository would have a variety of types of resources. She stated that she wanted to 'get away from textbooks and more toward personalized learning with students.' She defined personalized learning for students as a way 'to create learning environments that are more learner-centered, including learner choice of resources that incorporates their learning preferences and motivations.

HS also had ideas for repositories to counter his concerns. He wondered whether it was networks that were needed first, or a knowledge base for use of OER. Ultimately, he felt they were needed simultaneously. He described his personal context and needs for OER and stated, 'The kind of OER that I'm personally most interested in are lesson plans, discussion questions, classroom activities, educational strategies, and tools for teachers to use in the classroom that aren't digitally mediated learning experiences.'

Exploring these major concepts in the participants' own words led us to our final conclusions, a list of recommendations that US OER advocates, educators, administrators, and national policy-makers might consider when trying to increase both awareness and effective use of OER for PreK-12 teaching and learning.

11 A Discussion of Practice

Our experience and our dialogue with our participants for this study generated recommendations for practice related to the three main concepts, professional learning, community building, and the creation of effective OER repositories.

11.1 *Professional Learning for OER*

Professional learning can take many forms with respect to design, delivery models, and learning outcomes. Participants in our study indicated that PreK-12 educators sought learning experiences that would meet their professional learning interests and that would be relevant to projects and initiatives they were currently developing. Current forms of OER professional learning described by our participants were diverse and included regional summits, educational conferences, district-driven professional learning, self-directed professional learning, MOOCs, and professional learning communities. Participants indicated that all delivery models for professional learning should be timely, accessible (easy to understand and easy to participate with busy schedules), and contextually meaningful. In addition, communication channels that connected learners to a larger community of practitioners for real-time support and help generating an iterative body of knowledge over time would be important.

Although it was the initial focus of our research, the MOOC we reviewed and participated in did not seem well-designed to meet PreK-12 participant needs for preliminary professional learning about OER. It also seemed less-than-ideal for PreK-12 community building to help connect interested teachers and administrators. Despite its foundational title, *Introduction to Open Education*, the course was designed for more advanced post-secondary practitioners with well-established digital literacy and social networking skills. In order to design and deliver a MOOC that might be better-suited to introductory-level PreK-12 teachers, findings indicated that content should allow for greater choice and personalization to meet the needs of a diverse group of practitioners. Experiential learning designs were recommended, including project- and problem-based learning that might support learners to explore foundational knowledge and skills of OER, and apply their existing understanding of OER in their local contexts. Based on our findings, we recommended learning objectives that centered on the following areas:

- OER basics, including what they are and where to find them
- open licensing
- moving beyond textbooks and low-cost resources
- open pedagogy
- differentiation between open and free, and
- defining 'quality' in OER.

In addition to content related to these topics, and experiential assessments, our participants indicated that they desired guidance on how to network in digital spaces as a means of establishing digital PLNs. These recommendations for professional learning based on participant advice addressed our first exploratory question, 'What do PreK-12 practitioners need to learn in order to find and use OER in ways that align with their contexts?'

11.2 *OER Community Building*

Participants in this study emphasized the importance of a sense of community for OER professional learning. They felt that creating safe and social learning spaces in professional learning contexts might help embed community knowledge. Twitter, Facebook groups, and blogging platforms were the most common ways that PreK-12 educators in our study connected before, during, and after their professional learning experiences. Participants recommended the following:

- Explore mobile, easy to use digital networking solutions that make it easier for teachers to quickly connect with each other at school and district levels. Slack is one example of software designed for this purpose.
- Encourage state-level administrators to establish or expand digital statewide communities of practice.
- Strengthen capacity for self-advocacy, by designing and promoting professional learning related to use of social media for networking and community building among teachers.

- Intentionally create and support post-workshop or post-conference opportunities for practitioners to stay connected (blended approach).
- Leverage the power of professional associations such as ISTE to support digital community engagement.

Recommendations in this section addressed the second exploratory question for the study, 'What types of communities support PreK-12 practitioners to find and use OER?'

11.3 *OER Repositories*

While not a specific question for this study, the importance of easy-to-search, high quality OER repositories was raised repeatedly by participants. One of the challenges they identified, related to awareness and use of OER, was searching for and discovering high-quality and standards-aligned OER. They recommended that OER repositories needed to be well-organized (by grade-level, state-specific standards, subject, and type of resource), easy to navigate, accessible, and peer-reviewed. A specific example of a well-designed resource for finding and acquiring high quality paid content was Teachers Pay Teachers, a PreK-12 commerce site. PreK-12 OER repositories that could mimic the search and download model that this site represented (minus the commerce) might provide a solution for the challenge of creating awareness and increasing use of OER.

Figure 12.1 represents the culmination of concepts from our study. Professional learning for OER, combined with community building and a well-designed OER repository may lead to engaged, supported, well-informed, abundantly resourced, open PreK-12 advocates.

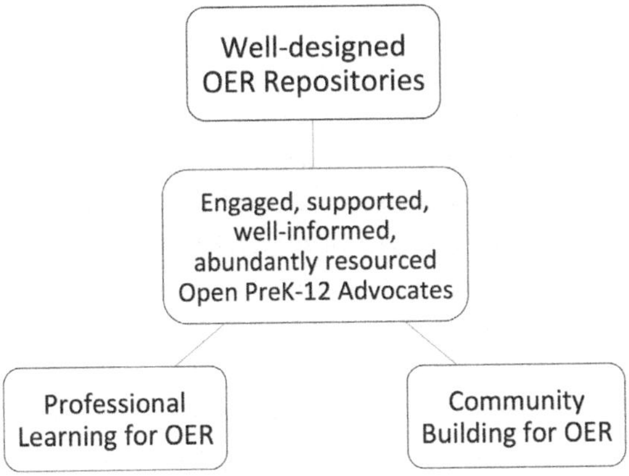

FIGURE 12.1 Three-concept diagram of recommendation. How to increase use of OER among PreK-12 advocates

12 Final Thoughts

Our enthusiasm for this study, the generosity of our participants, and the value of the *Introduction to Open Education* MOOC as a professional learning opportunity for interested #GoOpen advocates led to an extremely engaging and valuable process. Although very few PreK-12 educators took advantage of our Twitter-based call for participation, a small, insightful group of practitioners enriched our data. The challenge of locating literature about PreK-12 use of OER established an ongoing opportunity for continued exploration and future publication. It was clear from dialogue with our participants that significantly greater awareness, and support at grassroots and senior administrative levels was needed for use of OER to increase among US PreK-12 teachers. While participants felt that MOOCs might have value, if they were specifically designed for PreK-12 educators and administrators, they felt that any large-scale, open course would require more active facilitation, the opportunity to localize and contextualize content and assessment activities, and effective, active channels for building and sustaining PLNs.

Practitioners, whether they are teachers, librarians, instructional designers, instructional technologists, or administrators, need support, learning networks, and excellent resources for success in any change paradigm. As shown here, the critical need for well-organized, high quality resources in easy-to-access repositories, for funding and time for professional development, and for channels through which to develop community – factors identified over and over again as pillars for success – are possible with the introduction of open educational resources in the PreK-12 sector.

References

Allen, I. E., & Seaman, J. (2014). *Opening the curriculum: Open educational resources in US higher education* [Research report]. Retrieved from http://www.onlinelearningsurvey.com/reports/openingthecurriculum2014.pdf

Allen, I. E., & Seaman, J. (2017). *What we teach: K-12 school district curriculum adoption process* [Research report]. Retrieved from https://www.onlinelearningsurvey.com/reports/k12oer2017/whatweteach_2017.pdf

Boeije, H. (2010). *Analysis in qualitative research.* London: Sage Publications Ltd.

Boston Consulting Group. (2013). *The open education resources ecosystem: An evaluation of the OER movement's current state and its progress toward mainstream adoption* [Presentation slides]. Retrieved from https://www.hewlett.org/wp-content/uploads/2016/08/The%20Open%20Educational%20Resources%20Ecosystem.pdf

Canvas.net. (n.d.). *(HE/K12) Making the transition to open: The easy way to create, license, and share free materials* [MOOC]. Retrieved from https://www.canvas.net/courses/making-transition-to-open

Couros, A. (2010). Developing personal learning networks for open and social learning. In G. Veletsianos (Ed.), *Emerging technologies in distance education*. Athabasca: Athabasca University Press. Retrieved from http://www.aupress.ca/books/120177/ebook/06_Veletsianos_2010-Emerging_Technologies_in_Distance_Education.pdf

Cronin, C. (2017). Openness and praxis: Exploring the use of open educational practices in higher education. *The International Review of Research in Open and Distributed Learning, 18*(5). Retrieved from http://www.irrodl.org/index.php/irrodl/article/view/3096/4301

Crowley, B. (2016, April 29). *3 Steps for building a professional learning network* [Web article]. Retrieved from https://www.edweek.org/tm/articles/2014/12/31/3-steps-for-building-a-professional-learning.html#

de los Arcos, B., Farrow, R., Pitt, R., Weller, M., & McAndrew, P. (2016). Personalising learning through adaptation: Evidence from a global survey of K-12 teachers' perceptions of their use of open educational resources. *Journal of Online Learning Research, 2*(1), 23–40.

Duke University. (2014, November 19). *DOE endorses Duke MOOCs for teacher professional development* [Web page]. Retrieved from https://online.duke.edu/doe-endorses-duke-moocs-teacher-professional-development/

edX. (2014). *edX privacy policy* [Web page]. Retrieved from https://www.edx.org/edx-privacy-policy

edX. (2018). edX terms of service [Web page]. Retrieved from https://www.edx.org/edx-terms-service

edX. (n.d.). *Course search on the terms 'open education.'* Retrieved from https://www.edx.org/course?search_query=open+education

Flanigan, R. L. (2012). Professional learning networks taking off. *Education Digest: Essential Readings Condensed for Quick Review, 77*(7), 42–45.

Garrison, D. R., Anderson, T., & Archer, W. (2000). Critical inquiry in a text-based environment: Computer conferencing in higher education. *The Internet and Higher Education, 2*(2–3), 87–105. Retrieved from http://cde.athabascau.ca/coi_site/documents/Garrison_Anderson_Archer_Critical_Inquiry_model.pdf

Hewlett Foundation. (n.d.). *Open educational resources* [Web page]. Retrieved from https://www.hewlett.org/strategy/open-educational-resources/

Jones, M. L., & Regner, L. (2016). Users or students? Privacy in university MOOCS. *Science & Engineering Ethics, 22*, 1473–1496.

Kauffman, H. (2015). A review of predictive factors of student success in and satisfaction with online learning. *Research in Learning Technology, 23*. http://dx.doi.org/10.3402/rlt.v23.26507

Kimmons, R. (2015). OER quality and adaptation in K-12: Comparing teacher evaluations of copyright-restricted, open, and open/adapted textbooks. *The International Review of Research in Open and Distributed Learning, 16*(5), 39–57.

Moreillon, J. (2016). Building your Personal Learning Network (PLN): 21st-century school librarians seek self-regulated professional development online. *Knowledge Quest, 44*(3), 64–69.

Nunez, J., Caro, E., & Gonzalez, J. (2017). From higher education to open education: Challenges in the transformation of an online traditional course. *IEEE Transactions on Education, 60*(22), 134–142. Retrieved from https://www.ieee.org/publications_standards/publications/rights/index.html

Office of Educational Technology. (n.d.). *Open education* [Web page]. Retrieved from https://tech.ed.gov/open/

Parrish, P. (2009). Aesthetic principles for instructional design. *Educational Technology Research and Development, 57*(4), 511–528. Retrieved from https://link.springer.com/article/10.1007/s11423-007-9060-7#citeas

Powerful Learning Practice. (2012). *Connected educator month starter kit* [Web article]. Retrieved from https://dl.dropboxusercontent.com/u/8413898/CE14/connected-educator-month-starter-kit-2014.pdf

Roberts, V., Blomgren, C., Peters, K., Graham, L. (2018). *Open educational practices in K-12 online and blended learning environments*. Manuscript in preparation.

Robinson, T. J., Fischer, L., Wiley, D., & Hilton III, J. (2014). The impact of open textbooks on secondary science learning outcomes. *Educational Researcher, 43*(7), 341–351. https://doi.org/10.3102/0013189X14550275

Sergis, S., Sampson, D. G., & Pelliccione, L. (2017). Educational design for MOOCs: Design considerations for technology-supported learning at large scale. In M. Jemni, K. Kinshuk, & M. K. Khribi (Eds.), *Open education: From OERs to MOOCs*. Berlin: Springer-Verlag.

Siemens, G., & Wiley, D. (2017a). *Course activities overview. From introduction to open education* [Archived online course]. Retrieved from https://courses.edx.org/courses/course-v1:UTArlingtonX+LINK.OEx+3T2017/course/

Siemens, G., & Wiley, D. (2017b). *Course syllabus. From introduction to open education* [Archived online course]. Retrieved from https://www.edx.org/course/introduction-open-education-utarlingtonx-link-oex

Siemens, G. (2005). *Connectivism: A learning theory for the digital age*. Retrieved from http://www.elearnspace.org/Articles/connectivism.htm

Stefaniak, J., & Baaki, J. (2013). A layered approach to understanding your audience. *Performance Improvement, 52*(6), 1–10. Retrieved from http://www.wileyonlinelibrary.com

Trust, T., Krutka, D. G., & Carpenter, J. P. (2016). Together we are better: Professional learning networks for teachers. *Computers & education, 102*, 15–34. Retrieved from https://www.sciencedirect.com/science/article/pii/S036013151630135X

Twitter. (n.d.). *Twitter privacy policy* [Web page]. Retrieved from https://twitter.com/en/privacy

USED (United States Department of Education). (2015, October 29). *US Department of Education launches campaign to encourage schools to #GoOpen with educational resources* [Press release]. Retrieved from https://www.ed.gov/news/press-releases/us-department-education-launches-campaign-encourage-schools-goopen-educational-resources

Veletsianos, G., & Shepherdson, P. (2016). A Systematic analysis and synthesis of the empirical MOOC literature published in 2013–2015. *The International Review of Research in Open and Distributed Learning, 17*(2). Retrieved from http://www.irrodl.org/index.php/irrodl/article/view/2448/3655

Vivian, R., Falkner, K., & Falkner, N. (2014). Addressing the challenges of a new digital technologies curriculum: MOOCs as a scalable solution for teacher professional development. *Research in Learning Technology, 22*. http://dx.doi.org/10.3402/rlt.v22.24691

Wiley, D. (2013). What is open pedagogy? [Blog post] Retrieved from https://opencontent.org/blog/archives/2975

CHAPTER 13

Openness across Disciplines: Reflecting on a Multiple Disciplinary Summer School

Ilaria Torre, Klara Łucznik, Kathryn B. Francis, Diego S. Maranan, Frank Loesche, Roberto B. Figueroa Jr., Aska Sakuta and Tara Zaksaite

Academic disciplines – bodies of knowledge and skills – change over time for a variety of reasons, from the systematic integration and convergence of knowledge to the application of skills to reach an evolving goal. While separate disciplines were taught as far back as Roman times, contemporary academic disciplines are far different in form and number (Alvargonzález, 2011). Today, disciplines range from the general study of human behaviour to the specialised study of consonants and vowels. The academic world reflects this division of disciplines. For example, university degrees are typically mono-disciplinary, and researchers are often grouped in institutional organisations that follow the disciplinary boundaries. With the multiple disciplinary summer school 'ColLaboratoire,' we observe an exceptional example of addressing messy and ill-defined problems through several disciplinary lenses. In particular, we discuss the requirements and conditions under which this approach is an effective and appropriate alternative to mono-disciplinary research.

This chapter is structured as follows: first, we critically reflect on the role of openness in multiple disciplinary research. Because ColLaboratoire was modelled heavily on the organisers' experiences of working across the disciplinary boundaries within CogNovo, we subsequently review selected features, activities, and outputs of this doctoral training programme. We then discuss the organisation of ColLaboratoire, including how its decisions drew on the experience from CogNovo as a multiple disciplinary work environment. Following this, we reflect on the experiences of the ColLaboratoire participants and evaluate the outcomes of individual projects and the summer school as a whole. Within this chapter, we define openness as 'an accommodating attitude towards new, unconventional, and useful ideas and experiences,' and we reflect on the key factors that contributed to the realisation of ColLaboratoire. We conclude that these were enabled by what we identify as three forms of openness: multi-perspective, inter-perspective, and trans-perspective openness.

With the growth of human knowledge and technology, disciplines have fragmented into smaller and more manageable units. For example, science divides

 | DOI: 10.1163/9789004422988_014

into Natural and Social Sciences; the Social Sciences now include Economics, Psychology, and Linguistics; Linguistics includes Philology, Phonetics, and Syntax; and so on. As human life expectancy lengthens and population increases, so does the 'workforce' that contributes to expanding knowledge, leading to increasingly specialised disciplines.

There are some limitations to our narrow specialisations, as 'most scientific puzzles do not fit into disciplinary silos' (Yegros-Yegros, Rafols, & D'Este, 2015, p. 3), such as addressing the control of climate change and epidemic diseases. New disciplines, such as Psycholinguistics, Computational Neuroscience, and Bioinformatics, have emerged, where strands of research have joined forces. Scientists are aware of this trend: as Sung et al. (2003) point out, 'the most exciting science in the 21st century is likely to evolve among, not within, traditional disciplines.' This idea extends to learning environments; pedagogically speaking, Kysilka (1998) pointed out that 'knowledge in the real world is not applied in bits and pieces but in an integrated fashion' (p. 198), thus suggesting that learning should cover different disciplines from the very way in which school curricula, and indeed, university programmes are designed (see also EURAB, 2004). Furthermore, creativity and innovation have been noted to emerge from the interaction between disciplines. As Robinson (2001) notes,

> creativity depends on interactions between thinking and feeling, and across different disciplinary boundaries and fields of ideas. New curricula must be evolved which are more permeable and which encourage a better balance between generative thinking and critical thinking in all modes of understanding. (p. 200)

In resonance with these authors' views, we take a critical view towards the strictly laid disciplinary boundaries and shed light on the values and efficacies of cross-disciplinary collaborations. We do this by presenting a case study on how ColLaboratoire, a multiple disciplinary summer school, offered a space for students and researchers to engage in an open and collaborative research context.

1 ColLaboratoire: A Case Study

Our case study of the ColLaboratoire summer school was a multiple disciplinary event which took place at the University of Plymouth in August 2016. It was organised as part of CogNovo, a multiple disciplinary doctoral training programme, funded by an EU Marie Skłodowska-Curie Initial Training Network grant and the University of Plymouth. CogNovo included 25 doctoral research fellows, spanning the disciplines of the Arts, Humanities, Social Sciences, and Technology; their multidisciplinary supervisory teams; and industry partners. It aimed to equip each fellow with experience beyond conventional disciplinary borders and intended to address 'new ways to link scientific research in cognition with social and technological innovation' as 'cognitive innovation' (Denham, 2014, p. 202). CogNovo itself was an exploratory and open-ended enterprise that encouraged the investigation of disciplinary boundaries, collaboration with other disciplines, and the discovery of new ways of enquiry and dissemination with the goal of sustainable innovation (Denham, 2014). Therefore, the programme was an ideal environment in which to organise the summer school. Its name, ColLaboratoire, a merging of 'collaboration' and 'laboratory,' was meant to provide an explicit reference to the types of skill that we would be practising. As we will argue, the inherent openness and curiosity which were deliberately incorporated into the structure of this summer school and which encouraged in its participants provide an example of a sustainable multiple disciplinary learning environment, which is still producing new publications, source code, and societal impact almost two years later, as illustrated in Tables 13.1 and 13.4. In the following sections, we will reflect not only on what characterises an 'open' researcher but also on what characterises an 'open' learning environment, such as ColLaboratoire; and how such an environment can foster and instil an attitude of openness in its participants. By linking these two aspects, we aim to present a systematic way of implementing openness in the linear and multifaceted process of interdisciplinary research, in the hope that it will be beneficial for young researchers, learning institutions, teachers and established academics alike. Our critical reflections could be used in the future by other institutions and research groups who are interested in creating an environment-centred around multiple disciplinary collaboration.

2 Openness and Multiple Disciplinarity

The terms multidisciplinary, interdisciplinary, and transdisciplinary (amongst others) are frequently used interchangeably and without specific definitions. However, there are differences in their intended meanings (Schmidt, 2007). Multidisciplinarity draws on information from several disciplines while remaining within disciplinary limits; interdisciplinarity both unites and synthesises links between disciplines to form a 'coherent whole' (Choi & Pak, 2006, p. 351); and transdisciplinarity brings disciplines together in new contexts, transcending any existing disciplinary boundaries. However, for this chapter, we use the term 'multiple disciplinary,' suggested by Choi and Pak (2006), as an umbrella term that encompasses all of these meanings. (See Figure 13.1 for a visualisation of these four terms.) Here, we recognise that in multiple disciplinary collaborations, individual openness functions as a pathway to move from the first aspect of multidisciplinarity (i.e., a gathering of disciplines) to addressing interdisciplinary research questions and further transgressing disciplinary boundaries to transdisciplinarity. Particularly in these research settings, an attitude of openness is crucial to the collective formulation of a new research procedure, so that individuals do not limit their discussions to debates over mono-disciplinary facts and methods.

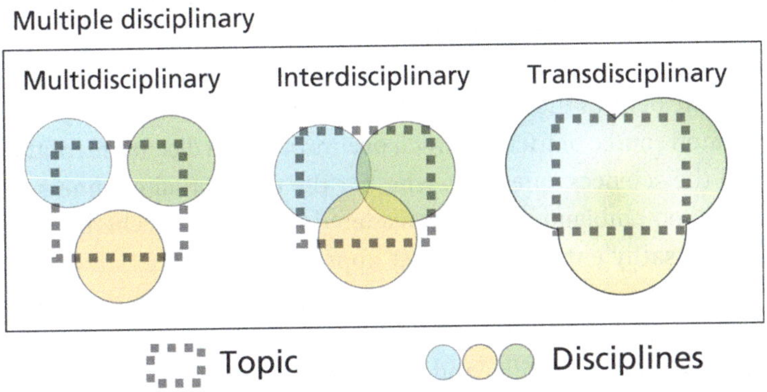

FIGURE 13.1 Visualisation of multidisciplinarity, interdisciplinarity, and transdisciplinarity as instances of multiple disciplinarity

Multiple disciplinarity has been called upon continuously by newly emerging and valuable research topics, many of which address real-world problems (Callard & Fitzgerald, 2015). Its benefits in enriching research itself have also been identified extensively: from increasing creativity, developing new knowledge, and rectifying individual disciplines' shortcomings, to encouraging and preserving academic freedom as well as the 'unity-of-knowledge ideal' (Nissani, 1997, p. 211). While there are institutions supporting this movement towards multiple disciplinarity (Nissani, 1997), they do not represent the majority, considering that many institutions still choose to encourage the stability, prestige, and predictability of mono-disciplinary research and preserve its many benefits, including well-established methods, epistemological congruence, and the depth/wealth of specialised knowledge. Multiple disciplinary endeavours also come with added costs, such as difficulties in coordination and an association with a lack of positive status (Yegros-Yegros et al., 2015). On what, then, could multiple disciplinary research depend on for the retention of its momentum and success? Bridle, Vrieling, Cardillo, Araya, and Hinojosa

(2013) have argued that 'openness and communication between individuals' (p. 30) is a crucial aspect for overcoming disciplinary boundaries. After all, any multiple disciplinary collaboration is potentially considered a dynamic and iterative process of crossing disciplinary boundaries, an experience which 'has to be lived' (Horizon, 2020) by each individual, in order to reach its full potential. Concerning academic research, this entails the mutual acknowledgement towards, and preservation of, methodological and epistemological pluralism as a foreground to any multiple disciplinary research or collaboration (Bruhn, 1995; Miller, Baird, Littlefield, Kofinas, Chapin III, & Redman, 2008). While individual openness on its own may be insufficient to overpower the complex structures and power relations that govern academia, it nonetheless plays a role in the development of interdisciplinarity.

It is typical for collaborations between disciplines to elicit debates about how each discipline defines the value, validity, and impact of its research. For instance, a common source of friction which occurs between disciplines of the humanities and the sciences, questions whether the conceptual openness of the humanities is too ambiguous to be considered rigorous and whether scientific rigour necessarily entails a positivist approach (Callard & Fitzgerald, 2015). These frictions may also derive from differences that exist in the objective of the research itself (Bruhn, 1995): Is the research asking *why* a phenomenon occurs, or *how* it occurs? Miller and colleagues explain that 'in any given research context, there may be several valuable ways of knowing, and that accommodating this plurality can lead to more successful integrated study' (2008, p. 1). Here, we propose that an attitude of openness is an essential foundation in acknowledging this methodological and epistemological plurality, thereby bridging communication gaps between multiple disciplines. Later in this chapter, we will discuss how this element we are referring to as an open attitude plays a role in practice (i.e. in a collaborative research setting).

Research is often collaborative, possibly even more so when crossing disciplinary boundaries. Ensuring that all parties involved in the process maintain the aforementioned open attitude can be challenging. In an academic climate dominated by mono-disciplinary research, individual researchers receive pressure from various sources such as performance evaluation from their institution, peer pressure from the field, personal ambition, as well as some of the 'roadblocks' (Blassnigg & Punt, 2013, p. 3), to invest time and energy to publish work in prestigious journals within their respective disciplines. This pressure creates a 'collective action problem' (Nosek et al., 2015, p. 1422), wherein skilled researchers do not publish in journals covering multiple disciplines due to generally low impact, and as such, these journals remain low in impact due to the shortage of high-quality submissions. Such a distribution of publications is consistent with the findings by Solomon et al. (2016) who show a similar degree of interdisciplinary integration for individual articles in monodisciplinary journals as for *Science* and *Nature*. Their findings suggest that the accepted and published articles in leading multidisciplinary journals cross disciplines within one issue, but not within the same article. In addition to this reinforcement effect, Rafols, Leydesdorff, O'Hare, Nightingale and Stirling (2012) also name intellectual inbreeding, avoidance of complex societal questions, and the reduction of cognitive diversity in the research system's ecology as potential outcomes of mono-disciplinary publication practice. On the other hand, there can be a high price to pay for pursuing open, multiple disciplinary, and collaborative research, such as poor performance evaluation, or even isolation from colleagues in the field. Those who do pursue this direction exude an 'honest signal' (see evolutionary signaling theory, e.g. Zahavi, 1977) of commitment towards interdisciplinarity, actively paying the high cost in order to acknowledge and contribute to its value.

Another aspect of the current research culture in which openness plays a role is the transfer and sharing of disciplinary knowledge. It is easy to overlook the impact that discoveries in one discipline can have in another. For example, research in physics has had many significant applications for medical research, as exemplified in the textbook by Podgorsak (2016). However, when cited in the radically different context of another discipline, researchers based in the original discipline can perceive new interpretations as misrepresentations. Similarly, the accurate sharing of knowledge between disciplines requires another aspect of openness, which is open access to data, ideas, or sources. The accessibility and transparency of work has been regarded as one of the most crucial aspects in facilitating and developing a type of open, dialogical relationship between disciplines (Nosek et al., 2015), with open access research also generating more citations and a more significant impact (Eysenbach, 2006; Piwowar & Vision, 2013). Here, again, we identify the need for openness – willingness to extend the ownership of one's knowledge, allowing to shed new light on it.

Moreover, in such instances of transferring knowledge, both parties can benefit from an ongoing dialogical relationship, whereby each discipline closely examines the others' theoretical and methodological perspectives, thus creating a collection of mutually acknowledged approaches from which the subject area can be studied. In summary, we argue that openness – an awareness of methodological and epistemological plurality – is a crucial facet which governs the success of multiple disciplinary (and/or collaborative) research at the individual level. If such an attitude of openness was achieved collectively across disciplines and communities (e.g., publishers, academic institutions, funders), it could play a significant role in enhancing the quality and efficacy of multiple disciplinarity itself.

As much as the idea of openness centres around individual interactions and relationships, organisations also play an important role in fertilising the grounds for successful collaborative work across disciplinary boundaries (Stokols, Misra, Moser, Hall, & Taylor, 2008). Firstly, disciplines coincide with institutions that function as 'regulatory systems; as cognitive systems that control and develop their respective knowledge base, and as cultural systems with particular norms and values concerning how issues should be studied' (Buanes & Jentoft, 2009, p. 448). As such, the necessity of having an open attitude – not only to other disciplines, but also to the idea of multiple disciplinarity itself – extends beyond the core researchers who are conducting the research, to its facilitators, managers, advisors, and publishers. In this light, we argue that the gathering of agents, each trained to be competent researchers within their respective 'institutions' (i.e., disciplines), enables multiple disciplinary collaborations. These individuals are ready to engage with a different discipline, critically reflect on their disciplinary backgrounds, and embrace their particular roles in the collaborative research project. Secondly, it is also paramount for the organisation to provide opportunities for these agents to collaborate openly and flexibly. Consequently, this means that the environment provides the space and time necessary for researchers – who are experienced and competent in their fields – to explore, contemplate, question, and make mistakes as they venture into the world of interdisciplinarity (Loesche & Łucznik, 2017). Callard and Fitzgerald (2015) also point out how this open space emerges from the gaps created between disciplines which struggle to merge:

> … if there is now an invitation to 'the social' from (some) parts of the biological sciences, then there is simultaneously an openness to think biologically from (some) parts of contemporary social theory. And if such moves are often partial and contested, they nonetheless form a gap into which the researcher interested in interdisciplinary experimentation might insert herself. (Callard & Fitzgerald, 2015, p. 63)

Thus, we suggest that openness represents both a gap or an opening – created either intentionally or unintentionally – that invites the insertion of an interdisciplinary researcher, and the attitude required to fill in such a gap. As described in the following sections, ColLaboratoire entailed both aspects, where the learning environment was intentionally left unstructured, and participants and organisers displayed the curiosity and skills necessary to restructure it.

3 The CogNovo Programme

As mentioned earlier, CogNovo was a doctoral training programme, with fellows from several disciplines in the Arts, Humanities, and Sciences (Maranan, Loesche & Denham, 2015).[1] From 2014 to 2017, more than 12 events, aiming to promote interaction and openness among the researchers and the disciplines involved, were organised as part of CogNovo. Previous reflections identified generosity, interdependence, free exploration, and trust as principles contributing to the types of research pursued in CogNovo (Loesche & Łucznik, 2017). As ColLaboratoire was modelled using the CogNovo fellows' experiences, here we describe and evaluate three additional features which played a significant role in promoting openness in the design of ColLaboratoire: disciplinarity, mobility, and environment.

3.1 *Disciplinarity*

The CogNovo training programme included a series of workshops, as the aim of the programme was to create a foundation for multiple disciplinary works. With broad scope, each week-long event aimed to inform multiple disciplines about the research methods (e.g., information gathering) and experimentation practices from neighbouring disciplines. Designed to focus on information transfer, lectures and seminars were delivered by key experts in an extensive array of disciplines ranging from neuroscience to anthropology. The quality of information delivered in these workshops was rich and informative; CogNovo fellows engaged with a mixture of epistemic sources, from experimental data and written archives to works of art.

In a subsequent workshop on Computational Modelling, in addition to the talks and seminars delivered by experts, group work was scheduled into the week-long programme. This encouraged engagement with the seminar content from different perspectives, producing several outputs. These included robots that helped advance an analogue film in a programmable frame rate, a socially-interactive robot, and a grant proposal, then submitted as part of the StudentshIP Enterprise Award to the Intellectual Property Office, a national funding agency. This type of group work illuminated the value of actively exchanging information about one discipline's practice with another, thereby uncovering new and alternative ways of transferring the knowledge of methods across disciplines (Marzano, Carss, & Bell, 2006). Several fellows remarked that it became easier to connect with another discipline in a practice-based manner, as this made the discipline more tangible and accessible. Thus, these workshops also encouraged openness through such interactions and discussions. Furthermore, existing misconceptions that disciplines had about one another were addressed, preventing them from being harmful and obstructive (Campbell, 2005).

While these examples of events show development towards creating a space for multiple disciplines at CogNovo, there was no strict temporal continuity in this pattern of events. The development from one event to another that could, in hindsight, be perceived as moving from combining multiple disciplines to an integrated research space, was, in reality, an intuitive and exploratory process of finding an effective way to collaborate. In fact, one later workshop on Entrepreneurship was based entirely within the discipline of the Business School, at most referencing other disciplines as examples, and remaining mono-disciplined at its core; it did not increase the fellows' experience in multiple disciplinary collaborations, nor did it produce any measurable academic output, such as multiple disciplinary publications. However, this was the first time that the CogNovo fellows closely reflected on the impact that multiple disciplines may have on addressing complex research questions and on the fact that crossing disciplinary borders is not an automatic phenomenon that happens when people from differing backgrounds sit in the same room. Furthermore, it was the first time that the fellows provided organised feedback about the workshops. The CogNovo fellows recognised the significance of this feedback and its ability to help evaluate each event retrospectively and to improve future events. The feedback gained at the end of this event was particularly significant as it ultimately helped to shape the organisation of ColLaboratoire.

3.2 *Mobility*

In CogNovo, as in all Marie Skłodowska-Curie programmes, mobility was encouraged, through an initial relocation for the programme and then regular secondments to external partners. Crucially, relocating to a foreign country for the first time has been linked to increased creativity and openness to experience (Maddux & Galinsky, 2009). This openness involves being available to listen to new ideas, which in turn derives from merely being open towards the 'other'; as Pettigrew and Tropp (2008) suggest, interacting with people belonging to an 'other' group reduces out-group prejudice and increases social proximity, as initially observed by Allport (1954). Thus, we inferred that being in a multi-cultural environment contributed to reducing the naturally occurring between-group barriers, and to fostering a feeling of openness. Having CogNovo fellows from 15 countries willing to spend three years in Plymouth, and summer school participants from 14 countries willing to spend one week in Plymouth, highlights a motivation to travel to, experience, and learn about a new country. This willingness and drive to engage in novel experiences may be another foundation for, as well as a corollary of, openness. This willingness is also contingent upon the ability of societal, financial, and political contexts to share a physical or virtual space (Stokols et al., 2008).

3.3 *Environment – Space and Sociality*

CogNovo was a single-centre EU Initial Training Network, with all research fellows based in the same institution, and even the fellows who went on secondments spent most of their time in Plymouth.

Single-centredness was an essential driver in the success of CogNovo for several reasons. Firstly, single-centredness reduces the 'expenses to travel over geographical distances' (Yegros-Yegros et al., 2015, p. 4), one of the coordination costs of multi-centred programmes, thus making it possible for the fellows to dedicate time and energy to meet and integrate. Secondly, it allowed CogNovo fellows to share the burden of solving various administrative puzzles since they were all subject to the same organisational regulations (Cummings & Kiesler, 2005). Thirdly, and as a result of optimising the use of time and effort, single-centredness allowed for longer face-to-face interactions. Fellows had time and opportunities to discover one's own social and professional compatibility with others in the group: with whom one can work, and with whom one cannot. The fourth aspect was the establishment of a single, physically shared workspace. The spatial proximity for the fellows who shared the workspace possibly nurtured the relationship and therefore interpersonal openness. This observation is consistent with previous findings linking shared workspaces to a higher level of reported interdisciplinary collaboration (Stokols et at., 2008). The workspace was both open and modular, allowing for the creation of small environments that afforded both unobstructed movements as well as areas of concealment (see prospect-refuge theory of designing spaces, in Appleton, 1996). It had couches on which fellows could not only relax but even sleep on and congregate around to chat informally. It was a place that afforded both the opportunity to be alone and the opportunity to have face-to-face interactions. It hosted seminars, work groups, experiments, and social gatherings. It was what the director of CogNovo called a 'space for integration,' where one could gain exposure to ideas from other disciplines and cultures. The same space was used as a basis for ColLaboratoire and provided, on a much shorter timescale, similar functionality.

Relationships between people, places, and spaces have been investigated in multiple ways including the aspects of territoriality and belonging – as summarised by Vischer (2008) – providing psychological comfort and environmental control at the workplace. For the CogNovo fellows, this sense of place was particularly salient throughout their PhD programmes, given that they had a devoted working area and seminar room for all their activities. This permanent location created a strong group identity for CogNovo, and also a sense of control as the fellows could all access, utilise, and influence the physical space (Nova, 2005). Informal reports from the CogNovo fellows suggested that having this single physical space helped to foster a sense of collective identity. Furthermore, the fellows' personalisation of their working environment helped to establish their own identities in the surrounding community and a sense of belonging (Haynes, 2007).

Beyond the establishment of group identity, previous research has found that physical proximity is also related to a higher number of collaborations (e.g., Olson & Olson, 2000), as initiating conversations is not only easier but also more likely (Nova, 2005). Loesche and Łucznik (2017) additionally emphasise that both trust and free exploration are central principles in successful multiple disciplinarity. In CogNovo specifically, the proximity of the fellows enabled them to develop their ideas in informal settings and revise them as necessary without leaving their shared office space.

While physical proximity was integral to CogNovo's community, social proximity was also crucial. Many successful collaborations among the CogNovo fellows emerged organically, having been conceptualised and explored in non-work environments. A similar observation was made by Sawyer (2007) while discussing successful collaboration in business. Informal conversation became 'the cornerstone of collaboration' (Nova, 2005, p. 122) and many effective ideas were born out of trusting relationships that were not 'built on promises' but that needed 'time and action to grow' (Loesche & Łucznik, 2017, p. 15) in shared spaces. Reflecting on the social proximity of CogNovo, a visiting researcher remarked that the programme was naturally social, observing that 'you walk into the room and you can sense the sociality of the group' (Hancock & Jenkins, 2016). Thus, physical environments became a central consideration in the organisation of ColLaboratoire, for their crucial importance in facilitating sociality.

4 ColLaboratoire: Its Organisation and Success

ColLaboratoire was modelled heavily on the CogNovo fellows' experiences of working within a multiple disciplinary setting. It was designed to establish a collaborative environment that would best serve multiple disciplinary research. At the same time, it preemptively addressed some of the issues faced by the fellows at the start of the CogNovo programme, at which point many had not had previous collaborative experiences (e.g., communication issues across disciplinary boundaries, poor understanding of other disciplines' research methods, ways of gathering knowledge, and dissemination of knowledge). Modelling the summer school on CogNovo reduced the number of challenges that ColLaboratoire participants would have to face.

The ColLaboratoire organisational team consisted of four self-selected CogNovo fellows who were responsible for coordinating the logistics of the summer school. These members had regular meetings over the eight-month period until the summer school took place. While each member had various roles (e.g., IT, financial, logistical, advertising), the decision-making was undertaken as a cohort during the meetings. The organisational components included sending out the project calls, assessing project proposals, inviting and selecting participants, inviting leading academics, organising accommodation, arranging catering, choosing and booking venues, and ensuring that everything ran to plan throughout the summer school.

Several factors contributed to the success of ColLaboratoire, stemming from the experience of the CogNovo fellows. These include its project-based structure, the encouragement of mobility, shared spaces, and social aspects.

4.1 *A Project-Based Structure*

At the beginning of the organisational process, the organisers agreed that the summer school should be project-based and structured similarly to CogNovo workshops. Building from the sense of personal achievement created in previous events, ColLaboratoire aimed to generate intrinsic motivation to collaborate with people of different disciplines through peer-led and practice-based approaches.

Furthermore, research indicated that experience-based learning is often more fruitful than theory-driven approaches (e.g., Ruben, 1999; Stokols, 2006). Practice-based approaches, for example, for the project described in Table 13.1, facilitate individual engagement among people whose disciplinary backgrounds are different from one's discipline, and which can provide open and judgment-free platforms to discover and ideate collaboratively (Francis, Haines, & Briazu, 2017). Many graduate-level summer schools in academic settings are designed to offer discipline-specific skills and knowledge in more traditional formats, with lecturers and workshop leaders focusing on teaching as opposed to facilitating learning. The organisers of ColLaboratoire, however, went beyond these traditional approaches by delivering a novel, peer-led, and

TABLE 13.1 Description of project 'Remapping the Sensorium: Do You Hear What I See?'

Title	Remapping the Sensorium: Do You Hear What I See?
Disciplines	Cognitive Psychology, Computer Science, Music
Initial description and goals	In this project, we will develop real-time systems and data processing workflows to reveal hidden brain and bodily processes summoned through the collaborative production of a musical piece or the collective experience of a film. We will sonify and visualise a range of physiological measures collected during collaborative production and collective spectatorship to provide insights into perception, action, and social engagement ... With the findings, we aim to gain greater insight into the impact of a collective experience ourselves and providing a toolkit that can be deployed in live events to augment audience participation and immersion in the cinematic experience.
Process of collaboration and results	The idea, to translate experiences from one medium to another, (e.g., the visual experience to sonic one), remained from the initial proposal to the final project. During the preparation phase, a flexible system architecture was prepared to accommodate various developments of the project. As expected in interdisciplinary collaboration, each participant brought a unique approach to interpret the collected data from the experience of collective spectatorship. The final project had a particular emphasis on the quality of sound and eye tracking analysis, as a consequence of specific interests expressed by the participants.
Future developments / collaborations	The project had several follow-ups. The idea of creating a sonification platform consisting of hardware, software, and conceptualisation on how to make different types of real-time and recorded data audible was implemented into "The Exciting Synesthesia Machine" (exhibited, e.g., at OTLip16, and the ESRC Social Science Festival 2016). The same platform was used for multiple other science-art projects such as "Finger Music," "A Space to Wonder," and "Experiments in Sonified Magic," presented at academic, professional and public events, ranging from presentations at University Open Days, International Dance Festivals, the Bizarre Bazaar public engagement event, Off the Lip Conference, and ESRC Social Science Festival (Loesche, Lemarchand, Kristensen, and Bridges, 2016). Additionally, it inspired one of the facilitators to develop his PhD project in a new direction.

project-driven experience that was designed to give participants real-world collaborative opportunities. Furthermore, the organisers intended to foster collaboration between participants through a project-based, open-ended, and semi-structured approach. As Domik and Fischer (2011) note, adopting these flexible and goal-directed approaches allows 'students [to] practise meaningful collaboration with other disciplines' and fuels the transformation of students from educational consumers to 'socially competent, responsible, self-directed learners' (p. 2).

The first step for realising the organisers' vision of a multiple disciplinary, open-ended, and project-based summer school, was proposing the projects. The organisational team invited the CogNovo fellows to submit proposals for projects; this call was successful, and bids for seven interdisciplinary projects were received. After circulating the ideas among the project facilitators, some of them decided to merge, so that the final list included four projects. Tables 13.1 to 13.4 provide a detailed summary of the projects, describing their associated disciplines, their original purpose, and how they evolved during and after the summer school took place.

As ColLaboratoire was a peer-led summer school, the CogNovo fellows placed themselves as project facilitators, rather than leaders. Project facilitators were required to be from at least two different disciplines (see Figure 13.2) to achieve Choi and Pak's (2006) criterion for multiple disciplinarity. While outlining each project's structure and offering guidance and technical assistance when appropriate, project facilitators prioritised flexibility. For example, the organisers agreed that participants should navigate the research and be allowed to shape the processes and outcomes of the work. In addition to the project facilitators, leading academics who had professional collaborative experience were also invited to share their views and participate in some of the projects, providing valuable suggestions and input. Crucially, ColLaboratoire built on an intrinsic commitment to multiple disciplinary goals with the aim of nurturing productive and rewarding collaborations between disciplines (Loesche & Łucznik, 2017; Stokols, 2006).

4.2 *Participants: Recruitment and Mobility*

After finalising the project proposals, the next stage was the recruitment of participants. Even though Stewart (2006) found a positive effect of team size on performance in his meta-analysis, they observed a peak at around seven team members. Together with other factors such as available funding, space, and logistic constraints, the organisational team decided to keep the project size below seven participants. CogNovo fellows emailed invitations to their networks, institutions, and research groups with interest in collaborative

TABLE 13.2 Description of project 'Are Networks (Becoming) Conscious?'

Title	Are Networks (Becoming) Conscious?
Disciplines	Cognitive Psychology, Philosophy, Computer Science
Initial description and goals	Could highly-connected networks (such as the Internet) be conscious? Is such a network more likely to be conscious if it has a body? Does the Internet have a 'body' capable of sensing and acting on its environment? This project will take into account extended, situated, enactive, and embodied theories of cognition, investigating the possibility of modelling networked-based consciousness. The goal of this project is to compose a compelling (and potentially fundable) research proposal including research questions, initial literature review, discussion on methodologies, and proofs-of-concept.
Process of collaboration and results	During the project, the group spontaneously broke off into smaller working groups and explored the aspects of the topic, based on individual expertise and areas of interest. Towards the end of the summer school, these threads were brought together into a coherent theoretical framework and proof-of-concept, creating the conceptual foundation for a research grant proposal.
Future developments/ collaborations	While the initial idea of the project was not followed-up, this project resulted in several successful collaborations between the participants, e.g., RE/ME (Maranan, Haines, & Clarke, 2017). The results of this project were documented and are publicly available: http://cognovo.bobfigueroajr.com

research. Upon application for specific projects, the applicants were asked for a description of their research and experience, previous collaboration experience, and skills or knowledge that they would be willing to share with the project group. Applications from 42 people were received. The following two primary selection criteria were adopted for selecting participants: applicants' previous collaborative experience and/or their willingness to collaborate, and whether their existing experience provided valuable expertise within their preferred project(s). These selection criteria coincided with the 'degree of openness and interest of participants in interdisciplinary working' that was used by Bridle et al. (2013, p. 26) for the selection of participants within a similar context; these criteria led to the selection of participants who were open to interacting with people from other disciplines. While each organisational

TABLE 13.3 Description of project "Nao' That's What I'm Talking About'

Title	**'Nao' That's What I'm Talking About**
Disciplines	Robotics, Performance Art, Philosophy, Social Psychology
Initial description and goals	In this project, participants will have the chance to choreograph and stage a performance with one or more NAO humanoid robots, after a multiple disciplinary discussion on the nature and perception of the robot. Roboticists, performers, artists, philosophers and programmers are welcome to apply: true to the spirit of CogNovo; we want this project to be a fulfilling experience for all of its participants, who will receive stimulating inputs from experts in the fields that this project spans.
Process of collaboration and results	During initial brainstorming sessions, the group decided to produce a 'robotic theatre' performance. Additionally, participants decided to collect audience feedback alongside with data on social perception of performing robots. This idea, which was not included in the initial proposal, enriched the outcomes of the project and created the possibility of publishing the project results in the field of Human-Robot Interaction.
Future developments / collaborations	After the summer school, the team kept working together analysing the data collected from the audience; this resulted in a paper that was submitted to "HRI," one of the most important conferences in Human-Robot Interaction. Even though it was rejected, the team received three peer reviews which will be used to further develop and re-submit the paper.

team member completed the ratings independently, they made the final decisions at the group level and on a case-by-case basis. The final attendees were 20 PhD and Masters-level researchers with expertise in a variety of disciplines, including Music, Dance, Applied Arts, Philosophy, Communication Science, Cognitive Psychology, Computational Neuroscience, and Computer Science This distribution of topics was identified posthoc, reflect to some extent the disciplines within CogNovo, and certainly contributed to the success of the projects. (See Figure 13.3 for an overview of these disciplines and their distribution across projects.)

In the same way that the funding for CogNovo was designed to facilitate cross-border mobility, ColLaboratoire organisers decided to allocate a substantial amount of the funding to student bursaries, with the result that

TABLE 13.4 Description of project 'Let's Improv It'

Title	Let's Improv It
Disciplines	Cognitive & Social Psychology, Dance, Improvisation, Computer Science
Initial description and goals	This project aims to explore psychological theories of shared experience and its physiological basis. We will engage in playful dance and movement improvisational tasks, studying the notion of social entrainment, empathic projection and theory of shared flow experience through observation, visualisation and sonification of physiological changes and improvised scores. It is a practice-based research project, resulting in an improvised movement light and sound performance.
Process of collaboration and results	From the beginning, the group decided to shift the initial goal into providing "an experience" for the audience to engage with. As a consequence, the group explored how to share embodied knowledge and used an improviser's way of understanding the social reality with people who had no experience with dance or movement improvisation. The initial proposal of sonification and visualisation of physiological dynamics of movement was excluded as it did not fit the new goal. As a result, the group provided a participatory improvised experience that explored the notion of social, nonverbal communication through the experience of mimicry, touch, and kinaesthetic empathy.
Future developments/ collaborations	Most of the members of the group (both facilitators and participants) continued the development of the project in the following year. The idea and the practice of collaborative, interdisciplinary work, were disseminated at "Dance Fields," one of the largest dance research conferences. Furthermore, the group produced a participatory performance that was shared at "International Dance and Somatic Practices Conference." The project was also described and published in a paper (Łucznik, Jackson, Sakuta, & Siarava, 2017). The collaboration continues; the group is planning further performance work to be exhibited at dance festivals.

ColLaboratoire was able to cover travel from as far away as Southeast Asia and the Americas. This distribution of funding allowed participants to make contact with others from different cultures and backgrounds; as framed by

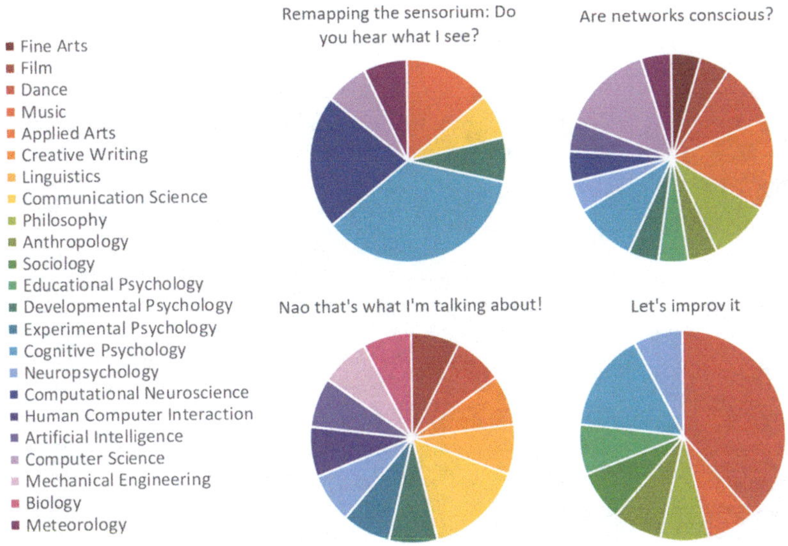

FIGURE 13.2 An overview of participants' and facilitators' disciplines and their distribution across the ColLaboratoire projects

Allport's (1954) Contact Theory, the organisers used this diversity of people as leverage for openness and creativity (Maddux, Adam, & Galinsky, 2010), both in social and in work settings.

4.3 *Environment: Space and Sociality*

As mentioned previously, the ColLaboratoire organisers decided to use the CogNovo workspace as the central location of the summer school (see Figure 13.3). Organisation centred on physical proximity: participants ate breakfast together every morning in a campus cafe, refreshments and snacks were supplied in a central location to bring teams back together in the late mornings and afternoons in between project work, and regular summary sessions also reunited project groups in a common place to share their progress with one another. Participants were also provided accommodation in a shared building where they had opportunities to meet and talk during their free time. With this approach of physical proximity, and by providing informal and unstructured time, ColLaboratoire instilled and nurtured openness to work across disciplines and summer school projects. It also enabled many face-to-face contact opportunities, and this 'allowed conversations to happen at dinner, at breakfast, at lunch' (Hancock & Jenkins, 2016). This exchange of ideas and relationship-building promoted confidential discussions and developed the trust necessary in multiple disciplinary communication (Bridle et al., 2013).

FIGURE 13.3 ColLaboratoire participants and organisers during project work. The photograph was taken by the ColLaboratoire organisers (2016)

For group work specifically, project facilitators were encouraged to take advantage of any available space on the university campus that they felt would foster creativity, openness, and trust. For example, in the 'Let's Improv It' project group (Table 13.4), this involved active movement in a dance studio and public spaces, while for the 'Are Networks (Becoming) Conscious' group (Table 13.2), it often involved close-knit discussions in smaller seminar rooms. These spaces were often in neutral or 'inspiring' locations, allowing the initiation of conversations during ColLaboratoire with less intimidation from organisational climates (Bridle et al., 2013).

Furthermore, existing evidence underlines the importance of social factors in multiple disciplinary work (e.g., Fiore, 2008; Klein, 2008; Marzano et al., 2006; Stokols, 2006), although a longitudinal study showed that social factors such as friendship did not predict success as much as intellectual ties (White, Wellman & Nazer, 2004). However, these findings may not necessarily be applied to a short and open-ended venture such as ColLaboratoire. To ensure successful open-ended collaboration, it may be more applicable to consider elements such as psychological safety – the 'shared belief that the team is safe for interpersonal risk taking' (Edmondson, 1999, p. 354). After all, multiple disciplinary collaboration is a social process which arguably involves higher levels of risk-taking than mono-disciplinary collaborations (e.g., Bridle et al., 2013). Therefore, together with the strong focus on physical proximity and own-group space, the summer school was constructed around unstructured time and a vibrant social programme to ensure that participants were able to interact and express their ideas informally and in low-risk settings. This plan involved the following activities across the week-long programme: research speed-dating, a social reception held at the National Marine Aquarium, a fireworks night, an international cooking evening, sports activities at a local climbing centre, a games night, shared daily breakfasts, and a group dinner.

5 ColLaboratoire: Processes and Outcomes

In the previous section, we described how ColLaboratoire was designed to replicate CogNovo's physical structure on a smaller scale, and from the perspective of the research fellows who had worked in close social proximity to one another for three years. In this section, we first discuss additional considerations in the process of facilitating projects, such as the management of teams and resources. We also note some objective and subjective outcomes from the event and individual projects.

5.1 *Management of Teams and Resources*

The project facilitators supported their teams with their research process in a variety of different ways. An event such as ColLaboratoire involves bringing together people with different cultural and disciplinary backgrounds, which inherently raises challenges in weaving together a diverse range of understandings and practices. Moreover, in an intensive one-week course, time management and resource availability are crucial factors for success. The facilitators were overseeing the work and helping participants to find a common point of contact, even when different parts of the team worked separately. It is notable that this was achieved in different ways by each project; for example, in the 'Do You Hear What I See' and 'Are Networks (Becoming) Conscious' projects (see Tables 13.1 and 13.2), the facilitators placed themselves as messengers and moderators between different segments of their groups. In contrast, the 'Let's Improv It' group worked closely throughout the week, dedicating daily time to group discussions centred round clarification of ideas and the direction of the project (see Table 13.4). In the 'Nao that's what I'm talking about' group (Table 13.3), facilitators assisted with task assignment and the moderation of group discussions in order to support the less experienced members of the group, ensuring that their ideas would be heard.

Projects were designed so that participants were required to acquire new skills to work towards the project goal. The facilitators, alongside expert guests, shared their knowledge in the practical sessions which were then immediately applied to the research problems in subsequent group work. Through practice, each group member could increase his or her understanding of how different perspectives from other disciplines could be applied, and their practical value. As discussed earlier, the CogNovo fellows' experiences indicated that opportunity for practice makes the perspective of another discipline more tangible and accessible.

The open-ended form of the research projects required facilitators to display flexibility and openness to participants' ideas. As Tables 13.1 to 13.4 illustrate, each project adjusted from its original proposal to reflect the specific interests of the participants. The facilitators accommodated this alteration in a variety of ways. For example, in the 'Nao That's What I'm Talking About' project, the group decided to provide extra materials and enrich their investigation by collecting perceptual data, as documented in Table 13.3. Alternatively, in the 'Let's Improv It' project (Table 13.4), group members decided to exclude some aspects of the planned research. After researching possible new technologies, the group decided not to engage with them. Another example of how the flexibility of the projects was useful, involved a participant who initially did not feel that she belonged to her project group, as she struggled to find a way in which her expertise could provide relevant insights into the topic. However, she was able to find the group to which she felt she could best contribute. Even then, a significant number of arguments, concepts, and the processes felt foreign to her, despite her sincere interest. Instead of treating this as a failure, the head of the programme appointed her as a general observer with the freedom to move from one group to another, identifying her critical eye as a valuable asset for the improvement of each project and the programme as a whole.

In the after-event feedback questionnaire, participants indicated that this additional effort was rewarding, with each of those changes resulting in stronger and more innovative projects. As mentioned earlier, ColLaboratoire reflected the CogNovo fellows' belief that successful collaborations are born out of a dynamic and iterative process. Thus, researchers wishing to facilitate this should be prepared to adapt their ideas and practice to the changing landscape afforded by interacting with people outside of their discipline (Loesche & Łucznik, 2017).

5.2 *Experiences and Outcomes*

The success of ColLaboratoire is evident in a variety of ways. Some of the outputs include peer-reviewed articles (e. g., Łucznik, Jackson, Sakuta, & Siarava, 2017), an engineered body-awareness-enhancing tool (Maranan et al., 2017), a sonification platform (Loesche et al., 2016) which was used in multiple other science-art projects, and conference workshops (e.g., Łucznik & Jackson, 2016) – including one that was organised by participants belonging to two different ColLaboratoire groups (Maloney & Sakuta, 2017). For further details, see the 'Future developments/collaborations' rows in Tables 13.1 to 13.4. These turnouts illustrate that interdisciplinary events such as these can result in innovative research projects leading to a variety of outcomes to raise the participants' research profiles. Importantly, many of the ColLaboratoire participants have continued working together. For example, the group of 'Let's Improv It' developed the ideas of their projects further, while elements from the project 'Do You Hear What I See' were the basis for 'The Exciting Synesthesia Machine,' a multimodal exhibition to make visual input audible in real-time (Loesche et al., 2016; also see Tables 13.1 and 13.4).

In addition to these outputs, which provide an objective measure of the continued success of the summer school, its positive impact can be evidenced by the participants' evaluations of the event. Many of these reactions mirrored a sense of stepping into new territory and feeling a strong sense of excitement. For example, one participant remarked that 'The project work was so outside of my comfort zone. I learned an awful lot and loved every second of it'; while another commented that, 'The summer school has taken me out of my comfort zone and allowed me to question many things.' These remarks about learning were often emotive, with one participant stating that 'This week resulted in a powerful experience. I've learned so much and found lots of pleasure in our collaborations.' These comments also provide evidence for the development of positive affect, mutual trust, and genuine openness towards other individuals in ColLaboratoire (Hancock & Jenkins, 2016). One participant wrote that '[ColLaboratoire] was an absolute hit with me and I have been telling people that it was one of the best weeks of my life.' In a final film interview with the participants, one remarked that, 'I've always dreamed of a place like this where everyone is curious, active, and where amazing ideas just emerge naturally … what I can take home, is that this does exist'; another concluded the interview by saying: 'This, ColLaboratoire, is life-changing.'

6 ColLaboratoire's Legacy: Multi-Perspective, Inter-Perspective, and Trans-Perspective Openness

Reflecting on the knowledge and experience gained throughout the organisation and execution of ColLaboratoire, we note that many collaborations between groups of participants are still on-going and are building on what was only a one-week long event. In this final section, we discuss how the aforementioned 'attitude of openness,' shared by both the organisers and participants, likely played a role in realising this richly condensed one-week programme and in producing a sustainable model of collaboration. We suggest that an attitude of openness entails the following three facets:

1. Multi-perspective openness: being open to the idea of interacting with individuals from other disciplines and listening to their opinions with an open mind to eliminate any prejudice against one another. This openness derives conceptually from Allport's Contact Hypothesis (1954), an ample duration of cooperative contact with the 'other' reduce prejudice between groups and enhances empathy and understanding, as shown in the meta-analysis by Pettigrew and Tropp (2008).
2. Inter-perspective openness: softening the disciplinary borders of philosophical perspectives and theoretical frameworks to allow multiple avenues of inquiry to surface together (drawing from Miller et al.'s 'epistemological pluralism,' 2008).
3. Trans-perspective openness: allowing for methods, data, and knowledge to transcend disciplines, so that they can be used and interpreted in new and different ways (drawing from Bruhn, 1995, and Nosek et al., 2015).

These three facets can be thought of as different, albeit intertwined, components of openness, whose content naturally overlaps. Some of these facets are part of the psychological construct of 'openness to experience,' generally defined as one of the Big Five personality traits (McCrae, 2009). Here, in particular, we refer to states that can fluidly change (e.g., through experience) within an individual. As such, we address these three facets as original ideas, independent from pre-existing definitions. In all three, there is a process of suspending disciplinary beliefs (and disbeliefs), wherein one's own disciplinary standards and traditions are loosened to entertain other perspectives. There is also an affective dimension in realising this open, inclusive environment, which is a sense of placid neutrality towards entertaining competing perspectives; an unbroken and collective delight in suspending traditionally accepted answers.

While it could be argued that the three facets of openness were already present in CogNovo, it might be premature to assess the outputs generated from a three-year initiative as opposed to a one-week event. The scope and impact of the CogNovo programme itself will be investigated in the future when its outputs come to fruition, and we invite readers to provide additional much-needed long-term analyses of similar programmes. Here, we focus our reflection on ColLaboratoire specifically. ColLaboratoire and its participants realised the three facets of openness in several aspects of the programme:

- Disciplinarity. Trans-perspective and Inter-perspective openness were established through the transference of knowledge and methods between disciplines, and consequently, a loosening of traditional disciplinary borders. Furthermore, the practice-based structure of the event encouraged trans-perspective openness by facilitating extensive interactions between participants from different disciplines. ColLaboratoire also serves as an example of how openness effectively facilitates the creation of new knowledge among participants through less restrictive interaction (multiple disciplinary), which is common among open learning environments and approaches, hinged on Vygotskian social constructivism (Bruner, 1996; Vygotsky, 1978).
- Mobility. Bringing people together from different regions facilitated multi-perspective openness, breaking barriers between individuals.
- Environment. Multi-perspective openness was facilitated through the physical environment, which was a combination of open and modular spaces. In this sense, the aforementioned CogNovo fellows' 'space for integration' was an immersive experience of multi-perspective openness.
- Sociality. The process of building relationships and establishing trust relates to the development of multi-perspective openness, and, more broadly, to the Contact Hypothesis (Allport, 1954; Pettigrew & Tropp, 2008); existing personal and disciplinary prejudices are overcome through direct social experiences between researchers and the development of empathy. These are essential components that have been found to foster positive intergroup contact (Beelmann & Heinemann, 2014).

Crucially, multi-, inter-, and trans-perspective openness are both enablers and outcomes. Already inherent in many of the summer school participants, these facets of openness enabled free discussions and motivated collaborations. Further, and as a result of explicit facilitation, participants emerged throughout the event having been inspired and nurtured in the summer school's organisation. As such, the venture of ColLaboratoire raises two important considerations for prospective and much-needed multiple disciplinary collaborations. Firstly, that collaborative successes may be more likely if researchers possess the three aspects of openness introduced here and secondly, that summer school initiatives such as ColLaboratoire can assist in the acquisition of such disciplinary openness. After all, the success of multiple disciplinarity lies with those who are not afraid to interact, learn, unlearn, and reshape in the face of challenge.

Acknowledgements

CogNovo was the Marie Skłodowska-Curie Innovative Training Network (ITN) FP7-PEOPLE-2013-ITN, grant number 604764, funded by the European Union's 7th Framework Programme (FP7) for Research and Technological Development and University of Plymouth, from 2013 to 2017. The authors would also like to thank the ColLaboratoire participants and organisers, and Sue Denham, Michael Punt, Martha Blassnigg and Rebecca Pearce for their role in establishing and supporting CogNovo and ColLaboratoire.

Note

1 For an extensive description, see https://CogNovo.eu

References

Allport, G. W. (1954). *The nature of prejudice*. Cambridge, MA: Addison-Wesley.

Alvargonzález, D. (2011). Multidisciplinarity, interdisciplinarity, transdisciplinarity, and the sciences. *International Studies in the Philosophy of Science, 25*(4), 387–403. doi:10.1080/02698595.2011.623366

Appleton, J. (1996). *The experience of landscape*. Chichester: Wiley.

Beelmann, A., & Heinemann, K. S. (2014). Preventing prejudice and improving intergroup attitudes: A meta-analysis of child and adolescent training programs. *Journal of Applied Developmental Psychology, 35*(1), 10–24.

Blassnigg, M., & Punt, M. (2013). Transdisciplinarity: Challenges, approaches and opportunities on the cusp of history. *Steps to an Ecology of Networked Knowledge and Innovation: Enabling New Forms of Collaboration among Sciences, Engineering, Arts, and Design, 8790*, 1–13.

Bridle, H., Vrieling, A., Cardillo, M., Araya, Y., & Hinojosa, L. (2013). Preparing for an interdisciplinary future: A perspective from early-career researchers. *Futures, 53*, 22–32. doi:10.1016/j.futures.2013.09.003

Bruhn, J. G. (1995). Beyond discipline: Creating a culture for interdisciplinary research. *Integrative Physiological and Behavioral Science, 30*(4), 331–341. doi:10.1007/bf02691605

Bruner, J. S. (1996). *The culture of education*. Cambridge, MA: Harvard University Press.

Buanes, A., & Jentoft, S. (2009). Building bridges: Institutional perspectives on Interdisciplinarity. *Futures, 41*(7), 446–454. doi:10.1016/j.futures.2009.01.010

Callard, F., & Fitzgerald, D. (2015). *Rethinking interdisciplinarity across the social sciences and neurosciences* (Vol. 1). Palgrave Macmillan.

Campbell, L. M. (2005). Overcoming obstacles to interdisciplinary research. *Conservation Biology, 19*(2), 574–577.

Choi, B. C. K., & Pak, A. W. P. (2006). Multidisciplinarity, interdisciplinarity and transdisciplinarity in health research, services, education and policy: 1. Definitions, objectives, and evidence of effectiveness. *Clinical and Investigative Medicine, 29*(6), 351–364.

Cummings, J. N., & Kiesler, S. (2005). Collaborative research across disciplinary and organizational boundaries. *Social Studies of Science, 35*(5), 703–722. doi:10.1177/0306312705055535

Denham, S. L. (2014). Marie meets Leonardo: A perfect match? *Leonardo, 47*(3).

Domik, G., & Fischer, G. (2011). Transdisciplinary collaboration and lifelong learning: Fostering and supporting new learning opportunities. In *Rainbow of computer science* (pp. 129–143). Berlin/Heidelberg: Springer.

Edmondson, A. (1999). Psychological safety and learning behavior in work teams. *Administrative Science Quarterly, 44*(2), 350–383.

EURAB. (2004, April). *Interdisciplinarity in research.* Brussels: European Research Advisory Board (EURAB). Retrieved from https://ec.europa.eu/research/eurab/pdf/eurab_04_009_interdisciplinarity_research_final.pdf

Eysenbach, G. (2006). Citation advantage of open access articles. *PLoS Biology, 4*(5), e157.

Fiore, S. M. (2008). Interdisciplinarity as teamwork. *Small Group Research, 39*(3), 251–277. doi:10.1177/1046496408317797

Francis, K. B., Haines, A., & Briazu, R. A. (2017). Thinkering through experiments: Nurturing transdisciplinary approaches to the design of testing tools [Special Issue]. *AVANT, 8*, 107–115. doi:10.26913/80s02017.0111.0011

Hancock, B., & Jenkins, W. (2016). ColLaboratoire – CogNovo summer school [Video, Version 1.0.0]. *Zenodo*. doi:10.5281/zenodo.1147125

Haynes, B. P. (2007). The impact of the behavioural environment on office productivity. *Journal of Facilities Management, 5*(3), 158–171.

Horizon 2020 portal. Retrieved November 20, 2017, from https://ec.europa.eu/programmes/horizon2020/en/news/fet-living-interdisciplinarity

Klein, J. T. (2008). Evaluation of interdisciplinary and transdisciplinary research. *American Journal of Preventive Medicine, 35*(2), S116–S123. doi:10.1016/j.amepre.2008.05.010

Kysilka, M. (1998). Understanding integrated curriculum. *The Curriculum Journal, 9*, 197–209.

Loesche, F., Lemarchand, F., Kristensen, M., & Bridges, D. (2016). *DYHWIS* [Computer Software]. GitLab.com Software Directory. Retrieved from https://gitlab.com/fr_nk/DYHWIS

Loesche, F., Łucznik, K., & OTLip17 Committee. (2017). Our GIFT to all of us: GA(Y)AM: Preface [Special Issue]. *AVANT, 8*, 13–16. doi:10.26913/80s02017.0111.0001

Łucznik, K., & Jackson, A. (2016, December 8–9). *A space to wonder*. Paper presented at Dance Fields Un-Symposium, Coventry, UK [Practical Workshop].

Łucznik, K., Jackson, A., Sakuta, A., & Siarava, E. (2017). Let's improv it: The embodied investigation of social collaboration. *AVANT, 8*, 301–310. doi:10.26913/80s02017.0111.0027

Maddux, W. W., Adam, H., & Galinsky, A. D. (2010). When in Rome ... Learn why the romans do what they do: How multicultural learning experiences facilitate creativity. *Personality and Social Psychology Bulletin, 36*.

Maddux, W. W., & Galinsky, A. D. (2009). Cultural borders and mental barriers: The relationship between living abroad and creativity. *Journal of Personality and Social Psychology, 96*. doi:10.1037/a0014861

Maloney, L., & Sakuta, A. (2017, July 7–9). *Mediated self-sensing – Live sonification of the mover's heart rate*. Paper presented at Dance & Somatic Practices Conference on Moving the Sensate: Questions of Affect and Embodiment for the 21st Century, Coventry University, UK [Practical Workshop].

Maranan, D. S., Loesche, F., & Denham, S. L. (2015). CogNovo: Cognitive innovation for technological, artistic, and social domains. In *Proceedings of the 21st International Symposium on Electronic Arts* (Vol. 2015). Retrieved from http://isea2015.org/proceeding/submissionsISEA2015_submission_97.pdf

Marzano, M., Carss, D. N., & Bell, S. (2006). Working to make interdisciplinarity work: Investing in communication and interpersonal relationships. *Journal of Agricultural Economics, 57*(2), 185–197. doi:10.1111/j.1477-9552.2006.00046.x

McCrae, R. R. (2009). The five-factor model of personality. In P. Corr & G. Matthews (Eds.), *The Cambridge Handbook of Personality Psychology* (pp. 148–161). Cambridge University Press.

Miller, T., Baird, T., Littlefield, C., Kofinas, G., Chapin III, F. S., & Redman, C. (2008). Epistemological pluralism: reorganizing interdisciplinary research. *Ecology and Society, 13*(2). doi:10.5751/es-02671-130246

Nissani, M. (1997). Ten cheers for interdisciplinarity: The case for interdisciplinary knowledge and research. *The Social Science Journal, 34*(2), 201–216.

Nosek, B. A., Alter, G., Banks, G. C., Borsboom, D., Bowman, S. D., Breckler, S. J., … Yarkoni, T. (2015). Promoting an open research culture. *Science, 348*(6242), 1422–1425.

Nova, N. (2005). A review of how space affords socio-cognitive processes during collaboration. *PsychNology, 3*, 118–148.

Olson, G. M., & Olson, J. S. (2000). *Distance Matters, 15*(2–3), 139–178. doi:10.1207/s15327051hci1523_4

Piwowar, H. A., & Vision, T. J. (2013). Data reuse and the open data citation advantage. *PeerJ, 1*, e175.

Pettigrew, T. F., & Tropp, L. R. (2008). How does intergroup contact reduce prejudice? *Meta-Analytic Tests of Three Mediators, 38*(6), 922–934. doi:10.1002/ejsp.504

Podgorsak, E. B. (2016). *Radiation physics for medical physicists*. Springer International Publishing. doi:10.1007/978-3-319-25382-4

Rafols, I., Leydesdorff, L., O'Hare, A., Nightingale, P., & Stirling, A. (2012). How journal rankings can suppress interdisciplinary research: A comparison between innovation studies and business & management. *Research Policy, 41*(7), 1262–1282.

Robinson, K. (2001). *Out of our minds: Learning to be creative*. Chichester: Capstone.

Ruben, B. D. (1999). Simulations, games, and experience-based learning: The quest for a new paradigm for teaching and learning. *Simulation & Gaming, 30*(4), 498–505.

Sawyer, K. (2007). *Group genius. The creative power of collaboration*. New York, NY: Basic Books.

Schmidt, J. C. (2007). Towards a philosophy of interdisciplinarity. *Poiesis & Praxis, 5*(1), 53–69. doi:10.1007/s10202-007-0037-8

Solomon, G. E. A., Carley, S., & Porter, A. L. (2016). How Multidisciplinary Are the Multidisciplinary Journals Science and Nature? *PLOS ONE, 11*(4), e0152637. https://doi.org/10.1371/journal.pone.0152637

Stewart, G. L. (2006). A meta-analytic review of relationships between team design features and team performance. *Journal of Management, 32*(1), 29–55. doi:10.1177/0149206305277792

Stokols, D. (2006). Toward a science of transdisciplinary action research. *American Journal of Community Psychology, 38*(1–2), 79–93.

Stokols, D., Misra, S., Moser, R. P., Hall, K. L., & Taylor, B. K. (2008). The ecology of team science. *American Journal of Preventive Medicine, 35*(2), S96–S115. doi:10.1016/j.amepre.2008.05.003

Sung, N. S., Gordon, J. I., Rose, G. D., Getzoff, E. D., Kron, S. J., Mumford, D., Onuchic, J. N., Scherer, N. F., Sumners, D. L., & Kopell, N. J. (2003). Educating future scientists. *Science, 301*(5639), 1485.

Vischer, J. C. (2008). Towards an environmental psychology of workspace: How people are affected by environments for work. *Architectural Science Review, 51*(2), 97–108. doi:10.3763/asre.2008.5114

Vygotsky, L. (1978). Interaction between learning and development. *Readings on the Development of Children, 23*(3), 34–41.

White, H. D., Wellman, B., & Nazer, N. (2004). Does citation reflect social structure? *Journal of the American Society for Information Science and Technology, 55*(2), 111–126.

Yegros-Yegros, A., Rafols, I., & D'Este, P. (2015). Does interdisciplinary research lead to higher citation impact? The different effect of proximal and distal interdisciplinarity. *PLOS ONE, 10*(8), e0135095. doi:10.1371/journal.pone.0135095

Zahavi, A. (1977). The cost of honesty: Further remarks on the handicap principle. *Journal of Theoretical Biology, 67*(3), 603–605.

CHAPTER 14

Open in the Evening: Openings and Closures in an Ecology of Practices

Leo Havemann

Versions and interpretations of 'openness' currently abound, such that it is said to have become 'one of the central contested values of modern liberal society' (Peters, 2014, p. 1). Contemporary products and practices that are said to be open are often also the subjects of advocacy by a range of self-described *movements* for open source software, open science, open government, open access, open data, and open education. These 'opening' movements tend to operate (somewhat counter-intuitively) as *silos* of practice within particular professional communities (Atenas & Havemann, 2015; Campbell, 2015). On the surface, their connecting thread is that they make a common claim on behalf of openness as a worthy value, yet they also share a significant but less explicit commitment to distinctly *digital* forms of openness.

The notion of the digital-as-enabler has underwritten current discussions of open education, which have tended to focus on the provision of digital content, such as open educational resources (OER), and massive open online courses (MOOCs). Yet, 'opening moves' in education also have a pre-digital history. In a variety of contexts, attempts have been made to reposition education as both public good and human right, and to democratise educational access and participation beyond the privileged strata of society, thereby enhancing opportunities for social and economic participation, for the working class, women and other traditionally underserved groups (Brennan, 2016; Jordan & Weller, 2017; Longstaff, 2014; Peter & Deimann, 2013; Peters, Gietzen, & Ondercin, 2012; Rolfe, 2017; Weller et al., 2018).

Recently a critical turn has emerged in the open education literature. In addition to voices which have critiqued open education as under-theorised (Bayne, Knox, & Ross, 2015; Edwards, 2015; Gourlay, 2015; Knox, 2013; Oliver, 2015; Veletsianos & Kimmons, 2012), another strand has called upon scholars and practitioners to refocus their attention on open educational *practices* (OEP). From this perspective, open forms of education (like education in general) are framed as a range of processes undertaken by human beings, rather than consisting specifically in the resources they create or amend. This framing appears

 | DOI: 10.1163/9789004422988_015

to offer the possibility of deeper insights into actual practices, but whereas the forms of openness afforded by OER or MOOCs are well understood, it is less obvious what exactly makes a *practice* open. However, this inherent ambiguity might be viewed as a strength rather than a weakness of OEP: while much of the literature discussing OEP has framed the concept in relation to OER, there is a more expansive concept of OEP which recognises other forms of openness and ways of opening (Cronin, 2017; Cronin & MacLaren, 2018; Havemann, 2016; Roberts et al., 2018).

Taking its cue from this line of enquiry, this chapter considers the question of what is open about (or opened by) open education, and how the concept of OEP can potentially aid this investigation. It focuses on a case study of practice at Birkbeck, University of London, which is an institution of higher education that itself grew out of a particular instance of opening almost 200 years ago. The case study will illustrate the senses in which Birkbeck, along with the particular case of practice under study, is characterised by an interplay of openings and closures.

1 Opening Moves in Education

> 'Open education' often carries the weight of describing not just policy, practices, resources, curricula and pedagogy, but also the values inherent within these, as well as relationships between teachers and learners. So is open education a slogan or a philosophy, a metaphor, model, or movement? (Cronin & MacLaren, 2018, p. 127)

The polyvalence of the term *open* has afforded it wide applicability in contemporary culture but also introduced a significant degree of ambiguity (Pomerantz & Peek, 2016). The application of this label suggests, but cannot in itself define, a worthy, positive goal. The actual nature of openness remains somewhat slippery. Indeed, Tkacz (2012) argues that forms of closure are both inherent to, and inevitably (re)produced by opening movements; consequently, he questions the utility of openness as concept, if not as rhetoric:

> All these individuals and groups understand their practices and ideas in relation to the open and use it to 'look forward'. [But] the open has not proven well suited to this task. Rather than using the open to look forward, there is a need to look more closely at the specific projects that operate under its name .... To describe the political organisation of all things open requires leaving the rhetoric of open behind. (p. 404)

While the open education movement is unlikely to welcome a call to expunge the use of 'open' from its discourse, it does appear that there is a troubling inconsistency in its application, and that the concept of openness warrants further investigation.

Certainly, in the higher education context, references to openness have recently proliferated, such that it is now differentiates apparently alternate versions of resources, courses, educators, and even practices. But before the turn of the millennium, mention of 'open education' or 'open learning' might very likely have called to mind an institution such as The Open University in the UK, Athabasca University in Canada, or UNISA in South Africa. Such institutions arose from a social mission to open up access to higher education study and qualifications, making use of distance and distributed education modes to reach students who either could not attend campus-based education at the places and times offered, or who lacked traditional entry qualifications (Peters, Gietzen, & Ondercin, 2012). The Open University is 'open' primarily in the sense that it seeks to extend the benefits of higher education to students who otherwise would not be served by the sector. Yet this university itself acknowledges and even celebrates the ambiguity of openness in its mission statement, which declares: 'The Open University's mission is to be open to people, places, methods and ideas' (Open University, n.d.).

Of late, a discursive shift appears to have introduced a markedly different notion of openness, which has quite rapidly become central to discussions of open education, and which is afforded through the granting of access to openly licensed or freely available digital content, delivered in the form of OER (including open textbooks), or MOOCs. Without discounting the value of such practices, it has been argued that in the process, openness is said to have 'acquired a sheen of naturalised common sense and legitimacy, and formed what seems to be a post-political space of apparent consensus' (Bayne, Knox, & Ross, 2015, p. 247). If open has become a value which is 'battled for,' whether because or in spite of its unstable meaning (Weller, 2014), it appears critical to interrogate the work that the label 'open' does in various contexts.

As Watters (2017) notes, stories and 'histories' can play a key cultural role as explanatory frameworks which account for how present conditions came about. Silicon Valley's educational technology narratives tend to be shaped in terms of the transformative and 'disruptive' roles technology has when acting upon education. At times in such histories (even when versions of them are taken up by champions of technology within institutions), education tends to be presented (along with the help of recurring motifs such as 'the Victorian classroom') as a conservative, essentially unchanging domain, lacking its own vision or drive to innovate.

While it is crucial not to confuse the goals of open educators with those which drive technology companies, it is noteworthy that open education narratives have tended to somewhat uncritically adopt a similar notion of the 'coming of the digital" as the great enabler and game-changer. Thus, accounts of open education's history tend to emphasise the dual influences of both the open access and free and open source software movements. It is also usual to highlight the decision by the Massachusetts Institute of Technology (MIT) to release large volumes of its learning resources as 'open courseware' as a model for the provision of open, modifiable educational materials in digital formats, leading to the coining of the phrase 'open educational resources' by UNESCO (2002). Such influences and milestones are of undeniable significance, and yet, strangely, until recently there appears to have been less discussion of the educational antecedents of today's digitally-focused open education movement, as if somehow education itself has contributed little to this project. In presenting a vision of educational openness that is necessarily digital, the existence of a necessarily *analogue and closed* opposite is implied, and while some practices appear widely accepted as legitimate exemplars of open education, while others are rarely discussed under this banner.

To describe something as being open is to rhetorically contrast it with that which is closed; perhaps even to raise a spectre of *closed-ness*, that only openness can exorcise. In essence, open movements, almost by definition, suggest that one must be *for* openness and, *against* closed-ness. Yet, open is not, after all, the true opposite of closed; rather, open indicates some degree of difference from closed. On closer inspection, openness is better understood a matter of degree or quality, rather than one half of a binary. The issues created by the apparent binary have not escaped the notice of the OER movement. Wiley (2009), for example, argues that openness is better understood as continuous. This conception of openness can be illustrated by the example of a door, which can be either open or closed, but where openness indicates many available degrees on a continuum. This continuum model certainly makes sense in the specific case of OER, which can be *more or less openly licensed* (for reuse or repurposing) depending on the permissions granted by the creator, but it fails to account adequately for exemplars which are *differently* open.

MOOCs provide a salient example of a different form of openness. The mainstream of MOOCs (sometimes known as 'xMOOCs'), can be characterised as content-driven online courses (as opposed to the community-driven emphasis of the original 'cMOOCs') (Weller, 2014). While MOOCs are therefore a form of 'open' digital content, their openness is often primarily one of enrolment – the learning materials contained within the MOOC platform may not be openly licensed (or, indeed, openly available, as one must typically register on the platform and enrol on the course). While some might consequently argue that MOOCs are not open, it is more accurate to say that their openness is different in form from the openness of OER (Czerniewicz et al., 2017). A MOOC typically creates an open opportunity for potential learners to enrol, to peruse the learning materials, to complete assessments, often to interact with other participants, and in some cases even to gain a degree of support in this process from facilitators. Yet this opportunity is nonetheless evidently also closed in certain other ways. It is closed to those who do not have reliable access to a device or connection that supports the use of the online platform, and it remains no less closed to those who have not yet gained the necessary levels of digital, language or academic skills to navigate, interact or learn within that environment. If one can surmount these barriers, the MOOC is open to be studied, but there can be further elements of closure. Those students who additionally wish or need to evidence their participation often must pay for a certificate, and after the MOOC ends, those who have not paid may not retain access to the course resources unless they have been made available or openly licensed for downloading, reuse or repurposing in other contexts. Attempting to determine whether MOOCs are less or more open than OER on a continuum appears futile; such cases evidence qualitatively different forms of openness, which are different again from the openness of an open university.

Adding nuance to this grey area: much of the discussion of openness has understandably focused on the modern phenomena of open courses, resources and universities, which have explicitly sought to appropriate the open label. Yet moves to widen educational access and participation can be traced back to the Middle Ages, and seen to recur under different guises, suggesting that openness has been an ongoing feature of educational practices, past and present, but that those practices have taken context-specific shapes (Peter & Deimann, 2013). Furthermore, alternate forms of openness continue to operate, for example in the sharing and reuse of resources 'without a licence' by educators who may be primarily concerned with the availability and applicability of resources, rather than with their legal openness (Amiel & Soares, 2016; Veletsianos, 2015). For Amiel and Soares (2016), there are two contrasting notions of 'the commons' in play: the legal versus the social.

While the sharing of unlicensed resources may not officially constitute engagement with OER, this can nonetheless be described as an open educational practice. Indeed, such practices would seem to be explicitly included under an open education umbrella by the Cape Town Open Education Declaration (2007), which stated:

> open education is not limited to just open educational resources. It also draws upon open technologies that facilitate collaborative, flexible learning and the open sharing of teaching practices that empower educators to benefit from the best ideas of their colleagues. It may also grow to include new approaches to assessment, accreditation and collaborative learning. Understanding and embracing innovations like these is critical to the long-term vision of this movement.

The Cape Town Declaration marked the beginning of a trend towards discussion of open education as a wider-than-OER set of 'practices,' which would be followed up by OEP definitions such as the following: 'practices which *support the (re)use and production of OER* through institutional policies, *promote innovative pedagogical models*, and *respect and empower learners as co-producers* on their *lifelong learning* path' (Andrade et al., 2011, p. 12, emphasis added). In this definition, OEP is positioned as inclusive of OER-openness (i.e., content that is openly licensed), but also as addressing aspirations to other *opens*, thereby encompassing a wider and more nebulous remit. This wider remit of OEP, untethered from a specific interpretation of open, is understood here to approach questions of pedagogic innovation, of educational power relations and empowerment, and also of the notion of lifelong (and perhaps we might add, life-wide) learning. This very 'open' definition of OEP consequently reconnects contemporary discussions of digital resources and practices with the values of open universities and suggests that education should neither be restricted to the young, nor focused solely on employment. OEP, understood in this way, has roots in OER, but also in networked, participatory scholarship and learning communities (Cronin, 2017; Cronin & MacLaren, 2018; Masterman, 2016; Nascimbeni & Burgos, 2016). These other open practices are sometimes likely understood by educators primarily as something else (blogging, social networking), rather than as 'OEP' or as something done in the name of openness.

While perhaps an emerging consensus now accepts that OEP encompasses a range of practices which act to open aspects of education, at the same time a kind of 'digital divide' persists. It appears that analogue forms of educational practice often tend to be regarded as self-evidently 'closed' – either unrelated to today's digital open practices or recognised only for ancestral roles. It is understandable that scholars and practitioners of digital education are particularly interested in digital content and practice, but this collapsing of open into digital is problematic. In addition to failing to account for multiple senses of open, it may unhelpfully serve to promote a perception of open education as something that occurs only within a particular silo of digitally-driven learning and teaching, thereby alienating colleagues who might be aligned, but focused elsewhere (such as widening participation or developing academic literacies).

Once an educational history is re-infused into the concept of openness, it becomes clear that openness does not simply flow inevitably from digitisation, and by implication, nor are analogue practices necessarily synonymous with closed-ness. As Edwards (2015) suggests, we must proceed from an understanding that educational 'openings' inevitably entail 'closures':

> Different educational practices involve … the interplay of openness and closed-ness which can be examined empirically. This is the case for all practices, whether face-to-face or digital. Initiatives to open education through the use of digital technologies therefore reconfigure rather than simply overcome the interplay of open-closed-ness. This is not to say that these initiatives cannot be beneficial, but they will be selectively so, as is the case with all educational practices. … An important question therefore becomes not simply whether education is more or less open, but what forms of openness are worthwhile and for whom. (p. 253)

This conception of an interplay of open and closed elements occurring across all instances of practice creates the possibility of a more holistic vision of practitioners, practices, and the spaces in which education takes place. Rather than casting the university as simply a site of traditional 'closed' education, it might perhaps be better understood as a complex ecology of practices. For Nardi and O'Day (1999), information ecologies are 'systems of people, practices, values, and technologies in a particular local environment' (p. 49). In an information ecology, systems and subsystems operate interdependently, supporting species diversity in different niches; keystone species are critical to the wider ecology; and as the ecology changes and evolves, species migrate in and out, and co-evolve (Nardi & O'Day, 1999). Drawing upon this model, Thorne (2016) argues that the open education movement has 'catalysed a revitalization of new developments within both open and for-profit educational sectors.' This notion can also be applied at the level of the individual institution, in which alternative learning and teaching modes may co-exist, occupying specific niches. Through this frame, a university is an ecology in which digital and analogue, and 'open' and 'closed' educational practices may well co-exist in interdependent, complementary ways rather than being positioned in opposition to each other.

2 Stepping Up: A Case Study

The complexity of openings and closures can be illustrated through examining a case study of practice within an institution which can be understood as at once, traditional, analogue and 'closed' in its emphasis on face-to-face mode teaching – and yet which perhaps should be understood as the UK's original 'open university.' This institution came into existence almost 200 years ago with the establishment of the London Mechanics Institute, by Dr George Birkbeck in 1823, and was later renamed Birkbeck College, before becoming popularly known as Birkbeck, University of London. While the college has evolved through numerous changes over the decades, it continues its original mission of making higher education available in the evening, in order to cater for an otherwise disenfranchised group of typically mature and part-time students who work during the day: a practice decried at the time as 'spreading the seeds of evil' (Birkbeck, University of London, n.d.).

Birkbeck, as an institution, might be described as largely untroubled by the modern-day, digitally-driven open education movement, but certainly emerged out of, and continues to pursue, an opening mission. Birkbeck is a university which is, quite literally, open in the evening. While this is quite a very specific form of openness, it is nonetheless a form. Unlike institutions which run classes during conventional business hours or asynchronously as distance learning providers, Birkbeck's historic approach openness recognises that many people who might wish to be students are at work during the day but may still prefer to attend face-to-face classes (notwithstanding the recent transformation to a default blended mode of provision supported by the digital content and platforms). Lower entry qualification thresholds compared with those at surrounding London institutions also act to enable access for a high proportion of mature and non-traditional students, as well as a substantial population of postgraduates who are often returning to study after many years away.

Of course, attending classes in the centre of London on weekday evenings is neither the only possible route to participation in higher education for such students, nor is it an option that is open to everyone. Birkbeck's evening students could instead opt for fully-online programmes (probably provided by other institutions), which would obviate the need for attendance at face-to-face classes.

For a variety of reasons, though, the majority of Birkbeck students prefer to time-shift their attendance at face-to-face classes into a slice of the day between six and nine p.m. – a time usually reserved for eating dinner, spending time with partners and friends, putting children to bed, working late, commuting home, or Netflix. The sacrifices involved in giving up such normal activities and bearing the significant costs of study in England suggest that these students value this face-to-face element, and survey results confirm that Birkbeck students rate the quality of their teaching highly.

In this context, face-to-face teaching in the evening has been seen and celebrated as the college's 'unique selling proposition.' Nonetheless, Birkbeck's digital education activity has quietly gone mainstream. Most modules[1] taught at Birkbeck now incorporate elements of online support or interaction, typically through Moodle and integrated services, so it could be said that 'blended learning' is already the norm; even so, Birkbeck modules have tended to remain face-to-face-centric, with supporting materials or assessment administration handled online. Unlike other institutions which have pursued digital delivery as a means to broaden enrolments beyond the immediate geographic area, at Birkbeck fully-online and online-led modules have remained the preserve of a small number of specific programmes. In between the face-to-face-centric and the fully online modules, there has been a mostly vacant ecological niche for online-led modules which contain face-to-face elements.

In 2012, with a view to investigating the potential of online-led blended learning, a cross-college group initiated a project in two phases. The group wished first of all to develop a generic, flexible, blended learning design compatible with Birkbeck's approach to teaching and student support. The second phase would involve the development of a pilot module, which would become known as 'Step Up to Postgraduate Study in Arts' (henceforth referred to as Step Up), and which would enable a trial run of the generic design. In doing so, the group also sought to address an issue of wider concern in the college at the time of the project's commencement, which was the recruitment, retention and success of students in postgraduate programmes. While acceptance into a postgraduate programme might usually be taken as an assurance of graduate-level academic capabilities, in practice many incoming Birkbeck postgraduates are returning to study after long breaks, while at the same time attempting to balance the demands of study with significant work and family commitments. Academic skills training for potential or accepted (but still pre-sessional) postgraduates was identified in the bid as a gap in existing provision, and addressing this gap appeared to offer a potential route to support recruitment, retention and achievement.

The team applied and were awarded several days of support from two consultants and during the first half of 2013 the project team met regularly. Discussions focused on the educational possibilities enabled by digital learning technologies, as well as the common or typical features of education at Birkbeck, and the needs and expectations of Birkbeck's diverse student population. The team were keenly aware of there being a difference between the values that underpin a Birkbeck education (which might be described as 'open') and a typical approach to teaching at Birkbeck. While evening face-to-face classes might be perceived as core to the experience, students also already tended to rely upon the use of the virtual learning environment to support delivery of learning materials, such as digitised readings and lecture slides. Coursework components, particularly assessment, marking and feedback, had become increasingly digital. Birkbeck students should not therefore be construed as opposed to the online, so much as devotees of the face-to-face. The project team were nonetheless wary of how a student who deliberately opts for a face-to-face-led programme would respond to the 'unexpected' inclusion of an online-led module, especially given that this would form a pre-sessional introduction to studying at the college.

Although aware and somewhat inspired by the pervasive 'MOOC mania' of the moment, the project team did not set out to create a massive, open, or fully online course. It was felt that opening the module beyond the target group of Birkbeck's own incoming postgraduates would present too great a challenge in terms of limited staffing resources to communicate with participants and mark submissions, which were judged as necessary features of the supportive experience the team were aiming to offer. Therefore, the module was designed to be free to invited participants rather than open, and mostly but not fully online, with face-to-face events launching and closing the module and acting as bookends of the study period. The guiding principle of the model's development was therefore *flexibility*, rather than openness, which as Oliver (2015) notes, 'has also been used to question the forms and practices of higher education and has arguably generated better-developed insights' (p. 369). The team drew on their own experiences of teaching and supporting learning at Birkbeck, as well as the expertise of the consultants, in order to frame some guiding principles of a bespoke flexible, blended approach:

- Class time is limited, and therefore is to be used carefully, mostly for interactive, community-building activities; information provision in class will be kept to a minimum, and all key information must be accessible online.
- Content delivery, self-access learning activities, and assessments can be accessed and completed online, asynchronously, in the order and at the pace of student's choosing.
- Multiple 'assessment opportunities' rather than a deadline will be provided, in order to support Assessment for Learning principles.
- The online environment should be designed to foster both reflection and interaction (e.g. through synchronous online events, as well as forums and journals).

The module first opened for students in July 2013, and thus far, has run again each subsequent summer. During the original run, members of the project team presented a conference workshop entitled 'Special Blend,' highlighting the ways in which a version of blended learning had been configured to work in the particular context of Birkbeck and its diverse student body (Havemann et al., 2013). Here, the team drew upon the typical, rather vague notion of 'blended' as indicating a mix of analogue and digital elements (Dziuban et al., 2018; Oliver & Trigwell, 2005). Yet the module might also be understood as blended in the sense of its blending of openness and closed-ness. Step Up is a taught module rather than an OER or a MOOC, and although the module does make use of OER from Birkbeck and elsewhere, its openness might appear dubious through the usual frames of open licensing or massiveness. However, when examined through the lens of OEP, it is possible to see that educational spaces are opened in the learning and teaching of Step Up.

For Pomerantz and Peek (2016), *open* is used to stand in for a wide range of distinct concepts. One of the most salient for this discussion is the notion of *open as participatory*. Where acknowledged barriers to participation in an educational context exist (for example, formal higher education programmes which charge fees or require entry qualifications), then these contexts can tend to be classified as 'closed' within the rhetoric of open education. Alternatively, OER and MOOCs are considered to widen the circle of participation, as access to them is free of charge. However, the implication that the ability to engage in OER reuse or MOOC-based learning is universal is problematic and elides the difference between access to learning materials and 'education' (Gourlay, 2015; Knox, 2013). Even leaving aside the disappearance of the teacher within such models, in order to access OER or participate in a MOOC, a learner requires digital devices and connectivity, coupled with a range of pre-existing literacies. The preponderance of English as a supposedly sufficient *lingua franca* for a global open education also belies universality.

The qualifying threshold of openness therefore surely cannot be a requirement to enable 100% access, let alone participation, even if this could actually be possible. The provision of freely accessible or modifiable learning materials represent a public good, even if such materials cannot claim or reasonably be expected to achieve universal reach. Thus, while a move towards openness may enlarge the circle of participation, it does not eliminate this boundary altogether which continues to both include and exclude. This suggests that acting to widen participation while recognising or imposing a particular set of limitations, is actually a normal, rather than aberrant, condition of openness.

In light of this, the case of Step Up is perhaps less closed than it might first appear. There are barriers to participation, in that students must be intending to enrol in a postgraduate programme at Birkbeck, but the module itself is free of charge. Keeping the module focused on the target group, rather than offering it as a MOOC, lowers the quantity of participation but arguably enables a more impactful experience for those who do participate, as this allows a small team of educators to interact online with the participants, give personal feedback on their assessments, and run face-to-face events.

Indeed, rather than operating from an assumption that more participants and higher levels of participation are always desirable, Step Up deliberately calls on students to participate only to the extent that they find productive or are able. In designing an optional, non-credit-bearing module to be studied over the summer, the team were concerned not to place unreasonable demands on students' time. Instead they are encouraged to engage selectively, in the order they choose. Self-assessment quizzes are designed to give an indicative sense of the student's prior knowledge of the topic of each learning unit. Students are encouraged to complete the marked assessments they find challenging in order to benefit from feedback, rather than target activities they are confident they can do. As such, the module might be described as less participatory than others where there is more compulsion and structure, but can also be understood, in keeping with some definitions of OEP, as empowering students to structure a personal pathway through the learning activities, with a view to the enhancement of skills but also the development of learner autonomy and independence which will be key to success in their postgraduate studies.

A further element of participation is students' active engagement in feeding back their experience of the module via the online 'reflection room' or social forum, as well as during the final face-to-face event. From the outset, the team presented Step Up as a work in progress; an experimental and evolving module which invited students as collaborators. Interestingly, the most frequent critique of the module has been to point out that no one realistically has time to complete all the material provided.

The openness of Step Up has also been evidenced in the commitment of the original team to share this evolving form of practice with colleagues, through workshops, invited talks and informal conversations, and through granting access to past iterations of the module. While the module itself has been successful in attracting a good proportion of those entering postgraduate programmes in Birkbeck's School of Arts over the past six summers, it has taken time for the flexible blended design it is based upon to propagate, but it is now evolving into different forms both within and outside of the original niche. Slowly but surely, this interest has grown, and elements of the approach have become more widely adopted, including the emergence of a sibling module,

'Step In to Undergraduate Study in Arts' and a cousin, 'Step Up to Postgraduate Study in Business.'

The intention in presenting this short case study has not been to claim that Step Up represents a cutting-edge innovation in the field of digital education, or that it necessarily pushes at the boundaries of openness. Instead the case study highlights that Step Up is remarkable in having taken root within a particular institutional ecology, one which can be understood as 'already open' in its mission to serve a non-traditional student community, but in which a blended, mostly online mode of learning and teaching has struggled to find a supportive niche in which to flourish. Step Up has finally established itself within the wider ecology and demonstrated that open practices can invite the migration of pedagogies as well as resources to new niches.

3 Conclusion

This chapter has questioned aspects of the rhetoric of the open education movement rather than the valuable work it does. Freely accessible and modifiable learning materials and free (even low-cost) online courses are public goods, even if they can neither claim – nor reasonably be expected – to achieve universal reach. However, in addition to generating these evident outputs, the open education movement has played a crucial role in 're-opening' the discussions about what it means to describe some aspect of education as *open*. The recent turn to practices, in particular, offers a critical lens through which to examine opening moves in education.

The purpose of the case study presented, similarly, was not to argue that Step Up to Postgraduate Study in Arts is any more or less open than an OER or a MOOC, but rather to question the utility of such claims. In rejecting a binary, either/or model of open and closed practices as oversimplified, neither should we readily accept the notion of a more/less continuum between these two poles. Instead, as we work toward a theory of open educational practices, it may be most productive to conceive of instances of educational practice as always *both/and*, deriving from an interplay of open and closed elements. Language evolves and gains meaning in use; it is therefore perfectly legitimate to apply the label 'open' to certain activities simply because they have become widely understood as such. Yet this should not be at the expense of other educational practices being unhelpfully labelled 'closed.' The close current association of the idea of openness with the digital allows a problematic slippage between digital and open, analogue and closed, which can lead to assumptions that simply embracing the digital is a sure pathway into a naturally and benevolently open future. Such techno-utopian tendencies now need to be tempered by observations that the wider social trend is that digital technologies are providing the key route to open up and exploit new markets for profit, at times at the expense of citizen privacy and the reduction of complex social phenomena to mere data points, at the risk of algorithmic redlining, and perhaps of irreparable damage to an already fragile public sphere.

Rather than using the language of open to 'look forward,' we might instead look to the present, imperfect world, and keep with us an awareness of the ways in which openings might harm as well as heal, and closures might protect as well as exclude. Simple binaries of closed and open, analogue and digital, where one half is always valorised, do not serve us well in navigating the choppy waters of contemporary education.

Note

1 In the United Kingdom, a single unit of study that contributes a specified number of credits towards a qualification is usually known as a 'module,' whereas the term 'course' might refer to an entire programme of study, such as a degree or diploma.

References

Andrade, A., Ehlers, U.-D., Caine, A., Carneiro, R., Conole, G., Kairamo, A.-K., ... Holmberg, C. (2011). *Beyond OER: Shifting focus to open educational practices: OPAL Report 2011*. Retrieved from http://duepublico.uni-duisburg-essen.de/servlets/DerivateServlet/Derivate-25907/OPALReport2011_Beyond_OER.pdf

Atenas, J., & Havemann, L. (2015). From open data to OER: An unexpected journey? In J. Atenas & L. Havemann (Eds.), *Open data as open educational resources: Case studies of emerging practice* (pp. 22–25). London: Open Knowledge – Open Education Working Group. http://dx.doi.org/10.6084/m9.figshare.1590031

Bayne, S., Knox, J., & Ross, J. (2015) Open education: The need for a critical approach. *Learning, Media and Technology, 40*(3), 247–250. http://doi.org/10.1080/17439884.2015.1065272

Birkbeck, University of London. (n.d.). *History of Birkbeck*. Retrieved from http://www.bbk.ac.uk/about-us/history

Brennan, K. (2016). The Victorian MOOC. *Hybrid Pedagogy*. Retrieved from http://hybridpedagogy.org/the-victorian-mooc/

Campbell, L. (2015). *Open Silos? Open data and OER*. Retrieved March 10, 2018, from https://lornamcampbell.wordpress.com/2015/06/08/open-silos-open-data-and-oer/

Cape Town Open Education Declaration. (2007). *The Cape Town open education declaration*. Retrieved from http://www.capetowndeclaration.org/read-the-declaration

Cronin, C. (2017). Openness and praxis: Exploring the use of open educational practices in higher education. *International Review of Research in Open and Distributed Learning, 18*(5), 15–34. http://doi.org/10.19173/irrodl.v18i5.3096

Cronin, C., & MacLaren, I. (2018). Conceptualising OEP: A review of theoretical and empirical literature in Open Educational Practices. *Open Praxis, 10*(2), 127–143. http://dx.doi.org/10.5944/openpraxis.10.2.825

Czerniewicz, L., Deacon, A., Walji, S., & Glover, M. (2017). OER in and as MOOCs. In *Adoption and impact of OER in the Global South* (pp. 349–386). Cape Town & Ottawa: African Minds, International Development Research Centre & Research on Open Educational Resources for Development. http://doi.org/10.5281/zenodo.1094854

Dziuban, C., Graham, C. R., Moskal, P. D., Norberg, A., & Sicilia, N. (2018). Blended learning: The new normal and emerging technologies. *International Journal of Educational Technology in Higher Education, 15*(1), 3. http://doi.org/10.1186/s41239-017-0087-5

Gourlay, L. (2015). Open education as a 'heterotopia of desire.' *Learning, Media and Technology, 40*(3), 310–327. http://doi.org/10.1080/17439884.2015.1029941

Havemann, L. (2016). Open educational resources. In M. A. Peters (Ed.), *Encyclopedia of educational philosophy and theory* (pp. 1–7). Singapore: Springer Singapore. http://doi.org/10.1007/978-981-287-532-7_218-1

Havemann, L., Johnston Drew, L., Barros, J., & Leal, J. (2013, July 22–23). *Special blend: Developing a model for technology-enhanced, flexible learning*. Can We Do It? Yes We Can: HEA/SEEC Conference, London, UK. Retrieved from http://eprints.bbk.ac.uk/8710

Jordan, K., & Weller, M. (2017). *Openness and Education: A beginners' guide*. Milton Keynes. Retrieved from http://go-gn.net/go-gn/openness-and-education-a-beginners-guide/

Knox, J. (2013). The limitations of access alone: Moving towards open processes in education technology. *Open Praxis, 5*(1), 21–29. http://doi.org/10.5944/openpraxis.5.1.36

Longstaff, E. (2014). The prehistory of MOOCs: Inclusive and exclusive access in the cyclical evolution of higher education. *Journal of Organisational Transformation & Social Change, 11*, 164–184. https://doi.org/10.1179/1477963314Z.00000000028

Nardi, B. A., & O'Day, V. (1999). *Information ecologies: Using technology with heart*. Cambridge, MA: MIT Press.

Oliver, M. (2015). From openness to permeability: Reframing open education in terms of positive liberty in the enactment of academic practices. *Learning, Media and Technology, 40*(3), 365–384. http://doi.org/10.1080/17439884.2015.1029940

Oliver, M., & Trigwell, K. (2005). Can 'blended learning' be redeemed? *E-Learning and Digital Media, 2*(1), 17–26. http://doi.org/10.2304/elea.2005.2.1.17

Open University. (n.d.). *The history of the OU.* Retrieved from http://www.open.ac.uk/about/main/strategy-and-policies/history-ou

Peter, S., & Deimann, M. (2013). On the role of openness in education: A historical reconstruction. *Open Praxis, 5*(1), 7–14. http://doi.org/10.5944/openpraxis.5.1.23

Peters, M. A. (2014). Openness and the intellectual commons. *Open Review of Educational Research, 1*(1), 1–7. http://doi.org/10.1080/23265507.2014.984975

Pomerantz, J., & Peek, R. (2016). Fifty shades of open. *First Monday, 21*(5). Retrieved from http://www.ojphi.org/ojs/index.php/fm/article/view/6360/5460

Roberts, V., Blomgren, C., Ishmael, K., & Graham, L. (2018). Open Educational Practice (OEP) in K-12 online and blended learning environments. In R. Ferdig & K. Kennedy (Eds.), *Handbook of research on K-12 online and blended learning* (pp. 527–544). Pittsburgh, PA: ETC Press.

Rolfe, V. (2017). Striving toward openness: But what do we really mean? *The International Review of Research in Open and Distributed Learning, 18*(7). http://doi.org/10.19173/irrodl.v18i7.3207

Thorne, S. L. (2016). Epilogue: Open education, social practices, and ecologies of hope. *Alsic, 19*(1). Retrieved from http://journals.openedition.org/alsic/2965

Tkacz, N. (2012). From open source to open government: A critique of open politics. *Ephemera, 12*(4), 386–405. Retrieved from http://www.ephemerajournal.org/sites/default/files/12-4tkacz_0.pdf

Veletsianos, G. (2015). A case study of scholars' open and sharing practices. *Open Praxis, 7*(3), 199–209. http://doi.org/10.5944/openpraxis.7.3.206

Veletsianos, G., & Kimmons, R. (2012). Assumptions and challenges of open scholarship. *The International Review of Research in Open and Distributed Learning, 13*(4), 166. http://doi.org/10.19173/irrodl.v13i4.1313

Watters, A. (2017, November/December). Memory machines and collective memory: How we remember the history of the future of technological change. *Educause Review.* Retrieved from https://er.educause.edu/articles/2017/10/memory-machines-and-collective-memory

Weller, M. (2014). *The Battle for open: How openness won and why it doesn't feel like victory.* London: Ubiquity Press. http://doi.org/10.5334/bam

Weller, M., Jordan, K., DeVries, I., & Rolfe, V. (2018). Mapping the open education landscape: Citation network analysis of historical open and distance education research. *Open Praxis, 10*(2), 109–126. http://doi.org/10.5944/openpraxis.10.2.822

Wiley, D. (2009). Defining 'open.' Iterating towards openness [Blog post]. Retrieved from http://opencontent.org/blog/archives/1123

CHAPTER 15

Fostering Openness within a Higher Education Institution: Tensions, Opportunities and a Work in Progress

Elizabeth Childs, Jo Axe, George Veletsianos and Keith Webster

At our institution, the authors have engaged in open practices and have sought to promote a culture of openness. In this chapter, we discuss factors that we have identified as fostering a culture of openness at school, faculty, and university levels, and we investigate the tensions and challenges experienced in developing a culture of openness.

We approach openness as a dynamic and negotiated space which encompasses 'collaborative practices [including] … the creation, use and reuse of OER, as well as pedagogical practices employing participatory technologies and social networks for interaction, peer-learning, knowledge creation and empowerment of learners' (Cronin, 2017, p. 10). Though openness is often assumed to be a democratizing approach to education, scholars have noted that its practice appears to be complicated and unequal (Gourlay, 2015; Veletsianos & Kimmons, 2012). This chapter contributes to the conversation about what openness looks like in practice. We believe that openness in practice is much more complex than advocates note, and we anticipate that by sharing our experiences, other practitioners who are exploring open practices at their own institutions will benefit. This chapter is divided into four sections: context, factors contributing to a culture of openness, tensions and challenges encountered in enacting openness, and the conclusion.

1 Our Context

Open practices are an emerging and sociocultural phenomenon situated in particular environments. As a result, open practices are shaped by the environments in which they are enacted, while concomitantly shaping those environments (Knox, 2013; Veletsianos, 2015). Therefore, this chapter situates its arguments in the context that framed our activities: the institution, the faculty, the school, and an MA degree within the school.

 | DOI: 10.1163/9789004422988_016

Royal Roads University (RRU) delivers predominantly graduate level programs to working professionals with an average age of 41 from a variety of sectors and geographic locations. Students bring a wealth of experience and connection to the world and their fields. After many years away from the formal education sector, many also have some trepidation about entering into an academic space as graduate learners, critical research consumers and creators. RRU degrees are delivered in blended format, with some programs being offered entirely online; and most programming is comprised of short on-campus residency experiences with the remainder of the degree being completed fully online using both asynchronous and synchronous approaches. Approximately 80% of courses are offered completely online, and at any given time about 65% of students are working in the online environment.

The university was established in June 1995. From its outset, it offered outcomes-based, blended and fully online programs that adopted a cohort model, placed team-based and applied learning as central to its educational approach, and used a learning management system (LMS) developed in-house. These approaches, while commonplace today, were viewed in 1995 with skepticism by some. As an institution that, for more than 20 years, has addressed challenges associated in widening access to non-traditional students, RRU has demonstrated a commitment to mediating the risks and building on the numerous affordances associated with using digital technologies in teaching and learning. From the earlier days using an in-house-created LMS, to its more recent designation as an Ashoka Change Maker campus (Royal Roads University, 2017a, para. 1), RRU has developed a culture that encourages experimentation, entrepreneurship, and innovation.

A key component of this culture, and one of the distinguishing features of RRU, is its institutional learning, teaching and research model (LTRM). The LTRM (Royal Roads, 2017b) identifies key elements that are common to RRU's distinctive learning, teaching and research activities including: outcomes-based; technology-enhanced; experiential and authentic; learning community; team-based; integrative; action and applied research; supportive and flexible learning. The model aims to foster the adoption of high-impact practices across the institution and is employed in course design as well as in strategic and academic planning. Having an overarching signature pedagogy (Shulman, 2005) that spans the university's programs and is taken up, in various degrees, by all units and aspects of the university, enables a variety of institutional stakeholders to work toward a common and shared goal.

Within this institutional context, the School of Education and Technology (hereafter the school), was launched in April 2013, with a mandate to offer related programming and pursue educational innovation. The opening of the school was itself a logical course of action for an institution of higher education with a unique provincial mandate to (1) offer certificate, diploma and degree applied and professional programming; (2) provide continuing education that is responsive to the needs of the local community; and (3) maintain teaching excellence and research that support the university's programs and are responsive to the needs of the labour market of the province of British Columbia (Royal Roads University Act, 1996).

In this context, the Master of Arts in Learning and Technology (MALAT) degree that is examined in this chapter is a variation of one of the earlier programs developed at RRU; it has been offered since 2000. The degree has been through several iterations since its inception and is currently offered in two formats: (1) fully online, and (2) blended, which has a two-week residency requirement including an online pre/post residency component; the remainder of the degree is completed fully online. The students from each format come together in the third course to work through the rest of the program as a larger community. Courses in the program are nine weeks long and each program offering runs consecutively for two years. The program has three exit pathways: thesis (primary research), research paper (secondary research), and a digital learning research consulting project.

In 2014, feedback provided by external reviewers identified that the MALAT program was in need of significant curriculum renewal if it was to remain competitive and relevant to potential students and employers. The program learning outcomes and assessment criteria required revisions in order to align with the requirements of the field and realities of the work environment, expectations of employers, and the competencies in use by professional accreditation bodies. The course content required updating and the course design was in need of a complete reconceptualization in order to reflect current understandings of creating engaging digital learning environments. Through extensive consultation in 2015 with multiple stakeholders, the program was redesigned based on the cross-curricular themes of openness, networked learning, and the development of a digital mindset. The current MALAT program is now founded upon principles of networked learning and open pedagogy, where students 'collaborate and contribute meaningfully to digital learning networks and communities in the field' and are equipped to 'create digital learning environments, and apply theoretical and practical knowledge to critically analyze innovations and assess their impact on organizations and society' (Royal Roads, 2017c, p. 1). The program redesign was informed by the following design principles: (1) personalization of learning – choice for students; (2) openness and the use of open educational resources; (3) collaboration and contribution to digital learning networks(s) and community(ies) using Web 2.0/3.0

tools and strategies; (4) digital mindset; (5) networked learning; (6) inquiry; (7) authentic learning and assessment; (8) inclusivity; (9) social justice; (10) contemporary, relevant learning outcomes; (11) academic rigor; (12) alignment with the school vision, and (13) alignment with the RRU learning, teaching and research model. These design principles emerged from a 2016 review of the research on open educational resources creation, adoption and use (Falconer, Littlejohn, McGill, & Beetham, 2016; Judith & Bull, 2016; Kimmons, 2016; Wiley, 2014); open pedagogy (Cronin, 2017; DeRosa & Jhangiani, 2017; Ehlers, 2011; Wiley, 2017); the development of digital capabilities (Beetham, 2015; Conference Board of Canada, 2016), and design thinking and intentional mindset (Crichton & Carter, 2015; Stanford University Institute of Design, 2016). It was the intention that upon completion of the graduate program, students would be able to engage more confidently in public discourse in an informed manner and from a critical education perspective in order to lead and support their organizations as they continually improve the learning experiences they offer. A series of research studies investigate faculty and student perception of openness, identifying faculty and student support requirements as they work and learn in more open, public spaces.

2 Factors Contributing to a Culture of Openness

In alignment with the RRU proclivity to adopt new approaches, tools, and techniques for the delivery of programs, the MALAT faculty began exploring openness as a design principle and considering the factors that would be critical to the success of a move towards openness. Openness as a design principle provided the lens through which all design decisions (for example, program, course, activities, assignments, readings, delivery, infrastructure, and interactions) were viewed. This ensured a consistent approach which allowed for more flexibility in the program design than if openness had been an 'add on.' The process of this redesign prompted reflections on the institution's culture of openness, the necessary levels of support for the MALAT redesign, and the tensions and challenges faced along the way. The factors contributing to a culture of openness are examined below and, while they represent the authors' authentic experiences at a particular point in time and within a particular context as they *modelled the model* of a program designed around openness, networked learning, and digital mindset, we are cognizant that this is not an exhaustive list. While the literature may expand on these factors, we have chosen to focus and discuss the issues based on our lived experiences of the journey into openness in the MALAT program at RRU. We hope that by doing so, we provide an authentic picture of implementation that can be used by others facing similar situations.

2.1 *Accurate Reading of the Institutional Culture to Identify Obstacles and Mediate Risk*

There are two aspects of this: (1) the school's ability to engage experts, both within the university and beyond; who would enthusiastically drive the design, development, and facilitation of courses, and (2) the ability and aptitude of the school to pursue this new direction and move ideas into action. These two considerations relied on the capability of the school to build on its existing strong working relationships with the Centre for Teaching and Educational Technologies, as well as with other key university units and committees, including the Library and the Curriculum Committee. These relationships, together with the ability to connect with external experts familiar with the challenges associated with open practices, provided a strong foundation for the discussions that ensued regarding pursuing openness as a design principle for the MALAT program. Some of the ways in which the power of these relationships was manifest included working with external stakeholders to identify potential difficulties and collectively brainstorming strategies to work around them or plan for them. A specific example of this was the challenge of finding associate faculty (sessional instructors) who had a similar understanding of the cross-curricular themes of openness, networked learning and digital mindset that were being taken up by the program; and who were willing and able to operate in this ambiguous, ill-structured space, while also designing courses that required them to operationalize this emerging definition.

2.2 *Insightful and Supportive Leadership at Multiple Levels of the Organization*

Having the school positioned as an innovation hub at RRU allowed the conversations, with various levels of leadership, about openness and the MALAT redesign to be approached with a sense of experimentation and possibility. Working with a cross-unit leadership team was critical given the emergent nature of the definition of openness and the need for the design of this program to align with the institutional pedagogical model. In this process, faculty from the school collaborated with individuals from the following units: Vice-President Academic and Provost, Centre for Teaching and Educational Technologies, the Library, and Information Technology (IT) services. By contextualizing the work of the MALAT redesign as a living example of a curricular innovation that was an alternative way of realizing the RRU teaching and learning model, the redesign team was able to demonstrate RRU's ability to continue to innovate in the area of digital learning. For example, the redesign was positioned as an opportunity to push the university to a different level of thinking, to explore new opportunities with regards to pedagogy, delivery, and the use of social media. The redesign elevated the need to be able to create learning environments that fostered the students' ability to become valued members of digital learning networks and communities in ways that extended beyond the traditional boundary of the institutional LMS. By having consultative relationships with key areas of leadership, the design team was able to illustrate the alignment of the redesign with achieving the goals of the LTRM, and in so doing, gain support and realize synergies. One example of this was the ability to piggyback on a WordPress eportfolio pilot that was occurring through the Centre for Teaching and Education Technologies and IT Services. This enabled the transfer of courses that were traditionally housed in the institutional LMS to a WordPress environment, in addition to the creation of individual WordPress blog instances for program students. Extending the RRU learning environment beyond the boundary of the institutional LMS constituted a major shift for the institution and, at the time of writing, would still be considered a pilot of an alternative learning ecosystem for RRU.

2.3 *Building Relationships with Those Who Are Charged with Pursuing Openness*

A main factor that has contributed to the development of a more open culture at the institution has to do with the trust that was placed in the capabilities of those who were in charge of pursuing open practices programmatically. Openness is an emerging practice at the institution, and as we will describe below, there are numerous tensions and challenges associated with its pursuit. Nonetheless, when school faculty and the cross-unit redesign team saw pedagogical opportunities in open practices and alignment with the LTRM, it immediately became apparent that the relationships that had developed over the years between various stakeholders would be extended to this endeavour. In particular, team members who were less experienced in open practices valued, involved, and drew upon colleagues who were more experienced to lead and support them in these endeavours. Importantly, individuals who were part of the redesign team explicitly expressed their trust in the team and the process they were following; in this case, trust was defined as shared goals, shared focus, respect, and value alignment. The end result was to pursue this initiative knowing that it was supported, valued and respected.

One of ways this was achieved was by having a thoughtful plan and an organized approach to the redesign that aligned and was supported by the university's internal processes for formalizing program development and ensuring quality assurance. With the support of the university executive, a redesign team participated in an intensive program planning workshop which resulted in the development of a clear vision and goals for the program. These goals directly aligned with the LTRM. The program vision and goals were then translated across the program learning outcomes, course goals, course learning outcomes, and aligned to course activities and assessments. Approaching the redesign systemically, the redesign team members then worked with members of their units to develop ways to achieve the program vision and goal. Drawing on, and valuing, the experiences of the different voices represented around the redesign table, as well as those external to it, allowed for a richer, more responsive program design to emerge. One of the ways in which this was achieved was by publicly sharing draft course design documents for feedback and input from the wider professional network through an open, comments-enabled Google document. This provided an opportunity for current faculty, associate faculty, alumni, external experts in the field, representatives from other disciplines and professions, and the general public to contribute their voices to the conversation. This act provided us with an early opportunity to test some of our own internal assumptions and beliefs about a more open approach to program design and resulted in the development of community of support for this work within and beyond the institution.

2.4 *Embracing Humility and Criticality*

Even though we saw pedagogical opportunities in an innovative approach to the redesign of MALAT, we were also cognizant of the fact that the history of pursuing pedagogical innovations and practices in education is fraught with tensions and challenges. Having an understanding of the history of educational technology, instructional design, and the pursuit of innovative practices in education ensured that we were approaching this endeavour without the rose-coloured glasses that are emblematic of the Silicon Valley ideology to educational technology (Veletsianos & Moe, 2017; Watters, 2015). From an early stage, therefore, the school accepted the fact that there would be risks in pursuing openness and potential mistakes that would need to be rectified.

In reflecting on these issues, we realized that a shared approach to our pedagogical endeavours embodied the idea of humility and criticality. Though we viewed the aim to re-imagine what a MA degree looks like with positive aspirations, we recognized that we could (a) learn a lot from others, and (b) not anticipate all outcomes and challenges. This recognition enabled us not only to support one another in these pursuits, but also to remain open to critical feedback from peers, administrators, and students. In going through this process, we realized that such feedback was consistent with our aspirations to 'be more open,' and to adopt not just frameworks to make content and materials reusable and remixable but also to embrace an open mindset to our adoption of open practices. Throughout the process, therefore, we sought to maintain a critical perspective, not only towards the curriculum and the design but also toward the idea of openness itself and the feedback we were receiving from others. We believe that our worldviews of humility and criticality contributed to developing not simply a culture of openness, but also a broader culture within the school as exemplified by William Pinar's (Kumashiro et al., 2005) contention that 'we scholars must treat each other with the same pedagogical thoughtfulness and sensitivity with which we claim to treat students in our classrooms, and with which we ask our students (prospective and practicing teachers) to treat theirs' (p. 266).

Critiquing the process used to enact openness, the outcomes of openness, as well as questioning openness itself, requires making caring and thoughtful reflections with an eye toward positive shared outcomes. Though we are only beginning to understand this shared quality at the time of writing, we recognize it in many of the interactions we had throughout the design and development of the program, and we realize its central position in fostering a culture of openness.

3 Tensions and Challenges

Of the many considerations associated with moving towards using openness as a design principle in the MA program, several areas of challenge – conceptual, practical and technical – were identified as we worked to develop a culture of openness. Examples of how these challenges are currently being navigated are discussed below.

3.1 *Conceptual Challenges*

3.1.1 Lack of Understanding of Terms

Early on in the development process, we identified a central challenge – a lack of understanding of terminology. Through a proliferation of terms associated with openness (e.g., open practices, open pedagogy, OER-enabled pedagogies, open access, and open science), lack of consensus in the literature (Wiley, 2017), confusion around the legal aspects of copyright vis-à-vis openness (Seaman & Seaman, 2017) and open-washing (Farrow, 2017), the average practitioner whose research is not in this area faces the daunting task of not only learning the language of open but also learning its associated nuances. In interacting with students, faculty, and administrators about our endeavours, we faced the three conceptual challenges discussed below.

There is a general lack of awareness of what the terms *open* means. When we in the school use the term *open,* we attach a specific meaning to it. When the term is used in day-to-day language outside of this community within our institution, we noticed that it was used to refer to one's willingness to be receptive and accessible to, or to be free, or offered at no cost. An example of this distinction could be an open course where debate is encouraged as opposed to an open course that allows individuals other than enrolled students to participate. In the context of the MALAT redesign, this challenge surfaced as the proposal moved internally through the various committees and approval bodies. While no formal change management process was used during the redesign, this multiplicity of definitions for what counts as open required ongoing discussions with all members of the redesign team as well as the internal approval bodies in order to inform, educate, and refine the terminology around open in the RRU context, as well as how it was being adopted in the MALAT program.

3.1.2 Open as a Continuum

The second conceptual challenge we faced was the tendency for individuals to view open as one state in a binary. Individuals perceived open and closed as two states, while we understood open and closed to represent a continuum of possibilities in which open and closed could be combined in myriad ways. Running in parallel was the tendency of learners, associate faculty and internal approval bodies to look to quantify open as a discrete thing with specific characteristics and applications. Moving to an understanding of a continuum of open (Kimmons, 2016) developed as we provided examples of course design decisions such as identifying the appropriateness of using the course WordPress blog and/or the Moodle discussion forums for various course activities, depending upon the perceived need for the product to be public or private.

3.1.3 Varied Perceptions of Openness

The varied understandings and differing perceptions of openness formed the third conceptual challenge. Though this challenge relates to the previous ones, we have categorized it separately to denote that even when individuals understood openness as a pedagogical practice, we encountered nuanced understanding of the term. Such nuanced perceptions of a shared goal posed challenges to developing a vision for an end-goal, but ultimately led to discussions that were necessary for the success of this endeavour. Working with our Centre for Teaching and Educational Technologies, we spent time delineating the various uses and types of understandings of open (for example, open access; open publishing; open scholarship; open educational resources; open pedagogy; open source) in order for the team to be able to make technical design decisions such as blog urls for the students in a way that was consistent with our intention for the program.

3.2 *Practical Challenges*

3.2.1 Risk of Reputation

Venturing into openness has been identified as being a journey into risk (Falconer et al., 2016; Judith & Bull, 2016). As is often a concern for organizations when adopting a new direction, there is a risk of blemishing the existing reputation; in this instance, the risk was not solely carried at the school level, but also had the potential for university-wide implications. Along with the aim to have students working more 'in the open' on their course activities came the fear that the RRU brand would be diminished; if students' work, with its potential imperfections, was on display, there was a possibility that there would be a negative impact on the university as a whole. To address this concern, work was done to re-examine the student Code of Conduct policy as the Social Media Consent policy was being developed in order to come to a clearer definition of student roles and responsibilities. This work resulted in changes to the course sign-on process, prompting students to formally accept these responsibilities.

3.2.2 Potential for Copyright Violation of RRU Library Resources

Another concern was the exposure of the university to copyright violation if students posted articles, in an open space, that they had downloaded through the university library database. In addition, there was a concern about student access to course readings if students and faculty were working in a non-password-protected environment. The topic of access to course readings arose due to the university process for confirming, prior to courses going live, that all links to readings and resources conformed to copyright requirements. If the readings were no longer housed in a password protected environment, then it would be possible for faculty and/or students to post additional resources that violated copyright constraints. Due to the severity of the potential implication of copyright violation, namely having the database rescinded from the RRU library, various mitigating strategies were developed and implemented. These included email communication to students; synchronous discussions about the topic at three points prior to the first course of the program; discussions with faculty and associate faculty to raise awareness and share processes for follow up, and involving the library in the online orientation to specifically speak to this issue. While addressing challenges relating to risk and liability was essential, there were other practical challenges that also required attention.

3.2.3 Resourcing

Factors relating to resourcing were of particular concern; in this context, resourcing took the form of support for faculty developing and teaching courses, support for students working in the open environment, the implementation of resources for different modes of delivery, and securing the resources necessary to ensure timely implementation. Given the nature of the proposed changes to practice, it was critical to ensure adequate resources were in place. The Centre for Teaching and Educational Technology staff worked closely with the school faculty as they moved forward with course design and development, providing guidance and supporting the faculty who had limited experience working in open environments. Faculty who were used to creating learning environments behind the walls of the institutional LMS were now being asked to shift their practices in ways that many had not yet experienced. The work done by Paskevicius and Forssman (2017), as outlined Figure 15.1, proved useful as a way to orient and guide discussions with faculty to provide them with the supports they needed in order to create courses exhibiting greater degrees of openness. In a similar vein, students were being asked to interact in a graduate setting in ways that many had not experienced before. Informed by the questions that were arising from faculty and students, the Centre for Teaching and Educational Technology staff developed documentation and resources to assist those using digital tools and working in more open, networked spaces.

When working in different delivery modes, concerns arose due to the need to house some resources and activities behind a password-protected wall within Moodle. In addition, institutional requirements to verify student access within the first seven days of the course required a Moodle timestamp. Therefore, the courses that were developed provided students with the ability to toggle back and forth between the open WordPress site and the closed Moodle companion site; while not ideal, it did allow the option for providing activities and resources in both open and closed environments.

In order to address these practical challenges, the university committed additional resources to aid in the timely development of courses, including assigning additional staff dedicated to the WordPress site development, as well as to faculty and student support. Given the complexity of the new direction for course development and implementation, these working partnerships were essential to the successful program launch; therefore, obtaining

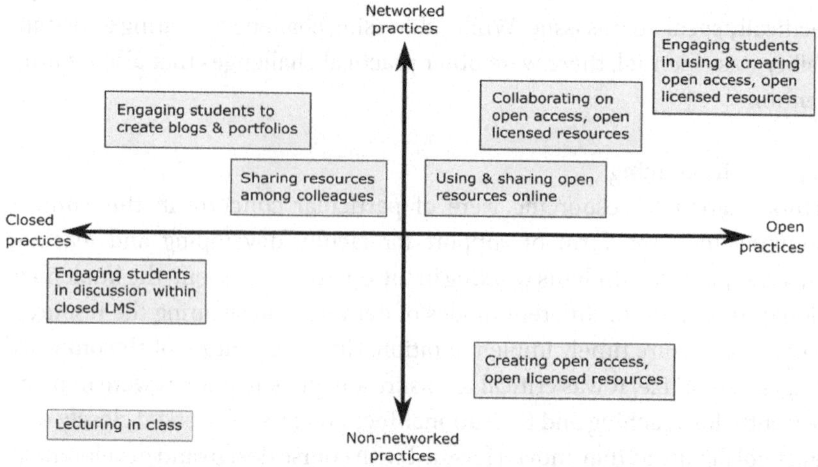

FIGURE 15.1 Openness and networked learning: From a developers' viewpoint (from Paskevicius & Forssman, 2017; https://www.slideshare.net/oeconsortium/the-role-of-educational-developers-in-supporting-open-educational-practices-72974912?ref=https://conference.oeconsortium.org/2017/presentation/the-role-of-educational-developers-in-supporting-open-educational-practices/; CC BY 4.0, https://creativecommons.org/licenses/by/4.0/;)

sufficient resources to ensure the course development and implementation was mandatory.

3.3 *Technical Challenges*

3.3.1 The WordPress Project

In implementing this environment, the MALAT program had the advantage of a WordPress project coincidentally underway to provide an eportfolio platform to several interested programs at the university. In expanding this WordPress project to accommodate an open MALAT program, the Centre for Teaching and Educational Technologies was able to provide instructional design and learning technologist assistance from staff with prior experience working with WordPress as an educational platform. Two MALAT WordPress instances, one for student sites, and one for course sites, were added to the official WordPress Project. The development and configuration of these WordPress instances was managed as a component of the larger project and, while the WordPress instances were kept relatively simple, full advantage was made of plugins and themes that enhanced their educational role. A key element of the design of this underlying platform was to keep as many options open as possible. For example, if an activity was too sensitive for discussion on the open Internet, then a forum within Moodle should still be a possibility. If an assigned project was mostly developed in the open as a stand-alone website, there might still be need for a discreetly submitted document in Moodle.

3.3.2 Learning Environment Integration

Three key spaces on the web for each student (Moodle, the course WordPress site, and his/her own WordPress site) plus the possibility of spending time on other student sites, meant that it was important that instructor communications arrive in a consistent form, in all the appropriate places, and in a manner that was timely but also retrievable later. The solution was for all instructor announcements to be made as posts within an Instructor Announcements forum in Moodle. This forum was configured to deliver each post to students by email. It also generated an RSS (real simple syndication) feed of these posts. The RSS feed could be used to republish the instructor announcements on the course WordPress site (using the WordPress plugin FeedWordPress) and, via a widget, in the side-bar menu of each student blog. This setup coincidentally furthered the principle of open – instructor announcements would be on the open course WordPress site, and the university's requirement to document the course – a record of instructor announcements – would persist on the course Moodle site. This was a critical requirement of the Office of the Registrar due to the RRU attendance policy.

As student use of the WordPress sites would mostly involve finding activities and resources on the course WordPress sites and creating materials, responses or engaging in discussion on the student blog sites, developing a way to connect these sites was important. There are typical methods of connecting these sites, such as lists of blog links and links back to course sites, but on the scale of a course with 30 students, how should a student or instructor efficiently navigate the emerging work and discussions occurring in so many places? RSS provided the bridge. Just as an RSS feed of instructor announcements could be used to re-publish these announcements on the course WordPress sites, RSS feeds of the relevant blog posts on each student's WordPress site could be used to re-publish them on the course WordPress site. The end result was a category of posts on the course site that included all blog posts placed by students in a specific course-related category on their own sites.

A more efficient method of reading and keeping track of student posts, as well as the comments on those posts, was still needed. By using a feed reader, students and instructors could easily track the new posts and comments they had yet to read. Using a web-based feed reader allowed users to collect and manage the content of many blogs in one place. Adding the RSS feed for relevant blog posts for each student site, and the RSS feed for comments on blog posts for student sites to their feed reader, gave each student, as well as the instructor, a single place to keep track of course activity.

Finally, in order to make the extensive use of RSS feeds by the instructor, students and support staff easier and less prone to human error, we used OPML (outline processor mark-up language) files to add many RSS feeds at once. These OPML files are collections of RSS feeds, and tools that make use of them can simplify the task of syndicating many feeds at once. Using OPML files syndicating all student posts for a specific course, or syndicating all comments on student posts, a student or an instructor can create a collection of feeds in a feed reader in seconds. This also enabled support staff to use this same OPML file of student posts for a specific course to establish the republishing of student posts in the course WordPress site. A feature of MALAT learning environment that can also be seen as a learning and teaching challenge is that students are free to discover the work of their peers at random. In some instances, discussion will emerge around one student post. With a feed reader syndicating comments from all student blogs, and presenting numbers of unread comments for each student blog, the instructor and other students are able to find the place where discussion is emerging and join in. Given the importance of learning community in the RRU institutional learning, teaching and research model, this was a critical technical challenge that had to be addressed.

Figure 15.2 depicts the MALAT learning ecosystem that was the result of taking these design constraints and technical challenges and viewing them in light of what could be done in order to achieve the program design principles and realize the shared vision for the program.

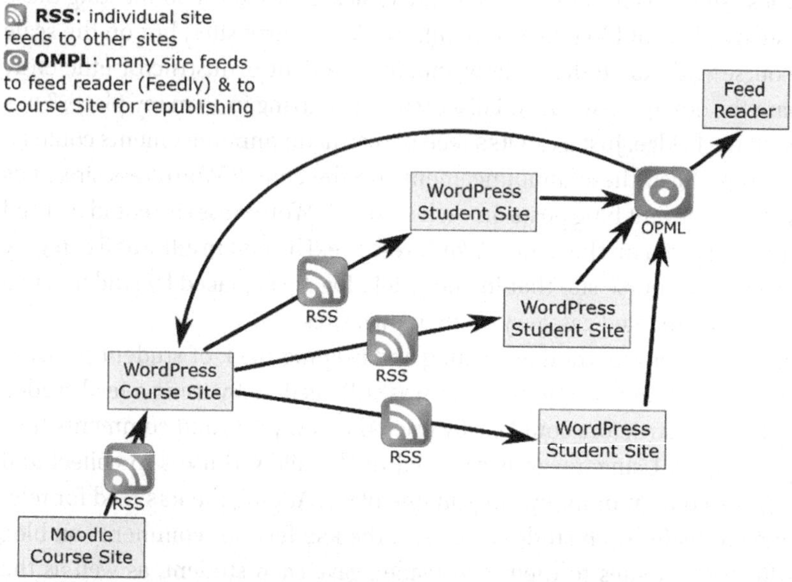

FIGURE 15.2 MALAT learning environment. (RSS Feed icon used under GNU license from the Mozilla Foundation. OPML icon used under a Creative Commons 2.5 license from Ken Rossi)

3.3.3 Privacy Issues

One factor unique to British Columbia's public post-secondary institutions is the FOIPPA legislation that governs the data privacy requirements for public institutions. This legislation requires that core web-based technologies used by students must reside on Canadian-based servers and that appropriate safeguards must protect students' personal information on these systems. To this end, a privacy impact assessment, completed for the WordPress project, found few serious risks to student privacy, and there were reasonable mitigation strategies for those that were found.

The WordPress instances established by the university were hosted at WPcloud which houses servers nationally. This, accompanied by typical safeguards, ensured that the WordPress systems were FOIPPA compliant. Users of the RRU WordPress instances authenticated with their RRU usernames and passwords. The Shibboleth protocol allowed university users to access third-party hosted WordPress instances with their institutional identity while sending only minimal identity data to the WordPress host. The use of WordPress sites as a connected learning environment invited differing levels of public exposure. Students were informed of data exposure possibilities upon logging into the WordPress system. One enhancement to the student blog system for MALAT was the adoption of numbered URL extensions in place of the username URL extensions applied to regular university WordPress sites. This allowed students that wanted to be substantially anonymous on the web to be so, while exploring the level of exposure they would eventually find comfortable.

3.3.4 Design Assistance to Leverage the Moodle/WordPress Ecosystem

The instructional design and technical challenges presented by the open MALAT program also offered an opportunity to develop a program-wide environment supporting learning that spanned traditional closed spaces and networked, connectivist spaces, where faculty and students mingled with outside experts and interested observers. The solution arrived upon was to use Moodle course sites as companion sites to WordPress-based courses and student WordPress blogs. This also presented the most flexible platform for as yet undiscovered learning design opportunities.

The desire to move towards open, along with the learning and technology content-orientation of the degree program, made WordPress an obvious choice. WordPress as a course site offered greater flexibility in displaying content and integrating outside resources, a place that easily included social media, simple re-publishing of content from student blogs and the course Moodle site, and a place for instructors to walk the talk of open. The design problem that then arose was 'what should reside in Moodle, on the course WordPress site, and on student blogs?' Further, in what ways should these places be connected? By walking through existing course activities and assignments, and then examining activities and assignments proposed for the revised program design, a map of the relationships between the course Moodle and WordPress sites and the student blogs was developed and was used to guide these design decisions.

The companion Moodle site also played an institutional role. It continued to be the place where assignment grades were submitted, and where final grades were calculated before moving on for formal approval. Moodle was the location for the copyright review, and the location of the course outline information that would form the official record of the course required by the Registrars Office. In these ways the revised MALAT program was able to retain an institutional footprint consistent with other university programs.

4 Conclusion

Embarking on the path of redesigning a graduate degree with cross-curricular themes of openness, networked learning and digital mindset has been rewarding and challenging. Institutionally, this work has raised awareness of the value and role of openness in cultivating innovative and responsive program design and delivery opportunities. It has demonstrated that there are a variety of ways in which learning environments can be designed that are consistent with the components of the institutional LTRM. It has also begun to cultivate a culture of openness by bringing together units across the institution to work on a shared goal and then consider how they might take up openness in their own unit. It has sparked a longitudinal research study investigating faculty and student perceptions of openness. The initial data analysis and preliminary findings have been presented at provincial, national and international conferences and used to inform design and revision decisions, student and faculty support, and a human-centred approach to program delivery. However, as identified above, entering into openness is complicated, in part due to the complexities involved in designing for an ill-structured, iterative and evolving space that is contextually constrained.

We recommend that those considering an openness initiative attend to relationships – both internal and external to the context. Take time to find and engage enthusiastic internal and external supporters and champions and build relationships with stakeholders. Identify and involve champions at all levels of the institution who: (1) have, and are able to support, a tolerance for calculated risk and ambiguity; (2) trust in the process and the shared goals that are cultivated when cross-unit teams work together towards a shared purpose, and (3) balance the pragmatics of the project with the requirement for thoughtful, caring and humble critical reflection. Foster an intentional mindset that is fuelled by curiosity and supported by nimble, lateral and connected thinking (Crichton & Carter, 2017). Ask for, and receive help when needed, and enter into the initiative with a fulsome understanding of research-informed lessons-learned that are relevant to your context.

The recommendations provided here are intended to help foster a culture of openness. They are a product of the lived experience of our journey on the continuum of openness. For those of you embarking on an openness initiative, we hope that these suggestions broaden your frame of reference of the possibilities and challenges and provide you with a more holistic portrayal of what is involved in cultivating a culture of openness at an institution with all of the complexities that are inherent in the act of implementation.

References

Beetham, H. (2015, November 10). Building capability for new digital leadership, pedagogy and efficiency [Blog post].

Conference Board of Canada. (2016). *Employability skills 2000+*. Retrieved from http://www.conferenceboard.ca/topics/education/learning-tools/employability-skills.aspx

Crichton, S., & Carter, D. (2015). Taking making into the schools: An immersive professional development approach. In M. Niess & H. Gillow-Wiles (Eds.), *Handbook of research on teacher education in the digital age* (pp. 412–438). IGI Global.

Crichton, S., & Carter, D. (2017). *Taking making into classrooms toolkit.* Retrieved from https://mytrainingbc.ca/maker/downloads/Taking_Making_into_Classrooms.pdf

Cronin, C. (2017, April, 20). *Open culture, open education, open questions*. Retrieved from http://ow.ly/L9ch30b2f41

DeRosa, R., & Jhangiani, R. S. (2017). Open pedagogy. In L. Mays (Ed.), *A guide to making open textbooks with students*. Rebus Foundation.

Ehlers, U.-D. (2011). Extending the territory. From open educational resources to open educational practices. *Journal of Open, Flexible and Distance Learning, 15*(2), 1–10.

Falconer, I., Littlejohn, A., McGill, L., & Beetham, H. (2016). Motives and tensions in the release of open educational resources: The JISC UKOER programme. *Australasian Journal of Educational Technology, 32*(4), 92–105. doi:10.14742/ajet.2258

Farrow, R. (2017). Open education and critical pedagogy. *Learning, Media and Technology, 42*(2), 130–146.

Gourlay, L. (2015). Open education as a 'heterotopia of desire'. *Learning, Media and Technology, 40*(3), 310–327.

Judith, K., & Bull, D. (2016). Assessing the potential for openness: A framework for examining course-level OER implementation in higher education. *Education Policy Analysis Archives, 24*(42).

Kimmons, R. (2016). Expansive openness in teacher practice. *Teachers College Record, 118*(9), 1–26.

Knox, J. (2013). The limitations of access alone: Moving towards open processes in education technology. *Open Praxis, 5*(1), 21–29.

Kumashiro, K., Pinar, W., Graue, E., Grant, C., Benham, M., Heck, R., ... Luke, C. (2005). Thinking collaboratively about the peer-review process for journal-article publication. *Harvard Educational Review, 75*(3), 257–285.

Paskevicius, M., & Forssman, V. (2017, March 8–10). *The role of educational developers in supporting open educational practices.* Paper presented at Open Ed Global, 2017, Cape Town, South Africa.

Royal Roads University. (2017a). *Royal roads designated Ashoka U Changemaker Campus.* Retrieved from http://www.royalroads.ca/news-releases/royal-roads-designated-ashoka-u-changemaker-campus

Royal Roads University. (2017b). *Royal roads learning and teaching model.* Retrieved from http://ctet.royalroads.ca/rru-learning-and-teaching-model

Royal Roads University. (2017c). *Master of arts in learning and technology.* Retrieved from http://www.royalroads.ca/prospective-students/master-arts-learning-and-technology

Royal Roads University Act Royal Roads University Act [RSBC 1996]. Chapter 409 Subsection 2. (2010). Retrieved from http://www.bclaws.ca/civix/document/id/consol21/consol21/00_96409_01#section2

Schulman, L. S. (2005). Signature pedagogies in the professions. *Daedalus, 134*(3), 52–59.

Seaman J. E., & Seaman, J. (2017). *Opening the textbook: Educational resources in the US higher education, 2017.* Retrieved from https://www.onlinelearningsurvey.com/reports/openingthetextbook2017.pdf

Stanford University Institute of Design. (2016). *Welcome to the virtual crash course in design thinking.* Retrieved from http://dschool.stanford.edu/dgift/

Veletsianos, G. (2015). A case study of scholars' open and sharing practices. *Open Praxis, 7*(3), 199–209.

Veletsianos, G., & Kimmons, R. (2012). Assumptions and challenges of open scholarship. *The International Review of Research in Open and Distance Learning, 13*(4), 166–189.

Veletsianos, G., & Moe, R. (2017). The rise of educational technology as a sociocultural and ideological phenomenon. *Educause Review.* Retrieved April 10, 2017, from

http://er.educause.edu/articles/2017/4/the-rise-of-educational-technology-as-a-sociocultural-and-ideological-phenomenon
Watters, A. (2015). *Ed-tech and the Californian ideology*. Retrieved from http://hackeducation.com/2015/05/17/ed-tech-ideology
Wiley, D. (2014). The access compromise and the 5th R [Blog post]. Retrieved from https://opencontent.org/blog/archives/3221
Wiley, D. (2017). OER-enabled pedagogy [Blog post]. Retrieved from https://opencontent.org/blog/archives/5009

CHAPTER 16

A Pedagogy of 'Small': Principles and Values in Small, Open, Online Communities

Tanya Elias, Laura Ritchie, Geoffrey Gevalt and Kate Bowles

Innovation in open teaching and learning has become increasingly attentive to the commercial potential for *scaling up* as witnessed by the growth of massive open online courses (MOOCs) since 2012 (Urrea, Reich, & Thille, 2017). This attention intensifies under conditions of austerity and disruption, as both educational institutions and their technology company partners search for new markets and new means of profitable operation, targeting learners locally and across the world to whom education can be delivered with maximum efficiency and minimum cost. Drafting open pedagogy into this effort is troubling and invites us to revisit poorly-cited open education theories from the 1970s (see Rolfe, 2016) in order to understand the ecologies that shape open learning in the present.

This chapter is influenced by early work in open pedagogy (Katz, 1972; Paquette, 2005; Spodek, 1970). Using two relatively small, non-profit platform projects as examples, our aim is to revisit the community-centered philosophy of open pedagogy found in this early work and to ask new questions about scale while searching for productive ways to release open learning practices from their current institutional harness. We begin with an introduction of key terms and then offer an overview of our two examples, #smallstories and Young Writers Project (YWP), and a brief description of our research methodology. Finally, using Paquette's (2005) value pairs as a foundation, we explore these case studies more fully using words gathered both directly from the sites and through interviews with participants. Combining these, we suggest and discuss the possibility that small open online communities enable peer-based pedagogy in ways that larger ones might not.

1 Ideas and Values

Before introducing the details of our research, it may be helpful to explore several foundational ideas and their underlying values that guide and serve as a framework for our research.

 | DOI: 10.1163/9789004422988_017

The foundational ideas drawn from Claude Paquette's (2005) summary of early open pedagogy provide a framework for this chapter and allow a structured understanding of the stories and processes that will be demonstrated in our examples. For Paquette (1979):

> Open pedagogy is centered on the class interaction between the student and the educational environment that is proposed. From this interaction, significant connections will be revealed for the student that will allow him/her to begin a learning process ... For the champions of open pedagogy, creating the educational environment has three levels: the creation of a physical class environment, learning activities, and instructor intervention. (p. 18)

Paquette (2005) further observes and reflects on three value pairs that constitute axes of negotiation in the open classroom: autonomy and interdependence, freedom and responsibility, and democracy and participation.

To summarize these value pairs briefly, autonomy and interdependence counterbalance one another creating the founding tension for peer-based open learning that requires learners to fashion their own autonomy in continuous negotiation with their community. Paquette then suggests that open learning is energized by student agency (freedom) but is tempered by the need for students to learn responsibility and to recognize that their choices interact with choices that others have already made or will make. Balancing freedom with responsibility extends the complementarity of autonomy and interdependence. Finally, democratic ideals bring the principle of freedom of speech to the open classroom including the freedom to speak controversially; this principle, however, requires ongoing active participation of students in the management of learning and in the resolution of disputes.

The online nature of our two examples amplifies these three tensions and transforms the context for their negotiation. Unlike traditional educational settings envisaged by the open pedagogy of the 1970s, open online spaces are asynchronous, translocational and even global in scope. Creating the possibility of group negotiation is a familiar challenge to any educator working in open, online spaces. In our two examples there are opportunities to moderate membership lightly or through blocking, and there are potentially both social and technical obstacles that users need to overcome. In general, however, these two small distributed communities do not offer the opportunity to gather users into a room to resolve a dispute.

Paquette summarizes open and participatory pedagogy as being constituted in the same tensions that enable communities like these to cohere: the balance that must be continuously adjusted between the operational values of the individual and the social or strategic priorities of the group. To Paquette, this focus on the negotiation between paired values defines open pedagogy as a community practice: continuously becoming, always incomplete, defended against complacency and radically opposed to standardization.

2 Ideas of Small

'Small' is a loose idea whose value is difficult to communicate with words especially in the current educational context, where institutional investment in efficiency combines with algorithmic innovation to promise economies of (massive) scale unbundled from labour cost. Much of this effort to scale up delivery without increasing costs ends up leveraging data and surveillance techniques used by commercial platforms. These include features such as personalization, automation, gamification and tracking that are familiar from what Chris Gilliard calls 'the only web most students know' (Gilliard, 2017, p. 64). Consequently, our definition of small includes what it is *not.* Small is not big and not commercial. It is not optimized or standardized; it is not derived, averaged, or calculated. Instead, it is personal, crafted and artisanal. Small is also often entails a delay in responses; it can be slow and inefficient.

Small offers an alternative to large, data-supported, corporatized approaches to education. It acknowledges the risks of scale and limits of quantification (Eisner, 2013) that have become normalized. Small offers a choice to those who have, either consciously or unconsciously, already experienced moments where 'the recipes [they have] inherited for the solution of typical problems no longer seems to work' (Greene, 2004, pp. 132–133).

What then might the potential of small be? Can small acts, small dollar amounts, small projects, small cultural shifts and small communities serve as paths to change or acts of resistance? Can small sites promote community and civility that foster learning and builds skills? What follows is a modest exploration of these questions using narrative and conversational enquiry within the online context of the #smallstories hashtag on the open-source social platform Mastodon and the community-led Young Writers Project (YWP).

3 Case Study Rationale and Significance

By using Mastodon's #smallstories and the YWP as our case studies, we chose two examples whose practices exemplify the principles of early work in open pedagogy, in particular the negotiation between individual and community needs which has been overlooked by recent analysis of open education (Rolfe, 2016). These two case studies serve as examples allowing us to connect the ideals and values of small communities and the potential for creating inclusive, sustainable, participatory peer learning environments in other contexts; by studying the ways in which smaller informal learning communities operate, we can see some new opportunities for these negotiations to be better managed in formal distance or classroom-based learning. As early adopters in Mastodon, we witnessed exploratory collaborative practices of prose, poetry, musical and creative remixing, and we noticed how small acts of monologue, provocation, and invocation led to rich dialogue. Within YWP, we noticed young writers making powerful connections with each other, demonstrating openness, learning, willing to take risks, and in effect, becoming one another's teachers.

4 Mastodon and #smallstories

Our first case is the #smallstories hashtag on the social platform Mastodon,[1] which is a relatively new, on-profit open source alternative to Twitter. It was built to connect users through a federated network of 'instances.' Each instance is an independent software installation run by its own administrator with its own focus, moderation policies, content hosting parameters, and language preference, each existing at its own scale. For example, the OERu, a nonprofit network that offers free online courses for students worldwide (OER, n.d.), has set up its own Mastodon instance and are fully in control of membership, its code of conduct and content moderation as stated explicitly on their instance homepage: 'This is the Mastodon instance for educators and learners involved in the OERu. Accounts of users not involved in OERu courses may be removed' (Lane, n.d.). Together, thousands of instances 'form a giant constellation of interconnected communities. Users from any server can read, follow, and reply to users on another server' (Lawson, 2017). Many Mastodon communities are small; federation makes an instance with a user of one quite feasible. Culturally, Mastodon favours strong moderation and community safety, in conscious opposition to Twitter's weak regulation of harassment (Cole, 2015). Its origins are connected to advocacy by and for LGBTIQ users (Hart, 2017). Some instances have a thematic focus, for writers or artists, for example. Mastodon also offers the potential to form loose communities around persistent hashtags, a practice that it shares with Twitter.

Though Mastodon is often compared to Twitter, there are several attributes that set it apart. The most often-cited difference is that Mastodon supports posts of up to 500 characters, with some Mastodon instances setting even higher character limits, as opposed to Twitter's recently extended 280-character limit. A Mastodon post can include up to four attached images as well as short videos. This has created a rich environment for visual artists, while the character length has also attracted many writers. Content warning labels support user autonomy in deciding what material they read; granular levels of visibility for posts express a nuanced understanding of the ways in which individuals and community negotiate what they choose to share, and with whom. Together, these features support users who choose to distribute explicit materials to do so in a way that ought not to abuse or traumatize others. None of these features is fully restrictive, however: the functionality of Mastodon's features depends on considerate use and awareness of potential sanction.

Mastodon has intermittently attracted attention from technology writers and social media commentators (see, for example, Newton, 2017, in *The Verge*). The early involvement of open and critical educators also led to articles on its potential to replace Twitter for educators concerned about harassment. Bali (2016) identifies reasons for educators to be interested in the project, including the fact that as open source software, anyone 'can contribute to how it works' and install and run it anywhere. She noted reflective conversations taking place and suggested value in content labelling. Lynds and Richards (2016) showed similar interest in the early potential of the project:

> Even if Mastodon is not long for this world, something with similar affordances will/should play into [Next Generation Digital Learning Environments]. As a GNU variant, we hope that more platforms and DIY solutions emerge. Our optics are around building competencies for users in environments that (hopefully) add value to people looking to engage and build meaning with others. (para. 1)

As well as offering educators user-control, Mastodon supports open and public networking in ways that are not possible on corporate-designed institutionally managed LMS platforms like Blackboard, Moodle, or Canvas. To educators concerned about students experiencing harassment, surveillance, or further erosion of privacy on social platforms or within learning management systems, an open source non-profit user-negotiated community platform may have significant appeal. Nevertheless, it is important to note that for many prominent open educators, Mastodon has not been convincing or engaging (Shaffer, n.d.). To the authors, this process of reflection and reservation is constitutive of the negotiation Paquette sees in open pedagogy: a willingness to entertain change while remaining critical of risks.

Between November 2016 and the end of 2017, the number of registered Mastodon users grew from under 10,000 to over one million on over 1,200 different instances (Grafana, n.d.). To avoid generalizing about the Mastodon project as a single entity, we have focused on a smaller, organic community of practice assembled around a persistent hashtag: #smallstories. This hashtag appeared modestly in late 2016, at a time when users actively explored the structure of Mastodon in conversation with one another and with its developer; tagging was another form of structural exploration. In a federated network, tagging functions differently than on a single-instance platform; its function as a lens on community activity is incomplete and varies according to networked connections made among followers across instances. Nevertheless, #smallstories fostered a small community of writers and readers who gather and celebrate stories of the everyday. By the end of 2017, more than 70 writers had contributed their stories and used the hashtag close to 800 times. #smallstories has also generated #smallpoems, with contributors sharing, commenting on or remixing found materials. We have chosen this example as the kind of outcome that open educators hope for and that is hard to design: the community that achieves independent identity and extends beyond the life of a particular course.

5 Young Writers Project (YWP)

Young Writers Project (YWP) was established with grant funding as an independent non-profit in August 2006, with a mission to help young people improve their writing skills. The organization has four program areas: a civil online community,[2] where young people share work, give and receive feedback, improve work for potential publication and take part in interactive workshops in writing and digital media; a Schools Project that includes a private digital platform, content and support for teachers to use in their classrooms; workshops both in school and after school; and publication of young writers' best work. Since 2006, YWP has connected with an estimated 110,000 young people; published or presented work of more than 17,000; provided professional development training – ranging from one-off workshops to yearlong master's credit courses – to 2,000 teachers; and has undertaken continuous self-review (Hall & Axelrod, 2014; Kotula, Tivnan, & Aguilar, 2014). Its founder explains its origins:

> In 1997, I was a newspaper editor and in a project we were working on I noticed that there was a profound difference between solicited submissions from students in 4th grade and those from 8th grade. The fourth

> graders' responses were fresh, emotional, interesting – and sprinkled with a few spelling, grammar and punctuation errors. The eighth graders' responses were similar, unemotional and boring – but they contained virtually no errors of grammar, punctuation and spelling. This led me to ask: What happens to the teaching of writing between 4th and 8th grades?
>
> I followed up. I interviewed teachers and students, and examined available research and data on the teaching of writing. I concluded that starting in about 5th grade, the teaching of writing in US schools tends to deaden interest and self-confidence, with resulting drop-offs in performance. ... This correlation between student attitudes to writing and writing performance has been borne out in subsequent years of surveys, statistics, observations and external research.
>
> So I started to look for a different way for young people to develop their writing skills and confidence. ... In 2006, Vermont Business Roundtable, a group of business and higher education leaders who recognize the importance of writing to success in school and business, offered a grant, and this enabled me to found the Young Writers' Project as an independent non-profit.
>
> YWP offers young people a non-judgmental and respectful space to accomplish four basic steps in writing: (1) explore and discover ideas until they find something that really interest them; (2) give and receive feedback and suggestions for improvement from peers and guides; (3) edit their work to make it better; (4) find authentic, external audience for their best work to affirm and motivate. In its school's platform, YWP encourages teachers to use their individualized, private digital classroom spaces for the practice of writing, for showing that writing can be *fun and for incorporating commenting into the curriculum.* (Gevalt, 2017)

For its first eight years, YWP only published work in a series of Vermont newspapers, radio broadcasts and websites. In October 2014, it developed a digital monthly publication,[3] and opened up its Web community to young people from anywhere. YWP has had over 40,000 users on *youngwritersproject.org* (Reid & Gevalt, 2017).

YWP is designed for user interaction; users can easily find and react to each other's work. Community members can sort by author name or genre, can comment and reply, and are notified via email or private message when one of their posts receives a comment; when their comment receives a reply; or when a post on which they left a comment has been revised. In YWP Workshops, a collection of interactive workshops – guided by experts or Community Leaders (approximately 50–60 youths are chosen each year based on their energy, activity and skill – each with a sequence of steps towards completion, content is not visible outside of the learning group, and all responses to the learning steps are coherently grouped and visible to promote interaction and to enable users to be less self-conscious about early drafts. YWP currently has approximately 4,000 active users whose ages typically range from 13 to18 years and whose skills are also wide-ranging.

In 2016, YWP founder Geoffrey and young writer Bridget presented to the annual conference of International Digital Storytellers:

> The most common question was, 'How do you keep it civil?' They were particularly intrigued given that young people are free to post whatever they want – there is no moderation. But the simple fact that the young people are civil to each other is such a relief – an oasis, if you will, in a desert of school/teen harshness – they value and protect it. And, in turn, they are more apt to take creative risk, knowing they will be supported. A deeper answer, though, is because it is small: small enough that users feel a part of it and a sense of ownership, small enough that users trust it, and small enough that they feel they have identity and control. It is inherent in young people to have strong values relating to equality, voice, and opportunity. They protect those values when trusted to do so.
>
> For a long time, I wanted the organization and site to be larger. I wanted as many young people as possible to join and work on their writing … But I now want it to stay small.
>
> Smallness retains the idea of community, that is a group of people who are different but who are bound by one common element. In the geographic world the commonality is the physical location. In the digital world, the commonality should be broad interests or goals, rather than beliefs. YWP is small and centered on a commonality of an interest to express, to grow, to learn. (Gevalt, 2017)

6 Significance of Rethinking Scale in Online Learning Communities

While Mastodon has been conceived as an alternative social network that somewhat accidentally began to host a collaborative writing project, YWP is more obviously driven by educational principles. These two small, open community-led environments are far from unique: they are examples of the kinds of loosely networked, collaborative projects that can be sustained at smaller scale by relatively informal negotiation and tacit cooperation, and that share some common attributes with small professional associations, cooperative platforms, and connectivist learning projects such as #rhizo14, #clmooc, or #ds106 (Hamon et al., 2015; Levine, 2013). Projects like these exist all over the Web as reactions to, and forms of resistance against, conventional, corporatized models for learning and social networking. Many open educators have had first-hand experience of these kinds of environments (Mackness & Bell, 2015).

Both Mastodon and YWP use open source software. Mastodon has been developed out of GNU Social; YWP's platform is built on Drupal. As von Krogh and von Hippel (2006) suggest, the case studies point to the ability of open source software project to create a culture of use that is attentive to continuous software improvement and favours governance and organization mechanisms that maintain open source software in the commons. Both Mastodon and YWP have semi-formalized groups of leaders in YWP and moderators in Mastodon. While the software is technically open, in governance terms, the administrative functions are reserved. Nevertheless, both projects rely on the labour and motivation of all users to maintain culture and values.

Moreover, both examples use non-profit business models and are grant-based or crowd-sourced. Mastodon's development is funded solely by very small monthly contributions by site and project users; YWP is a non-profit and relies on donations from individuals, businesses, and foundations. Both are advertising-free, and neither track user behaviour. Against a background of commercial and institutional investment in (relatively) open learning at massive scale, these smaller endeavours draw more heavily on voluntary contribution and participatory leadership. They offer a vision of alternative social media centered around cycles of experience and connection and are designed to give equal voice to all participants and to value the agency and safety of historically marginalized users. Their focus is neither scale nor optimization via the exploitation of user data. In a time of surveillance capitalism, these differences are critical (Gilliard, 2017). By choosing alternative financial models, they act as small examples of ways to challenge dominant socio-political and economic models (Battiste, 2013; Freire, 1977), and in small but consistent ways they deconstruct the way power has been traditionally and commercially orchestrated (del Guadalupe Davidson, & Yancy, 2009); they offer a concrete example of what Foucault (1982) described as the essential task of 'bringing into question … power relations and the 'agonism' between power relations and the intransitivity of freedom' (p. 792).

As alternative technology projects, Mastodon and YWP are also useful models for informal or less formal connectivist learning environments. Learning involves cycles of experience, whether active or cognitive; and reflections on, in, and about those experiences (Conrad & Openo, 2018). Downes (2008) explained, 'the learning process is influenced by the four elements of the semantic condition … diversity, autonomy, openness, connectedness' (para. 8). Similarly, Cormier (2008) explains that 'community acts as the curriculum, spontaneously shaping, constructing, and reconstructing itself and the subject of its learning' (p. 3). Community as priority is fundamental to understanding the first-wave emergence of open online courses that introduced 'massive' open-ended enrolment as a feature, and subsequently have been known as cMOOCs, to differentiate them from post-2012 xMOOCs. Reflecting on these principles, Downes (2017) emphasizes that the 'community, rather than the curation or transmission of any sort of content' should be at the heart of a connected, online learning experience (p. 166). Following the principle that community viability enables interaction and prompts thinking, resulting in both intentional and unintentional learning, we suggest that these two projects enable us to rethink an ecology for open pedagogy that finds value in small rather than massive scale (Conrad, 2008).

7 Exploring through the Lens of Individual Experience

The formation and development of these two participatory communities at small scale encourages us to explore the examples of #smallstories and YWP through the lens of individual experience. Staying true to small research principles, we pay attention to the ways in which individual users experience, contribute to, and learn in the context of their respective communities.

7.1 *A Methodology of Wondering, Becoming, and Generating*

Jackson and Mazzei (2017) describe 'thinking with theory' as a methodology that seeks to pose problems, open up thoughts, and to find newness. Somerville (2007) describes a 'methodology of postmodern emergence' that, with strong influences from Indigenous epistemologies, is centred around ideas of wondering, becoming, and generating within the research process. As users observing, discussing and analyzing environments where we also participate, we are practising a loose ethnography, consistent with Stewart's (2008) take on 'weak theory' (from Sedgwick):

> Theory that comes unstuck from its own line of thought to follow the objects it encounters or becomes undone by its attention to things that don't just *add up* but take on a life of their own as problems for thought. (p. 72)

Tentative process methodologies like these are helpful in approaching new or changing social formations, and in opening up ideas rather than seeking solutions. Our aim in this research is to begin and then to suggest further directions for reflection and discovery. In considering how best to engage our fellow users with research, we have chosen conversational methods – a semi-structured interview process guided by the principle that as researchers we wanted the flexibility to 'create contexts where participants and researchers create reciprocal relationships to help them develop and deepen critical consciousness' (Kincheloe, McLaren, Steinberg, & Monzó, 2017, p. 250), given that interactions within research are 'always complicated, mercurial, unpredictable, and of course, complex' (p. 245).

As Jackson and Mazzei suggest, observational research supported by conversational enquiry is 'not about what things mean but about how things work' (2017, p. 727). Extending Jackson and Mazzei, we note that this is not even about the mechanics of how things work, but about perceptions by individuals reflecting on their participation and how things are felt to be working. We are not fundamentally interested in counting numbers of posts or interactions, diagramming network relationships, or in classifying what users say. Our research follows the spirit of Paquette's commitment to a pedagogy of individuation 'qui mise sur ce qui distingue une personne d'une autre' – 'that rests on what distinguishes one person from another' (Paquette, 2005, p. 1). This is similar to Downes' (2017) distinction that '*personal* learning is something made to order' by the individual (p. 356), as opposed to something generic or 'off the shelf.' We are also tactfully seeking to avoid the flattening effect of 'coding, sorting, sifting, collapsing, reducing, merging or patterning' (Jackson & Mazzei, 2017, p. 723) – the traditional repertoires of qualitative research analysis that we find too heavy-handed for such a tentative exploration.

7.2 *Methods to Ensure Accountability and Structure*

The protocols of human research ethics approval, important to each of us, set up conditions of accountability around this relatively open-ended process. These protocols remind us to open conversations with a clear account of purpose and the likely destination of the words gifted to us. Our project began with an open call to participate in a collaborative writing document. This call had the effect of reframing our own activities as users, and of letting others know (including the creators of Mastodon and YWP) what we are doing. Through this process, we co-developed a list of questions to guide our investigative conversations and gained ethical approval from the Research Ethics Committee at the University of Chichester. These questions were:

1. How did you first hear get involved YWP or Mastodon #smallstories and why?
2. How long have you been involved & in what capacities?
3. Tell me more about (the above) participation. What benefits do you think you get from (reading, writing, remixing, leading etc.)
4. Do you think that your involvement as had an impact of your life beyond the YWP/Mastodon #smallstories? In what ways?
5. Are there things that you feel unwilling or unable to share?
6. Can you think of one event, story, phase, etc. that you think best describes your experience with Young Writers Project/Mastodon #smallstories?
7. Have you/would you encourage others to get involved?
8. Is there anything else you would like to add?

The same questions were used to guide the interviews for both #smallstories and YWP, though the interview processes themselves were varied. With #smallstories collaborators, we did not ask for identifying information, although we knew their published usernames. We also offered the opportunity to engage with us through video link or through written exchanges. One participant, someone who might not have participated otherwise, opted to participate via messages. Six additional interviews were conducted using a videoconferencing tool, and two were conducted through email. Where quotations from interviews are included below, they are anonymized as A, B, C, et cetera, according to our approved protocol.

With the YWP group, it was additionally important to respect the sensitivities of research involving young people. As a result, YWP data was gathered using two surveys (50 respondents) and a group interview with nine former and current participants. The group interview participants were selected and contacted by an YWP employee able to ensure parental consent was in place, although half were over 21 years old; direct quotes are attributed to authors with names as requested.

We then reflected on the material that we had gathered, and in what follows, we connect this with our own observations, experiences, and intentions as fellow #smallstories participants exploring the same environments.

7.3 *Acknowledging Important Value-Based Tensions*

Our aim here is to see how well our findings, observations and shared insights within #smallstories and YWP correspond to Paquette's framing of value pairs that hold small open communities in place. Like Paquette (2005), we believe open and participatory pedagogies emerge from the same tensions that enable communities to develop and be sustained by diverse individuals, as opposed to the '*collaborative principle* where every entity in the network becomes the same and, consequently, all dialogue, all meaning, ceases' (Downes, 2017, p. 90). The following section offers examples of each value pair from #smallstories and YWP and considers the tensions they create.

7.3.1 Autonomy and Interdependence

Paquette (2005) suggests that autonomous learning is a three-phase accomplishment that includes assisted autonomy, intermediate autonomy, and 'grand' autonomy. Assisted autonomy is a contingent or intermittent experience defined by the length of time that a learner can operate independently before needing help; intermediate autonomy represents the capacity to assemble and use resources of one's own and to participate fully and authentically on this basis; and 'grand autonomy' is an unachievable state of ethical coherence in which the learner operates entirely according to her own expectations and laws. Paquette connects all three states to the counterbalancing recognition that each autonomous learner acts with others interdependently. This is the founding tension for peer-based open learning, one that requires learners to fashion their own autonomy in continuous negotiation with their community.

Our two examples encourage autonomy in contribution, up to a point. Users do not write to instruction, to a curriculum, or to a deadline. Participation is self-directed, and draws on the users' own resources, motivation, and timing. The challenge emerges when new users need assistance. Educators who work in open online environments with students quickly notice that resources sustaining autonomy include user guides typically in written English, focusing on moderation expectations of a platform's culture and techniques; at the same time, users learn the tacit social rules of courtesy and offense. However, these are often learned through trial and error. In our conversations about #smallstories, C asked:

> What if I posted something on the #smallstories tag that didn't fit? I don't want to jump into a space that others are inhabiting and do it wrong. I don't know the rules of the thing, even though I know there are no rules.

This comment highlights the challenges that many users face negotiating autonomy and communal norms within online communities. Later in the conversation, C extends this idea explaining, 'I haven't quite figured out how I want to engage.' As this comment shows, the development of autonomy is a complex process of negotiating one's role within a community. In contrast, D entered the community with a higher level of autonomy, though the decision to enter with friends again points to the criticality of interdependence:

'I dragged in a couple of buddies in with me and we just started playing. I like the idea that there aren't really any rules.'

E has substantially separated the value he gets from writing from the value of being read:

> The result for other people reading it is incidental almost. It seemed like it was important to write for me. But I like it when I think that someone has read it. If I felt that no one was going to read it ever I would still write it.

Not surprisingly, E and D post, read, and comment often, while C rarely posts but often reads. Though none of these collaborators experienced these cultural norms of #smallstories as prohibitive and exclusionary, their comments illustrate that even in a supportive environment, the new learner experience can be difficult and vary considerably. Ultimately, the development of higher levels of autonomy relies on help-seeking behaviour, and an ethos of patience and assistance. More subtly, interdependent autonomy online is mobilized in the ways in which users pay attention to each other's presence by responding, commenting and sharing. For the #smallstories collaborators, this interdependent autonomy begins with noticing activity within the hashtag and contributing to a practice of noticing in the everyday. 'Writing a #smallstory has to do with the idea of noticing, particularly the small moments that if you take a step back have bigger meaning ... giving me a reason to pay closer attention' (A). This noticing also can extend beyond the #smallstory hashtag within Mastodon:

> There are hundreds of equivalent stories being told [on Mastodon] everyday, just not being seen by their authors with the tag of #smallstories. And sometimes I'll mention that, and they say, 'Oh yeah, I should probably do that, but I'm already writing,' says the person. (E)

For B, noticing extends far past the site and has begun to change the way they perceive others, promoting a higher awareness of their interdependence throughout the world:

> Some of the #smallstories have been pretty moving. Some of them very personal, some of them tragic or sad, and that impacts me. It's important for me to see these things ... it's important for me to know that there are other lives. There are 7 billion lives which means every day, 7 billion times however many numbers of small stories ... and the #smallstories tell me that sometimes. (B)

Moreover, noticing can change how one interacts with the world, empowering them to acknowledge and more fully acknowledge their autonomy to think and make small changes in their actions. Small communities with clearly stated ethical purpose can, therefore, create an opportunity for users to more deeply understand and embrace both their autonomy and interdependence, resulting in what A describes as 'a real generosity of spirit that flows through the hashtag; not just the stories but responses are so positive.'

Within YWP, interdependent autonomy develops as writers feed off each other's example and support. For example, one feature of the YWP community is called the 'sprout.' If a post triggers a memory or an experience or a story on the part of a reader, s/he post their own story as a 'sprout' of the original, and the two will remain linked. This can precipitate deep connections.

> A year ago, in December, I read a poem titled 'Green Eyes' ... and it sparked something in me. So, I started writing ... soon it became a poem titled 'You-Words.' Its publication thrilled [me] – people related to and enjoyed my piece. My experience with sprouting from 'Green Eyes' embodies the conversation of writers. The sprout is one form of compliment/conversation, the commenting on my post another, and my motivation (from receiving comments) to leave comments on other's work the third. (Janet, 2017)

Janet's comment demonstrates how her interdependent autonomy developed through the iterative cycle including the compliments/conversation of the sprout, and the responses of others to her post which ultimately motivated her to leave comments on the work of others within YWP.

Like the #smallstories collaborators, Rebecca also clearly articulates how the relationship between autonomy and interdependence discovered within a small online community has had far-reaching positive impacts: 'YWP helped me see art as something collaborative, and something that you have to support ... I have carried that with me into an MFA program, and I think it makes me a stronger and more dedicated member of that community (Rebecca, 2017).

By writing in a civil space, by knowing they can control what they write, and by knowing that any response will be supportive and non-judgmental, YWP writers explore their identities, emotions and ideas while gaining communication skills and confidence. They are, in effect, learning about themselves as they write in a space that is of manageable size, that respects the individual, and that is free of the bullying and/or negative responses by peers they receive daily in school or life environments. Likewise, those viewing notice and experience glimpses of the lives of others.

The relatively small troupes of active contributors within #smallstories and YWP is part of what allows for a *feeling* of interdependence. Just as in a co-created network developed through open learning, a smaller scale creates the possibility of users recognizing others and being affected by stories shared over time. It is the tension created between autonomy and interdependence that can cause new ideas to emerge and learning to occur.

> The small stories thing has sort of spun off into – someone was talking about pedagogy of small and pedagogy of slow, and that sort of thing – the specific effect it had on me is to coin for my own use the phrase 'pedagogy of harmony.' You can't plan ... and in general that's how my ideas develop. Something tweaks me and I go – oh, it's this. (B)

These acts of writing, responding, and noticing within both #smallstories and YWP seem to resemble the idea of mutual care that is described as the foundation of dialogue and radical education (Freire, 1977; Horton, Bell, Gaventa, & Peters, 1990). One of the characteristics of small might therefore be that it focuses on developing personal relationships first. Another characteristic might be that it recognizes that 'good teaching doesn't scale ... to move towards a more just world, we need to do a better job of finding out who [our students] are and what motivations shape their world' (Gilliard, 2017, January 31, para. 5).

7.3.2 Freedom and Responsibility

Building on the value pair of autonomy and interdependence, Paquette (2005) connects freedom to empowerment and suggests that open learning is energized by student agency. In formal educational settings, teachers establish the tasks that are to be undertaken in order to demonstrate that learning outcomes have been achieved. In the open classroom, students are empowered to choose the activities through which they will learn (Broom, 2015).

For many younger writers, freedom comes from the anonymity they are offered on YWP which is critical to the opportunity to explore sensitive issues. In most cases, other users, parents, teachers, and classmates do not know their usernames. Anna (2017): 'The feeling of anonymity was the ultimate power. I no one would judge me. I felt like my parents would never see it, my school would never see it, and like I could really freely express myself.' Similarly, Zoe admitted:

> I had a very abusive home situation growing up, and I was a bit cornered when it came to expressing that in my writing. I was able to work through a lot of the resulting mental health issues on the site, which the

> community was very, very supportive of and for which I am eternally grateful. (2017)

Anna and Zoe's comments demonstrate the challenging issues and disturbing and confusing thoughts that youth participating in YWP often have as they try make sense of themselves and illustrate the importance of the freedom to express them in a supportive space.

> YWP is a space where they can explore some of their darker or weirder thoughts without fear of retribution or derision or any repercussion. We'd much rather have them write about topics such as suicide and cutting and bulimia and figure them out than have them take some sort of rash action. (Geoffrey, 2017)

Paquette also counsels, however, that this freedom be tempered by the need for students to learn responsibility and to recognize that their choices interact with choices others have already made or will make. Balancing freedom with responsibility extends the complementarity of autonomy and interdependence, and strengthens the bonds enabling communities to sustain peer learning environments that value diversity and create a context for sensitive disclosure.

Within YWP, the freedom to canvas difficult topics is balanced by appreciation and strength of this small community. As Bridget puts it, 'YWP was my social media ... Facebook fills time and YWP fills my mind.' Bridget was one of the first informal leaders on the site, spending time commenting on others' work and posting her own impressive new work. The freedom she experienced came from knowing that she was part of an appreciative community that would often affirm, and even emulate her ideas and level of engagement. Over time, a sense of responsibility took over: 'As I got older, at first I objected to all these new, young middle schoolers coming onto my site. But then ... I began to give them comments and encouragement.'

Similarly, Ava felt 'an obligation to give back to the community even though it was a crazy year, I tried to get on as much as possible and give comments to the younger writers.'

For alternative social networks, the effort to value both freedom and responsibility is framed by the broad failure of commercial networks to achieve this balance at massive scale. The larger social platforms, especially Facebook, Twitter and YouTube, have notoriously failed to foster user accountability; they struggle with content moderation. Real names policies have not prevented the flourishing of fake identities, but instead have exposed vulnerable users to abuse. Account verification has been diverted into reputational currency and has not provided protection against harassment. All three platforms have been exploited as distributors of extreme material, political propaganda, and fake news. In this context, what policies support the possibility that users can responsibly care for the health of a network, and self-manage out of consideration for others? And does this support the hypothesis that scale is also a factor in creating sustainable open pedagogy?

As with the YWP participants, conversations with #smallstories collaborators identify a variety of freedoms and responsibilities both offered and accepted. Specifically, the acceptance of content labelling, and the designation of images and whole instances, such as NSFW (Not Suitable For Work) indicates a willingness to accept constraint on individual practice as potentially valuable to community. It is also modelled in the way users can contribute financially to the support of the project and in the open dialogue between community developers, moderators, and users.

> I remember thinking except for the fact that the platform is kinda of similar if you really get into it, it has a different kind of vibe. It's got the protection people are asking for on Twitter. It doesn't feel really like Twitter at all to me. (C)

It is not enough for the software to integrate features to protect users: in order to achieve the needed balance between freedom and responsibility, users must feel a sense of ownership and control; they must care enough to protect their community. B describes different kinds of freedoms afforded within a community without expectations or specific agendas, something different from other platforms: 'it fills a role that none of the other technology does, which is to be a part of a small informal, haphazard community that doesn't particularly have any particular goals ... that's not available on other platforms.'

D described another type of freedom offered by Mastodon #smallstories by contrasting it to the results of monoculture grazing among sheep:

> We raise sheep. When we brought the sheep in, we also had one we had kept separate. When we rejoined them, the wool of the ones that had been out was amazing. The other one had wool that was markedly different. Mastodon is a healthy pasture with lots of stuff to graze on. A lot of spaces have become monocultures. One of the things it does is makes me consider other possibilities, the 'adjacent possible.' There are only few

> digital tools that create serious 'adjacent possible.' It encourages you to take things outside the box – the walls are semi-permeable. It's all connected. It encourages wide grazing.

D describes honouring participation as an ongoing responsibility:

> This space is not for everyone ... The danger is becoming too big ... but it goes the other way too, then it becomes a club. That's why there's a need for constant invitation and openness to participate. Share with us. Come as often as you want.

For A, remixing the #smallstories of others into poems or videos is a practice of honouring, reflection and extension similar to YWP users who respond to a story by sprouting a story of their own. Remixing is conceived as way of paying attention: 'a way to honour the writer, a way to riff off what they have written' (A). Noting, however, that some writers have questioned this practice, A asks, 'Where is the line between the invitation to remix and just an invitation to read?' In an open, online community, anyone has the freedom to remix the content. Yet, in this community, users demonstrate an awareness and acceptance of responsibility to respect the wishes of other contributors. For open educators, this resonates with the need to consistently and patiently restate the principles of an open environment, and to recognize that the negotiation of respect in open communities that anyone can join requires an ongoing commitment of care.

7.3.3 Democracy and Participation

For Paquette (2005), democratic ideals bring the principle of freedom of speech to the open classroom. This is politically precise – not simply the freedom to choose what to do in order to learn, but the freedom to speak controversially. Paquette argues, however, that democratic opportunity demands democratic participation, requiring students to take an active role in the management of learning, and in the resolution of disputes.

Both Mastodon and YWP offer opportunities to explore the benefits and tensions involved in sustaining democratic ideals at small scale with minimum formal governance. In both spaces, as needs have been identified, the appropriate affordances have been developed in the software, the community ethos, and the content. Mastodon's early development community that was largely built for, guided, funded, and maintained by members of the queer community who 'looked into the software and saw themselves reflected back' (Hart, 2017, para. 28). Many of Mastodon's users 'were trans and/or nonbinary; many dealt with disabilities; many were victims of harassment. Certainly, the most vocal and most frequent of Mastodon's unpaid contributors seemed to invariably fall into one or more of these categories' (para. 28). It seems likely that the differences within Mastodon identified by the #smallstories collaborators as largely cultural rather than technological are derived from these roots.

> There's a friendliness ... Every once in a while I see someone focus on something that's off-kilter, but I don't think that's the fundamental presence ... the Mastodon experience seems intentional, not a chance occurrence. I think people are trying are trying to engage in a relatively honest way and are trying to be mildly friendly if not supportive. (E)

> It's a surprising population, a varied a group of people as I have ever been a part of. It's wild, wacky, and strange. (D)

The YWP site and larger project predate social media and were developed specifically to support the needs of youth. Because YWP is built on the value of respect and trust, users tend to feel agency to comment to others when they think a piece of writing – or a comment – might be construed as disrespectful. This becomes *de facto* moderation through reflection and dialogue; users think about it, and have a sense of their voice in how the community operates or considers its core values. While YWP staff make the final publishing and featuring decisions, YWP has community leaders to help identify powerful pieces for publication or special highlight and encourages community suggestions. Community leaders also can create writing challenges, and all members can make regular suggestions on how to improve their site.

In the case of YWP, smallness gives young writers a sense that their voice and their work as individuals matters within a respected community. They also recognize that the community's intrinsic value is that they are respected and not judged. This leads them to want to share and take creative risk.

> YWP was actually one of the only places where I felt comfortable sharing things I couldn't share anywhere else. Part of it was the pseudo-anonymous aspect of the site, where very few people knew me as a person and most knew me only as a username. There, I could share writing that came from my soul and expressed feelings, topics, and ideas that I kept hidden in my outward persona in my day to day life. Instead, people would offer their support and solidarity. The environment of YWP was so inspiring and comforting to me as a troubled young writer and showed me that I was not alone. (Tyler, 2017)

One result of this democratic participation is that the YWP community is openly supportive of diversity and self-development. Avi, a YWP user now in college, posted a personal essay when he was a sophomore in high school declaring that he was gay. The post received 24 positive comments and 1,600 views in two days. It had a profound impact on him and gave him courage to share his feelings, in person, with classmates.

YWP does not track demographics, but on the basis of school identification, it reasonably estimates that nearly 15 percent of its users are young people of colour compared with a five percent overall population of colour in Vermont. YWP has programs specifically directed at young people of colour and has generated creative projects including the slam poets Muslim Girls Making Change (Waqar, Adam, Ginawi & Abdikadir, n.d.), who have performed throughout Vermont.

Like the other value pairs, however, there remains a tension between democracy and active participation, particularly participation among traditionally marginalized groups. As Mastodon has grown, some early Mastodon users and developers have expressed concern about being pushed out by dominant groups (Hart, 2017). A flurry of other blog posts written in April 2017 echo Hart's concerns and hopes both from the perspectives of existing marginalized users and more mainstream newcomers (Brown, 2017; Drott, 2017; Jeong, 2017); Moreover, people of colour and other minority groups remain underrepresented within Mastodon.

Within YWP, the issue of sustaining democratic participation has been a cornerstone of its work. YWP regularly surveys all its users for suggestions on how to improve the site and programs; it seeks out volunteers for special projects; it rewards, publicly, the most committed users and writers with Senior Writer and Community Leader status which allows them the ability to designate stories for publication, choose daily prompts, organize special projects. Many of these projects have centered on student voice, social activism, societal injustices.

Since 2007, YWP has provided teachers with private digital classroom platforms and this program reached a peak in 2012 of being used by teachers in 60 schools with an estimated 8,000 students. Annual surveys of students using the platforms confirm that small community networks extend the classroom experience, allow students to gain a greater understanding and appreciation of each other, and allow teachers to gain a greater understanding of their students. However, limitations remain. As John, a teacher writes,

> Creating community through shared writing is a wonderful tool that I have used for over a decade. Yet, it has never been what it could be

> because I held a lot of the power. I decided who was chosen to read aloud, I made the copies of the 'good piece' to model. With YWP, kids are in the drivers' seats. They decide what to read, who to read, and what pieces should 'go viral' in the classroom. And of course, whenever learner feel in control, they are certainly more motivated to do what it takes to become better. (2013)

8 Final Thoughts

The cultures of open source and alternative social media-maker communities continue to evolve. Our conversations have led us to believe that while corporatized education focuses on enclosure, profit, reputation and efficiency, open source communities offer a counter-cultural model for learners to interact technologically, economically and socially in a complex world. Community-facing projects can appear small by some measures; we argue that this is because they restore capacity to individuals to negotiate and self-manage without having to move through a preset curriculum. We do not want to overstate or ascribe permanence to the value of these projects, however, as they are inherently vulnerable in a context where venture capital funding has become a standard for platform viability. We also recognize that small communities are constrained by human bandwidth and that this risks reproducing privileged networks in exclusive formations.

And finally, we recognize that Paquette's value pairs are not always able to be negotiated successfully. As we learn continuously from the Internet, communities and social groups that focus only on harmonization of ideas, politics or values will often struggle to appreciate dissonant views and their efforts can too easily be diverted to excluding or shaming; conversely, users who valorize the expression of dissenting speech as a mark of independent thought will often fail to appreciate the organic and tender efforts of groups to grow and change. The dissonance this can create is difficult to resolve at scale; in small communities, however, we continue to see a willingness to entertain cooperative struggle as the basis of learning from peers who do not think as we do.

Regardless of the future of the Young Writers Project or Mastodon's #smallstories activity, it is clear that for at least some users, the recuperation of online community from profit-based platform cultures within small open online communities re-instills hope – hope that strangers can be kind and learn from one another, hope that care-based communities are possible both online and in the real world, hope that there are alternatives to the status quo, hope that change is possible. To us, this cultivation of hope is an inherently pedagogical project that connects capacity to learn to the effort to live thoughtfully, and this is where we have found connection between these two platforms and our work as open educators.

As educators, we recognize the stories we have collected as accounts of learning taking place, and we believe that this account of learning is connected in important ways to openness of the two environments. We do not come to this position lightly or without reflecting on the tacit, informal ways in which welcoming communities can feel exclusive or unkind at times. Our analysis of Paquette's value pairs has helped us to identify that tension within communities, particularly around individual freedom, is an inherent feature of open practice. Nevertheless, on the basis of our analysis of these two less formal projects, we conclude that against an institutional context of investment in massive scale, artificial personalization and machine-led data analysis, educators have good reason to support a pedagogy of small whose measures are in the transformation of individual experience, one human step at a time.

Notes

1 Mastodon has been in operation since October 2016. See https://joinmastodon.org for more information.

2 See https://youngwritersproject.org

3 See thevoice.youngwritersproject.org

References

Bali, M. (2016, November 28). Are you on mastodon yet? Social network of our own [Blog post]. Retrieved from http://www.chronicle.com/blogs/profhacker/are-you-on-mastodon-yet-social-network-of-our-own/63261

Battiste, M. A. (2013). *Decolonizing education: Nourishing the learning spirit*. Saskatoon: Purich Publishing Limited.

Broom, C. (2015). Empowering students: Pedagogy that benefits educators and learners. *Citizenship, Social and Economics Education, 14*(2), 79–86.

Brown, E. (2017, April 17). *Is* Mastodon the new social media star, or imploding black hole? [Blog post]. Retrieved from http://www.zdnet.com/article/is-mastodon-the-new-social-media-star-or-imploding-black-hole/

Cole, K. K. (2015). 'It's like she's eager to be verbally abused': Twitter, trolls, and (en) gendering disciplinary rhetoric. *Feminist Media Studies, 15*(2), 356–358.

Conrad, D. (2008). From community to community of practice: Exploring the connection of online learners to informal learning in the workplace. *American Journal of Distance Education, 22*(1), 3–23.

Conrad, D., & Openo, J. (2018). *Assessment strategies for online learning: Engagement and authenticity*. Athabasca: Athabasca University Press.

Cormier, D. (2008). Rhizomatic education: Community as curriculum. *Innovate: Journal of Online Education, 4*(5). Retrieved from http://nsuworks.nova.edu/innovate/vol4/iss5/2

del Guadalupe Davidson, M., & Yancy, G. (Eds.). (2009). *Critical perspectives on bell hooks*. New York, NY: Routledge.

Downes, S. (2008, September 10). Connectivism and its critics: What connectivism is not [Blog post]. Retrieved from https://www.downes.ca/cgi-bin/page.cgi?post=53657

Downes, S. (2017). *Toward personal learning.* National Research Council Canada. Retrieved from www.downes.ca/files/books/Toward Personal Learning v09.pdf

Drott, J. (2017, April 9). Mastodon, pineapple, social media and other unanswered questions [Blog post]. Retrieved from https://medium.com/@sargoth/mastodon-pineapples-social-media-and-other-unanswered-questions-c5127c7c9aa0

Eisner, E. W. (2001). What does it mean to say a school is doing well? In D. J. Flinders & S. J. Tornton (Eds.), *Curriculum studies reader* (2nd ed., pp. 279–287). New York, NY: Taylor and Francis.

Foucault, M. (1982, Summer). The subject and power. *Critical Inquiry, 8*(4), 777–795.

Freire, P. (1977). Pedagogy of the oppressed. In D. J. Flinders & S. J. Thornton (Eds.), *Curriculum studies reader* (2nd ed., pp. 75–86). New York, NY: Taylor and Francis.

Gilliard, C. (2017, January 30). Educon 2.9 and 'student voice' or 'finding a glimmer of hope in a time of chaos' [Blog post]. Retrieved from http://hypervisible.com/post/educon-2-9-and-student-voice-or-finding-a-glimmer-of-hope-in-a-time-of-chaos/

Gilliard, C. (2017). Pedagogy and the logic of platforms. *Educause Review, 2*, pp. 64–65. Retrieved from http://er.educause.edu/~/media/files/articles/2017/7/erm174111.pdf

Grafana. (n.d.). *Mastodon monitoring project.* Retrieved from https://dashboards.mnm.social/dashboard/db/mastodon-network-overview?refresh=1h&orgId=1

Greene, M. (2004). Curriculum and consciousness. In D. J. Flinders & S. J. Thornton (Eds.), *Curriculum studies reader* (2nd ed., pp. 135–149). New York, NY: Taylor and Francis.

Hall, A. H., & Axelrod, Y. (2014). 'I am kind of a good writer and kind of not': Examining students' writing attitudes. *Journal of Research in Education, 24*(2). Retrieved from https://files.eric.ed.gov/fulltext/EJ1098193.pdf

Hamon, K., Hogue, R. J., Honeychurch, S., Johnson, S., Koutropoulos, A., Ensor, S., Sinfeld, S., & Bali, M. (2015). Writing the unreadable untext: A collaborative autoethnography of #rhizo14. *Hybrid Pedagogy.*

Hart, A. (2017). Mourning Mastodon [Blog post]. Retrieved from https://medium.com/@alliethehart/gameingers-are-dead-and-so-is-mastodon-705b535ed616

Horton, M., Bell, B., Gaventa, J., & Peters, J. M. (1990). *We make the road by walking: Conversations on education and social change.* Philadelphia, PA: Temple University Press.

Jackson, A. Y., & Mazzei, L. A. (2017). Thinking with theory: A new analytic for qualitative inquiry. In *The Sage handbook of qualitative research* (pp. 717–737). Thousand Oaks, CA: Sage.

Jeong, S. (2017, April 4). Mastodon is like Twitter without Nazis, so why are we not using it? [Blog post]. Retrieved from https://motherboard.vice.com/en_us/article/mastodon-is-like-twitter-without-nazis-so-why-are-we-not-using-it https://motherboard.vice.com/en_us/article/from-witches-to-dolphins-these-are-the-communities-that-make-mastodon-great

Katz, L. G. (1972). *Research on open education: Problems and issues*. Urbana, IL: ERIC Clearninghouse on Early Childhood Education.

Kincheloe, J. L., McLaren, P., Steinberg, S. R., & Monzó, L. D. (2017). Critical pedagogy and qualitative research: Advancing the bricolage. In *The Sage handbook of qualitative research* (pp. 235–260). Thousand Oaks, CA: Sage.

Kotula, A. W., Tivnan, T., & Aguilar, C. M. (2014). *Students' voices: The relationship between attitudes and writing outcomes for fourth and fifth graders.* Waltham, MA: Education Development Center, Inc. Retrieved from http://ltd.edc.org/sites/ltd.edc.org/files/WritingAttitudesandOutcomesArticle.pdf

Lane, D. (n.d.). OERu social – Mastodon [Blog post]. Retrieved from https://mastodon.oeru.org/about

Lawson, N. (2017, October 23). What is Mastodon and why is it better than Twitter [Blog post]. Retrieved from https://nolanlawson.com/2017/10/23/what-is-mastodon-and-why-is-it-better-than-twitter/

Levine, A. (2013, January 28). DS106: Not a course, not like any MOOC. *Educause Review Online*. Retrieved from https://er.educause.edu/articles/2013/1/ds106-not-a-course-not-like-any-mooc

Lynds, D., & Richards, S. (2016, November 23). OurChatSpace OR what Mastodon could do for #HigherEd [Blog post]. Retrieved from http://daniellynds.com/edtech/ourchatspace/

Mackness, J., & Bell, F. (2015). Rhizo14: A rhizomatic learning cMOOC in sunlight and in shade. *Open Praxis, 7*(1), pp. 25–38.

Newton, C. (2017, April 4). Mastodon.social is an open-source twitter competitor that's growing like crazy. *The Verge*. Retrieved from https://www.theverge.com/2017/4/4/15177856/mastodon-social-network-twitter-clone

OER Foundation. (n.d.). About OERu [Blog post]. Retrieved from https://oeru.org/about-oeru/

Paquette, C. (1979). Quelques fondements d'une pédagogie ouverte. *Québec français, 36*, 20–21 (T. Morgan, Trans.) Retrieved from https://homonym.ca/?s=paquette

Paquette, C. (2005). *La pédagogie ouverte et interactive: une brève histoire.* Retrieved from http://arc-en-ciel.csdm.ca/files/Pedagogie-ouverte-et-interactive.pdf

Reid, S., & Gevalt, G. (2017). About YWP | Young writers project [Blog post]. Retrieved from https://youngwritersproject.org/about

Rolfe, V. (2016, November). Open, but not for criticism? [Slide presentation]. Presented at #opened16, Richmond VA. Retrieved from http://www.slideshare.net/viv_rolfe/opened16-conference-presentation

Shaffer, K. (n.d.). Twitter is lying to you [Blog post]. Retrieved from https://pushpullfork.com/twitter-is-lying-to-you/

Somerville, M. (2007). Postmodern emergence. *International Journal of Qualitative Studies in Education, 20*(2). doi:10.1080/09518390601159750

Spodek, B. (1970). Extending open education in the United States. In B. Spodek (Ed.), *Open education* (pp. 64-77). Washington, DC: National Association for the Education of Young Children.

Stewart, K. (2008). Weak theory in an unfinished world. *Journal of Folklore Research, 45*(1), 71–82.

Urrea, C., Reich, J., & Thille, C. (2017). L@S '17. In *Proceedings of the Fourth (2017) ACM Conference on Learning @ Scale.* New York, NY: ACM.

von Krogh, G., & von Hippel, E. (2006). The promise of research on open source software. *Management Science, 52*(7), 975–983.

Waqar, K., Adam, H., Ginawi, L., & Abdikadir, B. (n.d.). Muslim girls making change [Blog post]. Retrieved from https://muslimgirlsmakingchange.weebly.com/

AFTERWORD

(In)Conclusion

Paul Prinsloo and Dianne Conrad

How does one conclude and close (however temporally) a book dedicated to open, openness, opening, opened, without giving the impression that the debate is now settled and closed? How does one conclude and yet, at the same time, keep the space open, and actually even destabilise the sense of 'ending?'

Our Call for Papers intentionally played with opening 'open' by referring to open, openness, opening, opened – to, from the very start, point to our claim that open is much more than just a status or process. In the context of education, specifically postsecondary and tertiary education, each of these terms offers glimpses of a tentative evolution of the notion of 'open' and can refer to, *inter alia*, admission requirements, registration periods, flexibility in choices, open pedagogies, curricula, professional development, curriculum resources, assessment practices, the scholarship of teaching and learning, and research.

In some of the debates on open education, there is also the unquestioned assumption that thinking about 'open' also almost automatically must call forth thinking about 'closed.' In some of the debates, the binaries – closed/open, good/bad, black/white – function as Medusa's gaze, keeping our thinking and practices locked in, and in our opinion, much poorer. Thinking in terms of binaries 'serves to flatten critique,' and we may miss the opportunity to engage with the notion of open as a 'sociomaterially and temporally situated practice' (Gourlay, 2015, p. 325). Open also calls forth the notion of space – whether enclosed spaces such as classrooms or gardens, boats or trains; and space as 'non-space' such as mirrors, as Foucault (1986) suggests.

While it is possible to see open, openness, opening, and opened as statuses or processes, we can also understand them in terms of multidimensional and sociomaterial relationships and networks. In these relationships and networks, the status or process of open, openness, opening, and opened evolve in relation to each other. These relationships are often mutually constitutive and often comprise incommensurable factors in overlapping ecologies consisting of human and non-human actors. A train, for example, can be seen as a particular space, but also, as Foucault (1986) suggests, as 'an extraordinary bundle of relationships' (p. 83); and as Gourlay (2015) suggests, 'a bundle of ideological signifiers' (p. 314). Foucault (1986) uses the example of a train which is, at the same time, 'something through which one goes, [but] also something by means of which one can go from one point to another, and then it is also something that goes by' (p. 24). Trains are therefore moving or stationary spaces, consisting not only of material relationships (the locomotive, coaches, etc.), but also relating to other materialities, e.g. the tracks, the station, the signals, etc. In addition to thinking about trains as spaces, we can also think of how humans, on the train, not only relate to the materiality of being on a train, but also to one another, being in and sharing the same space. It is therefore possible to think of trains as being more than *just* a train but indeed a 'bundle of relationships' (p. 83) that constitute an ecology of sociomaterialities and networks. In foregrounding open, opening, openness and opened, we aimed to open spaces where we could explore the interrelationships, the sociomaterialities, the different networks and ecologies that inform and shape our understanding and practices of open.

In the Call for Papers for this book, we proposed the possibility of understanding open, openness, opening, and opened open, openness, opening, and opened in terms of 'ecologies of open' that exist in the nexus of political, economic, social, technological, environmental and legal frameworks and agendas; and as entangled with contestation, incongruities and obstacles. Why ecologies? The word *ecology* originates from Greek and originally referred to 'house' or 'environment.' In the academic disciplinary context, it is found in the biological sciences and focuses on the dynamic inter-, and intra-relations between organisms and the environments in which they are found. In much of the current discourses on open education or OER, we think in terms of materials, policies, and licences, to mention but a few, while forgetting that surrounding these, there are human and non-human actors and networks. When we refer to 'ecologies of open,' we foreground the broader ecosystems that surround open education and that stimulate, support or curtail and frustrate open education. 'Ecologies of open,' therefore, aim to foreground the different processes, interactions, adaptations, and new forms of open that emerge or exist at any particular moment in time as a result of various, intersecting factors and human and non-human actors. Ecologies of open also rest on and flow from historical legacy systems and beliefs of how we understand the world and humanity's role in it; and how we define, teach, and share our understanding of knowledge. The notion of ecologies provides a useful interpretive lens on open as evolving, emerging, changing, and often liminal spaces/non-spaces.

Authors such as Gourlay (2015) and Knox (2013), as well as some authors in this book, point to the often unquestioned claims that open education and specifically open educational resources (OER) per se democratise education and are key to 'not only to solving the global education crisis but to unlocking sustainable global growth in the 21st century' (Daniel & Kilton, 2012). These claims position open education and OER in stark contradiction to the traditional university that is portrayed as 'exclusive, retrograde, and reproductive of social privilege' (Gourlay, 2015, p. 311). 'Central to many in the OER cause is the idea that the educational institution functions as a barrier to the egalitarian acquisition of knowledge' (Knox, 2013, p. 823). As such, traditional universities and teaching practices are 'reduced to a liminal site, and abstraction or a bundle of ideological signifiers which are not based on evidence from the particular, or from situated practice' (Gourlay, 2015, p. 314). As in defining open – where the temptation of thinking in terms of binaries, open/closed, good/bad – is a constant danger, we should also be careful as regarding open education and traditional education as homogenous and uniquely distinct spaces, and not connected like boats to harbours and the mainland; and overlapping with and connected to traditional and formal teaching and learning. There is ample evidence of open practices and open resources in traditional universities, while there is often a surprising lack of openness in the choice of prescribed materials in some courses at 'open' institutions. As Knox (2013) suggests, open education sometimes overlaps with traditional education, such as when the Massachusetts Institute of Technology (MIT) ventured into the open education space; and the OER University (OERu) claimed space as a university, albeit founded on OER. In its opposition to traditional higher education, the OERu functions as a 'parallel universe' (Taylor, 2007) 'in which the activities of teaching and learning take place independently of a centralised institution' (Knox, 2013, p. 824).

In imagining this book, we wished to open a space where authors from different geopolitical and institutional contexts could reflect upon and share experiences and insights on the different possibilities, if not universes Taylor (2007), that would help us to understand open, openness, opening and opened. Looking back at the various contributions in the book, the insights and shared experiences, we have a suspicion that underlying the quest for open, lies the rich history of how knowledge came to be defined, protected, shared, closed and opened. Each of the chapters in the book adds to our understanding of how knowledge came to be defined, formalised, and protected by gatekeepers and later on, by formal admission requirements and licencing agreements. Thinking about the evolution of humankind, it is interesting to consider, for example, how and when (as a continuum) did the tradition of sharing experience and knowledge through signs, gestures and later speech and oral traditions become only accessible to those *on the inside*, those of a particular gender, position in the hierarchy of the troop or tribe? When did knowledge become 'classified' as consisting of general secular knowledge and special or 'profane' knowledge (Muller & Taylor, 1995)?

We cannot, therefore, reflect upon open, openness, opening, and opened without considering and accounting for how issues and notions of open are connected to and often constituted by historical and current asymmetries in power relations, networks and ecologies of knowledge production and dissemination.

1 Open, Opening, Opened and Openness as Utopia?

Considering the evolution of humankind and knowledge, as well as the above-mentioned asymmetries, many still see open education as an (unattainable) utopia, an unreal space that cannot really confront and rectify the imbalances and injustices in knowledge production and dissemination. Despite the claim that open education is seen by many as a utopian dream, the chapters in this book bear testimony of the many individuals, alliances and organisations *doing* open. For many of them *doing* open – of opening, of breaking open, and of keeping and defending opened spaces; open education is anything but a utopian desire, but a very real, and often embodied, practice and sociomaterial space. There may be some individuals, alliances and organisations that do not recognise the flaws and contestations in the various nuances and practices of open education; many of them, however, are aware of how opening, breaking open, and keeping and defending opened spaces is often a compromised and entangled practice. For those who practice and embrace open, opening and opened, their practices constitute, in many respects a heterotopia as *counter-site* to a utopia (Foucault, 1986) or a 'parallel universe' (Taylor, 2007). *For them, opening education is not a utopia, but a real space.* As a site (whether a course, a book or as Foucault mentions – a mirror, a train, a ship, etc.), open education constitutes and is constituted by 'an extraordinary bundle of relations' and is, per se, heterogeneous (p. 23).

Many may scorn open education and its practices as only a utopian dream, as unachievable, and as merely a fleeting mirage in a mirror. We would propose that the chapters in this book provide evidence not only of deep and critical introspection on the limitations, challenges and potential of open education but also of open education practices and praxis.

Open. Openness Opening. Opened. This was our rallying call in the Call for Papers. The chapters following this introduction as well as the End Note provide a rich testimony of open education as heterotopia, a place of crisis and deviance, a place distinct but connected to the mainland of education, a space containing several, often incompatible spaces, a space where time accumulates and where time is flowing, a space that opens but also a space where 'open' is a process of opening; and a space, like a boat, that provides space for 'an extraordinary bundle of relationships' (Foucault, 1986) and 'a bundle of ideological signifiers' (Gourlay, 2015, p. 314).

References

Daniel, J., & Killion, D. (2012). Are open educational resources the key to global economic growth. *Guardian Online*. Retrieved from https://www.theguardian.com/higher-education-network/blog/2012/jul/04/open-educational-resources-and-economic-growth

Foucault, M. (1986). Of other spaces (J. Miskowiec, Trans.). *Diacritics, 16*(1), 22–27.

Gourlay, L. (2015). Open education as a 'heterotopia of desire'. *Learning, Media and Technology, 40*(3), 310–327.

Knox, J. (2013). Five critiques of the open educational resources movement. *Teaching in Higher Education, 18*(8), 821–832.

Muller, J., & Taylor, N. (1995). Schooling and everyday life: Knowledges sacred and profane. *Social Epistemology, 9*(3), 257–275.

Taylor, J. C. (2007). Open courseware futures: creating a parallel universe. *e-Journal of Instructional Science and Technology, 10* (1), 1–9. Retrieved from http://www.ascilite.org/archived-journals/e-jist/docs/vol10_no1/papers/full_papers/taylorj.pdf

Index